PERSPECTIVES ON THE ARMS RACE

Perspectives on the Arms Race

Edited by
David Carlton
and
Carlo Schaerf

St. Martin's Press   New York

© International School on Disarmament and Research on Conflicts,
Eleventh Course, 1989

All rights reserved. For information, write:
Scholarly and Reference Division,
St. Martin's Press, Inc., 175 Fifth Avenue, New York, N.Y. 10010

First published in the United States of America in 1989

Printed in Hong Kong

ISBN 0-312-02703-6

Library of Congress Cataloging-in-Publication Data
Perspectives on the arms race / edited by David Carlton and Carlo Schaerf.
p. cm.
Proceedings of the 11th International School on Disarmament and Research on Conflicts held in San Miniato, Italy, Aug. 20-30. 1986.
Includes index.
ISBN 0-312-02703-6
1. Arms race—Congresses.   2. Arms control—Congresses.
3. Strategic Defense Initiative—Congresses.   I. Carlton, David,
1938-   .   II. Schaerf, Carlo.   III. International School on
Disarmament and Research on Conflicts (11th:1986:San Miniato,
Italy)
UA10.P47   1989
327.1'74—dc 19   88-25136
                                                                       CIP

HIC LIBRUS EST SCRIPTUS, QUI SCRIPSIT SIT BENEDICTUS.
PROPTER CHRISTUM LIBRUM BENE CONDIDIT ISTUM.
QUI SCRIPSIT SCRIBAT, SEMPER CUM DOMINO VIVAT.
QUI SCRIPSIT SCRIBAT, ET BONA VINA BIBAT.
FINITO LIBRO PINGUIS DETUR AUCA MAGISTRO.
DETUR PRO PENNA SCRIPTORI PULCHRA PUELLA.

Explicit of the Twelfth Century
From C. H. Haskins: *The Renaissance of the 12th Century*

Contents

Preface ix
List of Abbreviations x
Notes on the Contributors xii
List of Course Participants xvi

1 Summary of Discussions
  William F. Gutteridge 1

PART I THE GENERAL ARMS RACE

2 The Pursuit of Security in the Nuclear Age
  Robert W. Malcolmson 11

3 Unstable Peace: Nuclear Deterrence
  Hylke Tromp 23

4 The Case Against Negotiations and For a Reconsideration of Strategy
  Robert Neild 36

5 Simulation of the Short-term Effects of a 'Limited' Nuclear War in Europe
  Andrea Ottolenghi 59

6 Conventional War in the Postwar International System
  Catherine M. Kelleher 100

7 Belief Systems and Arms Control Possibilities
  Jane M. O. Sharp 114

8 Technical Means of Verification of Arms Control Agreements
  Kosta Tsipis 135

PART II THE STRATEGIC DEFENCE INITIATIVE

9 Rendering Nuclear Weapons Impotent and Obsolete: The Origins of a Pipedream
  David Carlton 151

10	SDI and the NATO Allies *Robert d'A. Henderson*	169
11	The Technical Feasibility of Strategic Defence *Dietrich Schroeer*	191
12	Directed-Energy Weapons, Strategic Defence and Arms Control *Dietrich Schroeer*	220

PART III REGIONAL ASPECTS OF THE ARMS RACE

13	Nuclear Weapons and Coercive Diplomacy: Their Impact on the Developing World *K. Subrahmanyam*	255
14	The Concept of Nuclear-Weapon-Free Zones *Olga Šuković*	267
15	Brazil and Disarmament *Ernst W. Hamburger*	286
16	China's Defence Policy *Shu Yuan H. Chang*	293
17	Understanding China's Nuclear Disarmament Policy *Qian Xuefeng*	304
18	The Debate on Alternative Defence Policies in Italy *Paolo Farinella and Maria Clelia Spreafico*	310

Index   329

Preface

The chapters in this volume were presented to the eleventh course of the International School on Disarmament and Research on Conflicts (ISODARCO), held in San Miniato (Pisa), Italy, between 20 and 30 August 1986.

The organisation of the course was made possible by the generous collaboration and financial contributions of many organisations and individuals. For their financial contributions we wish to express our gratitude to The Italian National Research Council–National Committee for Juridicial and Political Sciences; The Italian Ministry of Cultural Affairs; The University of Rome I, La Sapienza, in particular Professor Antonio Ruberti and Professor Giorgio Tecce; The University of Rome II, in particular Professor Enrico Garaci; The University of Padua, in particular Professor Marcello Cresti and Professor Alessandro Pascolini.

We wish to acknowledge the dedicated collaboration before and during the course of Ariella de Rossi, Alba Faschetti, Lidia Paoluzi and Anna Prosperi. For administrative work our thanks are due to Fernando Pacciani and Luciano Fiore. For Hospitality in San Miniato we are indebted to the Cassa di Risparmio di San Miniato.

All opinions expressed in the chapters and in the summary of discussions are of a purely personal nature and do not necessarily represent the official view of either the organisers of the School or of the organisations with which the writers may be affiliated.

D.C
C.S.

List of Abbreviations

ABM	Anti-ballistic Missile
ADE	Armoured Division Equivalent
ASAT	Anti-satellite
ATBM	Anti-tactical Ballistic Missile
BMD	Ballistic Missile Defence
BMEWS	Ballistic Missile Early Warning System
CBM	Confidence-building measure
CCD	Charge-coupled device
CNR	National Research Council (Italy)
CTA	Centro Técnico de Aeronáutica (Brazil)
DEW	Directed-energy Weapon
EEC	European Economic Community
END	European Nuclear Disarmament Movement
IAEA	International Atomic Energy Agency
ICBM	Intercontinental Ballistic Missile
IRDISP	Istituto di Ricerche per il Disarmo, lo Sviluppo e la Pace (Italy)
ISTRID	Istituto Studi e Ricerche sulla Difesa (Italy)
KEW	Kinetic-energy Weapon
LRINF	Longer-range Intermediate Nuclear Forces
MAD	Mutual Assured Destruction
MIRV	Multiple Independently Targeted Re-entry Vehicle
NATO	North Atlantic Treaty Organisation
NNWS	Non-nuclear Weapon State
NOP	Nuclear Operations Plan
NORAD	North American Aerospace Defense Command
NPT	Non-proliferation Treaty
NSC	National Security Council (USA)
NTM	National Technical Means
NWFZ	Nuclear-weapon-free Zone
NWS	Nuclear-weapon State
OAU	Organisation of African Unity
OECD	Organisation for Economic Co-operation and Development
OPANAL	International Agency for the Prohibition of Nuclear Weapons in Latin America
OSI	On-site Inspection

List of Abbreviations

OTH	Over-the-horizon
PLA	People's Liberation Army (China)
R & D	Research and Development
RV	Re-entry vehicle
SAC	Strategic Air Command
SALT	Strategic Arms Limitation Talks
SAR	Synthetic Aperture Radar
SDI	Strategic Defense Initiative
SDIO	Strategic Defense Initiative Organisation (USA)
SIOP	Single Integrated Operational Plan
SIPRI	Stockholm International Peace Research Institute
SLBM	Submarine-launched Ballistic Missile
START	Strategic Arms Reduction Talks
TACT	Transition Arms Control Treaty
UCA	United China Airlines

Notes on the Contributors

David Carlton (*British*) (*co-editor*) is Lecturer in International Studies at the University of Warwick. He holds a Ph.D. degree from the University of London. He is author of *MacDonald versus Henderson: The Foreign Policy of the Second Labour Government*; of *Anthony Eden: A Biography*; and of numerous articles on modern international politics. He is co-editor of nine previous volumes in this series.

Paolo Farinella (*Italian*) is a physicist, working on space physics and planetary science at the University of Pisa, Italy. He is a member of the Italian Union of Scientists for Disarmament and a promoter of the study group on alternative defence concepts for Italy set up by the Florence Forum on the Problems of Peace and War. He is the author of many papers on technical issues regarding nuclear weapons and military activities in space.

William F. Gutteridge (*British*) is Professor Emeritus in International Studies at the University of Aston in Birmingham. He was formerly Senior Lecturer in Commonwealth History and Government at the Royal Military Academy, Sandhurst. He is author of four books relating to the armed forces in new states, with particular reference to Africa. He is editor of *European Security; Nuclear Weapons and Public Confidence*; and co-editor of *The Dangers of New Weapons Systems*.

Ernst W. Hamburger (*Brazilian*) is Professor of Experimental Physics at the University of São Paulo. He is author of numerous research papers on nuclear physics and on problems of education. He has served as Director of the Sociedade Brasileira de Fisica.

Robert d'A. Henderson (*Canadian*) is Assistant Professor of International Relations at the University of Western Ontario. He has also held appointments at the National University of Lesotho and at the University of Ife. He has published articles in various journals, including *The World Today, Orbis* and *Journal of Modern African Studies*.

Notes on the Contributors xiii

Catherine M. Kelleher (*US*) is Director of the Maryland International Security Project at the University of Maryland. She holds a Ph.D degree in Political Science from the Massachusetts Institute of Technology. Her governmental experience includes serving on the staff of the National Security Council. She is author of *Germany and the Politics of Nuclear Weapons*; and of numerous other publications in the field of International Security.

Robert W. Malcolmson (*Canadian*) is Professor of History at Queen's University, Kingston, Ontario. He is author of *Nuclear Fallacies: How We Have Been Misguided Since Hiroshima*, and of several publications on English Social History.

Robert Neild (*British*) is Professor Emeritus of Economics at the University of Cambridge and a Fellow of Trinity College, Cambridge. He served in the British Cabinet Office and Treasury between 1951 and 1956. He is author of *How to Make Up Your Mind about the Bomb*; and of numerous publications in the field of Economics.

Andrea Ottolenghi (*Italian*) is a physicist based at the University of Milan, where he is a member of the Research Group on Nuclear Weapons and Arms Control. Dr Ottolenghi has published extensively on the effects of nuclear war.

Qian Xuefeng *(Chinese)* is based at the Institute of International Studies in Beijing. He has also been a Visiting Study Fellow in International Relations at the University of Oxford.

Carlo Schaerf (*Italian*) (*co-editor*) is Professor of Physics at the University of Rome I. He was previously a Research Associate at Stanford University and on the staff of the Italian Atomic Energy Commission. With Professor Eduardo Amaldi he founded in 1966 the International School on Disarmament and Research on Conflicts (ISODARCO). He was appointed Director of ISODARCO in 1970. He is co-editor of nine previous volumes in this series.

Dietrich Schroeer (*US*) is Professor of Physics in the Department of Physics and Astronomy at the University of North Carolina, Chapel Hill. He is author of *Physics and its Fifth Dimension: Society*; of *Science, Technology and the Nuclear Arms Race*; and of a resource bibliography on physics and the arms race in *American Journal of Physics*, September 1982.

Jane M. O. Sharp (*British*) is based at the Stockholm International Peace Research Institute. She was formerly Resident Scholar on the Peace Studies Program at Cornell University. She has published articles on European security and arms control themes in such journals as *Bulletin of the Atomic Scientists; Arms Control; International Security;* and *International Affairs*. She is author (with David Holloway) of *The Warsaw Pact: Alliance in Transition?*

Shu Yuan H. Chang (*US*) is Professor of International Law at the North-West Institute of Political Science and Law at Xianin the People's Republic of China. She has also taught in Lesotho, the United States and Taiwan. She has published widely on Chinese themes.

Maria Clelia Spreafico (*Italian*) has recently completed a thesis at the University of Rome on the history of alternative defence concepts, in particular civilian-based defence. She has been active in the Italian Peace Movement, is a promoter of the Centro Studi Difesa Civile in Rome, and is a member of the study group on alternative defence concepts for Italy set up by the Florence Forum on the Problems of Peace and War.

K. Subrahmanyam (*Indian*) is Director of the Institute for Defence Studies and Analyses in New Delhi. He was Chairman of the United Nations Study Group on Deterrence, 1985–6. He has published extensively on defence and development issues and, in particular, on Indian security perspectives.

Olga Šuković (*Yugoslav*) is Senior Researcher at the Institute of International Politics and Economics in Belgrade. She has also been a Resident Fellow at the Institute for East–West Security Studies, New York. She has published widely on international security issues with particular reference to the United Nations.

Hylke Tromp (*Dutch*) is a Professor at the Polemological Institute of the University of Groningen. He has been a Visiting Professor at the Free University of Berlin. He was editor of the *UNESCO Yearbook on Peace and Conflict Studies* and has also published extensively in Dutch.

Kosta Tsipis (*US*) is Professor of Physics and Director of the Program in Science and Technology for International Security at the Massachusetts Institute of Technology. He is author of three books, co-editor of seven further books and author of 68 articles on international security issues.

List of Course Participants

Jürgen Altmann (West German) Peace Research Institute Frankfurt, Leimenrode 29, 6000 Frankfurt/M 1, West Germany.

Latiff Salawa Aminu (Nigerian) Nigerian Institute of International Affairs, GPO Box 1727, Lagos, Nigeria.

Stefania Argentini (Italian) Via Sabelli 55, 00185 Roma, Italy.

Gothom Arya (Thai) Faculty of Engineering, Chulalongkorn University, Phyathai Road, Bangkok 10500 Thailand.

Phil Austin (US) 5721-148th SW, Edmonds, Washington 98020, USA.

Dimitri Dino Batani (Italian) USPID Sezione di Milano, Dipartimento di Fisica, Università degli Studi, Via Celoria 16, 20133 Milano, Italy.

Mirjana Benic (Yugoslav) Seferova 4, 41000 Zagreb, Yugoslavia.

Rolf Björnerstedt (Swedish) Myrdalsstiftelsen, Munkbron 11, Stockholm, Sweden.

Angelika Brinkmann (West German) Freie Universität Berlin, Institut für Internationale Politik, Kiebitzweg 3, 1000 Berlin 33, West Germany.

Francesco Calogero (Italian) Dipartimento di Fisica, Università degli Studi, Piazzale Aldo Moro 2, 00185 Roma, Italy.

David Carlton (British) Department of International Studies, University of Warwick, Coventry, United Kingdom.

Antonio Castelli (Italian) Collegio Navale Morosini, Sant 'Elena, 30122 Venezia, Italy.

Xueyin Chen (Chinese) The Institute of Applied Physics and Computational Mathematics, PO Box 8009, Beijing, China.

Maria Clelia Ciciriello (Ialian) Dipartimento di Diritto Pubblico, II Università di Roma, Via Orazio Raimondo, 00173 Roma, Italy.

Giuliano Colombetti (Italian) CNR, Istituto di Biofisica, Via San Lorenzo 26, 56100 Pisa, Italy.

Maurizio Conti (Italian) Via Isonzo 234, 60100 Ancona, Italy.

Giuseppe D'Agosto (Italian) Via Ugo De Carlolis 59, 00136 Roma, Italy.

Silvana De Lillo (Italian) Dipartimento di Fisica, Università di Salerno, 84100 Salerno, Italy.

Brunellesco Dello Sbarba (Italian) Via Ricciarella 32, 56048 Volterra, Italy.

List of Course Participants   xvii

Eymert Den Oudsten (Dutch) Leidsekade 88/III, 1017 PN Amsterdam, The Netherlands.
Athanasios Drougos (Greek) The Polemological Institute, University of Groningen, Heresingel 13, 9711 Groningen, Netherlands.
Hugh C. Dyer (Canadian) Millenium Journal of International Studies, Department of International Relations, London School of Economics and Political Science, Houghton Street, London WC2A 2AE, United Kingdom.
Nabil Abdel Eissa (Egyptian) Physics Department, Faculty of Science, Al Azhar University, Nars City, Cairo, Egypt.
Mirko Elena (Italian) Istituto per la Ricerca Scientifica e Tecnologica, Facoltà di Scienze, 38050 Povo (Trento), Italy.
Gunner Eriksson (Swedish) Technical Peace Research Unit, Chalmers University of Technology, 412 96 Göteborg, Sweden.
Paolo Farinella (Italian) Dipartimento di Matematica, Università di Pisa, Via Buonarroti 2, 56100 Pisa, Italy.
Gil Isabel Ferrer (Spanish) Political Science Department, Autonomous University of Barcelona, Campus de Bellaterra, Barcelona, Spain.
Giuseppe Fusco (Italian) Via Francesco Pardi 18, 56100 Pisa, Italy.
Antonietta Graziani (Italian) Via Livio Salinatore 30, 00175 Roma, Italy.
Allen G. Greb (US) University of California, La Jolla, California 92093, USA.
Laura Guazzone (Italian) Istituto Affari Internazionali, Viale Mazzini 88, 00195 Rome, Italy.
William F. Gutteridge (British) 26 St. Mark's Road, Leamington Spa, Warwickshire CV32 6DL, United Kingdom.
Costas Hadjiconstantinou (Greek) Department of International Studies, Faculty of Law, Aristotelian University of Thessaloniki, Greece.
Gerd Hagmeyer-Gaverus (West German) SIPRI, Pipersväg 28, S-171 73 Solna, Sweden.
Marianna Halkia (Greek) 34–36 Aeolou St., Palio Faliro, Athens 17561, Greece.
Ernst W. Hamburger (Brazilian) Instituto de Fisica, Universidade de São Paulo, Caixa Postal 20516, 05506 São Paulo, Brazil.
Robert D'Arcy Henderson (Canadian) Department of Political Science, University of Western Ontario, London, Ontario, Canada, N6A5C2.

Brett Aaron Henry (US) Q-060, University of California, San Diego, California 92093, USA.
Frank von Hippel (US) Center for Energy and Environmental Studies, Princeton University, Princeton, New Jersey, USA.
Side Hu (Chinese) The Institute of Applied Physics and Computational Mathematics, China Association for Science and Technology, PO Box 8009, Beijing, China.
Xinsheng Hua (Chinese) The Institute of Applied Physics and Computational Mathematics, China Association for Science and Technology, Beijing, China.
Ali B. Jarbawi (Palestinian) Political Science Program, Birzeit University, Birzeit, PO Bank 14, West Bank, Via Israel.
Catherine McArdle Kelleher (US) The University of Maryland, School of Public Affairs, Morril Hall, College Park, Maryland 20742, USA.
Zoran Konstantinovic (Yugoslav) Pantovcak 172, 41000 Zagreb, Yugoslavia.
Juha Kotilainen (Finnish) Betaniankatu 3, Asunto 12, Turku 81, Finland.
Ignazio Lazzizzera (Italian) Dipartimento di Fisica, Università di Trento, 38050 Povo (Trento), Italy.
Francesco Lenci (Italian) CNR, Istituto di Biofisica, Via San Lorenzo 26, 56100 Pisa, Italy.
Evamaria Loose-Weintraub (West German) SIPRI, Bergshamra, S-171 73 Solna, Sweden.
Matteo G. Luccio (Italian) Center for International Studies, E38-600 MIT, Cambridge, Massachusetts 02139, USA.
Reneo Lukic (Yugoslav) IUHEI, 132 Rue de Lausanne, 1202 Genève 21, Switzerland.
David McKillop (US) 5169 Tilden Street, NW, Washington, DC 20016, USA.
Robert W. Malcolmson (Canadian) Department of History, Queen's University, Kingston, Ontario, Canada K7L 3N6.
Howard L. Mann (Canadian) Department of International Relations, London School of Economics, Houghton St, Aldwych, London, United Kingdom.
Mara Marinaki (Greek) Greek Ministry of Foreign Affairs, 1 Akadimias St, Athens, Greece.
Haider Mehdi (US) ELU Arts, Kuwait University, PO Box 13388, 71954 Kaifan, Kuwait.
Jan Melissen (Dutch) Polemologisch Institute, University of Groningen, Heresingel 13, 9711 ER Groningen, The Netherlands.

List of Course Participants

Blanche Isobel Merz (Australian) 23 Duke St, Kew 3101, Melbourne, Australia.

Kurt Karl Merz (Australian) 23 Duke St, Kew 3101, Melbourne, Australia.

Jorma K. Miettinin (Finnish) Department of Radiochemistry, University of Helsinki, Unioninkatu 35, 00170 Helsinki, Finland.

Daniela Minerva (Italian) Corso Trieste 95, 00198 Roma, Italy.

Guido Monterisi (Italian) Corso Trieste 199, 00198 Roma, Italy.

Yoko Nakai (Japanese) Aoyama Co-op 806, 3-27, Shiguya 4-Chome, Shibuya-ku, Tokyo, Japan.

Robert Neild (British) Trinity College, Cambridge CB2 1TQ, United Kingdom.

Sanaa Osseiran (Lebanese) 80 bis Rue de Sèvres, Paris 75007, France.

Andrea Ottolenghi (Italian) Dipartimento di Fisica, Università degli Studi, Via Celoria 16, 20133 Milano, Italy.

Dimitrios Papadopoulos-Tsayannis (Greek) 11 Tsimiki St, Salonica 54624, Greece.

Alessandro Pascolini (Italian) Dipartimento di Fisica, Università di Padova, Via Marzolo 8, 35131 Padova, Italy.

Arun J. B. Patwari (Indian) 759 Sudama Nagar, Indore (MP), India.

Qian Xuefeng (Chinese) 18 Jian Guo Rd (Middle), Shanghai, China.

Anna Scafati Reale (Italian) Istituto Superiore di Sanità, Laboratori di Fisica, Viale Regina Elena 299, 00199 Roma, Italy.

Armando Reale (Italian) Dipartimento di Fisica, Università di L'Aquila, 67100 L'Aquila, Italy.

Carlo Schaerf (Italian) Dipartimento di Fisica, Università degli Studi, Piazzale Aldo Moro 2, 00185 Roma, Italy.

Dietrich Schroeer (US) Department of Physics and Astronomy, 278 Phillips Hall 039A, University of North Carolina, Chapel Hill, North Carolina 27514, USA.

Jane M. O. Sharp (British) Center for European Studies, Harvard University, 5 Bryant St, Cambridge, Massachusetts, USA.

Shu Yuan Hsieh Chang (US) North-West Institute of Political Science and Law, Xian, People's Republic of China.

Maria Clelia Spreafico (Italian) Via G. Pezzana 102, 00197 Roma, Italy.

Jean Pierre Stroot (Belgian) CERN, EP Division, 1211 Genève 23, Switzerland.

K. Subrahmanyam (Indian) Institute for Defence Studies and Analyses, Sapruhouse, Barakhamba Road, New Delhi 110001, India.

Olga Šuković (Yugoslav) Institute of International Politics and Economics, Makedonska 25, 11000 Belgrade, Yugoslavia.

List of Course Participants

Johan Swahn (Swedish) Technical Peace Research Unit, Chalmers University of Technology, 412 96 Göteborg, Sweden.

Takashi Takagi (Japanese) 2-12-10 Narita-higashi, Suginami-Ku, Tokyo 166, Japan.

Giancarlo Tenaglia (Italian) Via Chiusi 2, 00139 Roma, Italy.

Hans Tolhoek (Dutch) Institute for Theoretical Physics, PO Box 800, 9700 AV Groningen, The Netherlands.

Hylke Tromp (Dutch) Polemological Institute, Heresingel 13, Groningen, The Netherlands.

Kosta Tsipis (US) MIT, Cambridge, Massachusetts 02139, USA.

Mikel K. Tsipis (US) 26 Egmont St, Brookline, Massachusetts 02146, USA.

Talitha Vassalli di Dachenhausen (Italian) Facoltà di Scienze Politiche, Università degli Studi, Via G. San Felice, 80100 Napoli, Italy.

Ben F. Weller (Sierra Leonian) Department of Political Science, Fourah Bay College, University of Sierra Leone, Freetown, Sierra Leone.

Andrew White (British) Department of International Relations, London School of Economics, Houghton Street, London WC2A 2AE, United Kingdom.

Marina Yarnell (US) Institute of French Studies, New York University, 15 Washington Mews, New York, New York 10003, USA.

Iradj Ziai (Iranian) 12 voie L. Terray, 94000 Creteil, France.

Paolo Zuffa (Italian) Largo Don Giuseppe Morosini 1, 00195 Roma, Italy.

1 Summary of Discussions
William F. Gutteridge

The eleventh course of the International School on Disarmanent and Research on Conflicts (ISODARCO) was held at San Miniato, Italy from 20 to 30 August 1986. A major part of the proceedings was devoted to two related questions: why has there been an arms race; and why have attempts at arms control and disarmament apparently failed?

Formal efforts to achieve disarmament have been going on for nearly a century and it is obvious that almost every nation state is much more highly armed than ever. It was suggested that in this process the search for a military balance, the establishment of balanced constraints by negotiation, has proved an illusion and a wrong way to seek peace. Balance, it was argued, implied symmetry to the point of identity and, because geopolitical conditions vary so much, it would never be possible to prove to the satisfaction of all parties the existence of a balance. Consequently more realistic objectives might be sufficiency rather than supremacy, and defensive rather than offensive superiority.

The adoption of overtly peaceful and co-operative aims by major powers seems to be the essential prerequisite. Though the need for continuing arms control negotiations or discussions was emphasised by some participants, bargaining-type negotiations in pursuit of balance in detail do seem to have proved counter-productive and likely to continue so unless there is a change in the international political climate resulting from a radical shift in popular attitudes.

This discussion was followed by an examination of prevailing belief systems and 'mind sets' in political and security establishments and the need for a shift from confrontational to more co-operative attitudes and how this was to be achieved. In such circumstances there seems to be a premium on unilateral initiatives, if the widespread prevailing national biases in favour of 'strong' that is confrontational stances are to be offset.

In this connection the origin in the United States of the attitudes leading to the nuclearisation of Western security policy were explained. Initial nuclear superiority forty years ago confirmed the American inclination to play from strength. (The view of the atomic weapon as the greatest single source of military strength was also in vogue in Great Britain by 1948). In the American case nuclear weapons came quickly to be seen not only as cost-effective but as an alternative to universal military training and conscription. Consequently a belief in the feasibility of perfect defence, in the face of an increased Soviet threat, has, several participants maintained, largely accounted for the apparent dissonance between American rhetoric and operational policy. A deliberately diplomatic and conciliatory stance has thus proved difficult to establish in the face of a long-standing assertion of superiority.

The problems posed by the incidence and character of the hundreds of conventional wars since 1945 in any attempt to encourage more co-operative oriented societies were used to demonstrate the complexity and long-term nature of any substantial process of change in international relations. The proliferation of independent states in the twentieth century has been accompanied by much more ready access to sophisticated weapons. The purchasers, almost as much as the suppliers, carry responsibility for this. On the other hand, major powers have no moral authority, in the light of their own records, to impose security arrangements in different parts of the world. In any case, the roots of third-world violence lie primarily in political and economic problems. The need to encourage firmly based regional security arrangements arising out of local initiatives was stressed.

A presentation on the military stance and attitude to disarmament of Brazil broadened participants' understanding of the processes involved. Brazil is a country which has developed virtual self-sufficiency in arms supply, in spite of not being subject to any real threat, and which is now exporting a very high proportion of its weapons production. Its recent experience illustrated very clearly the need to identify the social forces behind political aims. Though Brazil is not regarded as likely to become a nuclear power in this decade, the favourable attitude adopted by the military authorities there towards the scientific establishment has evidently provided scientists there with a privileged facility for criticism of government policies as well as financial backing for research.

China's defence policy and attitude to disarmament in their turn were shown to reflect clearly the special requirements of a country with a very large population, in the process of political and economic modernisation. A clear commitment to 'no first use' of nuclear weapons, while at the same time underlining the responsibility of the United States and the Soviet Union for real progress in arms control and disarmament, was regarded in discussion as realistic in the circumstances. Assessment of the factors encouraging a major reduction in personnel in the armed forces provided a significant illustration of the importance of identifying accurately the national interest and its capacity for survival in the face of external threats. The comprehensive political and social role of the military in China differentiates it from its counterparts in other countries: correspondingly the newly formed peace movement is more an agent than a critic of government policy.

Extended discussion on deterrence as a strategy led to a further debate on the general issues of peace and war raised earlier. One presentation took the form of a historical world view (from Agincourt to the present day) of the changing nature of war, based on the contention that the proposition 'if you want peace, prepare for war' has been rendered invalid by the destructiveness and lethality of modern weapons, their means of delivery and control. This and new political circumstances, it was argued, have undermined the cultural 'norms' surrounding so-called rational decision making which provide the common ground necessary for effective deterrence. Intervention in Vietnam and Afghanistan was not deterred.

It was argued that the choice lies between the elimination of nuclear weapons and learning to live with them. There was considerable doubt as to whether an alternative framework to deterrence for coping with these weapons could be readily devised. Real incentives to co-operate at a high level will be necessary if what some see as 'the overwhelmingly negative concept', in the nuclear age, of deterrence is to be replaced.

For this reason a discussion on 'finite' or 'existential' deterrence attracted much interest. A concept of deterrent sufficiency was considered which might be realised by a reduction of existing weapons overall to one-tenth of their present levels. There were, however, criticisms to the effect that crossing the nuclear threshold at all would be going most of the way to all-out nuclear war, that stocks of fissile materials, especially in the Soviet Union, would be difficult to verify and that parallel cuts in conventional forces might make the ensuing situation much less stable and even that nuclear warning shots might in new circumstances seem an attractive option. In general, however, deterrent sufficiency at a relatively low level seemed an idea worthy of further exploration.

In this connection the importance of evolving valid systems for evaluating the effects of nuclear weapons was stressed. Confidence about arms control measures might depend on reliable information of this kind. Similarly, continual revision according to the latest knowledge of the calculations relating to the extent and intensity of a 'nuclear winter' is vital to its credibility as a deterrent factor. Statistical semantics might prove in this as in other fields an obstacle to disarmament measures.

Chemical deterrence was presented as much more debatable than nuclear deterrence, largely because effective retaliation remains dependent on the existence of suitable weather conditions. The long history of chemical and bacteriological warfare goes back to classical times but only in the present century has it become a serious issue. Recently very lengthy and slow negotiations in Geneva, and the use of chemical weapons by Iraq, have generated more interest amongst the powers. Though a comprehensive international agreement appears a long way off, the negotiating atmosphere is improving partly because of pressures within the North Atlantic Treaty Organisation (NATO) and in the United States. Scientific investigations in Finland have made an important contribution to the general understanding. A joint US–Soviet general draft is now a possibility and may restrain tendencies to escalation through the procurement of a new generation of binary weapons. The special dangers of nuclear retaliation to the use of chemical weapons in Europe were underlined. In addition the controversy over the use of CS gas in domestic riots was reactivated: the distinction between such use and use in war still seemed widely accepted.

In military and political terms, international verification of agreements on arms control is necessary as an assurance, quite apart from detailed problems of legal compliance and determination of violations. Demands for verification have been used, however, to oppose or simply obstruct agreements and particularly to provide an excuse for not negotiating. For the purposes of national security, it is clearly important to understand at what level of clandestine activity by one state another's security might be jeopardised. Therefore adequate detection has to be defined and the limits of uncertainty and ambiguity determined.

Against this background, the technical possibilities, if supported by traditional intelligence gathering, were discussed. The general conclusions were that design, development, testing, underground testing and military activities could all now be satisfactorily monitored by a combination of means. Some areas for doubt remain. It was argued however, that new techniques of seismological measurement leave little doubt about underground tests, in spite of official US claims that it is difficult to distinguish between earthquakes and nuclear explosions.

Verification of the presence of nuclear warheads might in some circumstances be an issue in the maintenance or establishment of Nuclear-weapon-free Zones (NWFZs) in different parts of the world. Indeed the transit of the armed forces of nuclear powers or the existence of their bases within a particular region were seen by a number of participants as a major obstacle to the implementation of a denuclearisation policy by a group of neighbouring states.

In a review of developments in the last thirty years from the Latin American Treaty to the South African enigma, this factor, the question of nuclear explosions for peaceful purposes and problems of geographical limitation were emphasised. The Nordic and Balkan proposals were examined in more detail, and even the presence, in the latter case, of members of NATO and the Warsaw Pact was seen by some as a stimulus to the process of reaching agreement. The general, but by no means unanimous, view was the NWFZs were more important as confidence-building rather than as arms control or security measures, and that the discretion of individual countries to sign (as in the Tlatelolco Treaty) and the lack of necessity for initial unanimity in a region could provide a valuable model for international agreements more generally.

A discussion of coercive diplomacy on the part of nuclear-weapon states had obvious relevance to the establishment of NWFZs. It was argued that the threat of the use of nuclear weapons by nuclear-weapon states was not only inherent in strategic deterrence but had been regularly exercised in relation to the developing world. The Non-proliferation Treaty, it was asserted, amounted to a licence to proliferate for existing nuclear-weapon powers and worked against the security interests of non-nuclear states. Effectively it makes initiatives for NWFZs dependent on the convenience of the main nuclear-weapon powers. In all these circumstances, those developing states with the potential capacity to acquire nuclear weapons might be justified in keeping their nuclear option open.

That coercive diplomacy was often exercised by major powers against third-world countries was not contested, but the role of nuclear weapons in this connection was questioned in some detail. It was also suggested that exercising the nuclear option would undermine the economies of the countries concerned, however necessary it seemed to limit the dominance of the existing nuclear weapon powers.

A central issue of the discussions was the Strategic Defense Initiative (SDI)–its nature, feasibility and political implications. The historical perspective set out provided a valuable corrective to some of the fixed values and stereotyped images prevailing. The inherent contradictions implicit in President Ronald Reagan's own specific initiative were examined. There now seems little doubt that he initially proposed the creation of what amounted to a 'leak-proof shield' involving total population protection. How this had come about in the face of general scientific, as well as political, scepticism was discussed at length. Some were reluctant to accept the value attached to the more hawkish statements made by some advisers–the arguments were related back to the earlier discussion of the contradictions between apparently declaratory and actual operational positions.

The fact that there is little reference to the Soviet Union in Reagan's original speech served to confirm to some that this really was a 'utopian' proposal, and not so different from those made by other political leaders, including Mikhail Gorbachev. The danger that a utopian fantasy might be believed and become part of the strategic reality was stressed by others. There was considerable doubt expressed about the proposition that in the longer term SDI would come to seem of little importance, and only result in a new modified mix and balance between offensive and defensive provisions. Critics of this view maintained that it would greatly increase uncertainty by introducing many more variables into an already complex situation.

This debate took place against a background of technical knowledge provided at an earlier stage. The scientific experts differed about the feasibility of particular aspects of a defensive system, whether in space or at the points of departure and re-entry of missiles. However, they fundamentally agreed about the impracticality of a comprehensive 'perfect' system. In any case, with the exception of limited anti-missile technology, deployment of any networked system lay twenty or more years ahead and relatively simple counter-measures are already on the cards. As the population becomes more sceptical about the protection offered so politicians will have more difficulty in justifying expenditure. On the technical side, decoys and disguises for warheads and X-ray lasers were discussed in some detail. Terminal defence for point targets might be possible, but at other points relatively cheap counter-measures could be devised and effectively deployed. This might well account for the recently more relaxed Soviet attitude to SDI proposals.

The effects of SDI on arms control related mainly to the Anti-ballistic Missile (ABM) Treaty which some felt had to be radically revised in any case. In this area as in relation to the impact of SDI on NATO the obstacle presented by British and French nuclear forces was raised. In general the view of European NATO countries and of Canada was considered to be cynical, especially in regard to research contracts. Whether facilitated by government agreement or not, commercial firms in the computer and electronic industries were coming to terms with the fact that America is clearly not a charitable institution and they had no alternative but to take advantage of the crumbs from the rich man's table, while they lasted. Militarily and politically SDI seems to involve a move from deterrence to defence and as such presents NATO generally with a range of new uncertainties–strategic doctrine accommodation to this might be traumatic even if the SDI programme is never implemented.

Part I
The General Arms Race

2 The Pursuit of Security in the Nuclear Age
Robert W. Malcolmson

In November 1945, just three months after the bombing of Hiroshima, J. Robert Oppenheimer, the scientific director of the Los Alamos laboratory where the first atomic bombs were designed, made the following remark: 'We have made a thing, a most terrible weapon, that has altered abruptly and profoundly the nature of the world.'[1] Others at that time expressed similar views. The atomic bomb, they agreed, was undeniably a revolutionary tool of destruction; its creation marked a new departure in the world of power politics; and its implications, they foresaw, were likely to penetrate into all aspects of experience, nationally and globally. But, they asked, would these implications be widely and clearly appreciated? Would political thinking be able to come to terms with this extraordinary breakthrough in military science? These questions, of course, remain highly pertinent today. In the course of the following discussion, it is proposed to examine our longstanding approach, in the West, to the presence of this extraordinary power of destruction. In particular, one central question is raised: how has our pursuit of security been affected by, and related to, the existence of, as Oppenheimer put it, this 'most terrible weapon'?

Let us first recall some of the political choices that were made in the immediate postwar years. The United States, as the first nuclear nation, was destined, whatever it did, to set much of the agenda of the early atomic age, for better or for worse. The Soviet Union could react, but it could not initiate; it was in no position to influence significantly the terms of atomic energy policy. Washington, with its atomic monopoly, held all the technological high cards. And the United States chose, for various reasons, to play from what it saw as strength and to emphasise its nuclear arsenal as the centrepiece of its national security policy.

It is, in fact, abundantly clear that the years from Harry Truman to Lyndon Johnson were marked by a pronounced *nuclearisation* of American – and, more broadly, Western – defence policy. Some

American officials spoke of the atomic bomb as their 'winning weapon', politically speaking. As the Cold War intensified, increasing reliance was placed on the alleged 'deterrent' power of weapons of mass destruction and of their potential value in restraining and perhaps combating Communism. An early expression of this view is found in a letter of September 1948, written to the American Secretary of Defense by the British Minister of Defence, which staked out a position that became commonplace in both Europe and North America. 'The atomic weapon,' he asserted, 'is the greatest single source of military strength in the world at present, and it is in the interests of the security of the United States, as well as that of the United Kingdom, that both countries should develop it to the maximum of their ability, and with all possible speed'.[2] (The Americans were less than keen on the idea of a British atomic bomb). Communism, it was agreed, had to be contained; containment, from the late 1940s, was increasingly construed in terms of military might (as distinct from political and economic vitality); and the most robust and least troublesome bulwark of freedom was said to be the *deterrent power* of weapons of mass destruction. The goal was clear: create a healthy fear in Moscow of American destructive power and, by means of this fear, keep Communism in line (at a minimum) or even roll it back (a larger ambition).

An important development was occurring during these years: American policy (and, from around 1953, NATO policy) became committed to a very expansive vision of the role of nuclear weapons. These weapons came to be treated as the decisive factor in the conduct of Cold War diplomacy. Rather than showing caution and restraint in the face of their destructive power, American policy-makers thought largely in terms of their utility and of the messages of strength they would convey to Moscow. Even after the Soviet Union, to the surprise and consternation of American leaders, joined the nuclear club in August 1949, there was no rethinking of official policy. Indeed, with the decision in 1950 to develop the H-bomb, the stakes were increased. Although the monopoly might be lost, a decisive predominance, it was said, could still be maintained. As an official in the State Department put it in January 1950 (and this was a widely-shared opinion): 'I assume that we can maintain a wide superiority in atomic weapons over the Soviet Union, probably for an indefinite period of time.'[3] Such superiority was thought to be essential for US national security; indeed, it was commonly regarded as the foundation of a buoyant and flourishing American foreign policy. Thomas Finletter, a former Secretary of the Air Force, made this point forcefully in 1954. 'Much of our diplomatic strength in recent years,' he said, 'has come from our obviously overwhelming superiority in atomic weapons. Nothing but weakness will come from losing it.' He spoke of the mid-1950s as 'a time when the survival of the country calls on us to be vigilant as we never have been before in maintaining our air-atomic supremacy over the Russians.'[4] Vigilance, supremacy, staying ahead: these were watchwords of the brief era of Pax Americana.

The postwar years, we can now see, witnessed a dramatic reworking of the political agenda of fear. Immediately after Hiroshima, public consciousness was focused on fear of the bomb itself and the new weapon's implications for an insecure future. By the end of the 1940s this fear had been largely swept aside, to be replaced by the fear of Communism. The real threat to civilisation, it came to be believed, was not so much nuclear weaponry but rather Soviet barbarism and the Soviet quest for world domination. Paul Boyer, in a major study of nuclear consciousness during these years, has drawn attention to the orthodoxies that had become dominant by 1950. The fears and warnings of just a few years before came to be seen as excessive, alarmist, and unwarranted. The bomb, it was now said, 'was not so bad after all, and in any event it was here to stay'. 'The duty of the good citizen was to come to terms with it, and the best way to do that was to show enthusiasm for the peaceful atom and support civil defense.'[5] The challenge facing Americans was to learn how to cope with nuclear war, should it come, and to concentrate on dealing with the insidious evil of Communism. The 'terrible weapon' of 1945 had become, as Boyer puts it, 'the shield of the Republic by 1950.' 'America must have as many nuclear weapons as possible, and the bigger the better, for the death struggle with communism that lay ahead.'[6] The bomb, in this new climate of fear, was itself no longer seen as such a fearful thing.

This revised thinking helped to liberate nuclear weapons from previous constraints. Civilian controls were relaxed, nuclear tough-mindedness became fashionable, and there was a kind of normalisation of the status of nuclear weapons. To use them, it was suggested, would not be all that remarkable. John Foster Dulles, the US Secretary of State, made this position clear in a speech he gave to a closed NATO ministerial meeting in April 1954. The United States, he said, believed that nuclear weapons 'must now be treated as in fact having become "conventional". . . . It should be our agreed policy, in case of war, to use atomic weapons as conventional weapons against the military assets of the enemy whenever and wherever it would be of advantage to do so.'[7] Such a policy required a massive increase in the nuclear arsenal. In 1947 the United States possessed only 13 atomic bombs; in 1948 it had about 50. Thereafter the new weapons came to be mass produced. When Dwight Eisenhower was elected President, there were around 1000 warheads in the US nuclear stockpile. By the time he left office the arsenal totalled close to 20 000 warheads and was still growing.[8] The few efforts that were made to halt or slow down this extraordinary build-up were completely unsuccessful. Maintaining the nuclear advantage, it was said, was crucial for the security of free peoples.

But what did 'nuclear advantage' mean? Undoubtedly it meant different things to different parties, and some of these meanings would not have gone unnoticed in Moscow. We now know – and the Kremlin certainly would have assumed – that the Pentagon, in the immediate postwar years, developed a strong interest in nuclear first-strike strategies. While declaratory policy usually emphasised deterrence and retaliation, operational planning had in mind a more assertive posture. As the Joint Chiefs of Staff remarked in January 1950, '[we] cannot accept as a premise that either the super [thermonuclear] bomb or the atomic bomb is valuable only as a weapon of retaliation.'[9] Obtaining and preserving a first-strike capability was regarded by many military men as essential. Military officers, particularly in the US Air Force, were acutely conscious of the long-established advantages of striking first; and their emphasis on counterforce strategy (attacks against the military assets of the enemy) was inherently pre-emptive, since it only made sense if Soviet forces could be destroyed before they left their bases. As one historian has concluded, 'The notion that the United States and not the Soviet Union would be the first nation to use nuclear weapons in the next war was not only the expectation of the SAC [Strategic Air Command] planners; it was also the principal idea upon which most of their planning was based.'[10]

A strictly retaliatory view of 'deterrence', then, was certainly not dominant during the 1950s, partly because it was seen by many officers as dangerously constrictive and reactive. 'We don't build forces for deterrence . . .', observed Nathan Twining, Chairman of the Joint Chiefs of Staff from 1957 to 1960. 'We build forces for national defense – to fight. Their deterrent effect is only a peacetime by-product of their war waging capability.'[11] This outlook was common among military planners and strategists. In the words of a work completed in 1960 – and here its authors were expressing an orthodox opinion – 'The only effective military posture for deterring general nuclear war is an up-to-date operational capacity to wage such a war for the purpose of winning it should it be thrust upon us.'[12] It was, of course, simply assumed that any nuclear strike by the United States would be defensive and a legitimate reaction to Communist provocation, usually called 'aggression'.

The Pentagon's attachment to traditional strategy – to the prospect of fighting and winning wars, including nuclear wars – persists in the 1980s. Indeed, with the revival of a hardline, toughly nationalist foreign policy in Washington, this strategy is now taken more seriously than it was 20 years ago. Whatever talk there might be about 'unwinnable' nuclear wars, wars 'without winners' and the like, in the eyes of many military and strategic planners, in both West and East, striking first is seen as less bad than striking second.[13] The pressures to adopt pre-emptive postures have been growing, in the US Navy as well as in the Air Force.[14] First-strike options are being taken more seriously, and Star Wars will make them seem more plausible to anxious Soviet planners. As Thomas Powers has observed, 'With glacial inexorability, the fear of war is being pushed aside by the fear of being caught on the ground.'[15] In the face of much official talk about 'deterrence', we should take note of the view of one of today's most prominent nuclear strategists, and a US government adviser of impeccable hardline, anti-Soviet credentials. 'It is likely', writes Colin S. Gray, 'that it will be the United States which first feels moved to threaten and execute a central nuclear strike.'[16]

Official thinking about nuclear weapons in the 1950s did not go unchallenged. A highly militarised – indeed, nuclearised – conception of containment was certainly not cost-free, and it had its critics, both at home and abroad. One of the earliest and most probing of these challengers of orthodox opinion was George Kennan, the writer, diplomat, and originator of the policy of containment. Kennan conveyed the core of his objections in his 1957 Reith Lectures on the BBC:

> the weapon of mass destruction is a sterile and hopeless weapon ... which cannot in any way serve the purposes of a constructive and hopeful foreign policy. ... The suicidal nature of this weapon renders it unsuitable both as a sanction of diplomacy and as the basis of an alliance. ... There can be no coherent relations between such a weapon and the normal objects of national policy. A

defence posture built around a weapon suicidal in its implications can serve in the long run only to paralyze national policy, to undermine alliances, and to drive everyone deeper and deeper into the hopeless exertions of the weapons race.[17]

Political purpose, according to Kennan, was being weakened, not strengthened, as a result of the reliance on nuclear weapons. The power to destroy was being confused with the power to influence. Modern weapons of mass destruction, Kennan had pointed out several years earlier, 'reach backward beyond the frontiers of western civilization, to the concepts of warfare which were once familiar to the Asiatic hordes. They cannot really be reconciled with a political purpose directed to shaping, rather than destroying, the lives of the adversary.'[18] As Kennan and a few other observers could see, a special kind of illusion was taking hold within Western, and especially American, political culture: an illusion that equated nuclear weaponry with national strength.

The nuclear-based policy of the United States and its allies had a certain superficial credibility as long as the Soviet Union was nuclear-weak. For a few years, during which the Soviet Union was openly exposed to American nuclear strikes, the American homeland was invulnerable to Soviet strikes of any kind, nuclear or conventional. But such relative Soviet weakness, as some foresaw, could not last indefinitely. Nuclear weaponry had made killing spectacularly easy – so easy that no unilateral defence could be expected to prevent devastation. And it was only a matter of time until American society was exposed to nuclear weapons and their long-range delivery systems in the hands of a rival. It was obvious (or at least it certainly should have been) that Moscow had the strongest possible incentive to 'correct' the problem of the invulnerability of American territory. In fact, it soon became evident that Soviet leaders were determined to show that two could play the nuclear game, first under Nikita Khrushchev, with his rocket-rattling theatrics, and later under Leonid Brezhnev, when the Soviet arms build-up was particularly pronounced. The Kremlin demonstrated vigorously that it, too, could produce nuclear weapons in abundance. In response to the colossal American nuclear build-up, Moscow offered a colossal build-up of its own. And in so doing it completely deprived Washington of its previous nuclear 'advantage'.

American and NATO's dependence on nuclear weapons did not yield happy long-term results. For the United States became, objectively, more insecure, more exposed to crippling attack, than ever before. As two distinguished Americans, former Secretary of Defense, Robert McNamara, and Hans Bethe, a Nobel Laureate, have observed, 'Virtually every technical initiative in the nuclear arms race has come from the United States, but the net result has been a steady erosion of American security.'[19] High technology, in which Americans have put great faith, brought the United States, in a very few years, to a perilous point in its history. For in time the technology of mass destruction, on which the West came to depend so heavily, was mastered by those who are said to be our enemies.

This *mutual* vulnerability is not what the United States bargained for when it chose, shortly after the Second World War, to pursue a technological armaments race. There was general confidence that this competition could be managed to American advantage. But this faith was misplaced. So-called improvements in military technology have resulted in a precipitate decline in global security. And, while numerous political commentators and no small number of electors have concluded that this nuclear competition serves no useful purpose, powerful forces within the American government have always been deeply committed to this competition. The pursuit of nuclear advantage, partly with the intent of increasing Soviet insecurity, has been central to American policy for forty years, and it flourishes still. It underlay the strong American hostility in the mid-1980s to a ban on underground nuclear tests, despite overwhelming evidence that Moscow was keen to negotiate a ban and that adequate means of verification were available. Washington was wedded to nuclear weapons, and this knot of dependency was being tied even tighter during the 1980s.

The legacy of the pursuit of nuclear advantage weighs heavily on current decision making. Bureaucracies, after all, do not welcome fundamental change; inertia, while not necessarily decisive, is extraordinarily powerful; and these forces of inertia are closely allied with ideologies of fervent Anti-Communism – ideologies that continue to identify nuclear firepower with national well-being.

This, then, is one inheritance. And yet in the face of this formidable nuclear addiction, certain uncomfortable conclusions became virtually self-evident. The nuclear age has revealed, for all to see, an extraordinary ambiguity in the notion of power. Power no longer means what it used to mean. As Henry Kissinger once remarked, 'Until the beginning of the nuclear age it would have been inconceivable that a country could possess too much military strength for effective political use; every addition of power was – at least theoretically – politically useful. The nuclear age destroyed this traditional measure.'[20] For while we now have virtually unlimited power to destroy, this capacity implies very little power to get anyone to do anything. This remarkable power has been, in most respects, politically useless. Moreover, it has been accompanied by the emergence of the fact of absolute vulnerability; for our lives are now inescapably in Soviet hands, just as their lives are in American hands, and there is nothing that either side can do to alter this fundamental fact of life.

Unless, that is, one believes in Star Wars. For President Ronald Reagan's vision of space-based defences promises that the world can be remade. It assures us that the mutuality of vulnerability can be overcome. It imagines that new revolutions can undo those of nuclear physics. Star Wars holds forth a comforting dream: a dream that America can, by means of science, turn the clock back, regain the capacity for meaningful self-defence, and (perhaps) totally disarm 'the enemy'. It promises that, in the face of modern technologies of destruction, the United States can actually repeal the nuclear age, and that it can do this by itself, regardless of what the Soviets think or do. The glittering promises of Star Wars did not dim during the three years after March 1983. Indeed, in his State of the Union Message in February 1986, Reagan raised the rhetorical ante. He assured his countrymen that

> the same technology transforming our lives can solve the greatest problem of the 20th Century. A security shield can one day render nuclear weapons obsolete and free mankind from the prison of nuclear terror. America met one historic challenge and went to the moon. Now, America must meet another – to make our strategic defense real for all the citizens of Planet Earth.[21]

Of course, many American planners know that Star Wars is being oversold. After all, the essence of defence is attrition, not perfection; and nuclear weapons ensure that attrition is now irrelevant, a concept without meaning. It may well be that few of these planners and strategists actually believe, with their President, that nuclear weapons can be made 'impotent and obsolete' (notwithstanding the fact that some of the Star Wars technologies are new versions of nuclear weapons!). However, many of these people are highly attracted to plans for the intensive militarisation of outer space. Space, for them, is the new frontier. Now that the Soviet-American rivalry has reached a kind of stalemate on earth, the best 'terrain' for restoring an important degree of American military superiority, they think, is beyond the earth's atmosphere. It is 'out there' that the Soviet menace can be countered advantageously. Two Air Force officers put this priority clearly in 1981, writing in the *Naval War College Review*. It is essential, they said, 'to engage the Soviets aggressively in a race for the high ground of space in order to secure for ourselves a position of space superiority.'[22] According to two other USAF officers, also writing in the early 1980s, 'Space constitutes America's best opportunity... to get out in front of and shape what will eventually become *the decisive arena of military competition.*'[23]

We, in the West, have had and still have two principal choices in dealing with the nuclear peril. One alternative emphasises that this *common* peril has to be handled politically, in some collaborative manner. It stresses diplomatic over military solutions. According to this view, there is only one way that the United States and the Soviet Union can save themselves from each other's warheads, and that is together. Or, to put it differently, we can have either mutual security or mutual insecurity, either mutual survival or mutual destruction; whatever we get, it will be mutual.

The other view asserts that we can save ourselves by ourselves – by unilateral action. This has often been tried in the past. Indeed, it has been a central impetus behind the arms race. Going it alone has been and still is a major ideological commitment in the American body politic. Star Wars is the latest scheme to embrace this faith in unilateralism, this 'can-do' confidence that no challenge is too great for the greatness of the United States. As former US Secretary of Defense, James R. Schlesinger, has remarked: 'The American psyche believes that perfect defense *should* be attainable. In that we differ from all other nations. It is this unique belief that underlies the current hope for the SDI.'[24] The United States, it is popularly felt, should be a completely free agent. The United States is thought to be capable of just about anything; it can transcend what limits other nations. As for vulnerability, it is considered to be both unendurable and un-American. These are deep beliefs. And such beliefs comprise the ideological underpinnings of the make-believe of Star Wars.

Technology has been made to promise a great deal throughout the nuclear age. Now it is being forced to promise Utopia. The fact that such promises are sometimes taken seriously is, perhaps, a symptom of the malaise of our times and testimony to the desperation induced by a nuclear dependency that has undermined rather than promoted American security.

The late Averell Harriman, US Ambassador to the Soviet Union during the mid-1940s, once observed: 'The weaponry that came out of World War Two, nuclear weapons, is what changed the world. We can no longer shake fists the way we used to.'[25] In the nuclear age, threats have an entirely new meaning. Displays of muscularity have lost much of their plausibility. Restraint, in fact, is now more likely to pay dividends. Most importantly, it is no longer clear that war can serve as a tolerable arbiter of disputes between sovereign states.

It is worth recalling, in conclusion, the reflections of a participant from a middle power in the birth of the nuclear age, Lester B. Pearson. In November 1945, Pearson, then Canada's Ambassador in Washington, prepared a top secret document, entitled 'Canadian Memorandum on Atomic Warfare', in which he spoke of the prospect of a nuclearised future. If no international agreements for restraint can be reached, he predicted:

> there will be competition. Such competition in the development of atomic energy for destructive purposes would be the most bitter and disastrous armament race run. Like every other armament race in history, it would follow the same course, of fear, suspicion, rivalry, desperation and war; only in this case the war would probably mean international suicide.[26]

Pearson's warning would undoubtedly be applauded in many circles today. There is little evidence, however, that his or similar warnings have carried any weight in those places where power most resolutely resides – that is, in the world's various so-called 'national security' establishments. In these establishments the nuclear addiction is deeply rooted. So too is the passion for military solutions to political problems. These are addictions that are sustained by inertia, huge vested interests, and ideological fervor. Withdrawing from them will not be easy. But unless we do so, time will not be on our side.[27]

Notes

1. J. R. Oppenheimer, 'Atomic Weapons', *Proceedings of the American Philosophical Society*, vol. 90, no. 1 (January 1946) p. 7.
2. US Department of State, *Foreign Relations of the United States, 1948: Vol. I, Part 2* (Washington, DC, 1976) p. 750.

3. Memorandum of John D. Hickerson, Assistant Secretary of State for United Nations Affairs, 11 January 1950, in US Department of State, *Foreign Relations of the United States, 1950: Vol. I* (Washington, DC, 1977) p. 11.
4. Thomas K. Finletter, *Power and Policy: US Foreign Policy and Military Power in the Hydrogen Age* (New York, 1954) pp. 298–9. It should be noted, however, that in the same sentence from which the latter quote is taken he speaks of his age as 'a time when science has made war truly incompatible with civilization'.
5. Paul Boyer, *By the Bomb's Early Light: American Thought and Culture at the Dawn of the Atomic Age* (New York, 1985) p. 327.
6. Ibid., p. 349. Chapters 26 and 27 of Boyer's book are particularly informative on this changed sensibility.
7. US Department of State, *Foreign Relations of the United States, 1952–1954: Vol V, Part 1* (Washington, DC, 1983) p. 512.
8. Thomas B. Cochran, William M. Arkin, and Milton M. Hoenig, *Nuclear Weapons Databook, Volume I: US Nuclear Forces and Capabilities* (Cambridge, Mass., 1984) p. 15.
9. Thomas H. Etzold and John Lewis Gaddis (eds), *Containment: Documents on American Policy and Strategy, 1945–1950* (New York, 1978) p. 370.
10. Gregg Herken, *Counsels of War* (New York, 1985) p. 96; see also Ted Greenwood, *Making the MIRV: A Study of Defense Decision Making* (Cambridge, Mass., 1975) p. 58. For evidence on American nuclear warwinning strategies, see David Alan Rosenberg, 'Toward Armageddon: The Foundations of United States Nuclear Strategy, 1945–1961' (Ph.D. thesis, University of Chicago, 1983) pp. 260–1, 303–4 and 307; and Herken, *Counsels of War*, pp. 96–8, 143–4, 159–61, 164–5 and 268–9.
11. Nathan F. Twining, *Neither Liberty Nor Safety: A Hard Look at US Military Policy and Strategy* (New York, 1966) p. 100. 'Unfortunately,' he wrote, 'the conviction that no one can win a nuclear war does much to pull the force, drive, and sense of urgency from American research and development programs and it also adversely affects US force structure in being. There is no question that a nuclear war can be "won", as wars of the past have been won – by the side which is best prepared to fight it' (p. 112).
12. Robert Strausz-Hupé, William R. Kintner, and Stefan T. Possony, *A Forward Strategy for America* (New York, 1961) p. 161.
13. For evidence concerning pre-emptive first-strike strategies, see Daniel Ford, *The Button: The Pentagon's Strategic Command and Control System* (New York, 1985) especially pp. 105–8 and 233–42; and Stephen M. Meyer, 'Soviet Perspectives on the Paths to Nuclear War', in Graham T. Allison, Albert Carnesale, and Joseph S. Nye, Jr. (eds), *Hawks, Doves, and Owls: An Agenda for Avoiding Nuclear War* (New York, 1985) especially pp. 178–182 and 200.
14. Desmond Ball, 'Nuclear War at Sea', *International Security*, vol. 10, no. 3 (Winter 1985/6) p. 23.
15. Thomas Powers, 'Spontaneous Combustion', *The Sciences*, September/October 1985, p. 52.

16. Colin S. Gray, *Nuclear Strategy and Strategic Planning* (Philadelphia, 1984) p. 56.
17. George F. Kennan, *Russia, the Atom, and the West* (London, 1958) p. 56.
18. George F. Kennan, 'International Control of Atomic Energy' (20 January 1950), in Etzold and Gaddis (eds), *Containment*, p. 380. Years later, in 1983, Kennan found no reason to revise his basic position. One 'of our great postwar mistakes', he said, 'had to do with our embracing the nuclear weapon as the mainstay of our military posture, and the faith we placed in it to assure our military and political ascendancy in this postwar era ... And by this commitment to a weapon that was both suicidal and unsuitable to any rational military purpose we incurred, in my opinion, a heavy share of the blame for leading large parts of the international community into the most dangerous and fateful weapons race the world has ever known.' ('American Diplomacy and the Military', in his *American Diplomacy* (Chicago, expanded edition, 1984) pp. 171–2).
19. Robert S. McNamara and Hans A. Bethe, 'Reducing the Risk of Nuclear War', *Atlantic*, July 1985, p. 47.
20. Henry Kissinger, *White House Years* (Boston, 1979) p. 66.
21. *New York Times*, 5 February 1986, p. 10.
22. Lieut. Col. Dino A. Lorenzi and Major Charles L. Fox, '2001: A US Space Force', *Naval War College Review*, vol. 34, no. 2 (March–April 1981) p. 64.
23. Quoted in Thomas Karas, *The New High Ground: Systems and Weapons of Space Age War* (New York, 1983) p. 24 (emphasis added).
24. James R. Schlesinger, 'Rhetoric and Realities in the Star Wars Debate', *International Security*, vol. 10, no. 1 (Summer 1985), p. 6.
25. Studs Terkel, *'The Good War': An Oral History of World War Two* (New York, 1984) p. 331.
26. Public Archives of Canada, W. L. M. King Papers, MG 26, J1, vol. 389, p. 349941.
27. This is a slightly revised version of an essay first published in *Queen's Quarterly*, vol. 93, no. 3 (Autumn 1986).

3 Unstable Peace: Nuclear Deterrence
Hylke Tromp

'Si vis pacem para bellum': who wants peace should prepare for war. The original Latin sentence dates back more than two thousand years. Latin, however, is a dead language now and the Roman Empire exists only in history books. Apparently not much has changed since then in fundamental beliefs and theories about how to influence or regulate human behaviour. Relations between individuals, groups or states continue to be conducted on the assumption that the old Roman proverb formulates a basic law about human relations, comparable to other basic laws, like those in physics. The most recent variation on the theme is well known: 40 years of NATO is 40 years of peace and the best peace movements are the armed forces, so let us continue this effective peace policy and we will rest in peace.

It is, however, not a stable peace. 'Stable peace' is characterised as a situation where there is no preparation for war, no expectation of war and where nobody sees war as a realistic alternative for deciding a political issue.[1] It is not a utopian term. It is a description of the present state of international relations between the majority of states in the international system. There is, for example, such a 'stable peace' between the states now belonging to the European Economic Community (EEC). It is even difficult to remember that these states were fighting each other in the most devastating war in history less than fifty years ago. Even more interesting is that Japan and the United States, Germany and Great Britain, France and Italy, and all the other major antagonists in the Second World War, with the exception of the Soviet Union, are now co-operating in the Organisation for Economic Co-operation and Development (OECD). One can hardly imagine that war will erupt again between these states. Nobody wants it and nobody prepares for it. War has become as unthinkable as it was in the territory of the United States after the Civil War. Hundreds of millions of people live now in organised and stable peace in the same territory where for ages wars were fought continually between the few millions then living there.[2]

'Unstable Peace': there is no better description of the present state of relations between East and West. Nobody wants war. 'Peace is our Profession' is the established credo of the Strategic Air Command of the United States. Translated into an operational policy, however, this means deploying means of mass destruction all over the world to shorten the delivery time and to increase the perfection of annihilation. It is a peace based on the threat to kill and to destroy. It is an unstable peace: it is peace by deterrence. Peace by deterrence is based on preparing for war and on threatening with war. War is not unthinkable. Threatening war is a major tool in the politics of deterrence. Peace is reduced to the absence of organised violence. Still, war is always possible and in the long run probably inevitable.

Much has changed since Caesar conquered Gallia. Deterrence theory, however, neatly summarised in 'si vis pacem para bellum', is still the foundation for security and peace policy. The theory is simple and logical, and therefore easy to understand and to believe. 'It seems to be widely believed by influential politicians, military leaders, and segments of public opinion in many countries: and it summarizes and synthesizes elegantly and wittily many of the folk beliefs held by these groups', Karl Deutsch concluded in a widely used textbook.[3] The theory seems to satisfy the basic requirements for a good theory: it describes, explains, predicts and prescribes. 'Entia non sunt multiplicanda praeter necessitatem' (there is no need to look for a complicated explanation when there is a simple one available) as William Ockham (1285–1349) stated.[4]

Deterrence theory is based on the assumption that threats can influence behaviour decisively. In that respect, there is no fundamental difference between the basic assumptions underlying education, criminal law and international politics. It is the threat to punish that is supposed to guarantee law and order within the state and to keep peace between states. Criminal behaviour will be punished by jail sentences if not the death penalty. Aggression will be punished with a devastating counter-attack, or in the modernised strategical jargon, a 'second strike'. If both sides accept the basic assumptions of the theory, the first inevitable result is an arms race to ensure a 'military balance'. Deterrence policy will be narrowed down to measuring and calculating how much is needed and how much is enough – an enterprise that will again inevitably lead to the discovery of unexpected gaps and windows of vulnerability. As long as the process does not end in war, there will never be enough, and there will never be a military balance. In the meantime, the absence of war is described as peace, proving the theory: deterrence works.

A simple theory, however, is not necessarily a realistic theory. Deterrence theory is so simple, logical and easy to understand because it is derived from real-life situations that are simple and easy to understand. Even small children have no difficulty in calculating the benefits and costs of one or the other behavioural alternative. The costs of stealing a cake will in general be seen to outweigh the benefits of eating it, if one is caught in the act. On the other hand, if one can get away with it unnoticed, it is worth a try. These are the simple calculations to which deterrence theory can be applied, and which make it so logical and easy to understand. All the factors are known: the cleverness of the mother guarding the cakes as well as the slyness of her child in picking a moment that will be unnoticed. They know each other so intimately that there is hardly room for misunderstanding about intentions and capabilities. There is no doubt about flexibility in response, either. The mother will not kill the child if the child strikes out to acquire the cake, even if this is clearly an act of illegitimate behaviour in violation of official agreements.

In international politics, however, real-life situations are not simple but extremely complex. They are even difficult to define. Verified and relevant information is hard to get. Decision making is more often than not guided by guesses and intuition, if not emotions, attitudes and ideology. Even after disasters and catastrophes such as war have happened, historians may not be able to find out what precisely went wrong where and why, and who did it.

Deterrence theory fits perfectly, so it seems, into the culture of education where important lessons for life are learned. In science, it is called 'induction'. A general theory is derived from a single case. The 'general theory' of deterrence is already clearly failing in the other example mentioned: in deterring criminal behaviour. The basic assumption is the same as in education: the costs of criminal behaviour should surpass the eventual benefits. The uncertainties produced by a much more complex situation, however, are so many that there is room for manoeuvre. The penalty, even if it is a death sentence, is actually a calculated risk. Contrary to what endless television series suggest, criminality pays. The benefits outweigh the losses. Deterrence theory as applied in criminal law fails consistently and completely. Most criminal acts are committed without being noticed. In the case of those that are detected it is almost impossible to get sufficient proof to lead to a conviction. And when that occasionally happens it is so exceptional that its deterrence value is almost zero and certainly not sufficient to deter the next criminal act. This demonstrates that the theory, whatever its merits, does not always and under all circumstances explain and predict behaviour. Elevating a failing theory into official policy does not make in infallible. One may argue that this does not make the theory invalid, and that only the operationalisation is insufficient. That is true. Deterrence theory, however, is irrelevant for real-life situations unless certain specific conditions are fulfilled. Even then, it is not possible to predict behaviour with absolute certainty – deterrence theory is a theory about human behaviour, not about hardware.

For an effective and fail-safe deterrence policy, at least three conditions have to be considered. They are simple to formulate and easy to understand. First, there must be no doubt about the availability of the means to deliver the threat. Secondly, the possibility of misunderstanding should be excluded and both parties should always be in complete and continuing control of their behaviour. Finally, such behaviour should under all circumstances remain guided by perfectly rational calculations.

There is hardly any doubt about the availability of the means of delivery. Weapons ranging from small handguns to chemical or nuclear means of mass destruction are universally available. Even nuclear weapons are now expected to surface at some time in the arsenals of terrorists. Moreover, there is no doubt at all about the efficiency and lethality of the available weapons.[5] To avoid misunderstanding and to ensure full information on every movement, billions of dollars have been spent to improve information channels and to broaden the spectrum of communication. Satellites cover the surface of the earth. In theory, nothing goes unnoticed. Communication networks span the same globe, enabling information to be dispersed over the whole world in seconds. Information can be verified by a broad spectrum of technical means as well as other methods. The general assumption is that these gadgets have effectively solved the problem of command, control, communication and information. Nuclear and other wars can therefore be directed from war rooms in nuclear-free shelters. The highest political and military authorities are supposed to sit there behind desks looking at screens, occasionally pressing a button. In this clean and clinical environment, where the battle casualties cannot be seen, where human suffering and the eventual collapse of societies will only appear in figures on computer screens, the level of emotional involvement would remain low enough to allow perfect rationality in political decision making. Moreover, the decision-makers themselves are supposed to personify perfect rationality. That is the reason that they were elected, selected or appointed. At least, this is the implicit assumption – otherwise nothing else would make any sense. So, from the official point of view, there is hardly any reason to doubt the effectiveness and credibility of deterrence theory. All conditions are fulfilled. The weapons are in place and can be delivered within minutes, in any number, on any target, with high precision. The resulting destruction can be witnessed or recorded immediately. Decision-makers will know precisely what to do and they can do it. As long as the other side knows this and plays the same game, deterrence works and everybody should feel reassured.[6]

In principle, science is not a religion. Scientists are not supposed to be disciples and proselytes, believing in dogmas and occasionally delivering a credo. Their function is to ask questions and to try to answer them. Sometimes they have to formulate the questions nobody else wants to ask. Here questions arise about the validity and range of deterrence theory, and about its translation into an operational policy.

Deterrence theory presupposes complete, verified and always up-to-date information: this is a condition that is impossible to fulfil and it is surprising that its disastrous consequences for deterrence have been unrecognised, ignored or kept hidden for so long. In theory, satellites cover every square metre of the globe. In theory, they can deliver precise pictures, registering movements of troops down to a single vehicle, and if they are not yet able to read the licence number of a car, this is only due to the fact that licence numbers are in a vertical position and satellites cannot lean over. This is new. Caesar conquered Gallia without having a map. The battle of Poitiers in 1356 was fought when the armies encountered each other accidentally. In 1945, the commander-in-chief of one of the alliances was sitting in his bunker under the ruins of his capital, moving imaginary armies over a map without having access to the information that they no longer existed. Consequentially, excitement must have been rising with the advance of the new technologies. Unfortunately, there is a catch. The system works, and it can even work almost perfectly if enough satellites, spy planes and other equipment are used. The catch is that it is impossible to sort out the information acquired. American intelligence agencies are reported to have taped the orders (coming from

Iran to Beirut) for that devastating terrorist suicide attack by car-bomb on the Marine Headquarters in Beirut which killed more than two hundred marines and enforced the hasty retreat of American forces from the Lebanon, sealing another fiasco of American foreign policy. Their intelligence agencies were, however, too late in sorting out this relevant information to warn Marine Headquarters.

There is simply too much information. It is of no use to be able to inspect every square metre for traces of the enemy. There are too many square metres. So selections have to be made, and they have to be made in advance, which again means that detection can be avoided. In effect the information overkill prohibits decision-makers being informed in time, appropriately and effectively. In addition, there looms another problem that for a long time has almost escaped attention: the system has never been tested in war. Satellites can be as easily launched as destroyed. Space-mines can be placed next to satellites in peacetime, to be exploded at zero hour. Even if this is not done, the whole communication system will probably break down in the first hour, dependent as it is on vulnerable gadgets varying from radios to telephones. Explosions of nuclear weapons have devastating consequences for vulnerable equipment that is needed for communications. The 'electromagnetic pulse', especially when it originates from a high-altitude nuclear explosion, may silence all communication equipment, in addition to destroying or damaging electronics in computers over a wide area. As a consequence, nuclear war cannot in all probability be fought as a co-ordinated and well organised battle. It will run out of control, probably within minutes. Screens will go blank. Radio lines will go silent. Telephones will be dead. What will remain is the autonomous capacity of certain nuclear forces to deliver their missiles independent of orders from their commander-in-chief, like the nuclear submarines which, precisely because of the expectancy of a deafening silence from a destroyed or vaporised headquarters, have been empowered to strike back on their own if communication fails.[7] The collapse of information channels and communication lines is almost inevitable. So is the collapse of control. This is partly a direct consequence of the breakdown of the communication-network. Orders cannot be given or received. Military units will find out that they are on their own – which is not unusual in warfare.[8]

The collapse of control is already embedded in the command-and-control system as it has been devised and developed since the Second World War. The main characteristic (in the Soviet Union as well as in the United States) is the idea that there should be complete overall political control. Warfare with nuclear weapons was seen as too important to leave to the generals. The commander-in-chief had to be the person (or group of persons) who was politically responsible. This was felt to be necessary, because the use of nuclear weapons was regarded as a quantum jump, even in warfare. So it should not be decided on military considerations alone. This implied that the political authority should, from the beginning, be in charge of all military operations – even the smallest, because of the danger of escalation. So, for eample, the attack on a prisoner-of-war camp in Vietnam, which was discovered on 9 May 1970, got Presidential approval on 18 November of the same year. The military operation was well prepared by then and the attack on 21 November was afterwards described as a complete success from the military point of view. The camp, however, was found to be empty: everyone had left a long time before. In 1979 another US President tried to direct a military rescue operation for American hostages held in the Embassy in Tehran. The operation collapsed and was aborted in the Iranian desert before the Iranian government discovered that it was on its way. This demonstrates that it is simply impossible to conduct warfare by remote but perfect control, as if military units are children's toys, moving around following radio signals. Declaring war means abandoning politics and handing control over to the military. It is an illusion that political control will be kept intact by formally appointing the political leadership to military positions. The politicians will have to follow the directives given by the military, who will be in overall control. They will select, evaluate and present the information in such a way that the course of action preferred by the military seems inevitable.

Abandoning political control is as much the consequence of technological progress as it is necessitated by political considerations. Technological progress has given the political authorities the possibility to communicate at any moment with even the most distant places on earth, which they can see from pictures brought in by satellite coverage. Military communication networks span the globe.[9] Pictures and messages are instantly available. The result is a peace-time illusion concerning information, communication, command and control during war. Even in peace-time, however, communication channels fail frequently, and the system has been proved to be unreliable. The breakdown of the lines of command and control is obviously the first result of war. It is no consolation that such a breakdown will, in all probability, at first be only partial. A partial breakdown means that the war room map will show blind spots. Nobody will know what is going on there. That situation is not abnormal in the history of warfare. One is reminded of Field Marshall Douglas Haig's unawareness of what was going on in the trenches near the Somme on 1 July 1916, or Hitler's command and control of the Wenck army that he ordered to liberate Berlin in April 1945 but that did not even exist.[10] For effective political control, the high command has to be informed of all developments, it has to be able to transmit orders and see them executed.

Warfare has become increasingly more complex in recent times. Technological progress has created only the illusion that complete control is guaranteed. This has devastating implications for public and political awareness of the danger of nuclear war. The result is that nuclear war is discussed in terms that are as suggestive as unrealistic, such as 'limited nuclear war', 'control of nuclear war', 'escalation dominance'. Such discussions have nothing to do with the pending reality. Political considerations have, in addition, undermined the possibility of complete control, as in the classical example of *Catch 22* (a book that is as realistic as it is prophetic).[11] Official security policy is full of paradoxes. For example, to make nuclear war unthinkable and impossible, nuclear weapons had to be devised that make nuclear war thinkable and possible, such as mininukes, enhanced-radiation weapons, and battlefield nuclear weapons. The catch is the credibility of the threat: if nuclear war was completely unthinkable and impossible, nuclear deterrence would not exist. So nuclear war was made thinkable and possible again – which undermined deterrence of nuclear war. Here the catch is predictable, for the same logic is applied. Complete political control at the highest level is absolutely necessary for deterrence and, in order to ensure it, it has to be delegated. Otherwise, a 'surgical decapitating first strike' could destroy the political high command as well as military headquarters, nobody would be left in a position to order a second strike, and deterrence would be non existent. Centralising the political and military command would be an invitation to disaster. The obvious and logical counter-measure has been to delegate political control over at least a sufficient part of the nuclear forces to the local military command, who have to be in a position to press enough buttons to retaliate with an equally devastating second strike. So the nuclear submarines of the United States are equipped with the autonomous ability to take the decision to destroy the Soviet Union. The logic of nuclear deterrence has overruled the necessity of political control: in order to enhance the credibility of deterrence in peace-time, wartime control has been given up in advance. It is an ironic, and in a sense a paradoxical development that, with the increase of technological means to command and control, the actual command and control during hostilities and war has become theoretically as well as practically highly illusory. This marks the end of a historical development. For thousands of years, armies were commanded from the front. The commander-in-chief (whatever his actual title) led his men into battle and actually set an example by fighting in the front line. Alexander the Great was wounded repeatedly in battle. It was normal for a general to die on a battlefield. As firepower and the lethality of weapons increased,[12] the commanding generals were gradually removed from the front line to the rearguard. As the number of soldiers in the armies grew, commanding a battle became primarily a problem of information (how to know what happened on the battlefield) and secondly of communication (how to give orders to the troops). Since the eighteenth century, kings and generals (usually one and the same person) are depicted standing on hills overlooking the battlefield, equipped with binoculars and surrounded by dispatch riders. As armies grew beyond the somewhat critical size of 30 000 men it became impossible to survey the battlefield by eyesight. Fighting a battle became dissected into separate fights by separate units, loosely and perhaps intuitively directed by a central command, which was more often than not so ill-informed that it took the wrong decisions: a handicap that was usually equally divided between both adversaries. At Jena, Napoleon defeated a part of the Prussian army and it was only after the battle that he was informed of the much more decisive victory of his third Corps under Davout, which he did not command. Starting a war and fighting a battle now, more than ever, resemble participating in a lottery, if not playing Russian roulette. The outcome is completely unpredictable. One may argue that this is precisely the reason why war is declared and battles are fought: to enforce a decision. This underestimates expectations and strategical calculations made before battles are waged. Only rarely was a battle offered or started by a party which did not expect to win or at least to have a reasonable chance of winning. Warfare has suddenly, that is, within one century, become so complex that there is no way to predict the outcome. There are too many interacting variables. Command and control, information and communication belong to those factors that have undergone the most fundamental changes within a few decades.

The differences are appalling. Napoleon in 1815 was actually in

Waterloo, trying to command his army and, owing to a failure in information, he was defeated. One century later, the commanding generals (not to mention their sovereigns, Kaiser, King and Czar) did not even see the battlefield. They were generally located tens to hundreds of kilometres behind the trench lines of the First World War, planning breakthroughs while surveying maps, and relying on information from field commanders who were generally sitting in comfortable country houses far from no man's land. None of them was fit for battle. They fought a bureaucratised war, and an imaginary one. Today the reliance on technology and bureaucracy is almost total. The command centres are located in sheltered war rooms far from the battlefield. The distance may be more than ten thousand kilometres. The commanding generals will in all probability be blind, deaf and mute within a matter of minutes of war starting – if they are not immediately killed: the command centres are pinpointed on the target lists on both sides. Deterrence theory, however, assumes perfect command and control, as well as equally perfectly operating information and communication channels during war. This is a condition that cannot be fulfilled.

The last condition concerns rationality in decision making before and during war. Deterrence theory presupposes that decision-makers always and under all circumstances behave with perfectly rationality, without interference from emotions, attitudes or even moral considerations. In short, deterrence theory presupposes the existence of a 'homo strategicus', as naive economic theory once presupposed the existence of a 'homo economicus'. They do not exist – not even part of the time. The theory, however, can only describe, prescribe and predict, if the human decision-makers fit the requirements of a theory which actually reduces a decision-maker to a computer and the field of political and military decision making to a chessboard where all pieces can be seen and perfect knowledge exists as to how they can be moved. This is a level of abstraction that may have its virtues for explaining and understanding afterwards. It has its limits when applied to predicting and prescribing. It is impossible to predict how people will define the situation they are in, before they have done it. It is subsequently even more difficult to predict what course of action they will see as the most 'rational' for that particular situation. Moreover, there is no such thing as the 'perfect rational solution' for a political problem, or a 'perfect rational behaviour' in a certain situation. This is an intrinsic and perpetual cause of misunderstanding, confusion and – in the political dimension – of the escalation of mistrust and fear into conflict and, finally, war. Rationality is not an objective category. It cannot be separated from culture, emotions, ideologies, world views. If it seems irrational to commit suicide for political purposes in one culture, it may be the ultimate rationality in another culture or religion. If a cost-benefit analysis shows dramatic losses during a military offensive, and if therefore the rational decision would be to withdraw from the battlefield, another kind of rationality transcending the battlefield death toll may prescribe continuing the battle and the war, if not starting a new offensive. This is not a prediction. It is a description of what happened during the First World War (the 'war of attrition') as well as the Second.

Deterrence theory presupposes, moreover, continuity of rationality over time. Decision-makers are not only expected to be cool, rational and detached in the beginning; they are not supposed to become emotionally involved, least of all to get angry during a war. This is exactly what has happened time and again. Rationality, whatever it may be, changes over time. What seems impossible, unthinkable and completely irrational at the starting-point of a crisis, may be the rational thing to do as the intensity of hostilities escalates. The use of nuclear weapons may, for example, be ruled out as unthinkable when a crisis starts. When the ambassadors have been recalled, when divisions have been mobilised, when the first deaths have been counted after some skirmishing at a border, when a city has been bombarded and when napalm and chemical weapons have annihilated a few hundred thousand civilians, the exemplary use of a 'nuclear device' may seem to be the rational next step.[13]

Deterrence theory and its product, deterrence policy, are so easy to understand because they assume that reality is equally simple and easy to understand. It is not. It is highly complex. The factors guiding human behaviour are not in the first place 'rational'. Rationality as far as it influences behaviour is defined subjectively and changes over time. In the complicated political process where signals are given by manoeuvering troops, sending flotillas, deploying nuclear weapons and targeting means of mass destruction on each other's population centres, the messages are easily misunderstood and do not lead to the predicted and expected outcome. Deterrence policy is only effective in the simple situations where all information is available and verifiable at short notice, and where the threat is credible. It is not in more complicated human relations, specifically in international relations. It is doomed to fail when it is really needed – as history shows.

In the meantime, deterrence theory has been elevated to the status of a secular religion or an ideology, shared by decision-makers in the East and West, North and South. Their deterrence policies have led to the raising of defence expenditures and have institutionalised a process that is usually described as 'a global arms race'. These policies have made their countries highly indebted and have not added anything to their security. That deterrence theory can only be adapted to real-life situations when certain conditions are fulfilled has escaped their attention, if they have not purposefully ignored it. They have in practice narrowed down their attention to the two simple requisites that are seen as the essence of deterrence policy: keeping a military balance according to the dogma of keeping the peace by preparing for war; and diminishing the risks caused by this policy by negotiating arms control. If peace depended on deterrence theory and deterrence policy only, war would be inevitable and imminent.

Notes

1. Kenneth Boulding, *Stable Peace* (Austin, Texas, 1978).
2. See Bruce Russett and Harvey Starr, *World Politics: The Menu for Choice* (San Francisco, 1981) pp. 399 *et seq.*
3. Karl Deutsch, *The Analysis of International Relations* (second edn, Englewood Cliffs, New Jersey, 1978) p. 157.
4. The British philosopher William Ockham, who is quoted here, is the model for William of Baskerville in Umberto Eco, *The Name of the Rose* (London, 1983).
5. William M. Arkin and Richard Fieldhouse, *Nuclear Battlefields* (Cambridge, Mass., 1985).
6. Some of the recent studies on deterrence which are directly relevant for this contribution are Richard Ned Lebow, 'Deterrence Reconsidered: The Challenge of Recent Research', *Survival* (January–February 1985) pp. 20–8; Michael MccGwire, 'Deterrence: The Problem–Not the Solution', *International Affairs* (Winter 1985–6) pp. 55–71; Michael Howard, 'Deterrence, Consensus and Reassurance in the Defence of Europe' in International Institute for Strategic Studies, *Defence and Consensus: The Domestic Aspects of Western Security*, Adelphi Paper no. 184 (London, 1983) pp. 17–27.
7. Many of the following comments on command and control in warfare are based on Martin van Creveld, *Command in War* (Cambridge, Mass., 1986), as well as on the recent and important studies on the present command and control structure for warfare, especially nuclear war. See Desmond Ball, *Can Nuclear War Be Controlled?*, Adelphi Paper no. 169, (London, 1981); Paul Bracken, *The Command and Control of Nuclear Forces*, (New Haven, Conn., 1983); Bruce G. Blair, *Strategic Command and Control: Redefining the Nuclear Threat* (Washington, DC, 1985); and Daniel Ford, *The Button: The Pentagon's Strategic Command and Control System* (New York, 1985).
8. Ball, *Can Nuclear War be Controlled?*
9. Arkin and Fieldhouse, *Nuclear Battlefields*, p. 77.

10. On the disastrous conduct of battle at the Somme, see for example Martin Middlebrook, *The First Day on the Somme* (London, 1971). See also John Keegan, *The Face of Battle* (New York, 1976).
11. Joseph Heller, *Catch 22* (New York, 1955).
12. See T. N. Dupuy, *The Evolution of Weapons and Warfare* (Indianapolis, 1980).
13. Herman Kahn, *On Escalation: Metaphors and Scenarios* (New York, 1965).

4 The Case Against Negotiations and For a Reconsideration of Strategy
Robert Neild

INTRODUCTION

If one considers why we have an arms race and why negotiations over arms control and disarmament fail, one can trace the trouble to one precept of strategy that is commonly accepted without question: that the way to keep the peace is to maintain a military balance *vis-à-vis* one's potential opponent. There follows from it the belief that the way to improve stability and to check the arms race is to seek balanced constraints on arms by negotiation.

This chapter examines these beliefs, what is wrong with them and what should be put in their place. The conclusion reached is that if the political aim is the preservation of peace, the appropriate strategic objective should be, not Balance, but 'Sufficiency' in nuclear weapons and 'Defensive Superiority' in non-nuclear forces, two concepts that are developed in the analysis. The way to achieve these aims and ease the arms race is by independent (that is, unilateral) changes in strategy. Consultation and debate with one's opponent to persuade him that he too should change strategy may help to improve security and ease the level of arms. Negotiation of conditional changes can be counter-productive and is appropriate only in special circumstances. A basic principle arrived at is this: if there is a change in the level or character of one's forces that would help one attain nuclear 'Sufficiency' or non-nuclear 'Defensive Superiority', *regardless of whether one's opponent made a similar move*, there are no grounds for seeking reciprocity through negotiation. It will be advantageous to make the move independently.

This chapter is in two parts. The first part contains an examination of the notion of 'Balance' and what alternative strategic objective should be put in its place. In the second part consideration is given to the ways in which the alternative objectives should be pursued, how one side can influence the other and what should be the role of negotiation.

It must be emphasised that this chapter is not addressed specifically, let alone exclusively, to the policies of the United States and NATO. The object is to suggest a new general way of thinking, applicable to any confrontation, applicable to the policies of the Soviet Union and the Warsaw Pact just as much as to those of the United States and NATO. The reader is urged to think how it might be applied, starting, for example, by modest steps taken in the European theatre by the side that in his view has the greatest scope for a change of strategy in the directions proposed, be it the Warsaw Pact or NATO.

'BALANCE' EXAMINED

Introduction

The notion that the way to keep the peace is to maintain a military balance with your potential opponent rests on a seductively simple line of reasoning: If your opponent is stronger than you, he will be able to defeat you; therefore to defend yourself, you must keep up with him in arms; you must be as strong as he is, or stronger; you must pursue balance in arms for the sake of your security. It is a notion that is subscribed to by 'armers', 'disarmers' and 'arms controllers' alike. Armers argue that their nation must have more arms to maintain a balance. Disarmers argue that balanced reductions in arms must be sought by negotiation. Arms controllers argue for a negotiated balance whether that is to be achieved by increases in force levels, decreases or ceilings. None of them questions the pursuit of balance. Consequently, it is a concept which government leaders have used, sincerely, to achieve compromises between the advocates of big and small arms programmes and between the advocates of tough and soft negotiating positions. To justify those compromises they have appealed to the need for 'Balance', and have done so with an elasticity as great as the elasticity of the forecasts that could be made of their opponents' present and future armouries.[1]

Yet the notion that one must pursue balance in arms for the sake of one's security does not bear critical examination. There are objections to it of two kinds – practical and theoretical.

The Practical Objections

The practical objections concern 'Asymmetry' and 'Biased Perception'. Even if information was complete, a balance of military strength between two nations could be defined *precisely* only if the two nations were symmetrical – if they had the same weapons, the same sized armies, navies and air forces, with men of the same age, training and morale; the same arms industries, the same geography and the same allies (or none); and so on. Only if the conditions of symmetry were fulfilled to the point where there were two nations (or alliances) that were *identical* could we declare without risk of contradiction that there was a precise military balance. If there are asymmetries, if for example there are differences in weapons and in the period of training of the forces of two nations, there is no precise way of measuring those differences and reducing them to a common mathematical unit of 'strength', so as to arrive at a precise answer to the effect that, on balance, A is stronger than B by so much. In the language of the economist, there is no set of weights that one can observe, let alone use without dispute, to combine into a single aggregate measure the disparate variables that make up military strength.

In practice, nothing is symmetrical. There is no possibility of precise measurement of the balance of strength. Added to which, information is incomplete and uncertain, partly because intelligence is imperfect, partly because some things cannot be known: you cannot know how your potential opponent's forces, or yours, will perform in the event of war; and you cannot have sure information about future strength, which is what must guide your decisions to acquire new weapons and forces. One has to rely on judgement. And in the exercise of judgement, biased perception comes in. Each analyst or journalist who attempts to judge the balance and advise politicians and the public about it must decide what variables to select, what interpretation to put on the data for each and their relative importance. Each politician or member of the public who looks at what the analysts and journalists have to offer must decide which of them to follow and what interpretation to put on his work. Alarmists will pick on the analysts whose work suggests the opponent is stronger. Escapists will pick on the analysts who suggest the opposite. In one period, escapism may prevail: the 1930s are an example. In another, alarmism will prevail: the postwar arms race is an example.

But even if there is nothing one could call alarmism, only caution, the pursuit of balance is enough to generate and perpetuate an arms race. The cautious man, following the precept that balance brings security, which carries with it the notion that too little is dangerous and too much adds to safety, will over-insure: he will go for a margin of safety. But if only one of two opposed nations does that, the result, inescapably, will be an arms race. The first, trying to get ahead by a safety margin, forces the other to race in pursuit of balance.

The effect on disarmament and arms control negotiations is no less predictable. Since balance cannot be measured precisely, it will be extremely difficult to agree in negotiation what is a balanced reduction or a balanced level of arms. To isolate one category of weapons or forces and try to agree numbers for that category will not help much since the geography, alliances and enmities of the negotiating nations will never be symmetrical. For example, NATO and the Warsaw Pact are extremely asymmetrical in ways that affect both nuclear and non-nuclear forces. Moreover the military effect of setting numerical limits for one category will depend on the levels of arms in other categories which will not be symmetrical either.

Agreement will be possible only if the negotiators acknowledge that there cannot be precise balance and go for something rough and ready. But if they go for something less than rigorous balance, they are vulnerable to the accusation that, since balance is the touchstone of security, they are playing fast and loose with national security. And even if they sincerely stick to the pursuit of balance in as rigorous an interpretation as is possible, any agreement they reach will be vulnerable to the criticism that it is unbalanced. Within each negotiating nation, those who set themselves up as the guardians of national security will be able to pick on one or more dimensions of a proposal and claim that in this respect it is unbalanced and favours the other side, therefore it is unacceptable. So long as it is believed and accepted that balance is what brings security, there is no way out. It is impossible to prove that there is balance. It cannot be measured. So long as those who advocate and seek disarmament and arms control subscribe to the notion of balance, they will be hoist by their own petard.

The Theoretical Objections

It is essential to consider nuclear and non-nuclear forces separately. The theoretical objections to the pursuit of balance differ sharply in these two categories of forces.

Nuclear Forces
Nuclear weapons are so destructive that there is a saturation point beyond which there is no point in acquiring more. If your enemy can knock out your main cities and other significant targets twice, five times or ten times, there is no military point in your following him to similar levels of 'overkill'. To be able to kill your opponent many times over is not militarily useful. To pursue balance beyond saturation level is therefore not militarily sensible.

If your aim is totally peaceful, meaning that militarily you seek only to prevent your enemy attacking you and politically you do not seek to put economic pressure on him by generating an arms race, the only purpose for which nuclear weapons will be kept is to deter your opponent from attack. For this purpose the numerical objective of your weapons policy will be 'Sufficiency', not 'Balance'. To decide how many nuclear warheads you need for 'Sufficiency', you must start by asking how many of your opponent's cities and other tagets you must be able to destroy in order to deter him from making nuclear threats or attacks on you. I assume a 'nuclear setting', that is, a setting where two nations possess enough nuclear weapons to be able to inflict unacceptable damage on each other. In such a setting it is questionable whether extended deterrence, that is, the use of nuclear weapons to counter sub-nuclear threats or to protect allies, is credible. If one side alone possesses nuclear weapons, it can, however, practise extended deterrence without lack of credibility, since it does not risk retaliation. Moreover 'Sufficiency' will inevitably be the criterion by which it decides how many nuclear weapons it needs: if the other side has no nuclear weapons, there can be no question of balance. But once you are in a nuclear setting these conditions cease to hold. For the purposes of the present argument, it does not matter, however, whether extended deterrence is practised or not. If it is, the number of targets to be threatened, and hence the number judged to constitute 'Sufficiency', may be increased, but it will still be an absolute number, not a notion of matching the other side in pursuit of 'Balance'.

We can say X is the number of targets that we judge we need to be able to hit with nuclear warheads in order to deter the enemy. Each person will have his own view as to the right value of X. He may think it is one city, ten cities, a hundred targets, or more. It does not matter. Whatever the value assigned to X, we need to add to it a margin to allow for weapons that will not work and for weapons that can be expected to be knocked out by the other side before being launched – or in the air, if the other side has defensive systems. To this extent the margin, and hence the number of weapons required for 'Sufficiency', does depend on the size and characteristics of the opponent's nuclear armoury. But it does not do so in a manner that implies that 'Balance' is the right objective. It is conceivable – though it would be a fluke – that the number required for 'Sufficiency', arrived at from the formula

'Sufficiency' = X + M

where X is the required number of delivered warheads and M is the margin to allow for unserviceable weapons and losses would come out equal to the number possessed by the other side. But there is *no* reason why this should be so. If your weapons are invulnerable to your opponent's armoury (for example, if they are in hidden submarines) and he has no defences with which to obstruct them, the margin will be small, and 'Sufficiency' may be a number much smaller than his armoury. On the other hand, if your armoury is highly vulnerable to your opponent's weapons (for example, if you have missiles in silos threatened by multiple independently targeted re-entry vehicles: MIRVs) or it is vulnerable to his defences, 'Sufficiency' may be a number greater than your opponent's armoury. If at the same time his armoury is vulnerable to your weapons and defences he, similarly, will find that he needs more than you. Neither side will be able to be satisfied. Both will race for more. There will be instability. But the essential point is that, militarily, 'Balance' is a nonsensical objective to pursue with nuclear weapons. 'Sufficiency' is what makes military sense if your aims are peaceful, and where it will lead you depends on the vulnerability of your nuclear arsenal to attack, and the extent, if any, of your opponent's defences – and the number of your nuclear opponents.

Although a moment's thought tells us there is a saturation point beyond which relative numbers of nuclear weapons have no military significance and therefore cannot contribute to the achievement of political aims by military means, it is frequently said or implied that there is political value in relative strength in nuclear weapons at levels above 'Sufficiency'. Failure to keep up in the pursuit of 'Balance' is seen as lack of resolution, even as a sign that you lack the political will to use nuclear weapons. Nuclear weapons are seen almost as status symbols: we cannot let them have more than we have. There is a belief in the psychological effects of nuclear superiority and nuclear inferiority. In this vein, it has been argued that people *perceive* (albeit foolishly) that it matters whether numerically one is superior or inferior in nuclear weapons and hence that it actually does matter. These notions, like the emperor's clothes, are sustained by belief alone. But, as Steven Kull showed in an excellent analysis recently, they are notions that have real political force in sustaining the pursuit of balance in nuclear weapons, and they will continue to do so until they are punctured.[2] Understandably, these beliefs appear to be most powerful in the Soviet Union and United States, the two contestants for ownership of most nuclear weapons; the lesser nuclear powers perforce set their sights by reference to 'Sufficiency' in one version or another.

If your aims are offensive, meaning that you seek to attack, or threaten to attack, your opponent with nuclear weapons without risk of unacceptable retaliation in kind, there is in theory another objective you might pursue in a nuclear setting, namely 'Supremacy', through the acquisition of first-strike weapons, and defences against nuclear weapons, to the point where you were confident that the amount of damage your opponent could do to you was reduced to the level where it was acceptable. In other words, the objective would be to achieve a quasi-monopoly, so that mutual deterrence was ended; you would escape from a nuclear setting; and you would be free, from a military point of view, to make nuclear threats or attacks, or to practise extended deterrence unconstrained by the risk of unacceptable retaliation by your opponent. The trouble is that once two nations have acquired enough nuclear weapons to achieve mutual deterrence, an attempt by one to achieve 'Supremacy' can be relied upon to cause the other to race rather than risk losing its capability to deter; added to which, if both sides acquire nuclear forces with a counter-force capability, there will be pressure to attack pre-emptively or on warning.

The main argument for the pursuit of what amounts to nuclear 'Supremacy' has come from those in the military, notable the US Air Force, who have argued for a counterforce capability. Their line of argument, which was first propounded 20 or 30 years ago, is that the American strategic nuclear forces should be so large, so invulnerable and so accurate that, if those forces were attacked by the Soviet Union, the United States would still have the capability to strike back at the remaining Soviet nuclear forces (which would remain a threat to American cities) and knock them out. A force that could strike back only at Soviet cities would leave the remaining Soviet forces intact and available to attack American cities. In short, a counterforce strategy means acquiring forces of such a size and character that you can reduce to an acceptable level the damage your enemy can inflict on you – though in the arguments for this stragegy the notion of acceptable damage is raised to levels quite unacceptable to any ordinary mortal; indeed it is sometimes turned into a notion of relative damage – the United States would be driven less far towards the Stone Age than the Soviets and could recover more rapidly: another case, like balance in nuclear arms, of relative magnitudes being introduced where absolute magnitudes should rule.

If 'Sufficiency' were adopted as the aim, there would of course be political debate about what number of weapons was required: what is the right value for $X + M$? The armers and disarmers would pull in the usual directions. But if 'Sufficiency' was the touchstone, there would be the great advantage that debate, instead of being focused on 'Balance', as it is now, would be focused on the question, what abolute number is enough? It could be brought back to the question, how many nuclear weapons of what kinds are needed to induce fear in the minds of the other side and to produce stability? There might be a greater chance that counterforce capabilities and defences against nuclear weapons would be seen to be provocative and destabilising, and that it would be seen that 'Sufficiency' in countervalue weapons was what mattered.

Non-Nuclear Forces
With non-nuclear forces the considerations are entirely different. The difference lies in the different scope for defence, indeed in differences in the very meaning of the term 'defence' with respect to nuclear and non-nuclear forces.

There are two ways in which a nation, through the possession of armed forces, can dissuade another from attacking it. It can hold out the prospect of *retaliation* against his territory, armed forces or population, or *denial*, meaning that your armed forces prevent his from taking over your territory and population, if he attempts to enter it, or from bombarding you into submissiom. Nuclear weapons preserve the peace by threat of retaliation. They are so destructive that to use them for denial, that is, to use them against enemy forces on your own territory, is extremely self-destructive and therefore of doubtful credibility. Moreover, since nuclear weapons deter your opponent from attacking you only by threat of retaliation, it follows that to introduce nuclear defences, meaning systems that obstruct the delivery of nuclear weapons, is a strategy which, if it were successful, would weaken the nuclear deterrent of your opponent. For this reason, the introduction of defences against nuclear weapons by one side in a nuclear setting is a threatening strategy, likely to be interpreted as a move in pursuit of 'Supremacy', an indication of offensive aims.

By contrast, non-nuclear forces deter an opponent from attack by holding out to him the prospect of denial, possibly combined with a prospect of retaliation. (There is little sense in a non-nuclear strategy of pure retaliation, whereby you plan not to attempt to stop your opponent if he attacks, only to attack his territory in retaliation.) It follows that what serves at the non-nuclear level to prevent nation A attacking nation B is that the defensive capability of A should be greater than the offensive capability of B.[3] We shall call this 'Defensive Superiority'. As John Mearsheimer has emphasised, the temptation to attack is strong when a nation thinks it can swiftly defeat another on whom it has designs and run little risk of getting bogged down in a war of attrition;[4] when, in other words, the nation with offensive designs is confident that its offensive capability exceeds the defensive capability of the other (including any retaliatory capability the latter may possess). That condition we shall call 'Offensive Superiority'. The requirement that, for security, a nation's defensive capability should exceed its opponent's offensive capability may not be as difficult of attainment as might appear at first sight; and it has implications very different from the pursuit of balance in non-nuclear forces. Let us consider each of these points in turn.

There are some inherent advantages that can be exploited by a defender and one important advantage that can be exploited by an attacker. At the tactical level, the defender can enjoy the advantages of being dug-in, knowing the terrain, having pre-positioned supplies to hand, enjoying the support of the local population and having the possiblity of bringing more forces into play as he falls back. One expression of these advantages is the rule of thumb that is often repeated – though that does not prove that it is right – that to be confident of victory in an engagement in a mobile war in Europe you need numerical superiority in the engagement of three to one or some such number. At the strategic level, the defender has the long-term advantage, if his country is large, and so long as his will to fight is not broken, of being able to withdraw and mobilise the resouces of his hinterland, and perhaps of allies, whilst the attacker becomes increasingly extended and worn down. The prime advantage of being an attacker is that you may achieve surprise. On the other hand, the defender may reduce the chance of surprise by good intelligence and, more important, he may reduce the possible gains from surprise by ensuring that his forces are deployed neither in a thin line that can be broken nor in concentrations that can be knocked out by surprise bombardment.

Non-nuclear forces can be designed so that in their training, equipment, infrastructure, deployment and logistics they exploit these advantages so as to be better adapted to defence *or* to offence. For example, the forces of the neutral countries of Europe – Austria, Finland, Sweden, Switzerland and Yugoslavia – are designed for defence. The small size of these countries *vis-à-vis* any likely enemy makes a defensive strategy a choice of necessity as much as of virtue. On the other hand, the forces of the Soviet Union in Europe appear to be well adapted to offense – which is consistent either with the view that the political aims of the Soviet Union are offensive or with the view that they are peaceful but the means of non-nuclear deterrence chosen by the Soviet Union places strong emphasis on retaliation or pre-emption.

Just *how far* forces can be given, by design, 'Defensive Superiority' is an open question. It depends on geography, technology and other factors, about which it is not possible to be precise. By and large, the scope for 'Defensive Superiority' appears to be greatest where the country to be defended provides natural obstacles, good cover and is not too small. And where that is so, but not where it is absent, current trends in non-nuclear weapons technology, of which increasing accuracy and lethality of weapons is the key feature, will probably help the defender.

The reason for this is that a high kill probability per shot (which is what high accuracy and high lethality together provide) puts a premium on shooting first, something which scarecely matters if accuracies are low and you have to shoot repeatedly to have a high probability of killing your opponent. If there is good cover and forces are not in fixed positions known to the other side, the tactical advantage of shooting first can be reaped by the defender. He can conceal himself, whereas the attacker, to seek out the defender, must move forward and in doing so expose himself to the defender. On the other hand, if each side knows the positions of the other, because there is no cover or because positions are fixed and known to both sides, then the advantage of shooting first can be seized by the attacker before he advances.

I shall assume, for the purposes of the following analysis, that we are considering an area where there is significant military scope for varying the defensive capabilities of a nation's forces relative to its offensive capabilities. This is a *crucial* assumption on which the argument about non-nuclear forces stands or falls. This assumption is probably broadly valid for Europe, but perhaps not so for the Middle East.

To think about the scope for reducing the offensive capabilities and increasing the defensive capabilities of forces in Europe, or any other area, it is best to think about the forces of the opposing side, for one is conscious of their offensive capabilities, which are emphasised and made the starting-point of defence planning, in a way that one is not conscious of the offensive capabilities of one's own forces. One can then ask, how could the opposing nation reduce its offensive capability and increase its defensive capability? For example, from Western Europe we will pick on the large tank forces and other features of the Warsaw Pact forces and see ways in which the Pact might dispense with them without reducing their security.

The most important implication of a non-nuclear strategy of 'Defensive Superiority' is that its adoption by one country in a two-country confrontation can improve the security of both. Suppose that there are two nations A and B whose intentions towards each other are peaceful and who to start with have equal forces that have an all-round capability, not designed expressly for defence or offence. Suppose country A now changes its forces so as to increase their defensive capability while reducing their offensive capability, without diminishing its security. For example, it might increase its dispersed anti-tank forces and reduce its tank forces. Whilst country A remained equally secure or more so, country B would find it was more secure than before: the offensive forces facing it would have been reduced, added to which the pressure for pre-emptive attack would be less than before. Country B could therefore reduce its forces, *without* changing their offensive–defensive mix, and be as secure as it was to start with. This in turn would permit A to reduce its forces (with the same new mix) and be as secure as before; and so on. A cumulative downward arms race could be generated by a move towards a more defensive stance by one country only. If both shifted to a more defensive stance, the cumulative process would be more rapid.

Here is a way in which two countries or alliances that are locked in an arms race but do not have offensive aims against each other can get out of the race. So far we have considered it mechanically. But the political aspect is plainly of the greatest importance. To give your forces an offensive stance when your aims are peaceful is to provide grounds for doubt as to your intentions in the minds of your potential enemy: your capacity to attack he can see; your intention not to attack he must take on trust. On the other hand, to give your forces a defensive stance will reassure him: the limits to your ability to attack will be visible; and your declared intention not to attack will be confirmed by the evidence of your military stance. Reassurance to your opponent that you do not intend to attack him can be seen as an extension of Michael Howard's proposition that your strategy should provide reassurance to your own people and allies, not alarm them and divide them politically.[5] By this criterion, the strategy of the Warsaw Pact, with its apparent reliance on an offensive capability, is wrong. So, on the NATO side, is the strategy of 'deep strike'; and so is the idea, recently put forward by Samuel Huntington, that NATO should add to its deterrence by giving its non-nuclear forces an offensive capability.[6]

We can conclude that if your aims are peaceful the right military stance to pursue at the non-nuclear level is not 'Balance' but 'Defensive Superiority'. If your aims are offensive, then clearly your strategic objective at the non-nuclear level will be 'Offensive Superiority.' Whether you will succeed in achieving a great enough 'Offensive Superiority' to give you a high probability of victory will depend on the size of the opposing country relative to yours, and on many other things.

Plurality and Mixed Objectives

So far we have considered, subject to a few asides, two countries or alliances of fairly equal size; and we have assumed that, in accordance with whether their aims are offensive or peaceful, they should choose between the strategic objectives we have arrived at. In practice, matters are not as simple as that.

In general, the larger the number of armed countries or alliances that are potentially hostile to one another the harder it will be for any one of them to achieve its strategic objective, for the larger will be the number of countries that could combine against it and against which it must arm. The assumption that there are two countries or alliances is not a bad approximation, however, to the confrontation between NATO and the Warsaw Pact, where the Soviet Union and United States numerically are dominant at the nuclear level, and the forces of the member countries – or at least their forces in Europe – can be treated as single entities at the non-nuclear level.

The assumption that political aims are either offensive or peaceful also needs to be qualified in two ways. In the first place, political aims may be mixed and confused, being a compromise in domestic politics between groups with different views. Secondly, when two powers confront each other in different parts of the world, or have opponents in addition to each other, it may be appropriate for them to follow different strategic objectives in different areas. For example, the Soviet Union and United States maintain a capacity to intervene militarily in the third world, if for no other reason than to keep each other out of countries which they perceive to be in their respective spheres of influence. The forces kept for that purpose must have an offensive capability, a capability to intervene. On the other hand, in Europe, where frontiers are settled and the forces of the Soviet Union and United States are *in situ*, forces with defensive superiority are appropriate to each side if its political aims are peaceful. There is no logical difficulty here. There are simply different military requirements for different areas. But there may be a problem in organising non-nuclear forces that are expected to follow different doctrines, and practise different modes of fighting, in different areas.

Recapitulation

We can sum up the argument so far as follows:

1. The pursuit of balance in arms is a poor way to try to preserve the peace. It is likely to lead to an arms race and to alarm rather than reassure your potential opponent.
2. If your aims are truly peaceful, meaning that you seek neither to attack your enemy nor to generate an arms race so as to put economic pressure on him, the appropriate strategic objectives are 'Sufficiency' in the case of nuclear forces and 'Defensive Superiority' in the case of non-nuclear forces.

3. If your aims are offensive, or you wish to be able to go on the offensive, then the logical strategic objectives are 'Supremacy', meaning quasi-monopoly in the case of nuclear weapons (so that you can inflict unacceptable damage on your enemy while he cannot do so to you) and 'Offensive Superiority' in the case of non-nuclear weapons.
4. These alternative strategic objectives appropriate to alternative political aims can be tabulated as follows:

	Peaceful	*Offensive*
Nuclear Forces	'Sufficiency'	'Supremacy'
Non-nuclear Forces	'Defensive Superiority'	'Offensive Superiority'

5. The pursuit of the strategic objectives associated with offensive aims – nuclear 'Supremacy' and non-nuclear 'Offensive Superiority' – is likely to lead to an arms race and to the temptation to attack pre-emptively. Nuclear 'Supremacy' is not an objective you can expect to attain once your opponent has a substantial nuclear armoury. Non-nuclear 'Offensive Superiority' may be attainable depending on the size and characteristics of the opposing nation or alliance.
6. Nuclear 'Sufficiency' should be attainable, provided your nuclear weapons are not very vulnerable to your opponent's nuclear weapons and defences.
7. 'Defensive Superiority' in non-nuclear weapons will be attainable provided the relative military potential of the two countries (or alliances) is not too uneven and provided the terrain and other conditions are reasonably favourable to the defence.
8. The larger the number of separate armed countries or alliances that confront one another the harder it will be for each to achieve its strategic objectives and the less the likelihood of stability.

ACHIEVING THE OBJECTIVES

The next step is to consider how, by influencing the conduct of your potential opponent as well as by direct steps, you can achieve your strategic objective: 'Sufficiency' or 'Supremacy' in the nuclear realm; 'Defensive Superiority' or 'Offensive Superiority' in the non-nuclear realm.

There are three principal ways in which a nation may influence the arms policy of another. First, it may do so by *independent acts* of arms policy, that is, by unilaterally changing the level and characteristics of its forces, nuclear and non-nuclear, so that they demonstrate which of the military objectives it is able to pursue – and hence what are its possible political aims. Secondly, it may do so by *discussion*, that is, by discussing with its opponent, and by discussing in domestic forums which the opponent can follow, the logic and merits of alternative strategies, in particular the case for 'Sufficiency' and 'Defensive Superiority' if its aims are peaceful and the possible steps each can take, and proposes to take, unconditionally, towards those objectives. Thirdly, it may do so by *negotiation* that is, by attempting to strike bargains in which a change in arms policy by it is made conditional on a change by its opponent, on the grounds that it is not in one's interest to modify one's policy unless one's opponent reciprocates by doing likewise.

The process described as 'discussion' could be termed 'positive dialogue': one side says, 'We are going unilaterally to undertake these steps that will made us both more secure; we suggest you take those steps.' The exchange is primarily informative and persuasive in design. Conversely, the term 'negative dialogue' could be applied to negotiation, a process in which one side says, 'We will not do this unless you do that', thus putting both parties into adversary postures. Discussion is a concept that may require further refinement, but the essence of it will be clear from what has been said and what follows.

Peaceful Aims

Let us start by assuming that the aim of the nation (or alliance) under consideration is peaceful. It therefore seeks nuclear 'Sufficiency' and non-nuclear 'Defensive Superiority'; it seeks to reassure, not to deceive. This basic principle suggests itself: if there is a change in the level or character of your forces that would help you attain your (peaceful) strategic objective, *regardless of whether your opponent made a similar move*, there are no grounds for seeking reciprocity through negotiation. It will be advantageous to make the move independently.

Suppose two countries, for one reason or another, have acquired nuclear and all-round non-nuclear forces that are menacing to each other. Suppose that in this setting one side, country A, whose political aims are peaceful, decides to adopt as its strategic objectives nuclear 'Sufficiency' and non-nuclear 'Defensive Superiority', in order to reduce the risk of pre-emptive attack, ease mutual suspicion and ease the arms race. Without reciprocity from country B, A will improve its security by reducing the risk of pre-emptive attack, if it can re-shape its forces and change their level until the objectives of nuclear 'Sufficiency' and non-nuclear 'Defensive Superiority' are satisfied. A will wish to induce B to change its strategy in the same direction, since that will mean that mutual reassurance will be reinforced and that the *level* of forces (of the new structure) required by A in order to achieve security will be reduced.

For this purpose A can engage in discussion, as we have defined it above, with the hope of persuading B that, if his political aims are peaceful, it is in *his* interest to change his strategic objectives to nuclear 'Sufficiency' and non-nuclear 'Defensive Superiority' too, since in that way he will reduce suspicion and ease the mutual competiton in arms. The argument that a change in strategy will also reduce the risk of pre-emptive attack has less force when applied to the second than to the first of two countries to make the change. For if one has made the change and ceases to have an offensive capability, the *mutual* fear that, if I do not attack first, he will do so for fear that I will do so, is removed. However, since the distinction between offensive and non-offensive capabilities is not black and white and since perceptions of threats will be coloured, the argument must be reckoned still to have some possible force when applied to the second country.

If country B cannot be persuaded to match the changes that A has made, there seems to be nothing that A can do by way of changes in military strategy, except to continue discussion, hoping that one day it will bear fruit, meanwhile maintaining the new strategic stance of nuclear 'Sufficiency' and non-nuclear 'Defensive Superiority'

One possible move by A we should consider is that he might threaten to reverse his strategy and turn to the pursuit of nuclear 'Supremacy' and non-nuclear 'Offensive Superiority', which would have the following effects. First, it would fail to deter B and in that way increase A's security more effectively, since, *ex hypothesi*, the level of forces (and expenditures) maintained under the non-provocative strategy would be chosen so as to ensure no loss of security (and perhaps an increase) when A initially moved in that direction. (Otherwise it cannot be assumed that A would have made a change).

Secondly, it would diminish the security of A and B, by reintroducing the risk of pre-emptive attack. Finally, it would aggravate mutual suspicion and provoke competitive arming.

It would thus be a move that would be against the interests of A as well as B – unless B responded by reckoning that it was worth avoiding these *mutually* disadvantageous consequences and so was persuaded by this threat to change its strategic objectives to nuclear 'Sufficiency' and non-nuclear 'Defensive Superiority'. However, there would then be the problem as to whether A, having threatened and started to move in the wrong direction in order to persuade B to move in the right direction, could reverse engines. There is momentum in the internal political process of persuading a nation what is the right strategy to keep its potential opponent away and preserve the peace. But the main point is that, given the nature of the political processes that determine strategy, nation B would seem to be at least as likely to react perversely as favourably to A's threat. We are considering a nation (B), which, whatever its political intentions, has been pursuing the strategy of seeking 'Balance' or perhaps superiority of some kind. In such a nation, the martial spirit, hostility towards the potential opponent and suspicion of anything he does will not be negligible. Nation A seeks to allay that suspicion by adopting a non-threatening stance and trying by discussion to persuade B to do likewise. He fails. B's suspicion is too great, his political machine too inflexible, or his intentions too hostile. How, then, is B going to react to A going back to a more threatening stance? Will the interpretation that prevails be: 'Ah, this shows that we in nation B have been wrong in our strategy (and in our political intentions if these were offensive); we should adopt the strategy of nuclear "Sufficiency" and non-nuclear "Defensive Superiority" that A has been advocating'? Or will it be: 'Ah, this just shows that A was never sincere in all that talk about adopting a non-menacing strategy consistent with peaceful intentions. It was just an attempt to lull us into a false sense of security. The more offensive strategy that A is now adopting – or threatening to adopt – shows it was all humbug. We must redouble our efforts to keep ahead?' It would be a rash person who gambled on the former reaction. To threaten seems as likely to have a negative as a positive effect.

There remains the question whether negotiation will help you to induce your opponent to move. If, *ex hypothesi*, you have adopted nuclear 'Sufficiency' and non-nuclear 'Defensive Superiority' and, in pursuit of those objectives, your have gone to the limits of unilateral action consistent with the maintenance of security, and your opponent has not followed suit, you clearly cannot negotiate on the basis of direct reciprocity, of like for like. For you have already taken the action you want him to take. The only conceivable deal you could propose would be that if he moved, you would make a further move (such as a cut in your force levels), thus keeping one step ahead of him, at least as you perceive things. The trouble with this notion is that the deal amounts to a false bargain, in that if he shares your political aim of peace, it is in his interest to move unconditionally. Moreover it is a bargain with some risk, in that if you offer to move one step ahead of him your security will be at risk if he does not fulfil his side of the bargain. Hence suspicion and taut bargaining surrounded by propaganda would be likely, a process that could well be counter-productive, compared with that stance of sticking at the limits of the unilateral moves you can make consistently with the maintenance of your security, and persisting with discussion.

The question remains, when, if ever, is negotiation needed? The answer is, it will be needed if, when *both* sides have exhausted the unilateral moves they can make towards nuclear 'Sufficiency' and non-nuclear 'Defensive Superiority', including reductions in forces in response to each other's moves, they find that they still confront one another with forces that are threatening to each other's security and they still mistrust each other with those weapons. This implies that there are some types of forces, weapons or deployments that are threatening and cannot be neutralised in that respect by any defensive move. It may of course be possible to identify these before all the unilateral moves have been made.

At the non-nuclear level, chemical weapons are the category that comes to mind. The move to a defensive stance that one country in a confrontation could take would be to get rid of chemical weapons and concentrate on protective measures. But it may be the case (though this is open to debate) that a defensive stance is so ineffective, or so reduces fighting efficiency, that it canot be reckoned as more than a weak substitute for an offensive capability that provides a threat of retaliation and so deters the use of chemical weapons by your opponent. Therefore reciprocity, and hence negotiation, are needed.

At the nuclear level, the same argument applies. If your aims are peaceful you should go for 'Sufficiency', as defined earlier, and you should not threaten or obstruct your opponent's nuclear weapons since to do so will be destabilising, that is, it will make him less secure and cause him to arm more. If you start from a position where you and your opponent possess destabilising systems such as MIRVs you will increase your security – and his – by reducing the risk of preemptive attack if you remove those systems unilaterally, so long as you preserve 'Sufficiency', for example, through the possession of invulnerable submarine-launched missiles. There are no grounds for demanding reciprocity through negotiation so long as 'Sufficiency' is possessed, but there is a case for urging him to follow by means of consultation. Negotiation would become necessary in two sets of circumstances, analogous to the circumstances of chemical weapons discussed above: if you wished to go below 'Sufficiency' and get rid of nuclear weapons but, because of continuing mistrust, you were not willing unilaterally to join the nations that do without them and you therefore sought reciprocity; and if the only systems possessed by and available to both sides were so unstable (for example, land-based missiles many times MIRVed) that neither side enjoyed 'Sufficiency' and neither could de-MIRV unilaterally without risk of vulnerability to a disarming first strike. Both these contingencies are remote and academic.

Lessons of Negotiations

There are several lessons from the past which provide further grounds for not pursuing negotiation in the manner in which it has been practised, and indeed for pursuing it only in the special circumstances suggested.

First and foremost, negotiation over the balance in arms is arguably a potent way of perpetuating, rather than easing, an arms race, since it has the effect of both neutralising political opposition and intensifying the competition in arms. Negotiation neutralises opposition to the arms race by acting as a placebo. It does so in two ways. First, when agreements are reached, they tend, for understandable reasons, to be agreements not to do things peripheral to the main arms race, things in which the military have little immediate interest. Examples are the agreements not to militarise the Antarctic and not to fix nuclear weapons to the seabed. Such trivial agreements have been hailed as evidence that progress is being made to halt the arms race. The public feels reassured and relaxes – although the race goes on unabated.

Secondly, the very act of engaging in talks about arms has come to be regarded as reassuring, regardless of whether agreements are reached or security is improved. If talks are broken off, the world shudders and there are calls for their resumption; if they are joined again, there is a sigh of relief and it is assumed that something useful is happening. The question as to whether the talks are easing or aggravating the arms race, increasing or reducing security, is not addressed. It is taken for granted that talks are a good thing. It may of course be true that talking serves some ancillary purpose: opponents may be less likely to come to blows when they are engaged in talks than when they are not. But if that is the point it would be sensible to recognise it and ask whether a better approach could not be devised, an approach which combined the reassuring activity of talking with a greater likelihood of a positive outcome in terms of military security. Which is where our notion of discussion comes in.

The ways in which negotiation intensifies competition in arms have already been touched upon. It means that a category of arms or activities is picked out and 'Balance' in that category is put at the centre of the stage; it causes close scrutiny and sometimes wild propaganda about the other side's strength relative to one's own; and it causes the bargaining chip argument to be used to justify the development of new weapons and – though this is a corruption of the notion of a bargaining chip – to justify their deployment. (A new weapon is a bargaining chip so long as you threaten to acquire and deploy it. Once you deploy it, you have raised the stakes; the game has moved on).

An important example is the hurried deployment during the SALT I negotiations of MIRVs, the most destabilising of all weapons, since they are suited to first-strike attack and so give rise to fear and, as soon as two sides possess them, to pressure to strike pre-emptively in a crisis. Soon after the negotiations began, the US Senate and an advisory committee proposed delay, but the first deployment was pushed ahead with unexpected speed and the horse was out of the stable. Negotiation was the spur to this accelerated deployment. The logic of the pursuit of 'Balance', with its implication that relative strength is good for security and for bargaining, makes such things hard to prevent. One must ask what might have happened if, instead of pursuing 'Balance' and seeking to negotiate balanced changes, the policy had been to pursue nuclear 'Sufficiency', by means of unilateral acts that were calculated so far as possible to reassure the other side, and discussion.

Another lesson to be drawn about the dangers of negotiation is that when balance and reciprocity are sought, verification becomes a legal and technical issue, and one over which there is limitless scope for disagreement since total verification, like total knowledge, is unattainable. On the other hand, if the aim is independently to achieve nuclear 'Sufficiency' and non-nuclear 'Defensive Superiority', the visible military posture adopted by your opponent is what matters – the doctrine, equipment, training, logistics, deployment and all the other attributes of a nation's forces that show what kind of capability he possesses. It can be judged by national military experts, using good intelligence, such as is available by modern means of reconnaissance.

A further lesson is that negotiation totally to outlaw specified weapons, activities, deployments or types of forces is likely to be easier than negotiation to agree numbers of weapons or forces, because zero gives the appearance of offering no advantage to either side, even though that may not be quite true, whereas negotiation of numbers gives rise to disagreement over what constitutes 'Balance'. The postwar record of negotiations and agreements supports this view. The agreements made have nearly all been agreements to outlaw something. The only agreements to limit numbers were SALT I (including the ABM treaty) and SALT II, and the latter was challenged in the United States precisely on the grounds that in some dimensions the agreed numbers were unbalanced in favour of the Soviet Union.

A final lesson is that it would be a great mistake to try to outlaw 'offensive weapons' as a class and attempt to define them in general legal terms or to list them. That was tried in 1932 and led to insoluble disputes about definitions.

Offensive Aims

If your political aims are offensive, meaning that you aim to attack or to threaten to attack, your appropriate actions are very different and rather limited.

Whether you declare your aims publicly, like Hitler, or claim that your aim is peaceful, your arms policy will be directed at acquiring the requisite nuclear 'Supremacy' and/or non-nuclear 'Offensive Superiority'. In consultations, you may seek to calm your opponent. As regards negotiations, a government may walk out as part of a militaristic stance intended to intimidate its opponents and potential neutrals and to rouse its population at home; or it may play along, seeking to lull its opponent and gain advantage thereby. It is not obvious which tactic is better, nor that either will make much difference.

If your political aim is offensive in the more limited sense of seeking not to attack your opponent but to strain his politico-economic system by forcing him into an arms race, to intimidate him or to possess more status symbols, your strategy must be such as to create in his mind fear that your aims may be militarily offensive.

Recapitulation

Let us now sum up this part of the chapter.

1. There are three principal ways in which a nation may influence the arms policy of another: independent acts; discussion; and negotiation.
2. On the assumption that the political aims of a nation or alliance are peaceful, it will pay it to introduce independently (that is, unilaterally) a change in the level or character of its forces if that move will help it attain its strategic objectives (nuclear 'Sufficiency' and non-nuclear 'Defensive Superiority') *regardless of whether the opposing nation makes a similar move*. Reciprocity and negotiation are not needed.
3. If country A moves in that way and country B (its potential opponent) does not follow, it will be desirable, though not essential for security, for A to engage in discussion (as we define it) to persuade B to follow.
4. Negotiation is appropriate only if there are some types of forces, weapons or deployments that are threatening and cannot be neutralised in that respect by any defensive move. Chemical weapons are a possible example at the non-nuclear level. At the nuclear level, negotiation would be needed if nuclear weapons were to be reduced below the level of 'Sufficiency' with the object of their elimination; or if MIRVs were to be removed from two armouries so vulnerable that 'Sufficiency' was lacking and one-sided removal was unacceptable. Both are rather remote contingencies.
5. There are further grounds for demoting negotiation and avoiding it if possible. It is arguably a potent way of aggravating an arms race. It is needed only where balance and reciprocity are needed,

and that, precisely, is where verification will become an issue. (Broad changes in strategy do not require verification of the precise kind that is needed to satisfy those who, in pursuit of 'Balance', negotiate, draft and ratify treaties). In so far as negotiation must be pursued, it is likely to be easier to outlaw categories of weapons or activities than to limit their number. It would be a mistake to try to outlaw 'offensive weapons' as a class or to list them, a procedure that in 1932 failed in disputes over definitions.

CONCLUSION

If security is to be improved, the arms race is to be ended and we are to escape from what Henry Kissinger has called the 'impasse of thought'[7] about arms control, our attention and energies should be turned away from the pursuit of 'Balance' and 'Negotiation' and devoted instead to a reconsideration of strategy, defined quite simply as the study of how to achieve political aims, precisely specified, by the possession or use of military forces.[8]

Notes

1. The author is indebted to Jerry Wiesner for this point made in discussion.
2. See Steven Kull, 'Nuclear Nonsense', *Foreign Policy*, no. 58 (Spring 1985).
3. See Anders Boserup, 'Deterrence and Defence', *The Bulletin of the Atomic Scientists*, vol. 37, no. 10 (December 1981) pp. 11–13.
4. See John J. Mearsheimer, *Conventional Deterrence* (Ithaca, NY, 1983).
5. Michael Howard, 'Reassurance and Deterrence: Western Defense in the 1980's', *Foreign Affairs* (Winter 1982/3).
6. Samuel P. Huntington, 'Conventional Deterrence and Conventional Retaliation in Europe', *International Security*, vol. 8, no. 3 (Winter 1983–4).
7. Henry A. Kissinger, 'Should We Try to Defend Against Russia's Missiles?', *The Washington Post*, 23 September 1984.
8. Parts of this paper, notably the discussion of the theoretical objections to 'Balance', owe a great deal to lengthy discussions with Anders Boserup. An earlier version of this chapter appeared under the same title in *Arms Control: The Journal of Arms Control and Disarmament*, vol. 7, no. 2 (September 1986). Permission to reprint is gratefully acknowledged.

5 Simulation of the Short-term Effects of a 'Limited' Nuclear War in Europe
Andrea Ottolenghi

INTRODUCTION

There are more than 9 000 warheads deployed in Europe or facing Europe,[1] as well as several strategically important military installations like nuclear airbases, command, control and communication sites, and naval nuclear airbases (see Table 5.1). The presence of these warheads and installations and the possibility of limited nuclear wars have caused growing and manifest concern among Europeans.

There are several conceivable scenarios that could lead to a limited nuclear war in Europe. One can imagine a conventional conflict along the 'Central Front' where either deliberate escalation to the use of battlefield or tactical nuclear weapons is decided upon in order to countervail a possible 'conventional inferiority', or where a 'limited' nuclear exchange takes place in the fog of the battle, particularly if field commanders face the dilemma of 'using or losing' battlefield nuclear weapons. Alternatively one can consider a naval conflict in the Mediterranean or in the North Sea, where naval nuclear weapons are used in a 'selective' fashion, or a Middle East conflict which escalates into a European conflict and where again nuclear weapons are used in a limited way by both superpowers. Finally one can imagine a pre-emptive nuclear attack in Europe directed against nuclear bases, in a period of intense crisis.

The possibility of a nuclear conflict in Europe remaining 'limited' has often been discussed and mostly discarded by sensible analysts and politicians. Several points should be considered in this respect. First of all, different emphasis can be given to the word 'limited', We

Table 5.1 NATO/Warsaw Pact potential nuclear weapon systems, Europe

Category and type	NATO			WARSAW PACT	
	Countries deploying	Launcher total 7/86[a]	Launcher total 7/86	Countries deploying	Type
LAND-BASED					
ICBM			[b]	USSR	SS-11/-17/-19
IRBM					
SSBS S-3 D/TN-61	France	18	112	USSR	SS-4
			270	USSR	SS-20
GLCM					
BGM-109G	USA	128			
MRBM					
Pershing II	USA	108			
SRBM					
Pershing IA	FRG	72	(350)	USSR	SS-21/FROG
Lance	USA	108	(375)	USSR	SS-23/Scud A/B
Lance	Allies	55	77	USSR	SS-12 mod
Pluton	France	44	214	Allies	FROG-3/-5/-7
			143	Allies	Scud B/C

Artillery			
M-110	USA	500	
M-110	Allies	373	
M-109	USA	500	
M-109	Allies	1,659	M-1976, 2-S5, S-23, M-1955 (D-20), M-1973/2-S3, M-1975 how, M-1975 mor M-1955 (D-20) gun/how M-1973/2-S3 how
SAM (dual-capable)			
MIM-14B *Nike Hercules*	Allies	443	
SEA-BASED			
SLBM			
UGM-73A *Poseidon C-3*	USA	[a]	
Polaris A-3	Britain	64	
MSBS M-20/TN-60	France	80	
MSBS M-4/TN70	France	16	
			SS-N-5
	USSR	24	
SLCM			
BGM-109A *Tomahawk* (TLAM/N nuc mod to be installed in *Los Angeles* SSN (12); *Iowa* BBG (32); *Virginia, Ticonderoga, Long Beach, California* CGN/CG; *Burke, Spruance* DDG.)	USA	166	
	USSR	130[c]	SS-N-3[c]
	USSR	48[c]	SS-N-7[c]
	USSR	140[c]	SS-N-9[c]
	USSR	80[c]	SS-N-12[c]
	USSR	48[c]	SS-N-19[c]
AIR			
Land-based strike			
F-104 G/S	Allies	271	
F-4E	USA	96	
F-4E/F	Allies	167	
F-111E/F	USA	150	
F-16	USA	144	
	USSR	340	Tu-95, Mya-4, Tu-16, Tu-22, Tu-22M
	(Air Force)		
	USSR	235	Tu-16, Tu-22, Tu-22M
	(Navy)		
	USSR	1,190	Su-7, MiG-21, MiG-27,

Table 5.1 NATO/Warsaw Pact potential nuclear weapon systems, Europe

Category and type	NATO			WARSAW PACT	
	Countries deploying	Launcher total 7/86[a]	Launcher total 7/86	Countries deploying	Type
F-16	Allies	243		(Frontal)	Su-17, Su-24
Mirage IVA	France	30	90	Allies	Su-7
Mirage IIIE	France	30	40	Poland	Su-20
Jaguar	France	45	109	Allies	MiG-23
Tornado	Allies	358			
Carrier-based strike					
A-7/F-18	USA	48/40[d]			
Super Etendard	France	38			
ASW					
S-3A	USA	20[d]	(110)	USSR	Tu-142, Il-38, Be-12
P-3B/C	USA	(12)		(Navy)	
P-3	Allies	20			
Nimrod	Britain	28			
Atlantic	Allies	55			

[a] Listings for US assume deployment: Europe only, *not* incl reinforcements except in the case of 400 *Poseidon* SLBM warheads, assumed for planning purposes to be assigned to SACEUR from US central systems.
[b] A proportion of the launchers deployed is assigned to peripheral targets.
[c] USSR types and totals based on estimated naval deployments and equipment.
[d] Figures assume 2 US carriers in European area.
Source: The International Institute for Strategic Studies, *The Military Balance 1986–87* (London, 1986). Permission to reproduce is gratefully acknowledged.

can interpret this as meaning that the so-called 'collateral' effects on population are kept limited and in some way 'acceptable'. We can think about a limitation of the territory directly involved in the conflict (for example, Europe). We can think of a nuclear exchange avoiding the superpowers' territories. We can think of a nuclear exchange involving only selected counterforce attacks or we can think of a limited use of nuclear forces (typically tactical battlefield nuclear weapons). In any case all these interpretations of the word 'limited' imply the possibility of restraining the escalation of the war.

The probability of a nuclear war being kept at a 'limited' level – assuming it as a possible event – is not the same for all the scenarios considered above and for all the scenarios one can imagine. There are subjective and objective factors which must be considered. The objective factors are connected with the level of destruction already achieved that depends on number, yield and location of nuclear explosions. The subjective factors include the willingness of the two sides to terminate the nuclear exchange; also the capability of communicating such willingness to the opponent is a factor which should be taken into account.

It is important to distinguish, at least schematically, between a situation or a phase of the conflict in which both sides are willing to terminate a war and return to a pre-war condition and a situation – or again a phase of the conflict – in which one or both sides are willing to keep the 'collateral' damage limited, with the aim of forcing the enemy to yield in order to avoid complete destruction.

It should be pointed out that when people speak about the impossibility of 'controlling nuclear war' they generally mean that it is impossible to pursue objectives (which are militarily and politically meaningful) with the limited use of nuclear weapons. What is under discussion is not only the possibility of interrupting a limited nuclear exchange but also the possibility of prevailing (in any sense) in a limited nuclear war. Accordingly, it is clear that considering the scenario of a pre-emptive nuclear attack means assuming that one side considers the possibility of somehow winning a limited nuclear war.

If the collateral damages of a pre-emptive attack cannot be considered limited; if the enemy, after a pre-emptive attack, is not likely to yield; if it is very unlikely that the command and control system will enable the two sides to go through the various ladders of nuclear escalation in a 'controlled' way, then our conclusion will be that it is meaningless for any superpower to plan a limited nuclear strike in order to gain an edge over the opponent.

The above considerations are equally valid for a direct nuclear exchange involving the superpowers' territories as well as for a nuclear exchange taking place in Europe. In this sense the same constraints we discussed before apply to the case of a superpower conducting a nuclear attack against enemy European countries.

Discussions about the possibility of limited nuclear conflicts have, in the past, been very common in the United States, especially since the beginning of the seventies. There have also been several attempts to reassure Europeans that a nuclear war limited to Europe would be in any case out of the question for the United States, but these reassurances have not always been convincing. The neutron bomb controversy, the explicit inclusion of limited nuclear options in the US strategy or even the debate about the Euromissiles, which were also presented as a way of meeting the European anxiety, have increased the worries about a limited nuclear conflict in Europe.

As is well-known, one of the prevailing motivations for the deployment of the new Euromissiles was originally – at least for some Western European governments – the need to have a sort of insurance policy against a limited nuclear conflict. The argument was the following: if a limited nuclear exchange occurred, then the use of NATO medium-range missiles would hit Soviet territory directly, and it would hence trigger a global conflict. In this very simplified argument the mechanism of nuclear decision making was completely overlooked and important facts were not considered, in order to assuage European anxiety. Hence understanding better why a limited nuclear exchange cannot help any side in obtaining goals which are politically or militarily significant can have an important consequence in the political environment in Western Europe.

The Soviet Union has always said very clearly that it does not believe in the possibility of a 'limited nuclear war' and this argument has been used to support the idea that a limited nuclear war itself is impossible, since 'it takes two to tango'. The Soviets dismiss very clearly the possibility of having 'rules of the game' during a nuclear exchange, and emphasise that a limited nuclear confrontation in Europe will be followed, shortly afterwards, by a global war. Nevertheless the Soviets have substantially developed and deployed nuclear delivery systems which can possibly be used in a limited nuclear war. They possess the whole spectrum of 'limited' weapons, such as battlefield nuclear weapons, short-range missiles, and bombs for short-range aircraft. This is undoubtedly a sort of contradiction on the Soviet side that – despite generic assurance – affirms that short-range weapons are there only to deter the use of short-range weapons by the other side. These considerations suggest that the Soviets too admit the possibility of a limited use of certain kinds of nuclear weapons, in certain circumstances. At the same time there is every indication that the Soviets are not willing to abide by 'the rules of the game', especially if these rules are decided by the enemy. Hence the conclusion is that a war conducted according to certain rules is a very unlikely event.

In this framework studies have been conducted in order to estimate the consequences of possible pre-emptive nuclear attacks against military installations in Europe. By showing that such consequences are always very heavy in terms of number of casualties and economic and social damage, one can show that a pre-emptive strike does not guarantee any side the possibility of conducting a limited nuclear attack with impunity and that any 'militarily reasonable' pre-emptive attack is likely to contribute in a significant way to the escalation as opposed to contributing to the termination of war on favourable terms for the initiator of a pre-emptive nuclear attack. Last but not least, the results of these simulations give an idea of the level of risk we run in keeping thousands of nuclear warheads 'facing' each other on European territory, paradoxically in the name of the defence of territorial integrity.

THE MODEL

The most ticklish problem in a simulation is typically the construction of the model which, considering its very nature, involves a process for eliminating details not essential to one's aims. The subjective aspect always present in models requires special attention, particularly if one deals with questions like the 'feasibility' and 'credibility' of a strategy. That is why all the characteristics of the models must be available to anybody that wants to make his contribution or to control them. Moreover in a nuclear war there can be effects which are hardly predictable, since there is no precedent of several explosions within a short time; therefore models for such simulations lead to results that – for specific conditions and a specific scenario – must be taken as lower limits of the actual effects of a nuclear conflict.

The first simulations of the effects of a nuclear war were carried out with results based on several assumptions, often not expressed and on many occasions unjustified (officially because dealing with 'classified' matters). Since the late 1970s, as a consequence of new theories about the possibility of 'limited' nuclear wars, new studies have been developed with new approaches to the problem and with the publication not only of the results but also of the basic assumptions of the models. The development of a model to simulate the effects of a nuclear conflict in Europe (initially applied to the case of a counterforce attack in Italy[2]) is thus a part of these new studies carried out in various universities, independently of military research groups.[3]

The basic principles in developing the model derive from the need for an instrument that can be discussed with reference to all its components and can be enriched with further information without complete remaking. Hence the separation of various physical consequences of nuclear explosions and the use of continuous functions to describe the effects on population, thereby eliminating the need for using 'lethal areas' – a widespread method, in this kind of simulation, to describe synthetically the consequences of prompt effects.[4]

Figure 5.1 shows the structure of the base model: the prompt effects of the explosions (initial nuclear radiation, blast wave and thermal radiation, with their combination) are initially kept separate from the effects of radioactive fall-out. Subsequently, to quantify the consequences, the various effects are combined, trying to consider also the reinforcement derived from synergistic effects. Effects like the electromagnetic pulse are not expressly inserted into the model since they do not have direct consequences on population. However they cannot be disregarded since the complete lack of communication (at least between civilians) would render dramatic the impossibility of providing the injured people with medical care, besides the enormous number and seriousness of injuries anyway needing medical treatment.

To obtain the number of casualties, the whole area of Europe is divided into one kilometre squares. Within each square we assume an average value for the several variables, namely population density, thermal blast effects, and radiation exposure from fall-out. The total number of fatalities is obtained by adding together the deaths in all squares. A similar procedure is adopted in the calculation of the number of injuries, with the qualification that persons suffering injuries from both prompt and fallout effects, or those injured by more than one explosion are counted as fatalities.

We will now very briefly describe the various components of the model, starting from physical phenomena and then considering their effects on environment and human beings.

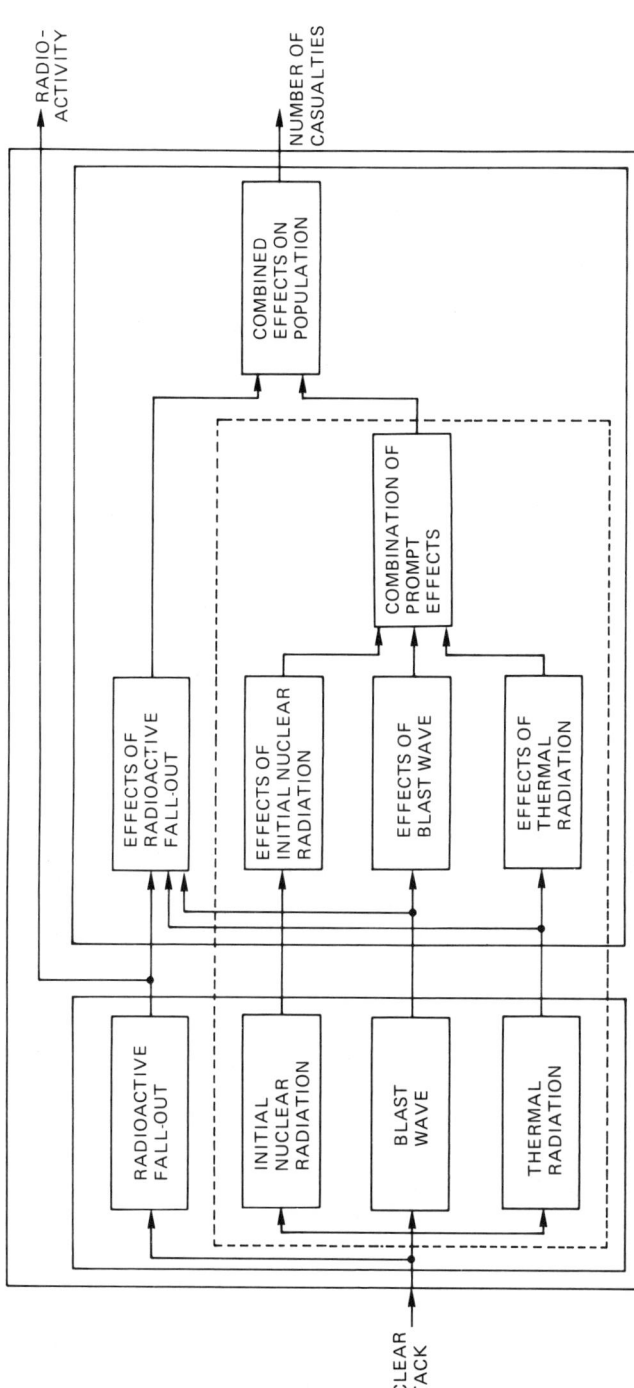

Figure 5.1 Structure of the model for the simulation of the short-term effects of a nuclear conflict (arrows from *blast wave* and from *thermal radiation* to *effects of nuclear radiation* are to describe the consequences of blast wave and thermal radiation on sheltering possibilities)

MODELLING PHYSICAL PHENOMENA

Prompt Effects

For the blast effect the overpressure model was used, mainly based on scaling laws as discussed in S. Glasstone and P. J. Dolan.[5] For the thermal radiation, the two parameters, radiation fluence and rate of delivery, were combined into one by defining the effective radiation fluence related to the experience from Hiroshima.

Fall-out

To estimate the effects of local fall-out a model is needed that describes the spatial distribution and the rate of the radioactive debris, as a function of the characteristics of the explosion and the meteorological conditions. Many studies on local radioactive fall-out have been carried out. Starting from theoretical considerations and experimental measures, a few models have been developed. One of the most important is the WSEG-10, developed in 1959.[6] This model – even though it keeps its validity within fixed limits – has a few defects, probably related to the yields of the warheads that during the 1950s were considered the most likely to be used (mostly greater than 1 MT). For yields of a few hundred kilotons and less, the WSEG-10 model seems to underestimate the highly radioactive area and overestimate the less contaminated area. The time taken for local fall-out to reach the ground also appears to be overestimated. In other words, the fall-out falling within a short time from the explosion and within a relatively short distance – typical of 'small' yields – seems to be partially disregarded.

During the 1970s detailed models were developed which considered the meteorological conditions point by point over the territory and taking into account the characteristics of small explosions. The complexity of these models requires such a large amount of data and computer time that it makes their use very difficult for a simulation of multiple explosions over a large territory. However, starting from one of these detailed models (DELFIC, 1979)[7] its author, H. G. Norment, has developed a simplified model (DNAF-1, 1981), and this model was used in this simulation.[8] The adequacy of this model was confirmed by the agreement between predicted and observed fall-out patterns following several US test explosions.

ESTIMATING THE EFFECTS ON POPULATIONS

Introduction

To estimate the effects on population, it is necessary to define the relationships between absorbed dose, peak overpressure and 'effective' thermal radiation, and the probability of death and injury due to these phenomena. Of course, this is the most ticklish part since hardly predictable aspects are involved, such as population behaviour. Moreover the problem is not only to quantify the effects of the individual physical phenomena, but also and especially to quantify the consequences of their combination due to synergism. Injuries due to single effects of explosions, that would produce almost no symptom and anyway no risk of death, might become fatal if effects were combined. This is particularly true of ionising radiations that reduce one's capability for defence and create the conditions for severe infections, even with only slight burns or injuries.

Biological Effects of Thermal Radiation and Blast Wave

As a reference, we have used Hiroshima's and Nagasaki's explosions to model the consequences on population of prompt effects. Unfortunately, not only modelling, but even collecting data, seems to be very much influenced by subjectivity. As shown in Tables 5.2 and 5.3, the data about Hiroshima are conflicting (68 000 fatalities according to *The Effects of Nuclear Weapons*[9] and 118 661 according to *Hiroshima and Nagasaki: The Physical, Medical and Social Effects of the Atomic Bombings.*[10]) (Data about Nagasaki are even more confused). These two sources (the first, American and the second, Japanese) are undoubtedly among the most qualified.

Table 5.2   Casualties in Hiroshima

Zone	Population	Density (per square mile)	Killed	Injured
0 to 0.6 mile	31 200	25 800	26 700	3 000
0.6 to 1.6 miles	144 800	22 700	39 600	53 000
1.6 to 3.1 miles	80 300	3 500	1 700	20 000
Totals	256 300	8 500	68 000	76 000

Source: Glasstone and Dolan, *The Effects of Nuclear Weapons.*

Table 5.3 Casualties in Hiroshima

Distance from Hypocenter (km)	Killed	Severely injured	Slightly injured	Missing	Not injured	Total
Under 0.5	19 329	478	338	593	924	21 622
0.5–1.0	42 271	3 046	1 919	1 366	4 434	53 036
1.0–1.5	37 689	7 732	9 522	1 188	9 140	65 271
1.5–2.0	13 422	7 627	11 516	227	11 698	44 490
2.0–2.5	4 513	7 830	14 149	98	26 096	52 686
2.5–3.0	1 139	2 923	6 795	32	19 907	30 796
3.0–3.5	117	474	1 934	2	10 250	12 777
3.5–4.0	100	295	1 768	3	13 513	15 679
4.0–4.5	8	64	373		4 260	4 705
4.5–5.0	31	36	156	1	6 593	6 817
Over 5.0	42	19	136	167	11 798	12 162
Total	118 661	30 524	48 606	3 677	118 613	320 081

Military personnel not included.

Source: The [Japanese] Committee, *Hiroshima and Nagasaki*.

However, comparing the percentage of fatalities as a function of the distance (see Figure 5.2) and comparing the lethal areas,[11] one can note a consistency between the two sources. Since the explosion over Hiroshima was an air burst (at about 500 metres from the ground), local fallout did not significantly influence the number of short-term fatalities. Therefore in those conditions the model to describe the effects of explosions can be reduced to the part enclosed by dotted lines in Figure 5.1.

To develop the model, we made the following assumptions. First, we assumed that most of the people who died in a relatively short time in Hiroshima were killed by thermal and blast effects. Secondly, we assumed that thermal and blast effects – as far as consequences on population are concerned – were of the same order of magnitude (see Figure 5.3). Thirdly, graphic data in Figure 5.2 can be assumed as reference to estimate the incidence of blast and thermal effects in the Hiroshima explosion. Fourthly, the probability of death at a fixed distance from the explosion can be expressed as follows:

$$P_D = 1 - (1 - P_{D_B})(1 - P_{D_T})$$

where P_{D_B} is the probability of death due to blast effects and P_{D_T} is the probability of death due to thermal effects. Thus the probability of

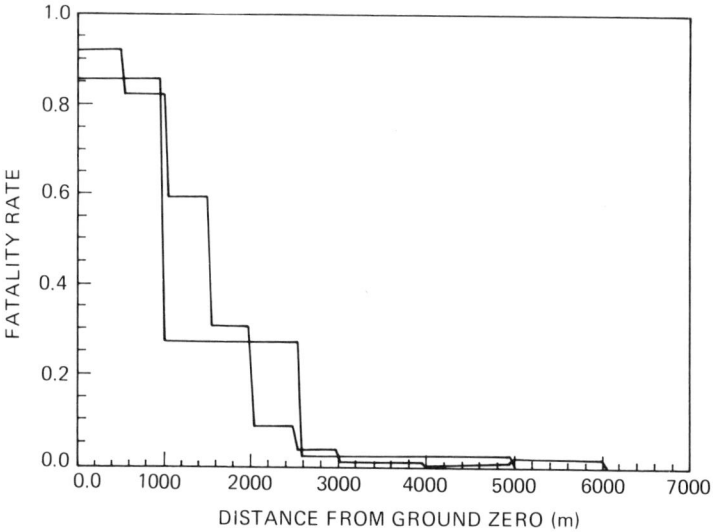

Figure 5.2 Percentage of fatalities versus distance from ground zero in Hiroshima

Sources: Glasstone and Dolan, *The Effects of Nuclear Weapons* and The [Japanese] Committee, *Hiroshima and Nagasaki.*

surviving an explosion is the product of the probabilities of surviving the two effects (blast and thermal), taken independently.[12] This obviously makes sense only for yields in the order of, or bigger than, tens of kilotons where, as already mentioned, the areas reached by initial nuclear radiation are completely devastated by thermal and blast effects.

The risk of this approach is to underestimate problems related to synergism. It seems to us, however, that it is certainly more adequate than either just considering the mechanical effects of the blast wave (like the US Department of Defense), or limiting the estimate of thermal radiation effects to directly exposed people, disregarding the consequences of firestorms (like the US Office of Technology Assessment[13]). As widely reported in several studies on these topics, both military installations and cities have such an amount of inflammable substances (including enormous amounts of fuel) that one can presume that firestorms and conflagrations would be very likely to develop in most cases.[14]

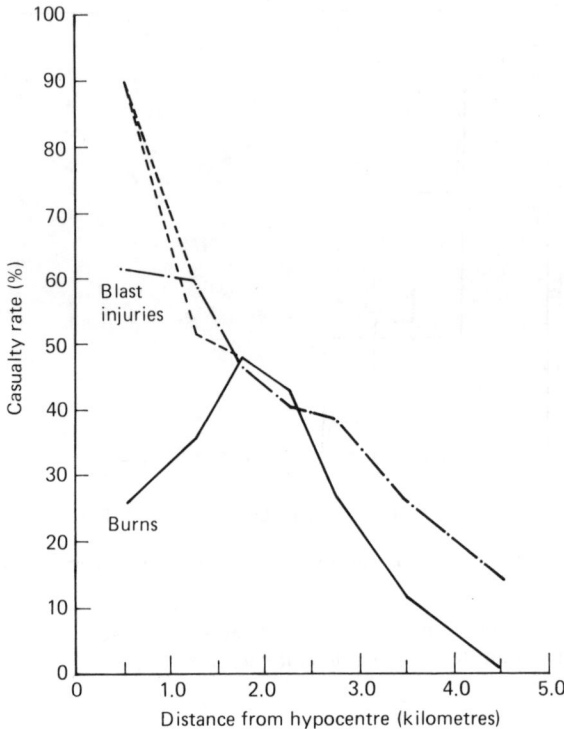

Figure 5.3 Incidence of blast injuries and burns by distance (probable incidence in the innermost zones, if one assumes that those who died were injured by blast and radiant heat)

Sources: Glasstone and Dolan, *The Effects of Nuclear Weapons*; The [Japanese] Committee, *Hiroshima and Nagasaki*; and A. W. Oughterson and S. Warren, *Medical Effects of the Atomic Bomb in Japan* (New York, 1956).

On these bases, we have obtained the following functions to express the probabilities of death as functions of peak overpressure and 'effective' thermal exposure.[15]

$$P_{D_T} = 1 - e^{-\ln 2 \left(\frac{T_{\text{eff}}}{22.14}\right)^{1.83}} \approx 1 - e^{-.69 \left(\frac{T_{\text{eff}}}{22.14}\right)^{1.83}}$$

$$P_{D_B} = e^{-\ln 2 \left(\frac{6.51}{p}\right)^{2.27}} \approx e^{-.69 \left(\frac{6.51}{p}\right)^{2.27}}$$

(T_{eff} in *cal/cm²*; *p* in *psi*).

Figures 5.4, 5.5 and 5.6 show the probability of death due to thermal and blast effects as a function of distance for yields of 150 KT (ground and air bursts) and 1500 KT (ground burst). As appears evident from the figures (and as appears from the physical models of the phenomena described above), thermal effects become more and more dominant as the yield of the explosion becomes bigger.

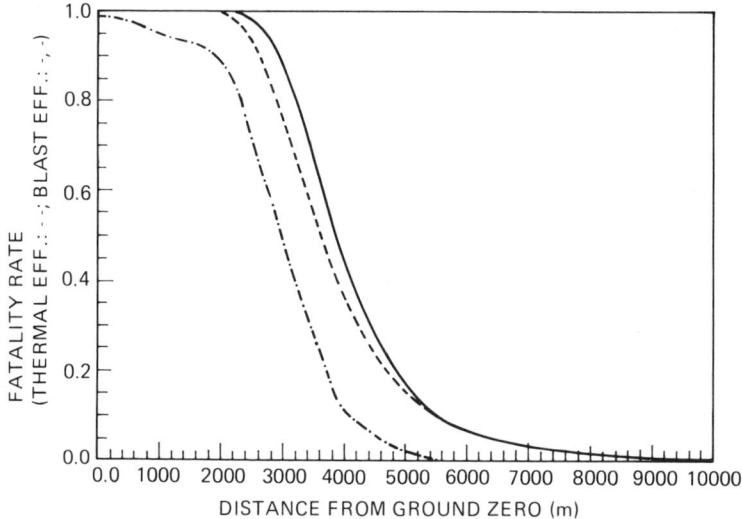

Figure 5.4 Probability of death – due to thermal and mechanical effects – as a function of the distance from ground zero, for a yield of 150 KT (air burst), according to the model. Height of burst is assumed to be 1180 metres.

Starting from analogous considerations, we have defined the probability of death or injury (P_{DoI}) as a function of the 'effective' radiant exposure:

$$P_{DoI} = 1 - e^{-.69 \left(\frac{T_{\mathit{eff}}}{6.31} \right)^{1.60}}$$

This relation is acceptable for yields greater or equal to 150 KT, in which thermal effects reach areas much larger than the areas damaged by blast effects. For smaller yields it is necessary to introduce the effects of the blast wave and eventually the effects of the initial nuclear radiation.

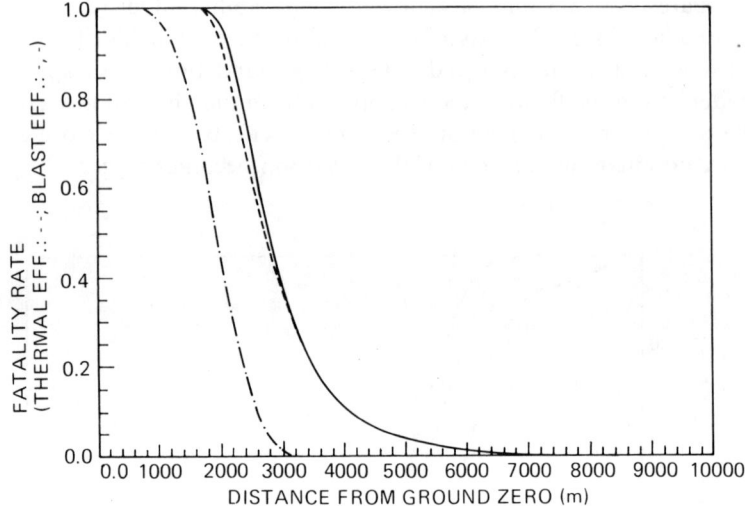

Figure 5.5 Probability of death – due to thermal and mechanical effects – as a function of the distance from ground zero, for a yield of 150 KT (ground burst), according to the model

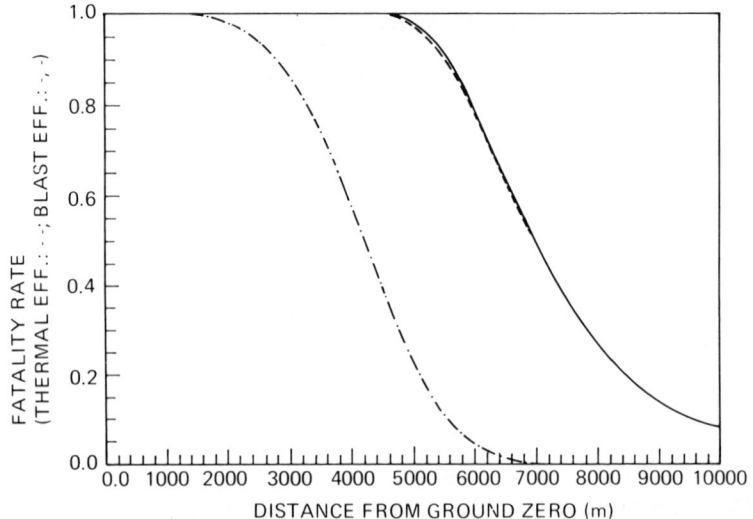

Figure 5.6 Probability of death – due to thermal and mechanical effects – as a function of the distance from ground zero, for a yield of 1500 KT (ground burst), according to the model

Biological Effects of Radiation

The correlation between the probability of death and the absorbed dose of radiation is one of the most confused questions concerning the effects of nuclear weapons. For many years an LD_{50} of 4.5 Gy (= 450 rads) had been assumed as correct, even though no evidence to support this value had ever been published. With regard to this problem, it is very interesting that C. C. Lushbaugh wrote as early as 1974:[16]

> There is a worldwide willingness to accept the estimate that the exposure that will kill the unattended normal man with 50% certainty within 60 days of exposure ($LD_{50/60}$) is 450 R[17] ... and that the mechanism of death is damage to his hematopoietic system and defense mechanisms against infection.... The degree of acceptance of this 450-R value is surprisingly high in view of its history and its lack of valid support from human reported data.

Lushbaugh, tracing this estimate to the end of the 1940s, remarked:

> The truth about how the 450-R estimate was made still lies buried in the personal notes of some of the 10 members of a distinguished committee of U.S. radiotherapists, radiation physicists, and pathologists who polled the U.S. community of practicing radiotherapists to determine what size of single total-body (photon) exposure was considered 'safe' and 'unsafe' ... there have been several attempts to check the 450-R estimate from human case histories after both accidental and intentional radiation exposures. These have been tabulated ... [see Table 5.4] to show how all studies have produced values lower than the original estimate ...

Most of the studies carried out in the 1970s produced results that put the LD_{50} in the proximity of 3.5 Gy, with a confidence of ±1 Gy. More recent studies carried out by Joseph Rotblat have further lowered this value, as a result of new, thorough analyses of data about irradiated people in Hiroshima.[18] In our model we have assumed a base value of 3.5 Gy as LD_{50}, while a value of 1 Gy is assumed as PD_{50}, which is the dose that gives a 50 per cent probability of having no short-term effects of radiation. The functions we have assumed are:

Simulation: 'Limited' Nuclear War in Europe

Table 5.4 Some clinical and statistical estimates of human total-body radiation tolerance

	Exposure to $LD_{50/60}$ dose
Normal men	
Warren and Bowers (1950)	450 R
Cronkite and Bond (1960)	350 rads
Langham (1967)	430 R (285 rads)
Jablon et al. (1969)	405 rem[a]
Patients	
Mathé et al. (1964)	400 R
Langham (1967)	380 R (250 rads)
Lushbaugh et al. (1966)	370 R (245 rads)
Normal men + blast and burn trauma	
Lushbaugh and Auxier (1969)	260 rem[b]

[a] Using RBE of fission neutron component = 4.
[b] Using RBE of fission neutron component = 2.

Source: C. A. Tobias and P. Todd (eds), *Space Radiation and Related Topics* (New York, 1974).

$$P_{D_R} = 1 - e^{-.69 \left(\frac{D_o}{3.5}\right)^{3.}}$$

$$P_{P_R} = 1 - e^{-.69 \left(\frac{D_o}{1.}\right)^{3.5}}$$

(see Figure 5.7).

The absorbed dose D_o must be expressed in Sievert (= 100 rem). In the case of γ or X rays, it is equivalent to express the dose in Gray (= 100 rads).

Taking into account the new studies mentioned above and as a sensitivity test of the model, we have repeated the simulation for fixed cases, keeping all the conditions identical, but changing the value of LD_{50} from 3.5 to 2.5 Gy and of PD_{50} from 1 to 0.75 Gy, using the following functions:

$$P_{D_R} = 1 - e^{-.69 \left(\frac{D_o}{2.5}\right)^{3.}}$$

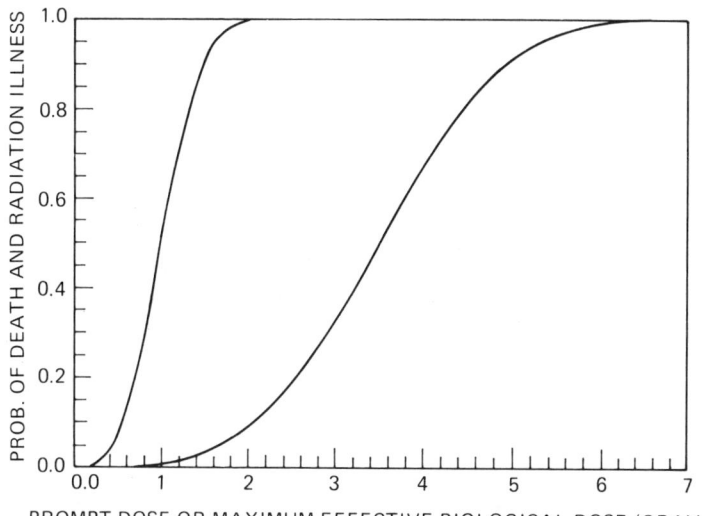

Figure 5.7 Probability of death and radiation illness as a function of the dose absorbed promptly, or the maximum effective biological dose, assuming $LD_{50} = 3.5\ Gy$ and $PD_{50} = 1\ Gy$

$$P_{P_R} = 1 - e^{-.69 \left(\frac{D_o}{.75}\right)^{3.5}}$$

(see Figure 5.8).

When ionising radiations are not absorbed instantaneously, it is supposed that a gradual and partial recovery is possible. That is why the concept of maximum effective biological dose is introduced: it can be defined as the equivalent of the dose that, if absorbed within a few minutes, would produce the same effects – as far as the short-term effects are concerned.[19]

Combined Effects

As already mentioned, to estimate the combined consequences due to prompt effects and fall-out, or due to multiple explosions, we have

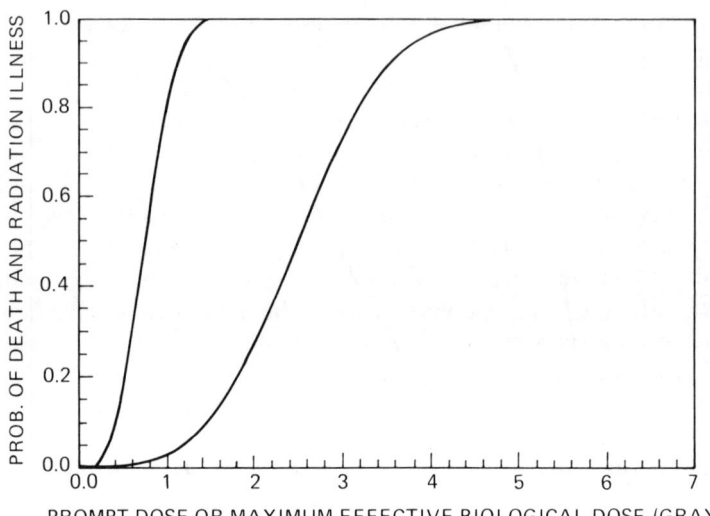

Figure 5.8 Probability of death and radiation illness as a function of the dose absorbed promptly, or the maximum effective biological dose, assuming $LD_{50} = 2.5\,Gy$ and $PD_{50} = 0.75\,Gy$

assumed as lethal the conditions that would either cause injuries due both to prompt effects and radiation illness, or multiple injuries produced by different explosions. The main risk of this approach is again the underestimate of the synergistic phenomenon.

DISTRIBUTION OF POPULATION, PROTECTION FACTORS AND METEOROLOGICAL CONDITIONS

Data about population density come from different sources; data about EEC countries are very detailed, while data about the other countries are not as good, but sufficiently accurate for the purpose of this simulation.

The behaviour of people after the beginning of the attack makes a big difference to the risk of radiation exposure. In this connection it must be pointed out that the first hours after fall-out deposition are the most dangerous, since radioactivity decreases very rapidly with time (as $t^{-1.2}$; t, in hours, is the time from the explosion). Therefore, computation of an individual's average protection factor must take into account the different weight of the different periods of time, considering the fact that it is very unlikely that people would shut themselves into basements or shelters (if available) right after the beginning of the conflict. In fact experiences from disasters of various kinds – including accidents with release of radioactive debris – show that most of the people try to reach their relatives and accumulate stocks of food and water, which means staying outside during the most dangerous periods. This is particularly so in the case where there is lack of communication and information on the dimension of the conflict and the level of involvement of the area. The experience of Chernobyl has shown very well that even in peace-time and with a low level of radioactivity – compared with the effects of a nuclear war – the information about the real situation can be dramatically inadequate.

Considering that in Europe very few countries have sheltering programmes for civilians, we have assumed the distribution of protection factors shown in Table 5.5. This is to assume that two-thirds of the people would do something to protect themselves from radiation. The value 1.4 is the protection factor used instead of 1 to consider the so-called 'ground roughness'. The apparently meaningless value of 0.7 was introduced to allow for an increase of radiation dose from beta-rays, especially in the case of people with fall-out debris on their body or their clothes.

Table 5.5 Distribution of protection factors – Case 1

Protection factors	0.7	1.4	2	3	5	10
Percentage of population	5	30	30	20	10	5

Sensibility tests were made, varying protection factors. Two other distributions were used: one relating to better protection levels (case 2), one relating to worse protection levels (case 3) (see Tables 5.6 and 5.7). In all three cases:

– 90 per cent of non-injured people in areas damaged by blast and thermal effects have been considered as having a PF = 1 and 10 per cent as having a PF = 2.
– all people already injured by blast or thermal effects have been considered as having no protection (PF = 1).

Table 5.6 Distribution of protection factors – Case 2 (better protection)

Protection factors	0.7	1.4	2	3	5	10
Percentage of population	5	20	20	30	15	10

Table 5.7 Distribution of protection factors – Case 3 (worse protection)

Protection factors	0.7	1.4	2	3	5	10
Percentage of population	5	40	30	15	10	0

The meteorological data were provided by the Global Weather Center (United States), in the form of typical monthly winds: speeds and directions were given at different levels over each point of a grid covering the northern hemisphere. The calculation of casualties was made for typical winds in four months, February, May, August and November.

THE SCENARIO: TARGET SELECTION

It must be pointed out that the scenario we shall consider in our simulation must not be considered as predictive. Any attempt to predict in detail how a war could start and develop is obviously impossible and anyway not among the aims of this simulation. Independently of the trigger of the conflict and its evolution, we made the following assumptions:

1. The conflict is characterised by a counterforce nuclear exchange.
2. The European countries directly involved in the nuclear exchange are those belonging to NATO and the Warsaw Pact.
3. The targets include the bulk of the nuclear forces of the two sides. As far as Western Europe is concerned this attitude is consistent with that part of the Soviet strategic thought which emphasises the role of surprise and of pre-emptive attacks, and sees a conventional war following an initial nuclear exchange. As far as Eastern Europe is concerned the bulk of nuclear forces is at the top of the targeting list of both the Single Integrated Operational Plan (SIOP) and NATO's equivalent to SIOP: the Nuclear Operations Plan (NOP).

4. The targeting list includes the main European nuclear installations and facilities, chosen among the following:
   – missile bases;
   – command sites;
   – nuclear storage sites;
   – air bases;
   – naval nuclear bases;
   – communication sites.

With very few exceptions, the following military installations were not attacked:
1. Nuclear and non-nuclear weapons research and production centres. Training centres. Nuclear test sites.
2. Nuclear artillery: range ≈ 30 km. Yield: from 0.1 to 12 KT.
3. Atomic Demolition Munitions. Yield: from 0.01 to 15 KT.
4. Surface-to-air missiles. Nike Hercules: range ≈ 160 km. Yield: from 1 to 20 KT.
5. Nuclear storage sites and command centres that appear to be devoted to controlling the military installations indicated above.
6. Military installations in or near large cities unless they have functions which are strategically very important, in order to minimise the so-called 'collateral' effects on population.
7. Political headquarters, to try to maintain the capability of controlling the escalation and stopping the war.
8. Airports devoted to VIP transport (for political leaders).
9. The hotline system (to permit communication between political leaders).

Many different kinds and yields of warheads would be used and it is hard to predict which weapon would be used on which target. An average value of 150 kiloton was then assumed. All targets were attacked by one ground burst, with the following exceptions:
1. 'Soft' targets like antenna (communication sites) were attacked by one low air burst (150 KT) at the 'optimum' height in order to maximise the area subjected to a peak overpressure larger than 70 kPa (≈ 10 psi): about 1180 metres for a yield of 150 KT.
2. The main command centres, excepting political headquarters, were attacked by a cluster of three 150 KT warheads.
3. The most important airports – chosen among those where strategic nuclear bombers are allocated – were attacked by a cluster of three 150 KT warheads.

4. Intermediate-Range Ballistic Missile Sites: SS-20 and SS-4 on the Eastern side; US cruise, US Pershing, French S-3 were attacked by a cluster of three 150 KT warheads.

According to these criteria, details of the targets attacked were as follows:
94 targets (3 in the Eastern countries and 91 in the Western countries): by one 150-KT air burst;
285 targets (94 in the Eastern countries and 191 in the Western countries): by one 150-KT ground burst;
91 targets (11 in the Eastern countries and 80 in the Western countries): by one cluster of three 150-KT ground bursts.

In total, about 98MT (652×0.150) were used to attack 470 military installations. The distribution of targets is shown in Figure 5.9.

We will now briefly consider the countries one by one, together with the targets chosen for the simulation. Targets are divided into categories (the same listed above) using a criterion in some way arbitrary, since many military installations have more than one function. We have chosen the function that appears to be the most important.

All military installations listed as communication sites are attacked by an air burst. All military installations attacked by a cluster of three 150-KT warheads are highlighted by an asterisk. Military installations inside the Soviet Union are not on the the list of targets because the effects of an attack against the Soviet Union are not considered in this simulation.

THE TARGETS: NATO

All the following countries are members of NATO. Denmark, Luxembourg, Norway, Portugal and Spain are countries that have a policy of not allowing nuclear weapons on their territories. However, most of them have important military installations. All nuclear warheads in NATO European countries are American, except the warheads of the French and British arsenals (between 500 and 700 nuclear warheads in both cases). Great Britain has chosen to integrate its weapons in the NATO structure and, besides its own arsenal, it has more than 1200 US nuclear warheads on its territory. France does not allow US nuclear weapons on its territory and maintains its nuclear independence (see Tables 5.8, 5.9 and 5.10).

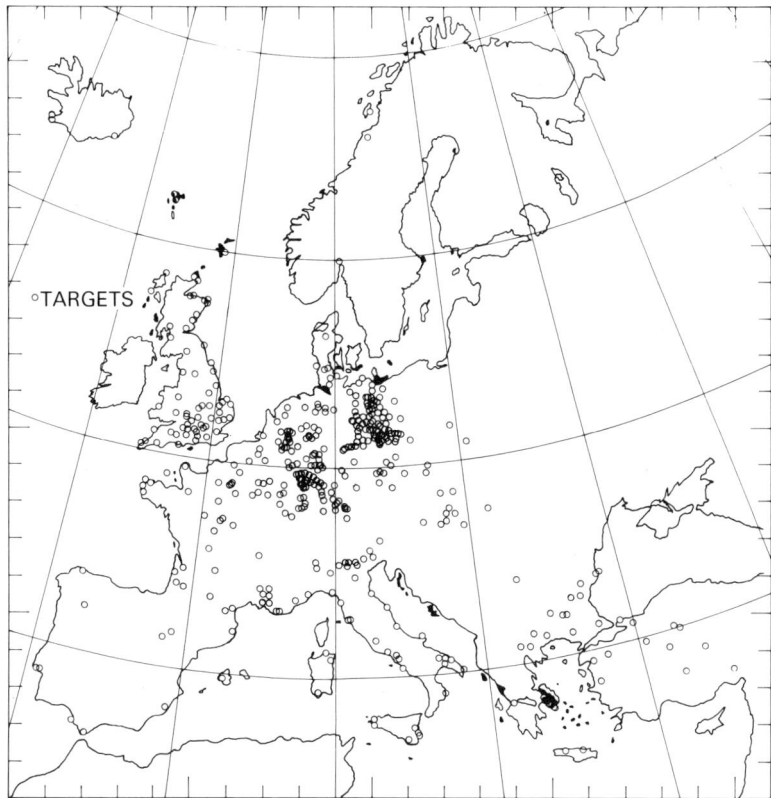

Figure 5.9 Military targets in Europe attacked in the simulation

Belgium (population: 9 890 000)

Missile bases: Florennes.*
Command sites: Casteau-Mons,* Maisieres.
Air bases: Kleine Brogel.
Communication sites: Kester.

Denmark (population: 5 150 000)

Command sites: Karup, Thorshavn – Faeroe.
Communication sites: Ejde – Faeroe Islands.

Table 5.8 US nuclear weapons in Europe

Nuclear weapon (warhead)	Number of warheads			Allied Users
	US use	non-US use	Total	
Bombs (B-61, B-57, B-43, B-28)	1 416	324	1 740	Belgium, Greece, Italy, Netherlands, Turkey, West Germany
Depth Bombs (B-57)	129	63	192	Italy, Netherlands, United Kingdom
Long-range Missiles				
Pershing II (W-85)	54	—	54	
GLCM (W-84)	100	—	100	
Short-range Missiles				
Pershing 1a (W-50)	120	100	220	West Germany
Lance (W-70)	324	368	690	Belgium, Greece, Italy, Netherlands, West Germany, United Kingdom
Honest John (W-33)	—	198	198	Greece, Turkey
Artillery				
8-inch (W-33)	506	432	938	Belgium, Greece, Italy, Netherlands, Turkey, West Germany, United Kingdom
155 mm (W-48)	594	138	732	Belgium, Greece, Italy, Netherlands, Turkey, West Germany, United Kingdom
Nike Hercules (W-31)	296	390	686	Belgium, Greece, Italy, Netherlands, West Germany
ADMs (W-45, W-54)	372	unk	372	Belgium, Netherlands, West Germany, united Kingdom
TOTALS	3 911	2 013	5 922	

Source: W. Arkin and R. W. Fieldhouse, *Nuclear Battlefields: Global Links in the Arms Race* (Cambridge, Mass., 1985).

Table 5.9 French nuclear forces

Delivery Mode	Number	Weapon System Type	Year Deployed	Range (km)	Warheads/ Yield	Warhead Type	Number in Stockpile
Strategic							
Land-based IRBMs	18	S3	1980	3 500	1 × 1 Mt	TN-61	18
Submarines (SLBMs)	80	M-20	1977	3 000	1 × 1 Mt	TN-61	80
	16	M-4	1985	4 000	6 × 150 kt	TN-70	96
Bombers[a]	34	Mirage IVA	1964	1 500	2 × 70 kt	AN-22	75
Aerial refuelers	11	C-135F	1965				
Non-strategic							
Aircraft[a]	45	Jaguar A	1973	720	1 × 6–8/30 kt	[b]	50
	30	Mirage IIIE	1964	800	1 × 6–8/30 kt	[b]	35
SRBMs	42	Pluton	1974	120	1 × 15–25 kt	ANT-51	120
Naval							
Carrier aircraft	36	Super Etendard	1978	650	1 × 6–8/30 kt	[b]	40

[a] The AN-51 warhead is also possibly a secondary bomb for tactical aircraft and the AN-52 is also possibly a secondary bomb for the Mirage IVA
[b] Warheads include ANT-51, ANT-52, and possibly a third type.
Source: Arkin and Fieldhouse: *Nuclear Battlefields.*

Table 5.10 British nuclear forces

Delivery Mode	Weapon System Number	Weapon System Type	Year Deployed	Range (km)	Warheads/ Yield	Number in Stockpile
Strategic						
Submarines (SLBMs)	32	Polaris A3	1968	4 600	3 × 200 kt	96
	32	Polaris A3TK	1982	4 700	2 × 40 kt	64
Non-strategic						
Aircraft	30	Buccaneer S2[a]	1962	1 700	2 × bombs	60
	36	Jaguar A[a]	1973	1 400	1 × bombs	36
	140	Tornado GR1[b]	1982	1 300	2 × bombs	280
Naval						
Carrier aircraft	30	Sea Harrier	1980	450	1 × bombs	30
ASW helicopters	69	Sea King	1976	—	1 × depth bombs	69
	16	Wasp	1963	—	1 × depth bombs	16
	35	Lynx	1976	—	1 × depth bombs	35

[a] Some 6 Buccaneer and 36 Jaguar aircraft withdrawn from bases in West Germany may be assigned nuclear roles in the UK
[b] 220 Tornado attack aircraft (GR1) are on order for the Royal Air Force, and continue to replace Jaguar aircraft.
Note: 34 Nimrod ASW aircraft, 12 Lance launchers, and artillery guns are also certified to use US nuclear weapons.
Source: Arkin and Fieldhouse: *Nuclear Battlefields*.

France (population: 55 170 000)

Missile bases: Apt-St. Christol,* Belfort, Laon-Couvron, Mailly, Oberhoffen, Reilhanette,* Rustrel,* Suippes.
Command sites: Aix-en-Provence, Bordeaux-Gironde, Cinq-Mars-la Pil, Contrexeville, Cotar, Doullens, Drachenbronn, Houilles, Hourtin, Metz, Mt. Angel, Mt. Verdun,* Prunay, Saint-Germain-En-Laye, Strasbourg, Taverny.*
Nuclear storage sites: Cambrai, Chateaudun, Toulouse, Varennes.
Air bases: Avord,* Cazaux,* Colmar, Creil, Evreux, Hyeres, Landivisau, Lanveoc-Poulmic, Limoges, Luxeuil,* Mont-de-Marsan,* Nancy, Orange, Roc-Amadour, Romorantin-Pruni, St. Dizier,* Savigny-En-Septa, Toul.
Naval nuclear bases: Brest, Chateaulin, Cherbourg, Ile Longue, Istres, Roches Douvres, Toulon.
Communication sites: Kerlouan, La Regine, Narbonne, Point d'Arcachon, Romilly-Sur-Seine, Rosnay, S. Assise.

Great Britain (population 56 020 000)

Missile bases: Greenham Common.*
Command sites: Barford St John, Basingstoke, Bentley-Priory, Brampton, Cheltenham, Croughton, Dundee, Goosnargh, Hawthorn,* High Wycombe,* Horsham, Mormond Hill, Northwood,* Oakhanger, Pitreavie Castle, Portreath, Portsmouth, Rudloe Manor, Slough, Upavon, Wilton.
Nuclear storage sites: Chilmark, Coulport, Dean Hill, Machrihanish, Plymouth.
Air bases: Alconbury, Boscombe Down,* Brize Norton, Coltishall, Cottesmore,* Culdrose, Fairford,* Honington,* Kinloss, Marham,* Mildenhall, St Mawgan,* Sculthorpe, Upper Heyford,* Waddington, Wittering, Wyton, Yeovilton.
Naval nuclear bases: Copenacre, Faslane, Gibraltar, Holy Loch, Plymouth–Devonport, Portland, Prestwick, Rosyth, Taunton.
Communication sites: Aberporth, Anthorn, Benbecula, Bentwaters, Boulmer, Buchan, Butt of Lewis, Chatham, Chenies, Cleethorpes, Criggion, Crimond, Defford, Edzell, Forest Moor, Fylingdales, Greatworth, Hartland, Inskip, Neatishead, Portsdown, Rugby, Saxa Vord, Shetland Islands, Staxton Wold, Thurso, Weathersfield, Wick.

88   Simulation: 'Limited' Nuclear War in Europe

Greece (population: 10 300 000)

Nuclear storage sites: Argyroupolis, Drama, Elefsis, Erithea, Karatea, Koropi, Perivolaki, Yannitsa.
Air bases: Araxos,* Hellenikon, Preveza, Souda Bay.
Communication sites: Iraklion, Kato Souli, Mt. Parnis, Nea Makri.

Iceland (population: 260 000)

Command sites: Keflavik.
Communication sites: Grindavik, Hofn, Sandur.

Italy (population: 57 150 000)

Missile bases: Comiso.*
Command sites: Affi,* Aviano1,* Decimomannu, Gaeta,* Grezzana, Martinafranca, Montecavo, Montevenda, Napoli,* Palombara, S. Vito dei Normanni.
Nuclear storage sites: Aviano2, Ghedi,* Longare.*
Air bases: Cameri, Gioia del Colle, Grazzanise, Grosseto, Istrana, Piacenza (S. Dam),* Rimini,* Sigonella,* Trapani, Villafranca.*
Naval nuclear bases: Augusta, La Maddalena, La Spezia, Taranto, Tavolara.
Communication sites: Andora, Bagnoli, Coltano, Concordia Sag., Crotone, Giugliano in C., Iacotenente, Marsala, Monte Sinauz, Mortara, Otranto, Pescara, Poggio Ballone, Poggio Renatico, Potenza Picena, Siracusa, Verona, Vicenza.*

Netherlands (population: 14 500 000)

Missile bases: Woensdrecht.*
Command sites: Brunssum,* Hoensbroek, Maastricht.
Nuclear storage sites: Havelteberg, 'T Harde.
Air bases: Valkenburg, Volkel.*
Communication sites: Soesterberg, Steenwijk.

Norway (population: 4 150 000)

Command sites: Bodoe, Kolsaas.*
Air bases: Andoeya, Oerland.
Communication sites: Helgeland.

Portugal (population: 10 280 000)

Command sites: Oeiras.*
Air bases: Montino.

Spain (population: 39 500 000)

Command sites: Estaca de Vares.*
Air bases: Zaragoza.*
Naval nuclear bases: Rota.
Communication sites: Estartit, Guardamar del Se, Humosa, Inogues, Soller.

Turkey (population: 49 500 000)

Command sites: Ankara*, Cakmakli,* Izmir.*
Nuclear storage sites: Corlu, Izmit, Ortakoy.
Air bases: Balikesir, Cigli,* Eskisehir, Incirlik,* Konya, Murted.*
Communication sites: Alemdag, Kargaburun, Sahin Tepesi.

West Germany (population: 61 200 000)

Missile bases: Arsbeck, Aschaffenburg, Bodelsberg,* Boettingen,* Crailsheim, Geilenkirchen,* Giessen, Hanau, Heilbronn,* Herzogenaurach, Kleingartach,* Landsberg Am Lec,* Lehmgrube,* Neckarsulm,* Neu ulm,* Oberoth,* Schwaebisch Gmue, Wiesbaden.
Command sites: Birkenfeld,* Darmstadt, Frankfurt,* Heidelberg,* Kalkar,* Kiel-Holtenau, Kindsbach,* Massweiler,* Moenchengladbach, Muenchweiler, Pirmasens,* Ramstein,* Rendsburg, Rheindahlen,* Seckeheim,* Sembach,* Stuttgart,* Worms.
Nuclear storage sites: Bergen, Bueren, Butzbach, Dahn, Deiling-

90 Simulation: 'Limited' Nuclear War in Europe

hofen, Dellbruck, Duelmen, Dunsen, Fischbach, , Flensberg, Flensburg, Grossauheim, Grossengstingen, Guenzburg, Hemau, Herbornseelbach, Kellinghusen, Kriegsfeld, Lahn, Leipheim, Miesau, Montabaur, Muenster-Dieberg, Muenster-Handorf, Nienburg, Paderborn, Pfullendorf, Philippsburg, Schwabstadt, Sennelager, Siegelsbach, Soest Hohnesee, Wackernheim, Weilerbach, Wearl, Wesel.
Air bases: Bitburg,* Bruggen,* Buechel,* Gutersloh, Hahn, Laarbruch,* Lechfeld,* Memmingen,* Norvenich, Rhein Main, Spangdahlem.
Communication sites: Adelheide, Altenbusek, Bann, Barme, Barnstorf, Dobraburg, Hamminkeln, Hinsbeck, Itzehoe, Jever Hohenkirch, Landstuhl, Linderhof, Pruem, Sylt, Treebeck, Zweibruchen.

THE TARGETS: THE WARSAW PACT

Bulgaria (population: 8 970 000)

Missile bases: Harmanli, Haskovo, Karnobat, Kavarna, Markovo, Plovdiv, Shabla, Vidin.
Command sites: Sliven.

Czechoslovakia (population 15 600 000)

Missile bases: Bruntal, Ceske Budejovice, Havlickuv Brod, Pilsen, Pribram, Slany, Susice, Taboa, Topolcany, Vysoke Myto, Zvolen.
Command sites: Milovice,* Mlada-Boleslav, Olomouc.

East Germany (population: 16 800 000)

Missile bases: Bernau, Bernsdorf,* Bruck, Dallgow-Doberitz, Dessau/Rosslau, Dresden, Dresden/Klotzsch, Eberswalde, Eggesin, Erfurt, Furstenburg, Grimma, Halle, Hillersleben, Jena, Kranpnitz, Leipzig, Magdeburg, Naumburg, Neubrandenburg, Neustrelitz, Ohrdruf, Perleber/Prigni, Riesa, Schwerin, Stendal, Vogelsang, Weimar, Wittemberg.
Command sites: Cottbus, Eggersdorf, Frankfurt Oder, Zossen.
Nuclear storage sites: Parchim.
Air bases: Alt-Lonnewitz, Altenberg, Annahutte, Bautzen, Bergen,

Brand-Briesen, Brandenburg-Brie, Drewitz, Finsterwalde,* Gorlitz, Grossenhain,* Janschwalde-Ost, Jocksdorf, Juterbog, Kamenz, Kothen, Marxwalde, Merseburg, Mirov-Rechlin,* Neuruppin,* Oranienburg, Prenzlau, Preschen, Putznitz, Rothenburg, Schoenwalde, Templin,* Tutow, Welzow, Werder, Werneuchen, Wittstock, Zerbst.
Naval nuclear bases: Peenemunde, Rostock.
Communication sites: Furstenwalde.

Hungary (population: 10 800 000)

Missile bases: Esztergom, Kecskemet, Szekesfehervar, Szombathely, Tatabanya, Veszprem.
Command sites: Matyasfold.*
Air bases: Debrecen.*

Poland (population: 37 500 000)

Missile bases: Borne, Swiebodzin.
Command sites: Legnica.
Air bases: Szprotawa,* Zagan.*
Communication sites: Kielce, Lodz.

RESULTS

As already mentioned, in our calculations we have not considered the effects of explosions on Soviet military targets. The number of fatalities in Western and Eastern Europe due to the blast and thermal effects was found to be 7.4 million. The total casualties from these effects (death plus injuries) amounted to 15.6 million. Tables 5.11 and 5.12 give the total numbers, including the effects of fall-out for four different wind conditions (typical monthly winds of February, May, August and November) and two values of LD_{50}, 3.5 Gy in Table 5.ll and 2.5 Gy in Table 5.12. The corresponding fall-out patterns are shown in Figures 5.10 to 5.13.

It should be pointed out that high as the casualty toll is, the numbers in tables may underestimate the actual numbers, since only short-term and predictable effects have been taken into account. Moreover, the days after the attack would probably be characterised

Table 5.11 Number of fatalities and casualties (fatalities + non fatal injuries) from thermal and blast effects, and from fall-out (assuming $LD_{50} = 3.5\ Gy$), millions

	February	May	August	November
Case 1				
Fatalities	67.3	70.6	67.7	64.0
Casualties	93.7	96.3	92.5	91.0
Case 2 (better protection)				
Fatalities	62.2	65.5	62.6	58.3
Casualties	88.6	91.2	87.5	85.2
Case 3 (worse protection)				
Fatalities	71.0	74.2	71.3	68.1
Casualties	97.1	99.7	95.7	94.9

Table 5.12 Number of fatalities and casualties (fatalities + non fatal injuries) from thermal and blast effects, and from fall-out (assuming $LD_{50} = 2.5\ Gy$), millions

	February	May	August	November
Case 1				
Fatalities	78.7	82.0	79.0	77.1
Casualties	104.8	108.1	103.0	103.2
Case 2 (better protection)				
Fatalities	72.9	76.0	73.3	70.2
Casualties	99.1	102.3	97.5	96.5
Case 3 (worse protection)				
Fatalities	82.9	86.0	83.1	82.0
Casualties	108.6	112.0	106.6	107.7

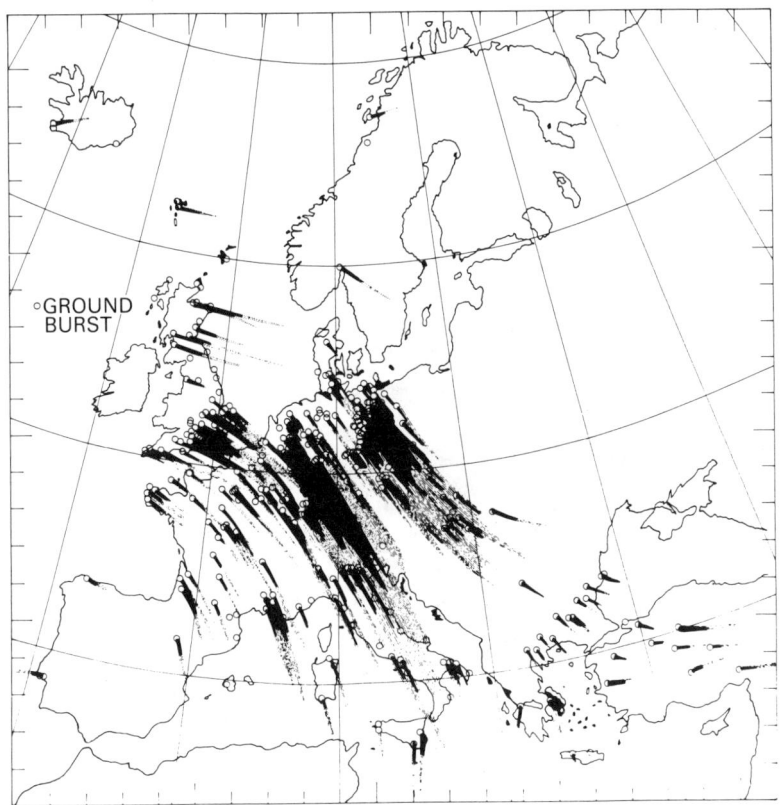

Black = more than 3.5 *Gy*
Grey = between 0.5 and 3.5 *Gy*

Figure 5.10 Fall-out pattern from a *limited* nuclear war in Europe, assuming typical February winds (fall-out from explosions inside the Soviet Union is not included); contours of maximum effective biological dose

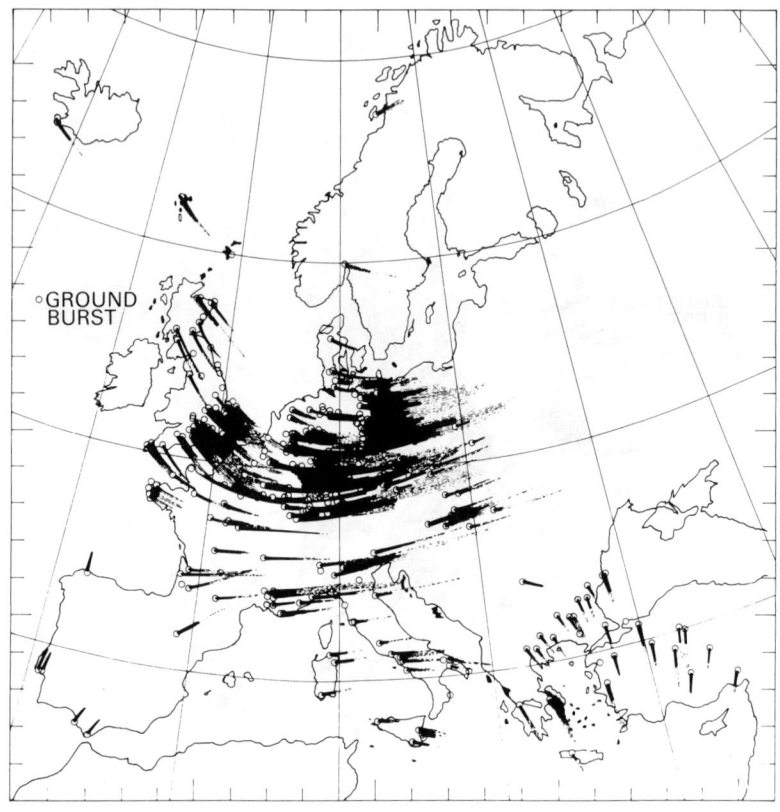

Black = more than 3.5 Gy
Grey = between 0.5 and 3.5 Gy

Figure 5.11 Fall-out pattern from a *limited* nuclear war in Europe, assuming typical May winds (fall-out from explosions inside the Soviet Union is not included); contours of maximum effective biological dose

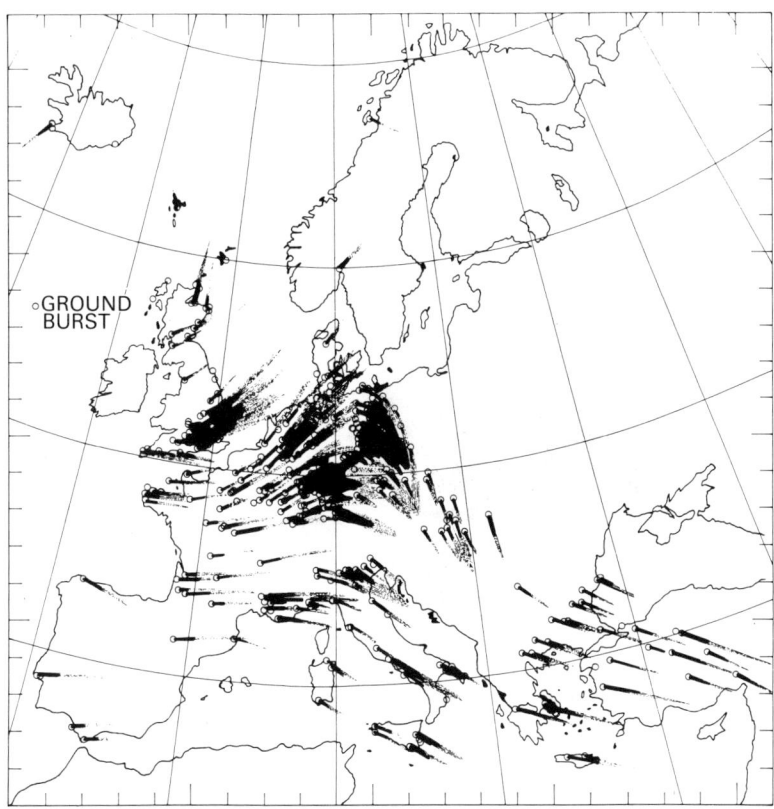

Black = more than 3.5 Gy
Grey = between 0.5 and 3.5 Gy

Figure 5.12 Fall-out pattern from a *limited* nuclear war in Europe, assuming typical August winds (fall-out from explosions inside the Soviet Union is not included); contours of maximum effective biological dose

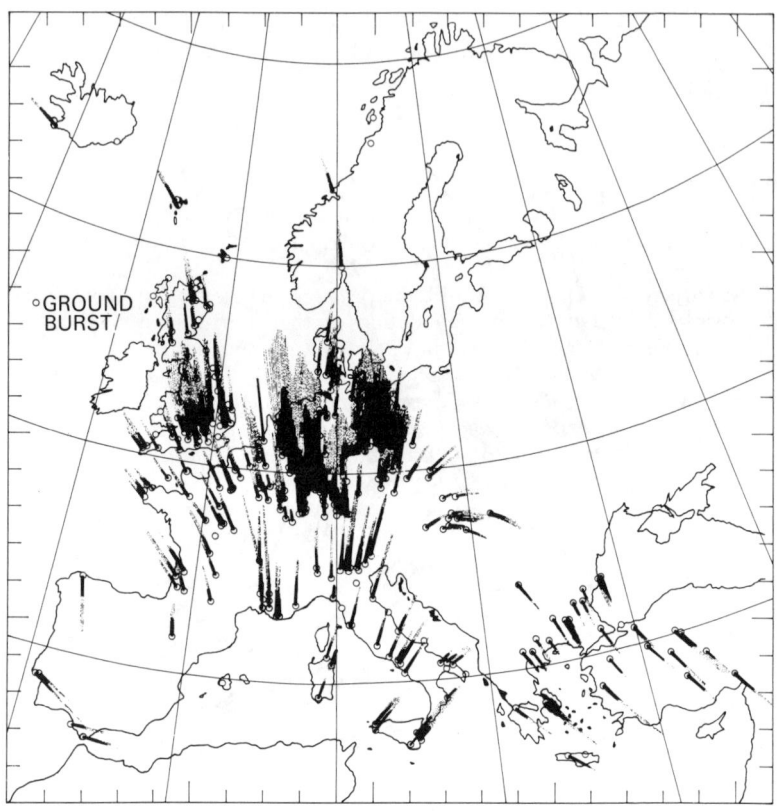

Black = more than 3.5 Gy
Grey = between 0.5 and 3.5 Gy

Figure 5.13 Fall-out pattern from a *limited* nuclear war in Europe, assuming typical November winds (fall-out from explosions inside the Soviet Union is not included); contours of maximum effective biological dose

by the presence of millions of injured people, most of whom would probably be without any hope. In fact the various effects of explosions (especially fall-out) have lethal consequences in a short time only for people very close to the explosions. Together with a total lack of communications, these would be the conditions within which the war should be kept *limited* and *controlled*.

In summary, the situation of a very limited nuclear exchange in Europe – against military targets only and using less than one per cent of the existing nuclear arsenal – has shown that it could result in the death or injury of more than 100 million people; a catastrophe of unimaginable dimensions.[20]

Notes

1. W.W. Arkin and R. W. Fieldhouse, *Nuclear Battlefields: Global Links in the Arms Race* (Cambridge, Mass., 1985).
2. A. Ottolenghi, 'Un'attacco all'Italia', *Sapere* (Bari), August-September 1986; and A. Ottolenghi, 'Simulation of the Short-term Effects of a Counterforce Attack in Italy', in P. Cotta-Ramusino and F. Lenci (eds) *Nuclear Weapons and Europe* (Scientia, Milan, 1986) pp. 435–54.
3. W. Daugherty, B. Levi and F. von Hippel, *Casualties Due to the Blast, Heat and Radioactive Fallout from Various Hypothetical Attacks on the U.S.* (Princeton, 1986); A. Ottolenghi, *Simulazione degli effetti di un attacco nucleare di tipo counterforce in Italia* (Milan, 1984); S. Openshaw, P. Steadman, and O. Greene, *Doomsday: Britain after Nuclear Attack* (Oxford, 1983); and A. M. Din and J. Diezi, *Nuclear War Effects in Switzerland* (Basle, Switzerland, 1984).
4. The lethal area is defined as the circular area within which the number of survivors is equal to the number of people killed outside that area. Mathematically the lethal area can be defined as follows:

   $$\text{lethal area} = 2\pi \int_0^\infty p(r) r \, dr$$

   where $p(r)$ is the probability of death at distance r from ground zero.
5. S. Glasstone and P. J. Dolan, *The Effects of Nuclear Weapons* (Washington, DC, 1977).
6. G. E. Pugh and R. J. Galiano, *An Analytic Model for Close-in Operational-type Studies*, Weapon System Evaluation Group, WSEG RM No 10 (Washington, DC, 1959).
7. H. G. Norment, *DELFIC: Department of Defense Fallout Prediction System: Volume I: Fundamentals*, Atmospheric Science Associates (Defense Nuclear Agency (DNA) 5159F-1, Washington, DC, 1979); and H. G. Norment, *DELFIC: Department of Defense Fallout Prediction System: Volume II: User's Manual*, Atmospheric Science Associates (DNA 5159F-2, Washington, DC, 1979).
8. H. G. Norment, *SIMFIC: A Simple, Efficient Fallout Prediction Model: Atmospheric Science Associates* (DNA 5193F-1, Washington, DC, 1979); and H. G. Norment, *DNAF-1 An Analytic Fallout Prediction Model and Code: Atmospheric Science Associates* (DNA 001-80-C-0197, Washington, DC, 1981).
9. Glasstone and Dolan, *The Effects of Nuclear Weapons*.
10. The [Japanese] Committee for the Compilation of Materials on Damage Caused by the Atomic Bombs in Hiroshima and Nagasaki, *Hiroshima and Nagasaki: The Physical, Medical and Social Effects of the Atomic Bombings* (New York, 1981).

11. Lethal area in Hiroshima:
    - calculated from data in Table 5.2

    $$\text{Hiroshima lethal area} = 2\pi \int_0^\infty f_1(r) r \, dr = 8.61 \text{ km}^2$$

    - calculated from data in Table 5.3

    $$\text{Hiroshima lethal area} = 2\pi \int_0^\infty f_2(r) r \, dr = 7.92 \text{ km}^2$$

    ($f_1(r)$ and $f_2(r)$ are the fatality rates at distance r from ground zero, according to the two sources.)
12. As is known, this formula is typical of independent events, while it is evident that the two events 'no injuries due to thermal effects' and 'no injuries due to blast effects' are not independent. If only the consequences of the two effects are known and the relation given above is used, two opposite errors can be made. First, the number of fatalities can be overestimated, due to the fact that in the area damaged by the explosion a person surviving from the first effect is likely to be sheltered also from the second effect. This statement is only partially true, since, for example, a good shelter against blast effects may be ineffective against firestorms. Secondly, the number of fatalities can be underestimated, due to the fact that in the area damaged by the explosion a person surviving from the first effect may have been injured by it. In fact, as a consequence of synergism, even non-severe injuries caused by the second effect – certainly not deadly by themselves – may cause death. On the contrary, if the confined effects of an explosion are known, and the relation given above is in some way used to deduce the consequences of the single phenomenon, the two errors are then made in the opposite way, underestimating the effects where they were overestimated, and vice versa. Independently of the starting-point, we assume that the two possible errors described above are, on the whole, of the same order and that they can be considered as compensating each other. We have then treated the two effects as if they were independent.
13. Office of Technology Assessment, *The Effects of Nuclear War* (Washington, DC, 1979).
14. H. L. Brode, *Fire Damage and Strategic Targeting* (Los Angeles, 1983).
15. In the functions of the kind $e^{-\lg 2 \left(\frac{x}{\tilde{x}}\right)^d}$ and $1 - e^{-\lg 2 \left(\frac{\tilde{x}}{x}\right)^d}$, $\tilde{x}$ is the value corresponding to 50 per cent fatalities, while α influences the slope of the curve.
16. C. C. Lushbaugh, 'Human Radiation and Tolerance', in C. A. Tobias and P. Todd (eds), *Space Radiation and Related Topics* (New York, 1974).
17. An exposure of 1 R(Roentgen) is approximately equivalent to an absorbed dose of 1 rad ($= 0.01$ Gy) in soft tissue.
18. J. Rotblat, 'Acute Radiation Mortality in a Nuclear War', in Institute of Medicine, *The Medical Implications of Nuclear War* (Washington, DC, 1986).
19. To estimate short-term survivability we have assumed the broadly-used concept of maximum effective biological dose. According to this ap-

proach, it is assumed that 90 per cent of total irradiation injuries are reparable with a repair rate of 0.1 per cent per hour of the residual reparable injury, while the remaining 10 per cent is irreparable. Since fallout radioactivity decreases as $t^{-1.2}$, there will be a certain time in which the effective accumulated dose will reach a maximum. The short-term effects are then assumed to be the same as the effects of a promptly-absorbed dose equal to the above maximum. We then have:

$$MEBD = max(EBD(T)) =$$

$$= max \left(\left(.1 \int_{t_a}^{T} t^{-1.2} dt + .9 \int_{t_a}^{T} t^{-1.2} e^{-.001(T-t)} dt \right) D_{h+1} \right)$$

Where:
- EBD(T) is the effective biological dose or relative biological dose at time T;
- MEBD is the maximum effective biological dose;
- D_{h+1} is the 'normalised' $h+1$ hour exposure rate, that assumes that all fallout is deposited at one hour from the explosion, regardless of whether this is actually the case or not;
- t_a is the fallout arrival time, in hours;
- T is time from the explosion, in hours.

20. The author wishes to express his gratitude to the Milan section of the Unione Scienziati per il Disarmo, to which the author belongs, and especially to Paolo Cotta-Ramusino, Dino Dimitri Batani, Massimo Ferrario and Patrizio Lubrini for the contributions made in the preparation of this chapter. He is also very grateful to Frank von Hippel and Barbara Levi for the information and data they gave and for the stimulating discussions. His best thanks also go to Joseph Rotblat for the comments and suggestions during the preparation of this work.

6 Conventional War in the Postwar International System
Catherine M. Kelleher

INTRODUCTION

Perhaps the most neglected area of postwar international security studies is the phenomenon of conventional war. In part, this reflects the continuing love–hate fascination of scholars, and officials and publics with nuclear weapons, the new revolutionary development of *their* time.[1] The scope and speed of the destruction possible in even a limited nuclear exchange has absorbed the analytic attention of military planners and those committed to war avoidance alike. For most in the advanced industrial world, conventional war is what happens before a nuclear escalation, or what happens somewhere else. Compared to the unthinkable horrors of nuclear warfare, even the bloodiest conventional conflicts pale – as only fifty million dead in the Second World War in contrast with the potential annihilation of nations and civilisations.

The result has been a curious intellectual, if not simple definitional, poverty which lumps together in a single category all that was known as *war* before 1945 and such post-1945 discoveries as insurgencies and counter-insurgencies, struggles for national liberation, and state-sponsored terrorism. There is, of course, an abundance of published lists cataloguing postwar conventional conflicts, especially those involving the use of violence in inter-state disputes ranging from one to several thousand days in duration.[2] However, there is remarkably little scholarly consensus on how to define conventional conflicts, beyond the simple indicator that nuclear weapons were not used; on how to specify data on frequency, types of participants, casualties, or even duration of conflict. And there is still less agreement on what lessons should be drawn for the purposes of promoting conflict avoidance, reinforcing regional stability, or even developing processes for war termination should conflict occur.

Recent events, however, suggest the urgent need for careful, systematic analysis of the nature of and the constraints on postwar conventional conflict. The prolonged blood-letting between Iran and Iraq has now led to escalation and the intervention of superpowers and third parties. The shattering of Lebanon as a viable state reveals the logical end of internecine inter-confessional conflict at the conventional level. Even such 'normal' conflicts as the continuing civil wars in Sri Lanka and the Philippines seem to have reached new levels of risk and destruction, and seem to be a threat to regional, if not global, security balances.

Most important of all, however, are questions now being raised about the role of nuclear weapons in the limitation of conventional conflict. It would seem that the threat of nuclear escalation has led to 'zones' and 'eras' of peace, or at least prevented direct military confrontation among the superpowers, the medium nuclear powers, and probably their clients.[3] In other words, nuclear deterrence has purportedly ameliorated the use of conventional forces across state boundaries, at least in the developed or industrial world. What is unclear, however, is whether nuclear weapons are either a necessary or a sufficient condition for these deterrent outcomes. The distinction has important implications for several contemporary policy debates. First, one needs to consider the long-run effect of reducing or eliminating classes or nuclear weapons – as proposed at Reykjavik and in the zero–zero Intermediate Nuclear Forces regime for Europe. Secondly, attention is focusing on the possibility of a threshold of conventional constraint specific to Europe with its large conventional force deployments. Thirdly, one must reflect on the nature of a 'substitutable' system of conventional deterrence for the present nuclear-based system, and what this would mean for both the frequency of conflict and the stability of present regional sub-systems.

These debates are clearly of vital importance in terms of future war and peace. If an important effect of nuclear deterrence has been to disqualify the nuclear weapons states and their closest allies from direct conflict among themselves, it does not seem to have had positive spill-over effects upon the non-nuclear states. It is probably too much to say that nuclear weapons have made the world safe for conventional war. But their existence has surely paralleled significant shifts in both battlefields and participants, perhaps even changes in the frequency and destructiveness of the numerous conventional conflicts since 1945.

At best, in this chapter one can only attempt to describe the trends in conventional conflict and suggest preliminary answers to these critical questions. But certain basic findings and conclusions emerge with considerable force. Conventional war since 1945 has had its own categories of unspeakable horror and high risks, of high costs in life and material, perhaps now cumulating to the levels of death and destruction equivalent to those suffered in the Second World War. The pace and deadliness of conventional wars have quickened many times over, in step with the pace of technology and the diffusion of political authority throughout what is now a truly global state system. Not surprisingly, even in the presence of the nuclear challenge, the processes of war-termination and war-avoidance seem no more calculable or comprehensible than in the violent period between 1914 and 1945. Moreover the role of the developed or industrial nations in conventional conflicts has been a complicated one, difficult to describe both in direction and in impact, especially given their aversion to direct confrontation with each other. No easy assumptions are therefore warranted or advisable as policy guides to what lies ahead in a marginally denuclearised world or in the total global battlefield.

PATTERNS OF CONVENTIONAL CONFLICT SINCE 1945

The present analysis relies heavily on five of what appear to be the most cited and the most credible catalogues of conventional conflict that are derived from empirical research (see Table 6.1). None of the lists can be viewed as exhaustive, and their definitions of conflict vary considerably. Nor does the amount of overlap in the cases included between any two lists inspire great confidence for rigorous secondary analysis.[4] Yet the data are sufficient to allow broad generalisations, permit the framing of questions about future patterns, and pose topics for further detailed research.

Frequency, Duration and Destruction

These five studies depict a fairly limited number (although a wide range) of inter-state conflicts between 1945 and 1980, namely 70 to 326. Clearly, definitions matter most here. The Kende list is perhaps the most complete in listing discrete inter-state encounters. The Gochman–Maoz list, which builds on the data-building efforts of J. David Singer, Melvin Small, and Richard Stoll, includes various

Table 6.1 Comparison of conventional conflict catalogues

		Period Covered	Total Cases	Casualties (millions)
1	Dunnigan & Bay	1945–85	70	51
2	Jongman	1945–85	223	
3	Kende	1945–82	148	26
4	Gochman/Maoz	1946–76	326	8
5	Sivard	1945–83	107	16

Sources:
1. James F. Dunnigan, and Austin Bay, *A Quick and Dirty Guide to War* (New York, 1985).
2. Berto Jongman, 'Quantitative Aspects of Armed Conflicts Since World War II' (Groningen Polemological Institute, mimeo, 1986).
3. Istvan Kende, *Kriege nach 1945: eine empirische Untersuchung* (Frankfurt, 1982).
4. Charles S. Gochman and Zeev Maoz, 'Militarized InterState Disputes, 1816–1976', *Journal of Conflict Resolution*, vol. 28, no. 4 (December 1984) 585–615.
5. Ruth L. Sivard, *World Military and Social Expenditures* (Washington, DC, 1983).

uses of violence and armed force (for example, blockade) as well as actual declared wars and formal interventions. All five studies concentrate on conflicts involving a span of participants and employing every level of available and emerging technologies. Just how much destruction of life and property has been caused by conventional wars since 1945 is difficult to estimate. Death and casualty reports are always subject to discrepancies in reporting, by both the victor and the vanquished, for reasons of either domestic or international political calculation. The estimates from the lists used for this analysis, however, are more conservative than many of the conflict lists examined. Several of these found that more than 1000 conflicts had occurred in the postwar period, and had assessments of increased damage associated with conventional war as a result reaching as high as perhaps 70 million dead.

The data available about conventional conflict confirm what Robert McNamara has repeatedly said: despite persistent illusions about nuclear peace, there has not been a day without war since 1945.[5] In this respect, the postwar period has continued the pattern first described by Raymond Aron as 'the century of total war.'[6] The data demonstrate a range of estimates which vary enormously, with the highest being perhaps the 50 million war-related deaths (including deaths from hunger or enforced flight) reported by James F. Dunnigan and Austin Bay.[7] Most estimates cluster with those of Ruth Sivard around the level of 20 million deaths, a level that approaches the total battlefield deaths (20 + out of 50 + million) in the Second World War.

Individual wars seem to have been somewhat less destructive than wars observed prior to 1945. Berto Jongman concludes, for example, that approximately one-half of his composite set of 223 wars involved less than 10 000 direct war deaths. Only twelve involved more than one million direct deaths – for example, the Chinese Civil War after 1945. Part of the explanation lies in what seems to be a greater number of conflicts of considerable severity but relatively limited duration and with fewer participants than prior to 1945. Charles S. Gochman and Zeev Maoz found that in their cases involving the use of violence short of war, most lasted less than a year. Duration became prolonged when major powers were involved or when the number of parties to the conflict was greater than two. Counting all Gochman–Maoz incidents that involved threats of force and displays of force with those in which force was used gave a median length of a dispute of 70 days with little variation over historical periods from 1816 to 1976.[8]

Geographical Distribution

The most dramatic shift in the pattern of post-1945 conflicts is the change in the geographic location of both battlegrounds and principal participants (see Tables 6.2 and 6.3). Conventional wars, especially those involving the greatest number of deaths and longest duration, have been wars in the third world. There has been only limited direct participation by the nations of the North in these conflicts. In contrast to the 1914–45 period, there have been few battle sites located in the North generally and in Europe, East or West, especially. Asia and the Middle East have experienced the most conflicts at both the intra-state and inter-state level, encompassing both major and minor regional actors. These conflicts have also spanned the longest and shortest durations recorded. Indeed, several authors assert that these two regions have suffered half (if not more) of all observed conflicts since 1945, and the vast proportion of human and material destruction.

Table 6.2 Regional distribution of postwar conventional conflicts

	1945–54	1955–64	1965–74	1975–86
Central & South America	7	14	5	12
Europe	4	3	5	2
Africa	2	14	13	24
Middle East/North Africa	10	14	10	20
Asia	16	14	16	17
GLOBAL	39	59	49	75

Source: Berto Jongman, 'Quantitative Aspects of Armed Conflicts Since World War II' (Groningen Polemological Institute, mimeo, 1986) pp. 34ff.

Table 6.3 Regional distribution of armed conflict 1945–86

Region	Number of conflicts	Total killed % Low	High	No. killed Low	High
Central/South America	6	3·5	2·5	> 122·0	> 129·0
Europe	1	0·073	0·049	> 2·5	> 2·5
Africa	12	11·2	7·6	> 384·5	> 388·5
Middle East	6	14·3	20·3	> 491	> 1041·0?
Asia	12	71·0	69·6	> 2436·3	> 2565·8
TOTAL	37			3436·3	5126·8

Source: Stockholm International Peace Research Institute, *SIPRI Yearbook 1987: World Armaments and Disarmament* (New York, 1987) pp. 310–17.

The political, ethnic and religious turmoil which have caused Asian and Middle Eastern conflict need little further commentary here. South and East Asia have seen a series of civil wars of enormous destructiveness and continuing severity. A list of only the most dramatic encounters would include: the Chinese Civil War (1945–50), the division of India and Pakistan (1946–56), North and South Korea (1950–3), turmoil in Kampuchea (1975–9), and Bangladesh (1971–2). Elsewhere, only the civil war in Nigeria from 1967 to 1970 or the conflict in the Sudan in the 1960s and the 1970s would seem to approach this level of severity in casualties inflicted and war-related deaths.

Third-world wars also present particular problems in interpretation – as for example, the thirty-plus-year war that the United States labels 'Vietnam.' For example, Aron's 'total war' yardstick would mean, at a minimum, also counting in the total description the struggles between 1940 and 1945 on the Indochinese peninsula against the Japanese, Chinese, and French; the constant fighting throughout the 1960s and 1970s over Laos and Cambodia; the civil war horror of Kampuchea under Pol Pot; and the continuing Chinese–Vietnamese border disputes. Moreover, assessment of the ultimate individual and social impacts remains confused. Little hard evidence exists on total numbers killed or dead due to war-related activities through this protracted Vietnamese war. And the consequences for overall security and development of the South-East Asian region (and perhaps for China and Japan as well) are only gradually unfolding.

War Participants

These regional distributions show a wide span of war participants over time – major states and minor powers, irredentist states and those filled with the fervour of revolutionary expansion. The process of decolonisation itself led to two different waves of war-participation – first, the struggle of armed nationalists against the colonial powers and, then, the struggles over succession among competing nationalist groups or political coalitions. In many cases there were also third wave disputes with neighbouring states over long-simmering ethnic, religious, or territorial issues that had been deliberately submerged during the colonial period.

Almost by any account, a handful of states that are newly-independent, ambitious, and relatively resource-affluent have accounted for a significant share of the conflicts recorded – perhaps as many as one-third. Gochman and Maoz list Israel, India, Pakistan, and Vietnam as the most involved in what they find to be the most frequent type of conflict: the two-party militarised dispute leading to escalation and war.[9] On the basis of the experiences of the late 1970s and 1980s, others might add several Central and South America actors (for example, El Salvador, Argentina, and Nicaragua); Iran and Iraq; and Somalia and Ethiopia.

A special case is involvement in what might be called *on-going* or protracted wars. In 1986, Jongman found there were 40 such continuing conflicts, ten in Africa, seven each in the Far East, Central and South America, and the Middle East, and six in Asia.[10] By contrast, McNamara noted in 1966 that at the beginning of 1958, there were 23 prolonged conflicts and by February 1966, perhaps some 40 continuing sociopolitical insurgencies.[11] These all involved low-level but constant violence to civilians, and fighting between regular and irregular (but still organised) forces.

The continuing Iran–Iraq conflict is an obvious example. For much of its course the pace of fighting has been more like that of the First World War – with, for example, trench warfare, intermittent mass offensives, and limited daily sorties – than most wars since 1945. Recent escalation suggests a more 'modern' tempo with increasing numbers of casualties and civilian involvement on both sides. More 'modern' too would be Sri Lankan, Afghan, or the Indonesian civil wars in their various phases.

Furthermore, when first world and second world participants have been involved in conventional conflicts, the pattern has tended towards both the escalation and the expansion of conflicts. At issue may be only basic postwar political tendencies – for example, American preferences for at least the rhetorical involvement of its allies in our-of-area disputes and the appearance of coalition warfare whether the case is Korea or the escorting of oil tankers in the Gulf. For the Soviet Union there is the objective of buttressing Communist rule, as in Eastern Europe and Afghanistan. But any conflict involving major powers, but especially the United States and the Soviet Union, has tended to be longer in duration and to have involved the greater use of violence over time, even if it has stopped at the 'display of force' level.[12] Disputes among minor powers, even clients of major states, have tended to encompass more frequent uses of direct violence but with a lesser probability of an eventual escalation to formal war.

Western states have also been engaged in some specific types of protracted conflicts. The long-running nationalist conflicts in Northern Ireland and among the Basques in Spain come quickly to mind, even though the levels of death and destruction involved are relatively low when compared to Asian cases. Of almost equal duration is the series of Greek–Turkish wars, over or around Cyprus, involving a relatively small number of deaths directly related to conflict but with particular importance for regional security.

THOUGHTS FOR THE FUTURE

On the basis of all this data, what are the prospects or lessons for the future? Most analysts and political observers believe the frequency of conventional conflicts throughout the state system is rising, and that the level of violence and destruction, particularly against civilians, is probably rising at least proportionally. Many scholars attribute this simply to the change in the composition of the international system. The wave of wars of decolonisation has simply been replaced by a greater number of 'old-fashioned' wars among the more than one hundred 'new' states that have emerged since 1945 – wars fought for territory or resources, for ethnic identity or political advantage.

The question remains: do mechanisms exist to stop, to limit, or to contain this level of warfare? Until the present, the developed world has remained largely outside these conflicts and has relied principally on three less-than-perfect instruments: public scrutiny and pressure through the United Nations; the extension or denial of direct political and military support (largely in the form of arms) to one of the warring states or groups; and the ultimate deterrent – the threat of direct intervention backed *in extremis* by all weapons at national command, including escalation to nuclear use. Not one of these instruments has proved effective or credible to contain the whole range of conflicts, or to minimise the risks of accident, miscalculation, or deliberate escalation.

This is particularly true in such high-risk, potentially high-cost disputes as the present phase of the Iran–Iraq war. At most, the developed nations can prevent or channel the form of external intervention and perhaps modify the pace and expansion of conflict (particularly as it affects the availability and price of oil). But the instruments by which to bring about conflict-termination on terms appropriate to a new regional stability and acceptable to the interests involved are simply not available or too risk-laden in terms of the future.

Those attempting to reduce the costs and the risks inherent in conventional conflicts in the third world face a number of severe constraints. First and foremost is simply the spread of ever more lethal technology to more and more nations. The consecutive postwar revolutions in terms of weapons speed, destructiveness and accuracy are now within the buying power and reach of at least one-half of the more than 160 states in the present international system.[13] Steadily increasing costs may keep quantities low and, except for a relatively small group of new states (perhaps 30), the levels of military effectiveness for protracted warface are highly questionable. But for many of the shorter conflicts or more limited regional rivalries, even small amounts of increasingly sophisticated weaponry may be enough. And for states of any size and level of wealth with preferential relations to a superpower, the constraints may be even less significant.

What can surely be foreseen is an increase in the proportion of national resources devoted by more states to this effort. In part this reflects increasing costs; in part it reflects the declining levels of economic growth and resource factor prices so vital to third-world economies. Indeed, cost levels in peace-time will in all probability continue to rise, as there is greater urgency to maintain sophisticated weaponry at required levels of readiness.

Put most simply, the international system has bumped up against an increasingly apparent inability to stop wars just as the significance of conventional conflicts has become increasingly clear. The list of continuing conflicts drawn from the 1987 *Yearbook* of the Stockholm International Peace Research Institute (SIPRI) underlines the urgency of the challenge (see Table 6.4). It also emphasises the need to develop a more systematic understanding of the various types of international behaviour described now simply as conventional war, and the various approaches that will be needed to achieve war-termination or minimisation of the destructive effects, especially *vis-à-vis* increasingly involved and vulnerable civilian populations.

Perhaps to be thought about, particularly given the new enthusiasm for conventional arms control, is whether there exist ways in which the mechanisms for limitation of conflict (and limitation of weapons in conflict) can be applied against a broader range of conventional conflicts. If one looks at the past thirty years, there seems little reason to hope that restraints on the international arms trade will accomplish what needs to be done. More hope might be gained from establishment of Nuclear-weapon-free Zones, or at least the exclusion of nuclear weapons or other weapons of mass destruction from areas in which regional stability now seems fairly well assured.

Beyond this there are a number of limitations, now being discussed in terms of Europe, that might well be applied. Perhaps the simplest to describe, but the hardest to implement, would be a series of confidence-building measures (CBMs) in which enduring rivals, those involved in continuing conflicts, might be given incentives to develop a set of exchange activities – monitoring; established ranges for acceptable levels of forces; limitations on mobility and readiness;

Table 6.4 Continuous regional armed conflict, 1945–86

Region	Government vs rebel group or nation	Beginning of conflict	Deaths (thousands)
Central–South America			
Colombia	M19, FARC, etc.	1978	8
Equador	Alfaro Vive	1985	2?
El Salvador	FMLN	1977	>60
Guatemala	URNG	1967	20 (1967–74) >21 (1979–86)
Nicaragua	Contras	1981	5–10
Peru	Sendero Luninoso	1980	6–8
Europe			
N. Ireland	IRA	1969	>2·5
Africa			
Angola	UNITA	1955	2 (1985)
Chad	Rebels; Libya	1965	721
Ethiopia	EPLF, TPLF	1962	>45
	Somalia	1964	38
Mozambique	MNR	1978	2 (1980–86) 2–3 (1985)
Namibia	SWAPO	1966	10
South Africa	ANC	1970s	3 (1984–86)
Sudan	SPLA	1983	3
Uganda	Obote, Okello, Amin	1981	>250
W. Sahara–Morocco	Polisario	1975	7–10
Zimbabwe	Dissidents	1980	>1·5
Middle East			
Iran	Kurds	1979	?
	Iraq	1980	350–880
Iraq	Kurds	1980	?
Israel	PLO, Syrian Troops	1948	>10
Lebanon	Christian, Muslim Militia	1975	>125
Syria	Sunni Rebels	1976	>6–26
Asia			
Afghanistan	Mujahideen	1978	>200
Burma	BCP, KNLA, rebels	1948	76–114
China (PRC)	Vietnam	1979	47 (1979) 1 (1980–6) ?
India	Separatists	1947	10 (1983–6)
Indonesia	Fretilin	1975	>0.1
Kampuchea	Khmer Rouge, KPNFL, ANS	1970	2000–3000 (1970–) 24 (1978–86)
Laos	National Liberation Front	1975	10–50

Malaysia	CPM	1945	4·1
Pakistan	Separatists, rebels	1972	>9?
Philippines	NPA, MNLF	1970	50–100
			10–15 (1983–6)
Sri Lanka	Tamils	1983	>3–4·5
Thailand	CPT, Separatists	1965	2·1

Source: Stockholm International Peace Research Institute, *SIPRI Yearbook 1987: World Armaments and Disarmament* (New York, 1987) pp. 310–17.

perhaps even as radical as the exchange of ground observer posts – that would, in fact, make clearer the onset of conflict, and avoid premature or pre-emptive moves based on miscalculation or misinformation. Some may indeed by 'negative' CBMs as well as those involving positive action. A specific example might be a set of penalties that would come into play if observers were not allowed in for the regular or challenge inspection of exercises, or perhaps penalties that could be taken out in terms of reductions in the agreed-upon 'acceptable' levels of forces.

The limitation is only that of the creative imagination, and of course, the ever-present political problem of negotiating the actual implementation. Here, however, the activities of the Contadora Group in terms of mobilising regional opinion about the Nicaraguan conflicts give reason for hope that regional powers may be willing to undertake this function when either the risk of war or the potential cost of war reaches a visible predictable level.

A set of what might be called 'defensive defence' measures have also been suggested for Europe, and there the direct pay-off in terms of conflict outcomes may be less certain. However, there may be applications in terms of third-world conflicts as well. Certainly the limitations on hardware, the deliberate attempt to make offensive systems less offensive, or at least less vulnerable, or susceptible to 'use them or lose them' calculations would seem to be the benefit of all those concerned with the mitigation of conflict.

Limitations on forces themselves, certainly in terms of quantity, would seem less significant or less possible in the areas where conventional manpower is, in fact, the largest resource most states can devote to such conflicts. Limitations on mobility and readiness, in terms of what might be called the software of force employment, would allow positive benefits in terms of the warning-time to the civilian population that might otherwise, through inadvertence, miscalculation or simple lack of information, be in the path of exchanges of violence.

None of these measures themselves represents a particular panacea or indeed a guaranteed result in the lowering of the frequency or the level of violence. The number of recurring conflicts, the number of enduring rivalries is in fact daunting, and one which suggests that these are problems that will constantly be with us, whatever the particular hardware or software solutions that are proposed or accepted.

The time seems more than apposite for rethinking the problem of the definition of conventional war, and for a search for new approaches to limitation and constraint. The prospects for change may still be slight; the pattern of increasingly frequent and destructive conventional conflicts may continue virtually unchanged. But the risks and the cost of simply waiting out the process will be increasingly high. Outcomes through attrition or exhaustion, particularly given the persistence of protracted conflicts and the spread of civil or social war, will place increasing strains on the stability and the flexibility of the present international regime. The search for more systematic understanding of the process of war-termination if not war-avoidance is and will continue to be as critical for the conventional as for the nuclear realm.[14]

Notes

1. See Bernard and Fawn Brodie, *From Crossbow to H-Bomb* (New York, 1962), for discussion of related developments around other new technologies; and George Quester, *Deterrence Before Hiroshima* (New York, 1966), for the specific case of the inter-war fascination with strategic bombing.
2. A comprehensive citation of the existing literature is to be found in the unpublished essays 'Quantitative aspects of armed conflicts since World War II', prepared in 1966 by Berto Jongman of the Polemological Institute, Groningen, and Milton Leitenberg, 'A Survey of Studies of Post-World War II Wars, Conflicts, and Military Coups'. Jongman finds, for example, that there are seven works that are most widely used. His own work builds on these with a composite number of independent cases totalling 223. Only 18 per cent or 38 wars were on all seven lists (Jongman, 'Quantitative Aspects', p. 31). Perhaps the most comprehensive listing of ethnic civil unrest (social war) will be the forthcoming work of Edward Azar of the University of Maryland.
3. For a nuanced analysis of this thesis, see John Lewis Gaddis, 'The Long Peace: Elements of Stability in the Postwar International System', *International Security*, Spring 1986, pp. 99–142.

4. Jongman, 'Quantitative Aspects', p. 30.
5. See, for example, Robert J. McNamara, 'Security in the Contemporary World', *US Department of State Bulletin*, 6 June 1966, pp. 874–81.
6. Raymond Aron, *The Century of Total War* (Boston, 1954).
7. James F. Dunnigan and Austin Bay, *A Quick and Dirty Guide to War* (New York, 1985) p. 10.
8. Charles S. Gochman and Zeev Maoz 'Militarized InterState Disputes, 1816–1976', *Journal of Conflict Resolution*, vol. 28, no. 4 (December 1984) p. 599.
9. Ibid., p. 608.
10. Jongman, 'Quantitative Aspects', pp. 41–3.
11. McNamara, 'Security in the Contemporary World'.
12. Gochman and Maoz, 'Militarized InterState Disputes', p. 601.
13. See Ruth L. Sivard, *World Military and Social Expenditures* (Washington, DC, 1983) and Stockholm International Peace Research Institute, *SIPRI Yearbook, 1987: World Armaments and Disarmament* (New York, 1987) for third-world buying patterns; and Alden Millins's seminal *Born Arming* (Stanford, California, 1986) for an examination of the process of diffusion of weapons and technology to newly-independent states. Elliot Cohen, 'Distant Battles: Modern War in the Third World', *International Security*, Spring 1986, pp. 143–71, is one of the few attempts to assess the impact of these technologies on conflict outcomes.
14. The author wishes to express appreciation to her ISODARCO colleagues for their encouragement and to Jill Jermano, Kori Schake, and Linda Staehli of the School of Public Affairs at the University of Maryland for research assistance.

7 Belief Systems and Arms Control Possibilities
Jane M. O. Sharp

INTRODUCTION

This chapter examines the ways in which the belief systems of policy-makers influence national bargaining strategies and the possibilities for concluding stable and equitable arms control agreements. The first part outlines five different belief systems as they affect the image of the adversary and the nature of international relations, draws the implications of each for broad defence and foreign policy goals (and specifically for the role nuclear weapons should play in advancing these goals) and suggests the most likely arms control bargaining strategies to emerge from each. The second part examines the hypothetical interactions between these strategies and suggests those combinations of negotiating partners likely to produce stable agreements and those for which negotiations would either be superfluous or counterproductive.

Arms control agreements rarely do more than codify some aspect of the *status quo*. Even this modest achievement usually requires an extraordinary alignment of favourable conditions not only between the main protagonists, but also among domestic and allied special interests. All too often negotiations consume and erode trust rather than build confidence, with each side employing increasingly coercive bargaining tactics that simply exacerbate the arms competition in the name of arms control.

Many factors influence the choice of bargaining strategies in arms control negotiations. These include a category of relatively immutable background factors like the polarity of the international system, the power differential and political climate between the negotiating parties, as well as the relations within the parties and between the principals and their alliance partners. A second category of more mutable factors includes the structural conditions under which negotiations occur: the formality of the setting, the number of parties and of issues at stake, and the stress of time and outside events. This chapter addresses a subset of the first category, namely, the factors that influence the political climate between the parties; specifically the belief systems and mind-sets of the decision-makers.

Members of the informed public reading accounts of arms control negotiations often ask why political leaders armed with the same data can draw widely differing conclusions about their significance and prescribe dramatically different solutions. One answer is that measurable facts, such as the raw figures about defence spending and deployed systems, are not as powerful determinants of bargaining policy and negotiating positions as the different belief systems, mindsets and operational codes of the elites in the policy-making community. How the facts are perceived, how the pay-off structure of a negotiation looks, how an adversary's proposals are interpreted, how intentions are gauged from capabilities and rhetoric, how previous encounters are remembered and analysed, all depend on the mind-set into which the information is fed.

This chapter tries to speculate intelligently about the ways in which the bargaining strategies determined by one state's elite images and belief systems will interact with the strategies determined by the dominant mind-set of the negotiating partner. Those with a Hobbesian view of international relations are likely to endorse quite different defence and foreign policies, estimate different force requirements, and adopt different arms control strategies from those with more flexible and optimistic attitudes.

BELIEF SYSTEMS

At least five different mind-sets can be identified in the political culture of most states: the Manichean, the confrontational, the competitive, the co-operative and the pacifist (see Table 7.1).[1] These are drawn primarily from the analyses and observations of US decision-makers, but Western analyses of Soviet defence and foreign policy-making elites suggest analogous categories exist in Moscow also.[2] In both Washington and Moscow, the two issue areas of most salience in formulating defence and arms control policies are, first, national security and the risk of war, particularly nuclear war; and, second, the risk of losing global status and influence to the other superpower, and at worst being taken over by the adversary's political

Table 7.1

Types	BELIEF SYSTEM		DEFENCE POLICY	
	Image of opponent	Nature of international relations	Overall strategy	Role of nuclear weapons
Manichean	• totally negative • illegitimate power with expansionist foreign policy • monolithic internally	extremely conflictual (Hobbesian)	roll-back to pre-1945	war-winning capability superior first strike
Confrontational	• largely negative • grudging acceptance of adversary as legitimate • foreign policy as expansionist • monolithic internally	highly conflictual	latent roll-back; manifest containment	damage-limiting need superior counterforce
Competitive	• mixed • accepts adversary as legitimate power • aggressive foreign policy • divided internally	deterrent model tends to worst-case analysis	containment	military denial needs countervailing force
Co-operative	• mixed • adversary as legitimate foreign policy as opportunistic • divided internally • suffers security dilemma	spiral model (Jervis) tends to best-case analysis	containment detente in both political and military relations	punitive denial nuclear minimalists sufficiency over balance as force-criterion
Pacifist	• neutral • legitimate power with defensive foreign policy • divided internally	potentially harmonious	accommodation defensive non-interventionist	nuclear abolitionists

Type of mind-set	ARMS CONTROL POLICY Main objectives	Likely bargaining strategies	COMPLIANCE DIPLOMACY Means of monitoring	Dealing with ambiguity
Manichean	• little faith in traditional arms control • zero-sum approach, needs to win and have adversary lose • arms control agreement to maintain superiority	bullying, blackmailing and coercive	• on-site inspection (OSI) as minimal requirement • little faith in national technical means (NTM), e.g. satellite reconnaissance	• requires absolute compliance in every detail • quick to denounce • ambiguity as deliberate violation
Confronta-tional	to curtail adversary's forces while maintaining own superiority and continued modernisation	coercive and competitive emphasis on bargaining from strength	more faith in NTM but concern re adversary encryption	• stringent standards of compliance • also quick to denounce ambiguity as violation
Competitive	seeks balanced limits to control both sides' pace of modernisation	• mixed competitive and co-operative tactics • strict tit-for-tat strategies • emphasis on reputation for commitment	OSI preferred NTM considered adequate	more willing to resolve ambiguity through diplomatic channels like the Standing Consultative Commission
Co-operative	• seeks more stable force postures on both sides • less concern with numerical balance as criterion	co-operative and integrative • benign tit-for-tat strategies • emphasis on problem solving	OSI if you can get it • NTM adequate • OSI useful mainly for domestic political reasons	• prefers quiet diplomacy • acknowledges both sides push treaty limits • sees need for constant consultation
Pacifist	• little faith in traditional arms control • objective to settle rather than to win	conciliatory and accommodating	• NTM adequate • least perturbed by asymmetries of open and closed societies	• prefers quiet diplomacy • sees adversary cheating caused by own side's hardliners and refusal to ratify agreements

system. Thus, at one extreme are those whose primary fear is of political change and who will run the risk of war to preserve their own political system, and at the other are those whose primary fear is nuclear holocaust and who will sacrifice their own political system to avert the risk of conflict that might lead to nuclear war.[3] Table 1 summarises each mind-set as it affects the image of the adversary and the nature of international relations; draws the implications of each for broad foreign and defence policy goals and specifically for the role nuclear weapons should play in advancing these goals; suggests the most likely arms control objectives and bargaining strategies consistent with each; and finally, suggests how each will conduct its compliance diplomacy once a treaty has been concluded.

Manichean

Joseph Stalin and Adolf Hitler exemplify Manichean or totalitarian thinking which sees the adversary in diabolical terms as the embodiment of evil. Neither the United States nor the Soviet Union has been dominated by this extreme perspective since the death of Stalin in 1953, but elements of Manicheanism emerge from time to time in both capitals. Ideologues like Mikhail Suslov and Boris Ponomarev, in Moscow, and some of the fundamentalist reactionaries associated with the Reagan Administration, like Patrick Buchanan, Senator Jesse Helms, Rev Jerry Falwell, and even on occasions Caspar Weinberger and Richard Perle, have expressed opinions suggesting primitive Manichean mind-sets.

Manicheans have often suffered persecution and may even be refugees from totalitarianism. They are highly ethnocentric and view the adversary in a totally negative light, regard its government as illegitimate, see its foreign policy as inherently aggressive and expansionist, and believe that its leadership is monolithic, and impossible to deal with or influence in any way other than brute force.[4] In his study of the early Cold War years, Daniel Yergin saw the more extreme cold warriors in the United States dominated by what he called the Riga Axiom, which viewed the Soviet Union as a 'world revolutionary state denying the possibility of co-existence, committed to unrelenting ideological warfare, powered by a messianic drive for world mastery'.[5]

Manicheans view international relations as Hobbesian and conflictual in all its aspects. Thus, in the United States, Manichean thinkers strive to return to the unambiguous American military superiority of the late 1940s and early 1950s and endorse a policy of rolling back Soviet political influence and military presence to its pre-1939 status: by force if necessary. This perspective generates requirements for manifestly superior military forces, and envisages many missions for nuclear weapons: to deter an attack on the United States or its allies, to prevail in any nuclear conflict that may arise, and to provide visible evidence of superiority in the global status game. Manicheans in the United States want nuclear forces to cover every conceivable target under the most difficult conditions and, at a minimum, to maintain a numerical edge over the Soviet arsenal in all categories.[6] They also favour the building of strategic defences to protect US populations and missile sites, while maintaining a massive offensive capability against the adversary.[7]

Given their view of the adversary as a basically illegitimate and expansionist power, Manicheans see no value in the pursuit of co-operative arms control regimes. If forced into arms control diplomacy by a more liberal public opinion such a leadership could be expected to see negotiations as a zero-sum game, to adopt extremely bullying and coercive tactics, and then to blame the inevitable failure of the process on the intransigence of the opponent.

Not surprisingly, Manicheans take an absolutist view of treaty compliance. Colin Gray and Richard Perle are good examples of this mind-set in their denunciations of alleged Soviet cheating at SALT and the chemical weapons provisions of the Geneva Protocol.[8] This viewpoint considers national technical means of monitoring adversary behaviour to be inadequate and claims that on-site inspections are vital for arms control to be worthwhile. Ironically, this would require a fair measure of co-operation with the adversary. Manicheans judge the adversary guilty until proved innocent and are quick to denounce publicly any suspected violations, however flimsy and ambiguous the evidence, rather than pursue quiet diplomacy.

Confrontational

Confronters are hardliners who also have a predominantly negative view of the adversary but, unlike Manicheans, do accept – albeit grudgingly – that the other side is governed by a legitimate power with whom diplomatic business can, and must, be conducted. Paul Nitze and George Shultz appear to fit into this category. They still suspect the adversary of being inherently expansionist in its foreign policy aims, and tend to view the adversary's internal decision-making elite as monolithic. Confronters are less paranoid than Manicheans, however. They endorse official US containment policy, as propounded by President Harry Truman and upheld by each succeeding administration, but often possess barely concealed 'roll-back' tendencies; particularly those with East-bloc emigre backgrounds. They believe that the best way to peace and stability lies in deterrence through the maintenance of superior military strength and see multiple missions for nuclear forces: deterrence, war-fighting and political coercion. Though not as conservative in their force requirements as the Manicheans, confronters also tend to favour the development and deployment of strategic defences.

Confronters are not totally resistant to arms control diplomacy but tend to see negotiations as zero-sum games to be won or lost. They favour coercive bargaining tactics and fear that any hint of conciliation will be exploited as weakness. The emphasis is on bargaining from strength and maintaining a reputation for resolve with little sensitivity to the risks of provoking the adversary.

Confronters have stringent requirements for the verifiability of treaty provisions, particularly for nuclear arms control agreements. This follows naturally from the belief that counterforce capabilities are necessary to maintain the credibility of nuclear deterrence and that numerical balance matters lest the Soviets gain a meaningful political and/or strategic capability. In the United States confronters tend to fret about the relative openness of the American weapons acquisition process compared to the relative secrecy of the Soviet process and believe this gives the Soviets an important advantage that actually encourages them to cheat. On-site inspection thus becomes necessary to overcome pervasive mistrust of the adversary. When the adversary engages in ambiguous behaviour which pushes right up to the treaty limits, the hardliner tends to favour some tit-for-tat kind of response. Quiet diplomacy is played down in favour of public denunciation designed – but rarely effective – to bring the adversary to heel.

Competitive

This is the mainstream mind-set that has dominated both superpowers' arms control diplomacy in the post-1945 period. Harold Brown, Secretary of Defense in the Jimmy Carter Administration, is a good example. Like the hardliners, the competitive mind-set has mixed views of the adversary, accepting its government as legitimate but still suspecting its aims as inherently aggressive if not necessarily greedy for more territory. The most important difference between the mainstream competitive view and both the Manichean and the hardline perspectives is an awareness in the former that the adversary's elites are as likely to be divided internally as one's own, and are thus open to influence. This view nevertheless still sees international relations as basically competitive and tends to make worst-case assumptions about ambiguous behaviour. International relations are perceived according to the deterrence model, namely that in order to deter aggression by the adversary a state must demonstrate both resolve and capability to prevail in any conflict that might arise.[9]

The competitive mind-set sees the need for balanced nuclear forces with the adversary, but is less confident than the confrontational and Manichean thinkers that nuclear superiority contributes to stability. It sees the need for counterforce as part of an effective deterrent force and tends to believe in limited nuclear options and escalation control once war breaks out. Such a force posture, while rationalised as defensive, nevertheless often looks offensive to potential adversaries and does little to dampen down the arms competition. Competitors are sensitive to the provocative and destabilising aspects of strategic defences that purport to protect populations from the adversary's nuclear weapons, while maintaining highly offensive strategic forces against that adversary. Nevertheless they tend to favour limited hard point defences to protect their own retaliatory forces. Some would like to amend the 1972 Anti-ballistic Missile (ABM) Treaty to permit land-based ballistic missile defences.

In arms control the emphasis on numerically-balanced agreements and strictly verifiable provisions constrains diplomatic possibilities. Before the 50 per cent cuts endorsed, in principle, by the 1985 summit, there was little willingness to go beyond a stabilisation of the *status quo*, to offer radical reductions, or to initiate weapons moratoria – except in manifestly obsolete or impractical weapons systems.

Mainstream competitors are less rigid about verification requirements than confronters and tend to define violations as those actions that give a manifest strategic advantage to the adversary. In the United States this group is concerned that the Soviet radar being built at Krasnoyarsk (which all groups agree will probably be a technical violation of the ABM Treaty if and when it becomes operational) might give the Soviets an advantage if both sides were to break out of the ABM Treaty. In general this group believes national technical means to be more adequate than do the confronters but nevertheless advocates on-site inspections to provide extra insurance. This group is more favourable to the concept of quiet diplomacy to resolve compliance ambiguities, as exemplified by the Carter and Gerald Ford Administrations' approach to the Standing Consultative Commission through the 1970s.

Co-operative

This belief system is characterised by sensitivity to the problems and requirements of the adversary as exemplified by policy-makers like Averell Harriman, George Kennan and Marshall Shulman. It tends to view an opponent's enmity as a transient rather than a permanent phenomenon, that can be transformed into a relationship of *détente* given the right kind of diplomacy. It is in tune with Yergin's Yalta Axiom which saw the Soviet Union as a traditional great power trying to achieve its objectives in the context of the existing international system rather than trying to overthrow it. In common with the spiral model of Robert Jervis – and in marked contrast to the confrontational and competitive mind-set – co-operative actors are aware that the actions of one's own state can affect the behaviour of others and should be moderated accordingly. Thus excessive military forces are eschewed as being dangerously provocative to political adversaries. Co-operators see strategic defences in general and the Reagan Administration's Strategic Defense Initiative (SDI) in particular, as likely to generate more offensive forces by the adversary and to undermine international stability.

In foreign policy, those with a co-operative mind-set still endorse containment of the other superpower's reach and influence but do so in the context of developing harmonious relations and relaxing tensions. In defence planning they see sufficiency as a more appropriate criterion than parity or superiority and see nuclear weapons as useful to perform one mission only – to deter a nuclear attack. They believe this deterrent mission requires only a minimal retaliatory force for which the primary criterion is invulnerability, not balance with the adversary. Many believe that nuclear weapons have no utility as instruments of war fighting and should not even be considered as military weapons, being unable either to gain or hold territory, nor to defend military positions or civilian populations.

Co-operative actors are the most optimistic about arms control, see negotiations as variable-sum games, and emphasise problem solving for both sides rather than one-sided gains. They are the most likely to initiate integrative bargaining and to respond to the other side's moves with benign tit-for-tat tactics. While sensitive to the political need for agreements that are equitable and verifiable, they do not make a fetish of nuclear balance in every force category or of treaty compliance in every last detail.

Co-operators believe that national technical means are adequate for the monitoring of each side's treaty compliance, noting that, despite the relatively closed nature of Soviet society, the Western intelligence community is rarely surprised by Soviet weapons development, having correctly predicted all new systems before they became operational. They believe that monitoring Soviet capability is enhanced by arms control agreements, the compliance provisions of which allow legal challenges of ambiguous behaviour. Co-operators believe in quiet diplomacy to resolve compliance problems and tend to blame both sides for pushing too close to treaty limits after SALT I.[10] While disappointed by Soviet recalcitrance to better explain technical violations like the Krasnoyarsk radar, co-operators do not judge the radar to be detrimental to Western security.

Pacifist

Few pacifists can be found among the decision-making elites of either superpower. Pacifists see the risk of war as much higher than the risks of political take-over. Their view of the adversary is more benign than that of the other four mind-sets outlined above, is more willing to credit the other side with legitimate foreign and defence policy objectives, and is more sensitive to the opponents' internal divisions. Pacifists emphasise common rather than conflicting interests between states and are prepared to invest heavily in measures to improve relations with their political adversaries.

Allies worried about security guarantees tend to be disturbed by pacifist tendencies in the decision-making hierarchies of their alliance leaders because pacifists tend to be accommodative in their foreign policy, minimalist in their military force requirements, and abolitionist with respect to nuclear forces, denying the need for even a minimal deterrent force.

Pacifists tend to favour radical disarmament measures and to be impatient with traditional arms control diplomacy, seeing the pursuit of formal treaties and agreements as more likely to drive the competition in armaments than to dampen it down. If engaged in negotiations pacifists would tend to adopt accommodative and conciliatory bargaining tactics without fear of exploitation; their objective being more to settle than to win. They would be more likely than others to engage in unilateral concessions, particularly on nuclear matters.

Pacifists are the most relaxed about verification requirements and consider the risks of cheating by an adversary small when compared to the benefits of mutual restraint and the risks of further unlimited accumulation of nuclear weapons by both sides. They are the most willing to give an adversary the benefit of the doubt in case of ambiguous behaviour and the least perturbed by asymmetries in openness. They tend to blame hardliners in their own government for recalcitrance in the adversary. Not surprisingly they deplore public denunciations of cheating and favour quiet diplomacy to resolve compliance ambiguities.

INTERACTIONS

The middle three categories of belief systems outlined above, namely confronters, competitors and co-operators, differ on many particulars but share a consensus on two general issues: the need to maintain strong military forces with a significant nuclear component, and the need to pursue arms control arrangements with the adversary. The two extreme points of view do not share this consensus.

Pacifists see little purpose for most military forces and none at all for nuclear weapons, and Manicheans see no purpose in co-operative arms control diplomacy. As Robert A. Levine noted in his 1963 study these two extremes share a simplicity in their approach and sometimes make strikingly similar policy recommendations despite their radically different political philosophies.[11] Thus anti-communist extremists and pacifists can both endorse the abolition of nuclear weapons and the building of a strategic defensive shield; neither of which are considered feasible by more sophisticated analysts. Similarly, in the debate over NATO's decision to deploy new American missiles in Western Europe in the early 1980s, the extreme left in western Europe and the isolationist right in the United States both advocated that the United States dissociate itself from Europe and let Europeans provide for their own defence; the American right believing Europe not worth the trouble and expense, the European left believing American 'support' too dangerous.

The potential for negotiated arms control – both in terms of reaching agreement on common goals and of concluding treaties that effectively limit armaments – can be assessed by examining how different bargaining strategies interact with each other.[12] Twenty-five interactions are theoretically possible between the five bargaining strategies that each of two negotiating parties might adopt, based on the preceding analysis of belief systems. Table 7.2 demonstrates that only a few of these are likely to produce stable and effective arms control agreements. In some, the mind-sets of the negotiating parties will preclude any recognition of common interests; in others, any agreements concluded are likely to be mere codifications of the *status quo*; and between conciliatory anti-war pacifists negotiations will be unnecessary. The following section briefly summarises the likely outcomes from these hypothetical interactions, beginning with those involving negotiating parties with a Manichean mind-set.

Interaction number 1, that between a pair of Manicheans, is unlikely to take the form of an arms control negotiation since Manicheans are indifferent to the welfare of others and insensitive to the benefits of co-operative diplomacy. In game theory terms the pay-off structure will never look worthwhile. A weak Manichean may nevertheless be unable to avoid coming to terms with a more powerful Manichean opponent, as Stalin was forced to negotiate with Hitler in the late 1930s. When Manicheans are engaged with each other, however, either diplomatically or in a situation of conflict, the prognosis is for a mutually destructive outcome as both sides tend to adopt bullying and coercive tactics, both are out to win, and neither is likely to reduce the other's demands.

Interactions between Manicheans and more flexible mind-sets present more potential for mutual influence but the changes may not always be in the direction intended, particularly if one side misreads the mind-set and the bargaining tactics of the other. In numbers 2 and 6, interactions between Manicheans and confronters, the confronters might have its belief systems and prejudices reinforced, and its positions even further hardened, by the bullying and coercive tactics of a Manichean negotiating partner. Latent acceptance of the legitimacy of the other's negotiating objectives could also be lost, for example, as appears to have happened in the Anglo-Argentinian negotiations on the sovereignty of the Falkland Islands.[13] The Argentine military government's attempted *fait accompli*, in taking over the

Table 7.2 Interactions between different bargaining strategies: likely outcomes

A \ B	Manichean	Confrontational	Competitive	Co-operative	Pacifist
Manichean	1. mutually destructive	2. A's Manichean stance moves B towards Manichean position	3. potential for B to move A into accepting B's existence, i.e. from Manichean to confrontational	4. A tends to take advantage of B's co-operative gestures	5. B likely to cave in
Confrontational	6. B's Manichean stance moves A towards Manichean position	7. positive outcome requires each to accept legitimacy of the other	8. B unwilling to give A the benefit of the doubt. Worst-case analysis of A's actions by B	9. B has potential to move A to more co-operative position	10. A takes advantage of B

	11	12	13	14	15
Competitive	potential for A to move B from Manichean to confrontational position	A unwilling to give B benefit of the doubt. Worst case analysis of B's actions by A	dangerous and mutually reinforcing interaction likely. Stalemate at best	positive outcome more likely if B is stronger than A	as A increases demands, B will move to competitive stance
Co-operative	16 B tends to take advantage of A's co-operative gestures	17 A has potential to move B to more co-operative position	18 positive outcome more likely if A stronger than B	19 mutually beneficial resolution of conflicts likely in all interactions between co-operative and conciliatory bargainers	20
Pacifist	21 A likely to cave in	22 B tends to take advantage of A's co-operative gestures	23 as B increases demands A becomes more competitive	24	25

islands by force, eliminated a considerable British tolerance for earlier Argentinian claims for eventual sovereignty over the Falklands, strengthened the hardliners in Britain, and generated overwhelming public support for British military countermeasures. In arms control negotiations the blatant accumulation of new weapons systems as coercive bargaining chips by one side has a similar blackmailing effect, toughening the negotiating positions of the other. As the United States bargains coercively it reinforces those in the Kremlin arguing against the feasibility of peaceful coexistence and strengthens those with a more orthodox Marxist–Leninist viewpoint of the final triumph of communism. Similarly, when the Soviets are intransigent – as when they walked out of the Intermediate Nuclear Force talks in November 1983 – those arguing against the virtue of a co-operative arms control are strengthened in the United States.

When a competitive bargainer negotiates with a Manichean – as in interactions numbers 3 and 11 – the Manichean may be moved into a position more accepting of the legitimacy of the adversary; particularly if the competitive bargainer is the more powerful. An example is the manner in which Israel was able to bring Egypt round to an acceptance of the state of Israel, and a willingness to negotiate a settlement in the Sinai.[14]

Co-operative bargainers interacting with Manicheans – numbers 4 and 16 – run the risk of exploitation by the bullying tactics of the latter. A firm co-operator employing a tit-for-tat strategy that rewards concession and punishes coercion will soon have to revert to a hard line if there is no conciliatory behaviour from the adversary. Efforts to play a benign game that does not respond to every defection with a corresponding one will be perceived by the Manichean as weakness and thus a measure of the success of his firmness, not as a concession requiring reciprocal behaviour.

Interactions between Manicheans and conciliatory bargainers of the anti-war pacifist stripe – numbers 5 and 21 – are likely to produce unequal and ultimately unstable agreements as the latter gives in to all the former's demands. Hitler's taking over of the Sudetenland, postwar settlements in which the victor demands unconditional surrender of the vanquished, and manifestly inequitable treaties, all fall into this category; usually with unfortunate long-term consequences.

In sum, Manicheans are unlikely to enter into serious arms control negotiations and, if engaged, are unlikely to generate the kind of climate conducive to the production of stable agreements. Fortunately, governments in Washington and Moscow since the Second World War have been largely made up of those with mind-sets and belief systems in the three middle categories outlined here. Nevertheless, while these policy-makers are not resistant to co-operative arms control efforts, not all forums involving various combinations of these moderate negotiations will produce effective agreements.

Negotiation between two confrontational bargainers, number 7, is more likely to occur than number 1, between two Manicheans. It requires each side to accept the legitimacy of the other and to recognise a common interest that threatens neither. Even then, the range of possible limits to which each side can agree is likely to be very narrow, since hardliners believe in peace through strength rather than peace through co-operation. Agreements are certainly possible but are likely to impose limits that have no effect on either side's arsenals. One case in point is the Limited Test Ban Treaty concluded in 1963 which bans nuclear testing in the atmosphere but permits testing underground and thus does nothing to slow the weapons development programmes of either superpower. Another is the Non-proliferation Treaty signed in 1968, and ratified by the two superpowers in 1970, which imposes limits on the non-nuclear weapons powers only.

Interactions between confronters and competitors – numbers 8 and 12 – are somewhat more conducive to productive arms control bargaining than between two confronters but negotiations are still constrained by a tendency on the part of the confronter to make worst-case analyses of the actions and rhetoric of the competitor. Both sides find it difficult to recognise areas of common interest and neither has the necessary confidence in themselves, or trust in the other, to make innovative proposals. Competitive bargainers who believe in deterrence by balanced nuclear capabilities are extremely fearful of being exploited by hardliners, and reluctant to make any move which could suggest giving the other side an advantage. Jerome Frank, writing of East–West disarmament negotiations in the 1950s and 1960s, observed that the risk that the other side might gain an advantage by cheating on an agreement was a far more potent determinant of both sides' negotiating behaviour than the far greater risk of a nuclear exchange that might destroy humanity.[15] And the pervasive mistrust of the Cold War years has been noted by many former officials. Louis J. Halle, who served on the State Department Policy Planning staff in the 1950s, admits that the United States was even more suspicious of reasonable Soviet proposals, believing them far more sinister and dangerous than proposals that were manifestly unacceptable. As Halle put it:

> Our instinct is to cast about for grounds on which to discredit the proposal instead of seizing it and making the most of it. Being distrustful of the Greeks bearing gifts, we are afraid of being tricked.[16]

In the 1980s, a similar Cold War distrust dominated American attitudes towards Soviet arms control proposals. A good example is the automatic rejection of Mikhail Gorbachev's test moratorium in the summer of 1985; not only by Reagan Administration spokesmen, but also by most of the media.[17]

Interactions between two competitive bargainers – number 13 – should theoretically be less risky than between two hardliners, but the prospects for innovative arms control are nevertheless slim. Competitive bargainers are overly concerned about numerical balance even as they claim to eschew offensive forces and strategies. Bilateral Soviet–American negotiations on strategic arms (SALT, START) since the late 1960s demonstrate the kind of progress that can be expected from this kind of interaction. It is possible to maintain sufficient sense of the common interest to keep the dialogue alive, but not to limit weapons programmes effectively. Some *status quo* agreements have been concluded but, since 1972, even these modest limits have proved impossible to ratify in the United States.

The interactions with the most potential for achieving equitable agreements are between co-operative bargainers and almost any kind of adversary except the lunatic fringe Manicheans and the most hardline confrontational bargainers. As noted earlier, the main characteristic of co-operative bargainers is their sensitivity to the security needs of others and of the dependence of one nation's actions on another. Unlike totalitarians, confronters and competitors, co-operative bargainers do care about the welfare of their negotiating partners and look for solutions that serve both sides' needs.[18]

Co-operators negotiating with either hardliners or competitors – numbers 9, 17, 14 and 18 – can move the adversary into more co-operative bargaining positions by a benign tit-for-tat strategy that always rewards concessions with concessions and generally, but not always, punishes coercion with coercion. Firm co-operators have the right mix of co-operation and strength that permits the bargainer to give its opponent the benefit of doubt when interpreting ambiguous moves, but will not cave in to the adversary's bullying behaviour. As noted above, however, the co-operative side of this strategy can backfire when tried against extremely hardline adversaries (interactions 4, 9, 16, and 17) who misperceive co-operation as weakness and are thereby reinforced in the appropriateness and effectiveness of their coercive behaviour.

Conciliators are unlikely to face conciliators in an arms control negotiation since disputes between them are likely to be settled tacitly. But any combination of conciliatory with co-operative bargaining tactics will reinforce the integrative aspects of each, as in interactions numbers 19, 20, 24 and 25. Arms control agreements that mop up loose ends after the otherwise tidy resolution of conflict are products of this kind of co-operative interaction. Two cases in point are the Anglo-American (Rush-Bagot) Treaty of 1817 that demilitarised the Great Lakes after the War of 1812 had been settled at the Treaty of Ghent in 1814; and the 1922 Washington Naval Treaty that set limits on capital ships after the First World War. Attempts to refine the 1922 agreement, in the late 1920s and 1930s, however, degenerated into competitive bargaining and concern over numerical balances.[19]

Purely conciliatory tactics work with friendly states to expedite the codification of common interests, but rarely work with an adversary more hostile than a firm co-operator; unless the interaction toughens up the conciliator. Bargainers lacking the interest or the capability to be firm in the face of bullying and coercive tactics do not fare well with totalitarians, confronters and competitors, who tend to pocket rather than reciprocate concessions, as in interactions numbers 5, 21, 10, 22, 15 and 23. That said, many opportunities for innovative arms control do appear to have been lost because potentially co-operative gestures were withheld by parties who misread negotiating partners with co-operative tendencies as competitive or confrontational bargainers on whom concessions would be wasted.

CONCLUSION

What lessons flow from these hypothetical bargaining interactions? First, the voting public, frustrated by the slow pace of arms control, should understand how the belief systems of their elected officials will limit the choice of national arms control bargaining strategies. It is thus quite unrealistic to elect leaders with either Manichean, confrontational or highly competitive mind-sets and then expect them to negotiate dramatic arms reductions treaties. *Status quo* agreements are the most that can be expected under these circumstances. These are non-trivial achievements especially when both sides have destabilising new systems on their drawing boards and in their weapons pipelines. But no one should be fooled into anticipating dramatic reductions or budget savings by arms control negotiations. Reductions usually occur as unilateral initiatives by confident leaders with strong co-ooperative instincts.

A second lesson for governments contemplating a set of negotiations is the need to invest more effort into assessing the nature of the adversary, since strategies that are effective with one party may be counterproductive with others. Manichean and confrontational strategies, characterised by coercive bullying and blackmailing, are obviously destructive to relations between negotiating parties and unlikely ever to produce useful stable agreements. Competitive bargaining strategies may be the only ones appropriate to standing up to totalitarians and confronters. Competition breeds competition, however, and such interactions are unlikely to produce effective arms control and may forfeit opportunities to soften the position of a latent co-operator. Co-operative approaches are optimum for dealing with all but the extremists, as these tactics allow most adversaries to shift one notch along the spectrum in a non-threatening environment. A firm tit-for-tat approach that punishes all defections is more likely to be effective in avoiding exploitation by confronters but a more benign approach that gives ambiguous moves the benefit of the doubt could be more effective with competitors and other firm co-operators. Purely conciliatory strategies are adequate for dealing with friendly partners, but are likely to be exploited by hardliners and might even encourage bullying.

Notes

1. Sources for Table 7.1 include Ralph K. White, 'Images in the Context of International Conflict: Soviet Perceptions of the U.S. and the USSR' in Herbert L. Kelman, *International Behavior: A Social and Psychological Analysis* (New York, 1965) pp. 238–76; Robert Jervis, *Perceptions and Misperceptions in International Politics* (Princeton, 1976); Robert Jervis, *The Logic of Images in International Relations* (Princeton, 1970); Alexander George, 'The Operational Code: A Neglected Approach to the Study of Political Leaders and Decision-Making', *International Studies*

Quarterly, vol. 13, no. 2 (1969) pp. 190–222; Glenn Snyder and Paul Diesing, *Conflict Among Nations* (Princeton, 1977) pp. 291–310; Charles Glaser, 'Why Strategists Disagree About the Requirements of Deterrence', paper delivered at a workshop on Explicating the Arms Control Debate, sponsored by the Center for Science and International Affairs, Harvard University, May 1984; and United States Congress, House of Representatives, Committee on Foreign Affairs, *Soviet Diplomacy and Negotiating Behavior: Emerging New Context for U.S. Diplomacy* (Washington, DC, 1979).
2. Rebecca V. and Daniel L. Strode, 'Diplomacy and Defense in Soviet National Security Policy', *International Security*, vol. 8, no. 2 (1983) pp. 91–116.
3. Robert A. Levine, *The Arms Debate* (Cambridge, Mass., 1963); and Daniel Yankelovich, Robert Kingston and Gerald Garvey (eds), *Voter Opinions on Nuclear Arms Policy: A Briefing Book for the 1974 Elections* (New York, 1984).
4. Richard Pipes, 'Why the Soviets Think They Can Fight and Win a Nuclear War', *Commentary*, vol. 64, no. 1, July 1977.
5. Daniel Yergin, *Shattered Peace: The Origins of the Cold War and the National Security State* (Boston, Mass., 1977) pp. 42–68.
6. Yankelovich *et al.*, *Voter Opinions*, pp. 50–69.
7. Daniel O. Graham, *The Non-Nuclear Defense of Cities: The High Frontier Space-Based Defense Against ICBM Attack* (Cambridge, Mass., 1983).
8. Colin S. Gray, 'Moscow is Cheating', *Foreign Policy*, no. 56 (Fall 1984) pp. 141–152; Richard Perle, 'SALT II: Who is Deceiving Whom?' in Robert L. Pfaltzgraff, Uri Ra'anan and Warren L. Milbury (eds), *Intelligence Policy and National Security* (London, 1981); and United States Senate Committee on Armed Services, *Hearings on Soviet Treaty Violations*, 98th Congress, 2nd Session, 1984 (Washington, DC, 1984).
9. Jervis, *Perceptions and Misperceptions*, pp. 58–113.
10. Michael Krepon, 'Both Sides Are Hedging', *Foreign Policy*, no. 56 (Fall 1984) pp. 153–72.
11. Levine, *The Arms Debate*, passim.
12. This section draws on the typology of interacting conflict strategies in Noel Kaplowitz, 'Psychopolitical Dimensions of International Relations: The Reciprocal Effects of Conflict Strategies', *International Studies Quarterly*, vol. 28, no. 4 (December 1984) pp. 373–400; on Thomas C. Schelling, 'A Framework for the Evaluation of Arms Control Proposals', *Daedalus*, vol. 104, no. 3 (Summer 1975) pp. 187–200; and on Svenn Linkskold, Pamela S. Walters and Helen Kartsourais, 'Co-operators, Competitors and Response to GRIT', *Journal of Conflict Resolution*, vol. 27, no. 3 (September 1983).
13. Kaplowitz, 'Psychopolitical Dimensions of International Relations'.
14. Howard Raiffa, *The Art and Science of Negotiation* (Cambridge, Mass., 1982) pp. 205–17.
15. Jerome Frank, *Sanity and Survival in the Nuclear Age* (New York, 1982 edn) pp. 191–224.
16. Louis Halle, *New York Times Magazine*, 15 November 1959.

17. For a contrary view see Eugene J. Carroll, 'A Useful Nuclear Step by Moscow', *New York Times*, 7 August 1985.
18. On the extent to which national leaders see their welfare dependent on others and vice versa, see Robert Keohane, *After Hegemony: Cooperation and Discord in the World Political Economy* (Princeton, 1984) p. 122.
19. Salvador de Madariaga, *Disarmament* (New York, 1929) p. 31.

8 Technical Means of Verification of Arms Control Agreements
Kosta Tsipis

There are many reasons why verification by technical means is important to arms control. Technology provides us with the capability to verify compliance with arms control agreements unilaterally, that is without co-operation from our treaty partner. 'National technical means' is the intentionally non-specific phrase used in treaty language for the systems that keep both sides informed about each other's doings. This capability is important to the United States for three reasons. First, for military reasons Americans should indeed know whether their opponent is complying with an agreement they have signed to limit a weapon or a practice. Secondly, verification is important politically; no arms control agreement will be ratified by the US Senate without the assurance that compliance by the Soviet Union can be verified. And there is a third, less discussed reason, which is that good verification acts as a deterrent to infractions. If the Soviets know that the Americans can tell if they violate an agreement, the Americans will believe that they will refrain from violating it. Being caught in a violation will threaten the agreement and risk international embarrassment.

It is important to make a clear distinction at the outset between 'verification', 'compliance' and 'sanctions'. What will be discussed here is the means of *verification*, which is essentially intelligence gathering. Intelligence is used by the US military, for example, to know what the Soviets are doing in order to plan forces; it is used by arms controllers to monitor whether the treaty partners are violating arms control treaties. When we are talking about verification, we are talking about intelligence gathering. *Compliance* deals with whether what has been observed constitutes a legal violation of a specific agreement, which is the province of the lawyers. Questions about what steps to take if a violation is observed, what *sanctions* to invoke, are the concern of yet another group. Here we are concerned only with verification and hence we will leave all arguments about compliance and sanctions to others.

In the past, verification has been used in the United States as a club to knock down arms control agreements. In the words of a former high official of the Central Intelligence Agency with responsibility for monitoring: 'Verification is like a heavy overcoat; if you don't want an arms control agreement, you put it on and say we cannot sign this because we cannot verify it. If you do want an arms control agreement, you take the coat off and get to work on the agreement.' The Ronald Reagan Administration has been particularly good at wearing this coat, using verification as an excuse to say 'no' to arms control. It is this Administration that has announced that 'adequate verification' (the description of the Jimmy Carter years) is no longer a valid measure. The requirement now is 'effective verification'.

Political labels apart, what is adequate verification? Must the Americans be able to see the slightest Soviet movement? Must they know how many times Mikhail Gorbachev brushes his teeth every day, or is it adequate to know whether the Soviets have 100 or 110 divisions, 1000 or 2000 missiles? The debate as to what constitutes adequate verification has been acrimonious in the United States. Those opposed to arms control insist that the United States must know every detail about Soviet activities. The people who believe that what we should be talking about is national security and not political competition with the Soviet Union have a different view. In trying to determine what 'adequate' means two questions need to be asked. First, what violations of a given arms control agreement will, if done clandestinely, damage national security? If one party has 10 000 nuclear warheads and adds 100 more without the other party's knowledge, would that put the first party at risk? If another 10 000 warheads are added will that threaten the other party's security? Secondly, can those violations be detected? There is a lot of argument about these questions. There is no need for either superpower to know in great detail what the other is doing, especially since the nuclear arsenals we now have are so large that they are, in fact, very stable. If you go from 10 000 missiles to 11 000 missiles, nothing in the strategic balance will be changed. Verification requirements become much more difficult and exacting when one gets down to smaller numbers of nuclear weapons. If in the future, by some miracle of co-operative arms control, we manage to lower the number of nuclear weapons in our arsenal to, say, 1000, verification requirements will be much more stringent. Then we should be able to detect small changes that are insignificant when the arsenals are large. If what one needs to detect is any change of more than ten per cent, ten per cent of 10 000 is obviously easier to spot than ten per cent of 1000. Adequate verification is thus meaningful only in the context of the size of the arsenals. It is not an absolute but a relative concept.

Let us take up the first question. If the Americans are to be secure in the knowledge that they will always be able to detect any Soviet violations of arms control agreements that would threaten security, what should they be able to detect? First, they should have notice of a new weapon being developed, through telephone intercepts, spies on the ground, or other means. Secondly, they should be able to see a weapon being tested – this is the easiest stage to detect, as it is almost impossible to test strategic weapons out of view of watching satellite eyes. Thirdly, they should be able to monitor production, through satellite pictures of factory activities. Finally, they should be able to see a weapon being deployed, and they should be able to see people training with the weapon.

Clearly these requirements have different time constants. For example, one must be able to detect a test as it is happening. If one's opponent tests a missile and one turns on one's detection system half an hour later, one has missed the test. But one does not have to detect deployment as it is happening. Is there a new radar in Siberia? Are they building a new submarine pen in Vladivostok? These one can discover at any time by comparing different sets of pictures, Before and After. A new radar or a new submarine pen are conditions, not events. Real-time detection is not required. So the systems that help the Americans monitor what the Soviets are doing in order to verify their compliance with arms control agreements are of two kinds: systems that monitor events and must reveal what is happening as it is happening; and systems that monitor conditions and show how something has changed. The US systems of both kinds are extremely good.

William Perry, Under Secretary of Defense for Research and Engineering in the Carter Administration, has said in Congressional testimony:

> We have never been surprised by the Soviets. We have always in the past been able to detect Intercontinental Ballistic Missiles (ICBMs) before they went into testing.

This means that the Americans must have the ability to tell that an ICBM is in development, which means that somehow they must know what is happening inside the laboratory, inside the engineering compounds of missile developing centres.

It is actually easy for the Americans to tell what is happening with Soviet strategic weapons, especially in a case of violation. A new missile must go through several stages: development in the laboratory, testing on a test range, production in a factory, and deployment in a silo or on a submarine or wherever it might be. Now, if this missile is forbidden by an arms control agreement, any activity detected relating to the development, testing, production and deployment of that missile will tell us that there is a violation. One does not have to see the entire process. Because the process of fielding a major weapons system is laborious, lengthy, and complex, there is a great confidence among American technical people and among the intelligence community that they can tell whether the Soviets are violating a missile prohibition.

The Americans use multiple means to gather intelligence from within the Soviet Union, and there is a synergy among them. For example, the Americans intercept a telephone call: somebody in Siberia talks to Moscow and mentions that something is happening. Now they know where to send their satellites to look for that activity. The process of gathering and interpreting information is complex, but in collating the various bits of information the sum is always larger than the parts. Now let us consider in some detail the three most important kinds of systems, the foundation of a verification capability, so to speak: optical cameras on the satellites; radars, especially the synthetic aperture radar; and seismic sensors. Then brief mention will be made of a few additional ways the Americans have developed to get the information they want without relying on the co-operation of the Soviets.

First, and still central, is the satellite, the proverbial 'eye in the sky'. What is on the satellite is a camera. Now, with an ordinary camera, one has a lens that collects light and sends it into the focal plane, where it encounters the film. In human vision, the sun sends down little packets of light called photons, which are waves of light, and they bounce off objects and enter one's eye and excite the cones and rods on the retina, and that is how one sees. That is why one cannot see in the dark; there are no light waves to bounce off objects and enter one's eye. The same thing is true with a photographic camera. There are objects on the ground, and the sun shines, its light reflects off them and comes through the lens of the camera and hits the photographic film, which is actually a dense collection of silver iodide crystals. When a light wave hits such a crystal, it turns black. The more waves of light that hit a crystal, the darker it becomes. If one takes a magnifying glass and looks at a picture, what one sees is little spots, some of them completely black, some different shades of grey, and some white, which means light did not get there, that they were not exposed at all. The film is a device that records how many light waves (photons) have hit a specific spot on the focal plane of the camera. The big problem with film on satellites is that one has to get it down to the ground to be developed. When the whole roll of film has been exposed, it has to be ejected from the satellite, caught by a friendly plane with a net and brought down to the lab to be developed. Another significant disadvantage of film is that when the supply that was launched with the satellite is used up, the satellite becomes obsolete.

We have a better way of using satellites now. It makes use of a recording device called a 'charge-coupled device' (CCD) that is a collection of many little boxes, 1000 boxes by 1000 boxes, say, that sits on the focal plane of the camera. When light hits the CCD, each one of these boxes receives photons and each one counts the photons that land inside it. The device then translates the number of photons in each little box into a proportional number of electrons. So what one has when one takes a picture is a million boxes, each one containing a number of electrons porportional to the intensity of light that hit that box. Now all one needs is a machine that very rapidly counts how many electrons are in each box and then transmits this information to the ground. At the receiving station on the ground is a machine that systematically transforms the count of electrons in each box back into values of light intensity. This proccess is then repeated for each of the million boxes, and because the exact location of each box on the focal plane is precisely known, at the end of the transmission process you have on the ground a duplicate of the picture in the array of boxes on the satellite CCD. Since each box is about the size of a crystal of silver iodide, this picture is as detailed as the picture made on photographic film.

The great advantages of the CCD are two in number. First, and most significant, it can transmit pictures almost as they are happening, so that somebody sitting in Washington DC or Langley, Virginia, or wherever it might be can see scenes in the Soviet Union a few minutes after they have been taken. Secondly, the CCD has metric accuracy, unlike film, which may bend and bulge. The CCD is like a fixed array, so that it is exquisitely accurate in the production of the picture. You get much better resolution with a CCD, especially now that the individual boxes are comparable in size to the grains of silver iodide on a film.

Resolution is important because one wants to see things on the ground that are very small, so that one can tell whether a given vehicle is a truck, say, or a tank. In order to see that one must be able to resolve details. The size of the smallest object one can distinguish on the ground is proportional to the distance of the camera from the ground and to the size of the picture element – the little box in the CCD array, called a pixel. The smaller the pixel, the smaller the object one can distinguish. Given that not much can be done about the height of satellites, it is important to make the pixels very, very small.

Here is a rough calculation. Let us say the satellite is 100 kilometres up, the individual pixel is two micrometres, and the focal length of the camera is four metres. One can quickly calculate that the resolution of the camera is five centimetres, which means that this camera can detect objects that are five centimetres in size. There have been stories that a hockey puck has been detected with such cameras, and that satellite cameras have been able to read licence plates on cars. There is also a story that two days after Nixon went to Moscow to sign the SALT I agreement, the Americans gave the Russians a picture of the welcome ceremony at the airport, taken from a satellite, in which faces could be distinguished. But this may be an apochryphal story.

How many pictures can one take and how fast can one transmit them? The issue here is that, as the resolution becomes smaller, down to five centimetres, the satellite must send one message down to the ground for every five centimetres squared it sees. Since one is looking at thousands and thousands of square kilometres of territory, that is a lot of messages, and the number that can be sent is limited by the size of the antenna and the electrical power of each satellite. Therefore, as one goes to higher resolutions, more of one's information must be stored, because it cannot be sent down as rapidly as it is taken in. What the United States has done is to turn the cameras off when they are passing over areas considered uninteresting. That is why the Americans missed the preparations made by South Africa for nuclear tests in the desert and had to be tipped off by the Soviets, whose cameras were not turned off.

When too much information comes down from the satellites, it is not possible for human photo-interpreters to look at it all, so machines have been developed to help with the load. When one is looking for a change in terrain that might signal an activity of interest, for example a hole in the ground, how does one detect it? One has a series of pictures of the terrain, and one compares each picture with the one before it. For a machine to make the comparisons the shadows in each picture must be exactly the same, which means that the satellite must pass over the same point at a time of day when the shadows are the same all year round. When the machine detects a difference, then a human interpreter looks at it. So it is not the number of pictures one can take that is actually important, but how many one can look at and analyse. To try to strike a balance, the Americans have two kinds of satellite cameras overhead. One kind takes wide-area pictures with rather poor resolution – a fishing expedition. The other kind, with higher resolution, zeroes in on things they have been alerted to and want to look at more closely.

Those Americans who favour signing arms control agreements have often faced the objection that for more than half the time it is not possible to monitor what is going on in the Soviet Union because of darkness (the Polar night) and cloud cover (very frequent in those latitudes). So how can one be sure one knows what is happening? Those wily Soviets will do things in the dark or when it is cloudy.

In the absence of photons from the sun, one must illuminate the object of one's picture with a different kind of electromagnetic illumination. One kind of radiation is the ordinary radar, but everyone has seen pictures of radar screens showing blips – there is something there, but one does not have any details about the shape and so on. The Synthetic Aperture Radar (SAR) takes care of the problem. SAR is a radar that can produce pictures of the terrain without visible light, with a resolution comparable to photographic resolution, so that one can see under cloud cover, through the leaves of trees, and in the dark. This is clearly a very important verification capability. In an ordinary radar, the resolution is proportional to the wavelengths of the electromagnetic radiation and is inversely proportional to the length of the antenna. The bigger the antenna, the better the picture one can take with the radar. But the wavelength of radar waves is so long that an antenna of ten, twenty, or even thirty metres is not going to improve the resolution significantly, and there is a limit to the length of antenna that is practical, even in space.

So synthetic aperture radar makes use of an ingenious technique. One puts a radar with an antenna on an aircraft or a satellite. While the radar is sending waves out, the plane or satellite carrying the antenna is moving. The radar wave comes back to the antenna, which has several dipoles, each of which receives the returns of the signals it has beamed out over a fixed period of time. The trick is to keep track of which dipole sends out which signals and receives them back once they have bounced off the object on the ground. If the signals received back can be stored while retaining both their size and their phase in proper order, then signals in each of the dipoles can be summed together with appropriate added phase shifts, namely the difference in the times each one has arrived, and that makes the antenna appear to the returning signals to be as long as the path the aircraft has travelled during the time the signals accumulated. The entire distance covered during that time now appears to the returning waves to be the length of the antenna. This is what enables SAR to produce photographic-quality resolution, since the distance the antenna has travelled can be many hundreds of metres.

For SAR to work properly, the antenna must know exactly where it is at any moment, and since the antenna may be on a plane that rises and pitches and changes velocity a little bit, that becomes very difficult. So there must be gyroscopes and accelerometers on the antenna to make sure it is always pointing in the right direction, and also to make sure that the right phase shifts are inserted into the signal. In the case of satellite-carried SAR one does not have these problems, of course, because a satellite moves much more smoothly than an aircraft. But one does need accelerometers to make sure that the phase shifts that one inserts are right.

Now what happens to the signals one receives on the antenna? One stores them, one sums them up, and then what one has is a series of electronic signals that have been produced by all the stored returns that have been added up on each dipole. Then one transforms the intensity, or amplitude, of the signals into intensity of light on a cathode-ray oscilloscope and one records it, generating a picture-like record of the landscape on either side of the aircraft path or the satellite path. This process has up to now involved recording everything on magnetic tape and then reconstructing it on Earth after that tape was returned, because it requires a lot of computational power. But now, with very small and powerful computers, this can be done on board the satellite. Therefore we can have SAR satellite radar pictures sent down to receiving centres on Earth very nearly in real time.

The Americans also make use of many other types of radar for verification purposes. They have a whole series of them around the perimeter of the Soviet Union to monitor activities connected with the testing of missiles or aircraft. They use two kinds of radar for this mission: ordinary radars, which just pick up the information that something is happening and send a signal without quite seeing or recognising the object, and 'over-the-horizon' (OTH) radar. Since radar beams propagate in a straight line, the beams from ordinary radars situated in Turkey, Pakistan, China and on ships in the Pacific would pass high above parts of the Soviet Union, beyond the curve of the earth. So there are places in the Soviet Union where the Americans cannot get an ordinary radar close enough to see what is happening on or near the ground. What they use then is the OTH radar, which bounces a beam of radar energy first off the surface of the sea and then off the ionosphere, so that the space over the Soviet Union is flooded with radar waves. Sending the radar waves from Cyprus or Finland or Great Britain and receiving them in Japan, one finds disturbances in the flow of energy, and the disturbances can be interpreted as a plane manoeuvring while being tested or as a missile in its flight that has not appeared above the horizon of the radars in Turkey or China. The OTH radars complement the other monitoring radars that surround the Soviet Union.

Another important category of event that it is desirable to be able to monitor is nuclear tests. The only nuclear tests currently permitted under the Limited Test Ban Treaty of 1963 are underground tests. To be absolutely certain first of all that they can tell if anybody is testing above the ground, the Americans have on satellites in outer space sensors of nuclear radiations (neutrons, x-rays, gamma rays, and of the nuclear electromagnetic pulse), so that they can detect whether the Soviets or anybody else are testing a nuclear device in or above the atmosphere. To detect underground tests, on the other hand, one must detect tremors in the ground. What the United States and the Soviet Union – and France and Great Britain and anybody else – now do when testing is dig a very deep tunnel several thousand feet underground, in which is put a nuclear explosive with the appropriate instrumentation. Then it is detonated and the yield and other nuclear effects are measured. When a nuclear explosive detonates underground, it releases an enormous amount of energy that creates a very strong shock wave that travels both within the crust and on the surface of the Earth exactly like an acoustical wave.

There are lots of other events that cause waves to travel like acoustical waves too: earthquakes, human pounding such as drilling and blasting for foundations of buildings, the pounding of oceans on shorelines, the motion of buildings and trees in the wind. The crust of the Earth is a very noisy place, and many of these activities generate acoustical waves that travel for long distances in the surface of the Earth and can be detected by devices called seismographs. There has always been concern that one may miss the waves coming from an explosion in the general hubbub if the waves from the nuclear detonation are very small, or, on the contrary, that if one makes one's seismometer very sensitive so as not to miss any waves coming from an explosion one will pick up hundreds of false alarms, things that may look like explosions but are not. This dilemma was eased by an ingenious way of arranging seismometers so that they would receive only the waves coming from one direction, dampening and attenuating waves from all other sources. That helped enormously, but it did not solve the problem of how to tell the difference between earthquakes and underground nuclear explosions. A partial solution to that problem was found in comparing the size and the ratio of the two kinds of waves generated by a nuclear explosion, one that travels on the surface of the Earth and one that travels inside the crust of the Earth, when the two waves are received at some other point on the Earth. The ratio of their amplitudes is different for nuclear explosions and earthquakes. But this method was not very effective for two reasons. First, one cannot use it to distinguish explosions of very low yield from earthquakes. And secondly, those who oppose a complete test ban treaty suggested that the Soviets might prepare a nuclear explosive for testing and then wait until an earthquake occurred in that region before triggering the explosion. The earthquake waves would then mask the waves generated by the explosion. That was an objection serious enough to give some pause to those who believe one must be able to detect even the smallest possible nuclear explosion.

Now a new and sophisticated technique has made it possible to distinguish tremors caused by earthquakes from those caused by nuclear explosions. Seismologists only very recently discovered that an explosion differs from an earthquake in that an explosion is a point source, and therefore most of its energy is going to go out in short waves of high frequency. If one tunes one's seismometers to listen only to the higher frequencies, say between 30 and 1000 Hz, there is no background noise to confuse them; nor is it possible to mistake earthquake tremors, which are at lower frequencies (1 to 10 Hz), for explosions. So scientists are now quite confident that they can both unambiguously discriminate between earthquakes and nuclear detonations and also detect the magnitude of underground nuclear tests of very, very low yields.

There is, of course, one problem. Short-wavelength sound, that is high-frequency waves, does not travel far in the Earth's crust. These waves are attenuated much faster than the long-wavelength low-frequency waves used for verification until recently. So if the Americans are to be absolutely sure that they can detect nuclear detonations on Soviet soil unambiguously, it will be necessary to have seismic stations on Soviet soil, near the potential detonation sites. The Soviet Union has already agreed to allow unmanned seismic stations on its soil, and scientists at Sandia National Laboratory have devised, tested and now have operating five such unmanned stations in the United States and Canada for practice and demonstration purposes. These stations communicate constantly by satellite relay with a central control facility in the United States, making them virtually tamper-proof. American scientists have already installed similar stations on Soviet soil and are monitoring them to see how they work. It must be noted that these scientists are sponsored by the Natural Resources Defense Council and funded by private foundations, and do not represent the US Government, which refused to adopt their effort. The last technical obstacle to an absolutely verifiable complete ban on the testing of nuclear explosives underground has, however, now fallen. It is indeed possible for us safely to ban all nuclear testing on the Earth. The one remaining barrier is political will.

There are of course many other means of monitoring acivities in the Soviet Union. But these three types of systems are emphasised here both because they are very important and because they give a measure of the sophistication that technology has made possible in monitoring for the purpose of verifying compliance with arms control agreements. Finally, then, let us give brief consideration to a few of the other things we can do, technically, to enhance our verification capabilities. Because we like to be able to look at things that are camouflaged or hidden or do not show in visible light, some satellites carry infra-red cameras and infra-red spectrometers, with which one can often tell what is being looked at even under these adverse conditions. Perhaps one spots a mound of material and one does not know what it is. With an infra-red spectrometer one may be able to tell whether it is a chemical mound, uranium, dirt, or garbage. It is very interesting technology to use when a satellite is passing over a factory in which one suspects something is going on. One looks at what is going into and out of the factory and one can examine the emissions from the chimneys; the chemical compositions of the materials going in and out can tell one a great deal about what the factory is doing.

Two kinds of electronic listening devices on satellites are also used for monitoring communications and for monitoring missile telemetry. These satellites have huge antennae, hundreds of metres long. Therefore they can receive very faint signals, and since most of the telephone communications in the Soviet Union are via microwave receivers and transmitters, the Americans can just listen to the microwave traffic. So with these devices they can listen both to signal traffic that has to do with military operations – the commander speaking to the sergeant, for example, over a field telephone – and to civilian telephone traffic. This is useful not only for hearing actual conversations, but for monitoring the volume, the number of communications. When an army division is stationed somewhere, there are very few exchanges between the division commander and the headquarters in Moscow, but when the division is being mobilised, there is a lot of traffic back and forth. By monitoring the density of traffic, one can tell a lot about a military operation.

There is also a different kind of listening device that listens for the signals that missiles send when they are being tested. If one is an engineer designing a missile, one wants certain information about what happens when the missile is tested. One wants to know how fast it is going, the rate at which fuel is being burned, how fast it accelerates, and whether the gyroscope and the accelerometers are working correctly. A missile under test carries sensors to measure all these things and an on-board radio to beam the information down to the engineers at the control centre. These signals are called telemetry. Telemetry is necessary in missile development because if something goes wrong and the missile crashes, one needs to know what happened so that the error can be corrected. So the Soviets receive telemetry signals from their missiles in flight – but so do the Americans. Thus by listening to their telemetry the Americans know in great detail how Soviet missiles work during testing. This is important information for the Americans to have, because the SALT II agreement allows modifications to missiles with quite specific limitations – a missile cannot be more than 5 per cent heavier, 5 per cent longer or wider, or carry more than ten re-entry vehicles. To verify that agreement, the Americans have got to be able to tell whether a missile differs in the specified parameters by more than 5 per cent, and that requires extremely sophisticated monitoring of the telemetry signals.

The Americans also like to know how things look when they pass overhead above their stations on the ground. For this they have very powerful optical telescopes situated in Hawaii that produce wonderful images of satellites. With them, they can see what a satellite is carrying, or even see a test missile's re-entry vehicle.

Now, despite all the foregoing assurances about how good the Americans are at the technologies of verification, it is true that there is always a measure of ambiguity. There are always some cases in which there is doubt as to whether the Soviets are doing something or not, and whether what they are doing is a violation of a treaty or not. The ambition of the technical community is to minimise this uncertainty. If, for example, one has a satellite that takes pictures that can only show a missile diffusely, one knows the missile is *there* but one does not know much else about it that would tell one whether it constitutes a violation – by how much it differs in size from the missile it might be replacing for instance. If the satellite picture has better resolution, that is, it produces a sharper picture of the missile, then the level of ambiguity goes down.

All the efforts to make better cameras and larger telecommunication antennae and bigger radars are efforts to limit ambiguity to insignificant levels, so that we can be confident of our means of verifying compliance. This fine tuning is not so important for military reasons, given the size of the current arsenals, but it is very important for political purposes. The American technical community has to be able to assure the political leadership that they see what the Soviets are doing in detail, in order to convince them that they can, without jeopardising national security, sign agreements to bring the arsenals down to the level where it will really be necessary to worry about verification of very small increments.

Part II
The Strategic Defense Initiative

9 Rendering Nuclear Weapons Impotent and Obsolete: The Origins of a Pipedream
David Carlton

INTRODUCTION

In the Presidential Campaign of 1976 President Gerald Ford in a crucial televised debate with Jimmy Carter indicated, in a reply to a question, that he considered Poland not to be a member of the Warsaw Pact. Of course, politicians being what they are, most members of his Administration would have had no moral objection to echoing their chief if he had asked them to do so. But, as luck or ill-luck had it, they were on this occasion spared from having to make idiots of themselves in public. For Ford's blunder was so crass and so easily demonstrable that he had no rational alternative but to admit his error. On 23 March 1983 President Ronald Reagan, in a celebrated television address, also revealed his fallibility when he said the following:

> What if free people could live secure in the knowledge that their security did not rest upon the threat of instant US retaliation to deter a Soviet attack, that we could intercept and destroy strategic ballistic missiles before they reached our own soil and that of our allies? ...
> I call upon the scientific community in our country, those who gave us nuclear weapons, to turn their great talents now to the cause of mankind and world peace, to give us the means of rendering these nuclear weapons impotent and obsolete.[1]

In Reagan's case, in contrast to that of Ford, however, his blunder was only self-evident to experts rather than to the American nation as a whole. Accordingly all members of his Administration were predictably required to endorse or at any rate refrain from contradicting the line of their chief. All appear to have been prepared to comply – with one notable and honourable exception. The exception was Richard DeLauer, then Under Secretary of Defense for Engineering. In May 1983 he pointed out that the proposed defensive system could not be achieved in the absence of Soviet co-operation. 'With uncontrolled proliferation' of Soviet warheads, he bluntly stated, 'no defensive system will work'.[2] And in the summer of 1983 he said 'There's no way an enemy can't overwhelm your defenses if he wants to badly enough. It makes a lot of difference in what we do if we have to defend against 1000 RVs [re-entry vehicles] or 10 000'.[3] He soon found himself out of office and has subsequently underlined in public his astonishment at the content of Reagan's speech.

The fact is that no significant number of independent scientists, whether for or against deploying limited strategic defences, have dissented from DeLauer's judgement. And many have also argued that even if the Soviets exercised restraint in producing further nuclear warheads, no US defensive deployments could ever guarantee 100 per cent protection against Intercontinental Ballistic Missiles (ICBMs). Moreover, there are other means of delivering nuclear weapons which Reagan's Strategic Defense Initiative (SDI) speech effectively ignored. Air-breathing cruise missiles present an obvious problem. And even if these could be neutralised by a non-space-based defensive system there would still be the 'suitcase bomb' to worry about: not only the Soviet Union but many other states might in the future succeeed in assembling a nuclear weapon in the United States simply by smuggling in the components. How, then, can nuclear weapons possibly be rendered impotent and obsolete?

In the course of a visit to Washington in 1986 the author asked an expert close to the Reagan Administration to comment on an unattributable basis on these arguments. He made no attempt to conceal his own belief that Reagan had indeed offered his nation a utopian vision that was simply unattainable. But he added that a 'lawyer's argument' might be made that the President had not really meant to hold out the hope that the United States could by its own unaided efforts achieve 100 per cent protection against nuclear attack. What he might have had in mind, according to this argument, was merely to create powerful if imperfect defences which could then be rendered perfect as a result of a subsequent nuclear disarmament agreement negotiated with the Soviet Union (and maybe other nuclear weapon states).[4] I agreed that the wording of his speech (on a strained interpretation) might just be held to be compatible with this version. But my rejoinder was to point out that the President had not subsequently explained in clear language that this was what he had meant and he had had numerous opportunities to do so. Moreover, Caspar Weinberger, his Secretary of Defense, stated on 27 March 1983:

> The defensive systems the President is talking about are not designed to be partial. What we want to try to get is a system which will develop a defense that is thoroughly reliable and total ... I don't see any reason why that can't be done.[5]

Confronted with this quotation my well-connected source could only offer the comment that the President might not have been best served by his over-zealous Defense Secretary! Perhaps not. But the fact remains that Reagan has not repudiated Weinberger's words; and, whether dishonestly or not, has permitted an unattainable utopian vision to confuse the only serious debate, namely the one about whether *limited* strategic defences are desirable.

In the remainder of this paper it is proposed to ask why Reagan saw fit to introduce this utopian note into his speech of 23 March 1983. Did he get the idea from any pro-ABM advocates or pressure group? Or did he bring the idea into the White House as a result of some earlier personal experience as Governor of California or as a presidential candidate? And, above all, there is the question of the scientific and technological advice he received as to the feasibility of rendering nuclear weapons impotent and obsolete. Did he seek such advice? If so, what was its nature? And did he ignore any such advice?

It remains to be acknowledged, by way of introduction, that any historian considering such a recent development faces obvious problems. But such is the open nature of American society and government that it is already possible to offer at least tentative answers to some of the foregoing questions.

REAGAN AS GOVERNOR AND PRESIDENTIAL CANDIDATE

Our first task is to try to decide whether Reagan brought his utopian vision with him into the White House in 1981 as a result of some earlier personal experience. Those who speculate that this could have been the case point to two episodes that conceivably could have been important.

The first episode occurred in 1966 shortly after he became Governor of California. He accepted an invitation to visit the weapons laboratory at Livermore, California, whose chief was the hard-line nuclear physicist Dr Edward Teller. According to Teller's own account:

> He [Reagan] listened carefully; not to a highly technical presentation, but to one that must have contained a host of completely novel ideas. He asked maybe ten or twelve questions which clearly showed that he followed – that he comprehended. Indeed, he was the only Governor who ever visited our laboratory.[6]

As is well known, Teller is opposed to Mutual Assured Destruction (MAD) and has long favoured research on various defensive capabilities. Could it be, then, that he became a guru for Reagan and that herein lies an explanation for the speech of 23 March 1983? It is indeed possible that Teller had much to do with Reagan's acceptance of the alleged bankruptcy of a strategy based on total mutual vulnerability between the superpowers. But this does not explain the utopian reference with which we are here concerned. For Teller appears never to have had any illusions of that kind. And in 1985 he categorically stated in an interview with the BBC: 'They say a complete defence is impossible. *Of course* it is impossible.'[7]

A second episode to which speculative attention has been paid concerns Reagan's visit to the North American Aerospace Defense Command (NORAD) while he was campaigning to become Republican presidential candidate. He was much struck by the implication of total US vulnerability to Soviet ICBMs which he appears to have fully grasped for the first time. He is said to have drawn anguished analogies with gunfighters in Western films.[8] He unburdened himself to a journalist, Robert Sheer of the *Los Angeles Times*, while on the campaigning trail in 1980:

> Norad is an amazing place – that's out in Colorado, you know, under the mountain there. They actually are tracking several thousand objects in space, meaning satellites of ours and everyone else's, even down to the point that they are tracking a glove lost by

an astronaut that is still circling the earth up there. I think the thing that struck me was the irony that here, with this great technology of ours, we can do all of this yet we cannot stop any of the weapons that are coming at us. I don't think there's been a time in history when there wasn't a defense against some kind of thrust, even back in the old-fashioned days when we had coast artillery that would stop invading ships if they came.[9]

But Sheer's account of the subsequent conversation, already in print *before* the SDI speech, has Reagan musing on the need for a US civil defence programme of the kind supposedly already possessed by the Soviet Union.[10] He did not, however, speak of the possibility of creating leak-proof shields over the two superpowers. It seems reasonable to conclude, therefore, that Reagan did *not* bring his utopian plan into the White House in 1981 as a result of the trauma caused by his visit to NORAD – even though the concerns about US vulnerability that led to it were clearly already present.

One other aspect of Reagan's pre-Presidential experience merits attention. It is that in the matter of national security issues he had a long-standing guru noted for his strong opinions but not generally greatly respected in the strategic studies community. This was Laurence Beilenson, a Californian lawyer who had advised the Screen Actors Guild when Reagan was its anti-Communist President in the immediate postwar years. He is author of a book entitled *The Treaty Trap* which Reagan commended to West Point cadets in May 1981. Its general thesis is that arms control agreements with the Soviets are futile. But while Beilenson favoured a US abandonment of the ABM Treaty of 1972, he does not appear to have contended that nuclear weapons can simply be rendered impotent as threats to populations by defensive technology. His outlook is summarised in an article he co-authored in January 1982 for the *New York Times Magazine*.

[A new nuclear strategy] will call for developing offensive weapons in great quantities, and exploiting mobility, concealment and dispersion to make them invulnerable to any conceivable nuclear strike. It will call for removing the shackles placed by the strategic arms treaty of 1972 on the development of antimissile weapons capable of protecting our population and economy. It will call for restoring of our emaciated air defense against bombers so as to meet an impending Soviet threat in that category of weapons. And it will require a program, following the Swiss example, for providing our cities with civil defense shelters, which can save enormous numbers of American lives ...[11]

The very fact that Beilenson envisaged the need for civil defence shelters and increased US offensive forces suggests that he did not foresee at this stage the creation of leak-proof shields over either of the superpowers. So Beilenson, however influential he may once have been, does not appear to have been the Svengali behind the utopian vision of the President's speech of March 1983. In short, the utopianism was almost certainly a product of developments in his thinking *after* he entered the White House.

THE ROLE OF US PRESSURE GROUPS

When Reagan entered the White House several prominent conservative pressure groups naturally assumed that their years in the wilderness were over and that they would soon see their cherished schemes translated into action. They had in fact more reason than similar groups in the past to travel hopefully. For Reagan and his immediate entourage appear to have been the most ideologically-motivated team to move into the Presidency in modern times.

In practice, however, the zealots have had their disappointments, not least in matters relating to defence and foreign policy. For entrenched bureaucratic interests in the Department of Defense, at the State Department and even at the Central Intelligence Agency have ensured a fair amount of continuity with the Jimmy Carter years. Hence one has heard calls to 'allow Reagan to be Reagan' and jibes to the effect that Alexander Haig and George Shultz have presided over the People's Republic of Foggy Bottom. Yet the zealots have not found the experience of the Reagan Presidency entirely negative. In short, *some* policies have changed since 1980. Moreover, large numbers of the personnel of the various pressure groups have been given positions of power and influence in or on the edges of the Administration and in some cases they themselves have played a part in accepting policies they disapproved of when in opposition. In the light of this general setting, let us now consider how the presssure groups and their leading personalities have conducted themselves in the matter of Reagan's utopian vision for rendering nuclear weapons impotent and obsolete. Did any of them sponsor the idea before or after Reagan came to power and how did they in the event react to his SDI speech?

The most important conservative pressure group concerned exclusively with national security issues in the pre-Reagan years was the Committee on the Present Danger, founded in 1976. Its acknowledged leader was Paul Nitze, an outstanding public servant since the days of President Harry S. Truman (to whom he had presented the famous NSC 68 analysis urging an active policy for the containment of international communism). Others involved included Eugene Rostow, Richard Perle, Edward Rowny, Fred C. Ikle, Richard Allen, Richard Pipes, William Casey and Jeane Kirkpatrick (all to become members at varying levels of seniority in the Reagan Administration when it was eventually formed). In opposition they undoubtedly helped to create a climate favouring robust approaches to national security policy; and in office they were usually to be found on the 'hawkish' side of the numerous debates within the Administration. What cannot be claimed, however, is that the Committee or any of its prominent personalities canvassed in opposition the idea of trying to render nuclear weapons 'impotent and obsolete'. Essentially they seem to have favoured a major US nuclear arms build-up to close the alleged window of vulnerability but with no particular collective bias in favour of defensive as distinct from offensive weapons. And in office they appear to have accepted a lead from Reagan in the matter of the SDI rather than to have been responsible for pushing him in that direction. Moreover most have been inclined in supporting the SDI to emphasise its medium-term implications rather than the long-term utopian goal with which we are here concerned.

A second conservative grouping was The National Institute for Public Policy based at Fairfax, Virginia. Its leading figures were (and are) Colin S. Gray and Keith Payne. This institute has long been associated with the hostility to the Anti-ballistic Missile (ABM) Treaty of 1972 and undoubtedly welcomed Reagan's SDI speech. Their support for the President, however, also seems to have been based on the entirely reasonable belief that the effect of his initiative would not be the establishment of leak-proof nuclear shields over the two superpowers but would rather be to create defences for hard-point targets, that is the American ICBMs, and maybe also provide some *limited* protection for the general population.

Gray and Payne, in their various writings before and after March 1983, have revealed great and consistent concern for maintaining and enhancing 'extended deterrence', that is the US guarantee of the security of Western Europe. To them the threat of a possible first use of nuclear weapons by the United States is a *sine qua non* for the maintenance of the credibility of such guarantees: and they even foresee circumstances in which the United States could prevail in a nuclear war. Accordingly, for example, Gray was a severe critic of the proposal for a NATO no-first-use declaration advanced by McGeorge Bundy, George F. Kennan, Robert S. McNamara, and Gerard Smith.[12] Gray wrote of this idea in 1982: 'Conflict in Europe must always be conducted in the shadow of nuclear weapons, no matter what NATO's declaratory policy may be.'[13] We may surmise, therefore, that Gray believes it to be neither possible nor desirable that Reagan's utopian vision should become a reality.

Payne, too, is in no way to be seen as an advocate of rendering nuclear weapons impotent and obsolete. In 1983, for example, he wrote an article urging revision of the ABM Treaty. But his aim was to see defences that would make ICBMs less vulnerable and afford a degree of population protection. He specifically added that 'this is not to argue that an impenetrable area defense system is now, or ever will be feasible'.[14]

The National Institute for Public Policy is thus clearly not to be held responsible for in any way contributing to Reagan's move towards utopianism. Indeed, we may conclude that this particular aspect of his SDI speech runs strongly counter to the general strategic approach of that institute. The National Institute for Public Policy is not noted, however, for having had any single-minded concern with promoting space-based nuclear defences. The organisation which has that reputation is High Frontier. So it may be particularly appropriate to examine its origins and outlook. It is in reality the creation of one possibly obsessive individual, namely, Daniel O. Graham, a retired Lieutenant-General and former Head of the Defense Intelligence Agency. He has long believed that the Soviets are determined to take the arms race into space and believes that the United States can and must do the same. He is, moreover, extremely optimistic about the technological feasibility of creating quite impressive space-based defences in the immediate future.

Graham launched his personal crusade for space defences while the Republicans were still in opposition and found some sympathetic listeners at the Heritage Foundation, the prominent Washington-based conservative Think Tank. Soon after Reagan's Inauguration, a panel was established, with Heritage Foundation funding, to attempt to draw up precise recommendations for the new Administration. Much to

Graham's chagrin, however, the panel came to be dominated by supporters of Teller. In particular, Karl R. Bendetsen emerged as its leading figure. Another key personality was Lowell J. Wood, a close associate of Teller and a principal figure in the Hertz Foundation. The result was a policy split which led to Graham forming his own organisation, namely the Washington-based High Frontier.

The split, however, was not about whether perfect defences could be established. Rather the dispute was about the type of space-based defence that should be recommended to the Administration and the likely timescale involved. Graham thought rapid moves could be made in the direction of selecting 'off-the-shelf' technology. Teller's supporters favoured an emphasis on longer-term research, believing that Graham's short-cut would be so technologically flawed as to be potentially useless for any serious defensive purpose.

Though Graham had a meeting with Reagan and subsequently received a friendly letter from him in June 1983 commending him for 'the important work that you and your colleagues have done to prepare the way for a more secure America',[15] it would appear that he had much less influence than the Heritage-based majority who supported Teller. And Teller personally had a number of meetings with the President which may indeed have been decisive in shaping the longer-term emphasis on research that has been the main practical outcome so far of the SDI speech.

Graham, however, continues to fight his corner and also claims to be a strong supporter of SDI in principle. For our purposes, however, it is important to note that neither before nor after Reagan's SDI speech did Graham raise hopes in the mind of the President or anyone else that leak-proof shields could be established. In 1983 he published *We Must Defend America and Put an End to MADness* in which these words appear:

> If effective strategic defense is defined as an impenetrable shield through which no nuclear weapons could penetrate, there will be no defense. Obviously, no defense in history has ever been perfect ... High Frontier rejected absolutist demands on strategic defense and looked instead for defensive systems, and programs which could add significantly to the US deterrent to nuclear war.[16]

This work was, however, written before the President's SDI speech.[17] How, then, did Graham react to its utopian element? With admirable consistency he has not overnight abandoned his former approach.

Instead, he has been able to support Reagan by seeing fit to suppose that 100 per cent defence was not envisaged in the SDI speech. For example, on 16 July 1986 he wrote as follows to a number of US legislators:

> The notion that only 100% perfect defenses can be considered protection for population is a false premise cultivated by the anti-SDI lobby and trumpeted in the media. It is a polemical device for undermining broad popular and political support for the defense systems. It allows anti-SDI spokesmen to support continuation of adherence to the MAD doctrine without saying so.
> Another false impression often heard of late is that the President originally called for a 'leakproof umbrella', but has changed his mind and now wants merely to protect missiles. Purveyors of this idea would have us believe that when General [James] Abrahamson, the SDIO [Strategic Defense Initiative Organisation] Director, states that we cannot achieve a perfect defense, or when Richard Perle says that we will start with defenses that reinforce deterrence more than protect population, they are at odds with Secretary Weinberger who stresses the goal of defending the people.
> This is all quite erroneous. President Reagan never called for perfection in strategic defenses, and neither has anyone else who is *for* SDI. Abrahamson, Perle, Weinberger all know, and have often stated, that the defenses will progress in stages, and that early stages will be more effective in the deterrent role than in the population role, but that the end goal of SDI is effective population protection – not perfect, but effective.[18]

Readers will realise that the present writer does not think that either Reagan or Weinberger has in fact taken the line attributed to them by Graham. But for our present purposes what is important is that Graham and High Frontier cannot possibly be held even partially responsible for the call to render nuclear weapons impotent and obsolete.

The majority group operating under Heritage Foundation auspices seems likewise to have been uninvolved in utopianism. For, as we have already seen, their principal inspirer, Teller, flatly stated to the BBC in 1985 that 'complete defence is impossible'.[19] In short, they have differed from Graham but not on this aspect of the matter. As for the Heritage Foundation itself, it was naturally in the vanguard of those anxious to see the abandonment of the constraints on defence enshrined in the ABM Treaty. But nothing in many pre-1983 Heritage Foundation publications dealing with this theme gave any indication that utopian aspirations were involved. And since 1983 the utopian issue has usually been glossed over – doubtless to avoid giving the appearance of differing from Reagan.

As well as these various pressure groups there were many individual strategic analysts arguing in the late 1970s and early 1980s in favour of a move towards nuclear defences in one form or another. The present writer has accordingly explored this literature on a quite extensive scale. But no article or book advancing the utopian goal embraced by Reagan has come to light. Overwhelmingly, the emphasis was on matching Soviet efforts; on protecting ICBMs; or on acquiring *limited* population defences for a variety of reasons including the possibility of countering accidental, catalytic or Nth power strikes.[20] It seems fair to conclude, therefore, that in the quest for the origins of Reagan's utopian vision, we must look to the inner sanctums of his Administration.

THE JOINT CHIEFS, THE NATIONAL SECURITY COUNCIL, THE CHIEF SCIENTIFIC ADVISER AND THE PRESIDENT

Any attempt to explain what happened in the White House in the period before March 1983 is bound to be tentative in character. For none of those centrally involved has so far written memoirs or published diaries. And two of the principals, the President himself and Robert McFarlane, have given only very sketchy press briefings on the matter. So we are very much dependent on one major source, namely, the then Presidential Chief Scientific Adviser George A. Keyworth II. And even Keyworth, in interviews with better-known US newspapers, has understandably shown an inclination to be less than totally candid.

I have not myself had an opportunity to meet Keyworth. But I was given a most helpful hint by one who was in a position to know Keyworth's side of the story. He pointed me in the direction of an article in a relatively obscure American newspaper, the *Philadelphia Inquirer*, and he gave me to understand that the revelations therein could be taken to be reasonably accurate. The journalist responsible for the article, Frank Greve, had had an interview with Keyworth who had apparently seen fit to be unusually forthcoming.[21] What follows is based partly on Greve's article, though some details have been independently confirmed by various 'insiders'.

The first aspect to consider is the role of the Joint Chiefs of Staff. Reagan's speech of 23 March 1983 contained this passage:

> Wouldn't it be better to save lives rather than avenge them? Are we not capable of demonstrating our peaceful intentions by applying all our abilities and all our ingenuity to achieving a truly lasting stability? I think we are. Indeed we must.
>
> After careful consideration with my advisers, including the Joint Chiefs of Staff, I believe there is a way. Let me share with you a vision of the future which offers hope.[22]

That the Joint Chiefs were in principle interested in intensifying the exploration of the possibilities for strategic defences is clear. Like many experts, they cannot have been happy with the way in which the strategic stability expected to result from the ABM Treaty of 1972 had not materialised as a result of the unexpected emergence of the threat posed to the American ICBM force by the vast array of Soviet MIRVed missiles. And they also could have been in no doubt that the Soviets had long been intensively involved in researching into defensive technology. But it is not clear, as Reagan implied, that they were properly consulted about his famous speech or that it reflected their own thinking. Greve wrote on the basis of his interviewing:

> 'We recognized that SDI was not a panacea' against nuclear threats of all kinds, said retired Army General John W. Vesssey Jr, then chairman of the Joint Chiefs. In fact, the Joint Chiefs had urged the President to consider strategic defense, but they had no specific plan in mind, simply considering it a concept worth careful study.[23]

As for presentation, they might well have preferred to 'sell' the matter of spending more on defensive research in the traditional 'action–reaction' way, that is to have called it not a Strategic Defense Initiative but a Strategic Defense Response – given what was known of intensifying Soviet efforts. Moreover, US research on defensive technology had actually been increased during Carter's time – so a further increase could have been presented more in terms of continuity than of strategic revolution. But the fact is that Reagan had his own ideas on presentation and in no way could the Joint Chiefs be said to have been responsible for this. In particular, the utopian aspect, which is our main concern in the present chapter, was not something to which the Joint Chiefs, with the possible exception of Admiral James Watkins who had had some prior meetings with McFarlane, appear to have been asked to give any serious and detailed consideration. The actual text of the SDI speech, according to Greve, was sent to them a mere two days before delivery.[24] It thus need not surprise us that the Joint Chiefs have not subsequently revealed any marked faith in the technological feasibility or even desirability of rendering nuclear weapons impotent and obsolete.

If the Joint Chiefs were presented with something like a *fait accompli* the same went for other key personnel. According to Greve, Secretary of State Shultz received two days' notice, while Ikle and DeLauer at the Pentagon received a mere nine hours.[25]

What, then, about the role of Chief Scientific Adviser Keyworth? He had been recommended to the President by Teller and was genuinely supportive of the idea of exploring strategic defensive possibilities. But he appears to have had serious doubts about the way in which Reagan's SDI speech was planned and launched. According to Greve, he received only five days' notice of the President's broad intentions and ' "he might have gotten less" according to a National Security Council (NSC) member, "had not we asked ourselves, 'How can the President go on the tube directing a major high-technology initiative and tell his scientific adviser nothing?' " '[26] Greve's account of Keyworth's role continued:

> His immediate reaction to the Star Wars idea, was, 'Give me time. It's big. Give me time,' Keyworth said in a recent interview.
> 'Most people saw the speech very close to the time of delivery and most – myself included, incidentally, – had the same reaction: "My God, let's think about this some more. Let's think about the implications for the allies. Let's think about what the Soviets are going to think. Let's think about what the scientists are going to think. Let's think about the command and control problems." '[27]

Keyworth's pleas for more time for exploration and preparation were, however, rejected. Reagan evidently believed, probably correctly, that a top-down lead was the only way to prevent the project being stymied by existing vested interests in the great bureaucracies of State and Defense, not to mention NATO. Whether his top-down lead needed to be quite so underprepared is of course another matter.

Reagan in fact made the decision on the final contents of his speech with an absolute minimum of expert counselling. Perhaps a few NSC staff, in particular McFarlane, gave some advice on the possible political impact, though they may have been more interested in seizing the 'moral high ground' from the Freeze Movement and the American Roman Catholic Bishops than in considering the impact on broad Western security concerns. But on the scientific and technological side almost nothing of a detailed nature seems to have been put to the President in the final and vital drafting stage. True, Reagan at one point asked Keyworth to prepare a text for his proposed speech. But he found the result too bland. The final draft, including the utopian passages, appears, then, to have been his own work – possibly assisted by a handful of NSC cronies who may have proposed a few minor amendments to take minimal account of last-minute reactions from those in the Administration hitherto kept in the dark. The competence of the NSC staff to be the sole guides to the President on the final form of so important a speech is, to say the least, not self-evident. But this point may need no underlining in the light of the disgracing of the NSC in the Iranian affair of 1986–7.

Keyworth did not resign over the SDI speech – though he quit later. For, as a protégé of Teller, he was, as stated, sympathetic to the principle of exploring defensive possibilities. But, like many others with that approach, he clearly wished that the matter had been handled differently.

One detects something of the same ambivalence in the work of the two study groups subsequently established by Reagan to explore some of the detailed implications of his speech. In particular, both groups, headed respectively by James C. Fletcher and Fred S. Hoffman, obviously had difficulty in taking entirely seriously the utopian aspects of the President's speech but loyally sought to gloss over this fact. Presumably most enthusiasts for strategic defences hope that the utopianism will be forgotten when the President leaves office but that the essentials of the SDI research programme will endure. In short, they hope that Reagan's cavalier approach to technological possibilities will prove in the end to have been of no lasting importance.

CONCLUSION

How important in fact was Reagan's lurch into utopianism? At this point only a tentative answer can be offered. But it does indeed seem possible that after an initial flurry it has largely ceased to matter. First, we may ask whether the utopianism made any difference to US domestic politics. Assuming a prime motive was to seize the 'moral high ground', was it successful in so doing? Certainly, the SDI vision had a strong appeal for many Americans. However, the present writer holds the somewhat unfashionable view that no decisive political advantage was gained overall. Most of those Americans who were impressed by the Freeze Movement and/or the Roman Catholic Bishops' Letter may well remain sympathetic to their ideas. In any case, they are unlikely, in the present writer's opinion, to have been converted in any large numbers, on the basis of one ill-prepared speech, to support for strategic defences. How, then, is one to account for the fading of the Freeze Movement? For the answer one should probably look at the history of similar mass movements in the United States and other Western countries, not least Great Britain and West Germany. The fact is that all such movements find it hard to maintain momentum. Vigorous, some may say fashionable, for a couple of years, they then tend to go into periods of hibernation as particular reasons sparking intense activity lose their immediacy. Reagan's SDI vision did allow him to take the political offensive in one of the few areas where he had previously been vulnerable – presenting alternatives to a nuclear arms race – and could therefore have hastened the decline of the Freeze Movement. However, his landslide victory in the 1984 Presidential Election was, we can now see, heavily overdetermined. His SDI line, in contrast to Walter Mondale's restrained and qualified endorsement of the nuclear freeze idea, would seem to have been at best of only marginal significance. This opinion is bolstered by examining the results of the Congressional Elections of 1986 when Reagan's attempt to use SDI to boost the chances of Republican candidates was unsurprisingly of no avail in circumstances when a big swing to the Democrats was also overdetermined for reasons largely unconnected with the arms race.

What, then, about the effect of Reagan's utopianism in creating tensions with the West European allies – sometimes seen as the most important result of his speech? To be sure, the initial reaction in NATO was one of incredulity and hostility. Various public attacks, in code or otherwise, were made by West European leaders and we may guess that behind closed doors fiercer rebukes were issued. Among West European strategic studies experts, too, strong disapproval was often expressed with vigour and indignation. Consider, for example, the case of the International Institute for Strategic Studies. It is said to have heard somewhat acrimonious exchanges in the course of its annual conference at Avignon, France, in September 1984 – something quite unusual in that citadel of Western 'establishment' defence thinking. And in its first quarter-century of existence few if any papers appeared under its auspices that were so unrestrainedly critical of the leader of the Western World as was that presented at Avignon by Lawrence Freedman, Professor of War Studies at King's College, London. In a memorable passage he delivered this severe verdict:

> President Reagan's speech of March 1983 may have launched a thousand research projects but it did not launch a strategic revolution. He was offering a false prospect of invulnerability, an illusion that he had some bold escape plan from the harsh realities of the nuclear age. This would have quickly been dismissed as the ramblings of a sentimental idealist had he not been President of the United States and had he not backed up this vision with the promise of a technical solution that was soon to be found wanting.[28]

Yet by Reagan's second term most West European leaders and strategic analysts had calmed down. For the realisation seems gradually to have dawned in Europe that mere words by Reagan could not alter technological realities. There will be no leak-proof shields over the superpowers. And thus 'extended deterrence' is not likely to lose whatever credibility it has – at any rate not on account of the utopianism in the SDI speech. Likewise the ability of the British and the French to deliver 'last resort' nuclear strikes on the Soviet Union is not about to disappear. True, Reagan has more than once caused further alarm in London and Paris by offering with droll consistency to share the US defensive capability with the Soviets. Yet as perfect defences are not what would be shared (if ever so unlikely a deal turned into reality), the two West European nuclear weapons states, which are both in the process of greatly strengthening their firepower, are probably in no real danger of losing the capacity to inflict unacceptable damage on the Soviet Union. That is not to say that the West Europeans are not justified in holding strong views about the merits and demerits of developing partial defences and of moving away from unqualified Mutual Assured Destruction. But they are arguments that do not relate to any totally transformed strategic environment in the foreseeable future.

There has, in short, been a gradual recognition throughout the West that utopianism in Reagan's mouth is still utopianism. After all, nearly every Western Leader for more than a quarter of a century has paid lip service in company with the Soviets to the idea of General and Complete Disarmament. And literally hundreds of diplomats have wasted thousands of hours in posturing at Geneva and New York in support of this unattainable objective.[29] Yet none of this has caused the slightest alarm to supporters of 'extended deterrence' or of West European independent nuclear capabilities. Probably the reason that many West Europeans reacted differently in the case of Reagan's speech is that they sensed that he might actually have meant what he said. But second thoughts seem to have led to the realisation that technological realities are not affected even if he did and does. The way is thus now clear for the only serious debate that has ever been relevant in this area, namely whether *limited* strategic defences are worth pursuing.[30]

Notes

1. The full text of Reagan's speech is conveniently accesssible in Office of Technology Assessment, *Strategic Defenses: Ballistic Missiles Defense Technologies; Anti-Satellite Weapons, Countermeasures and Arms Control: Two Reports by the OTA* (Princeton, New Jersey, 1986) Part One, pp. 297–8.
2. Quoted in Strobe Talbott, *Deadly Gambits: The Reagan Administration and the Stalemate in Nuclear Arms Control* (New York, 1985 ed.) p. 318.
3. Quoted in Lawrence Freedman, 'The "Star Wars" Debate: The Western Alliance and Strategic Defence', in International Institute for Strategic Studies, *New Technologies and Western Security Policy*, Adelphi Paper, no. 199 (London, 1985) p. 49, n. 50.
4. This line of argument, if Reagan actually believes it, is surprisingly close to that of Jonathan Schell, *The Abolition* (New York, 1984).
5. Quoted in Freedman, 'The "Star Wars" Debate', p. 37.
6. Quoted in Michael Charlton, *The Star Wars History: From Deterrence to Defence: The American Strategic Debate* (London, 1986) p. 95.
7. Ibid, p. 111.
8. Frank Greve, 'Out of the Blue: How "Star Wars" was Proposed', *The Philadelphia Inquirer*, 17 November 1985.
9. Robert Sheer, *With Enough Shovels: Reagan, Bush and Nuclear War* (New York, 1982) p. 104.
10. Ibid, pp. 105–7.
11. Laurence W. Beilenson and Samuel T. Cohen, 'A New Nuclear Strategy', *New York Times Magazine*, 24 January 1982, quoted in Sheer, *With Enough Shovels*, pp. 180, n. 86.
12. McGeorge Bundy, George F. Kennan, Robert S. McNamara and

Gerard Smith, 'Nuclear Weapons and the Atlantic Alliance', *Foreign Affairs*, vol. 60, no. 4 (1981–2) pp. 753–68.
13. Colin S. Gray, 'NATO's Nuclear Dilemma', *Policy Review*, no. 22 (Fall 1982) p. 109.
14. Keith Payne, 'Should the ABM Treaty be Revised?', *Comparative Strategy*, vol. 4, no. 1 (1983) pp. 1–20, esp. p. 10.
15. Ronald Reagan to Daniel O. Graham, 3 June 1983, quoted in Daniel O. Graham, *High Frontier* (New York, 1983).
16. Daniel O. Graham, *We Must Defend America and Put and End to MADness* (Chicago, 1983) pp. 47–8.
17. Interview with Daniel O. Graham, 17 July 1986.
18. Daniel O. Graham to various US legislators, 16 July 1986. I am most grateful to General Graham for making this letter available to me.
19. See note 7 above.
20. See, for example, numerous articles in a special issue of *The Washington Quarterly* entitled 'ABM revisited: Promise or Peril'. This resulted from the assembling of nine experts at the Center for Strategic and International Studies in Washington (*Washington Quarterly*, vol. 4, no. 4, 1981).
21. Greve, 'Out of the Blue'.
22. Office of Technology Assessment, *Strategic Defenses*, p. 197.
23. Greve, 'Out of the Blue'.
24. Ibid.
25. Ibid.
26. Ibid.
27. Ibid.
28. Freedman, 'The "Star Wars" Debate', p. 47.
29. See David Carlton 'International Systemic Features Inhibiting Disarmament and Arms Control', in David Carlton and Carlo Schaerf (eds), *Reassessing Arms Control* (London, 1985) pp. 28–35.
30. I am grateful to the Faculty of Technology at the Open University, of which I was then a member, for awarding me a travel grant that allowed me to carry out research and interviews for this chapter in Washington in the summer of 1986. My thanks are due to the following experts in the United States who granted me interviews either in person or on the telephone: Daniel O. Graham, Keith Payne, Jack Mendelsohn of the Arms Control Association, Robert L. Schuettinger and several persons who preferred not to be identified. None bears of course any responsibility for the conclusions I have reached. This chapter just appeared in Margaret Blunden and Owen Greene (eds). *Science and Mythology in the Making of Defence Policy*, published by Brasseys, London; and I am grateful for permission to republish here. I also wish to thank the editors of the volume for helpful suggestions, and the same applies to numerous ISODARCO participants.

10 SDI and the NATO Allies
Robert d'A. Henderson

INTRODUCTION

In his March 1983 nationally-televised speech, President Ronald Reagan proposed a 'Strategic Defense Initiative' (SDI) to research advance technologies which would provide 'the means of rendering nuclear weapons impotent and obsolete'. Such a long-term research and development programme would be 'consistent with our [Amercian] obligations of the ABM treaty and recognizing the need for closer consultation with our allies'.[1] His vision was to develop a high-technology defensive shield for 'our own soil or that of our allies' against Soviet strategic ballistic missiles armed with nuclear warheads – what has since come to be known as his 'Star Wars' proposal. Six days later in a press conference Reagan even hinted at sharing the emergent technology with the Soviet Union once it had been developed.[2]

It was proposed that the United States government would allocate US$26 billion over an initial five-year period for research into functional applications of 'emerging technologies'. If found to be successful, these technologies were to be used for developing a multi-layered ballistic missile defence (BMD) which could include space-based 'strategic defences'. But the resultant SDI programme with its accompanying promise of 'windfall' research funding has played havoc with America's alliance partners, partly owing to its undermining of NATO strategic doctrine and partly to American–allied clashes over SDI contracts and commercial rights.

ALLIED REACTION TO THE SDI PROPOSAL

From the initial SDI speech until the end of 1984, the Reagan

Administration argued that a SDI system would be an alternative to continued Western reliance upon nuclear deterrence which Reagan himself characterised as 'immoral'. This period of projecting SDI as an alternative to nuclear deterrence has come to be known as 'Star Wars I'. Although this argument stole part of the moral high ground from the American 'nuclear freeze' movement as well as the European peace movements, the initial reaction from European governments was of dismay. Such a change of alliance doctrine would undermine the already tenuous political consensus maintained by a number of allied governments in favour of the agreed-upon policy of nuclear deterrence. Their distress was not lessened by Reagan's blatant lack of alliance consultation prior to his SDI announcement. The political fall-out in Europe was sufficiently severe to prompt Reagan's staunchest alliance supporter, British Prime Minister Margaret Thatcher, initially to offer no public endorsement. Even the United States' northern neighbour Canada was hesitant to support the SDI proposal.

Was Reagan so naive as to suppose that such a massive research effort to create a defence shield would *not* be perceived by the Soviet leadership as threatening: a 'strategic shield' behind which to have the means to launch a pre-emptive 'strategic first strike'? Could NATO actually transform its doctrinal reliance on assured nuclear destruction into that of a technologically 'assured' area defence doctrine and, if so, could it do it without creating a period of strategic instability or nuclear crisis? Further, would such a ballistic missile defence over the continental United States and possibly Canada not result in an effective decoupling of American 'extended deterrence' from its West European allies?

Among the United States' allies, there was a perception of two distinct facets to Reagan's proposal. On the one hand, it was a multibillion dollar research investment by the American government along with the possible transfer of US technology, while on the other it was a proposed transformation of NATO's underpinning strategic doctrine. The resultant conflict between possible external funding for 'highly desired' high-technology research and jobs and the likelihood of domestic opposition to adopting a new 'destabilizing' doctrinal strategy led to the relative lack of interest by most of the NATO allies in Reagan's 'Star Wars I' proposal. Though the prospect of research funds met with at best a luke-warm response from alliance members including Canada, the proposed 'new' doctrine evoked a strongly adverse reaction, particularly from Europe.

An important source of this negative reaction in Europe was the prevailing political climate at the time. The West European governments, against fierce domestic opposition, had only just achieved a political consensus in favour of the 1981 deployment of new American Longer-range Intermediate Nuclear Forces (LRINF) when Reagan introduced his SDI 'vision'. The prime justification for deploying these Pershing II and cruise missiles was that they were part of a NATO 'dual track' policy agreed to in December 1979. On the one hand, the LRINF deployments were to counter the deployment of the Soviet theatre missiles, particularly the SS-20s, and on the other to encourage Soviet willingness to negotiate on a broad range of nuclear arms control. While the 1981 deployments could be seen by the Europeans as a reaffirmation of American commitment to Europe, the willingness of the European allies to accept the deployments had been taken by the Reagan Administration as evidence of Europ continued support for NATO's 'nuclear-first' strategy to deter the Soviet Union and its Warsaw Pact allies. As a result of the intense opposition from domestic peace groups and the European Nuclear Disarmament Movement (END) to the new missiles, none of the recipient countries was interested in having injected into its domestic political agenda a fresh 'issue' which would almost certainly evoke even stronger protest.

This initial Allied reaction might have been less adverse had the Europeans felt that the SDI proposal might have had merit on its own account. The general reaction, however, appeared to be that moving from reliance on nuclear deterrence to Reagan's 'vision' of strategic defences was a bad idea as it stood and an obstacle to future progress towards nuclear arms control. The combination of poor timing and perceptions of it being a 'fantasy' project appeared to doom the SDI proposal to an alliance-wide rejection, massive research funding notwithstanding.

In addition, the West Europeans feared that the SDI programme would jeopardise their security in a number of ways. The foremost concern was over 'decoupling' of American security interests from Western Europe. The Europeans feared alternatively that the United States, safe under its 'Star Wars' shield, would either be increasingly willing to engage the Soviets in a 'limited nuclear war' fought in Europe or unwilling to engage in a strategic nuclear exchange if such a limited European conflict began to escalate globally. The 'coupling' of American security to Europe was the basis of NATO's formation after the Second World War. In West European eyes, the doctrine of 'extended deterrence' was what bound the alliance together and it was the continuing credibility of the idea of a trans-Atlantic 'security community' which had been a major part of the argument for accepting the 1981 INF deployments.

As well as undermining 'extended deterrence', the SDI programme was seen as threatening the other foundation of European security: prospects for strategic and theatre arms control agreements between the United States and the Soviet Union. Europeans have always felt more secure when the two superpowers enjoyed cordial relations, or at least a 'lessening of tensions', and when their weapons competitions are restricted or limited by treaty. Apart from posing a direct threat to the 1972 Anti-Ballistic Missile (ABM) Treaty, the SDI proposal seemed to the Europeans to threaten the entire on-going East-West arms control process. As one of SDI's European critics pointed out, the deployment of defensive weapons in space 'will introduce into a remarkably stable strategic relationship between East and West an unprecedented degree of uncertainty and nervousness'.[3] In fact, some subsequent European support for SDI came from the so far mistaken perception that it would be used as an arms control 'bargaining chip': Soviet concessions on strategic and INF weapons in exchange for an American commitment *not* to develop strategic defences.

The final fear that SDI raised among West Europeans was that it would force the Soviet Union to increase its own efforts to develop effective strategic defences. This would reduce the American ability to retaliate against the Soviet Union, and therefore reduce the credibility of the US nuclear deterrent, undermining European security. However, the most serious repercussions of a Soviet-developed 'SDI' would be felt by Great Britain and France with their modest nuclear forces. Even if the Soviet Union did develop and deploy a partial though somewhat 'leaky' strategic defence system, as it almost certainly would be, at least in the early stages of development, such a system could well prove enough to nullify any deterrent effect of the small British and French nuclear forces. Such a possibility can be seen as undermining the national prestige and security planning of both countries which are rooted firmly in their claim to nuclear power status. Further, and possibly more important politically, both governments have recently embarked on expensive nuclear force modernisation programmes. These high costs would become particularly difficult to justify if the upgraded nuclear forces were to be perceived as obsolete even before being deployed. In the case of France, Defence Minister Paul Quiles announced in November 1985 that France was making a 'sustained and diversified' effort to develop a new, miniaturised nuclear warhead that would be 'virtually invisible' to enemy radar. He went on to say that 'the more the two superpowers emphasize programmes of strategic defence, the more will the penetration capacity of our missiles become the fundamental criterion of the credibility of our deterrent'.[4]

In the view of Christoph Bertram, 'for Europeans, the American strategic vision is one more expression of a shift in the American world outlook, away from coalition politics and towards an assertive protected United States acting on its own'.[5] Basically, allied governments, especially in Western Europe, chose to adopt a 'wait and see' attitude. But, as one former John F. Kennedy Administration official pointed out, if European governments' support for SDI could not be bought, it still might 'be rented'.[6]

STAR WARS II: OLD WINE IN NEW BOTTLES

In response to increasing European fears of the United States decoupling its security from the defence of Western Europe, the Reagan Administration began suggesting that a complete 'strategic defence' shield (or area defence) to protect American cities was a 'myth'. Rather it was now argued that SDI research was aimed at developing a more limited 'point defence' of America's land-based nuclear deterrent, in particular, ICBM sites and selected command headquarters. If a limited defence shield could be developed partly from enhanced existing technologies and integrated with off-the-shelf components, it would in fact provide a buttress to the present nuclear deterrent policy and continue coupling American security with Europe's. Further, such a limited 'point defence', if the technology could be enhanced and integrated together, could also have applications for creation of an anti-tactical ballistic missile (ATBM) defence against Soviet short- and intermediate-range missiles aimed at Europe. Thus developing SDI technologies would enhance current NATO deterrence strategy.

Following his second-term election victory in November 1984, Reagan re-affirmed his personal commitment to continuing research into strategic defences. He began playing down his earlier calls for a SDI system as an 'area defence' of the United States while encouraging allied participation in SDI research. Research into 'strategic defences' was projected as a way of enhancing NATO deterrence policy. The following month, at the Camp David presidential retreat, Reagan held substantial discussions on SDI and arms control issues with British Prime Minister Thatcher. At the end of their meeting, they jointly announced four specific points with regard to SDI research upon which they agreed:

1) that the United States' and Western aim was not to achieve superiority but to maintain the balance, taking account of Soviet developments;
2) that SDI-related deployment would, in view of treaty obligations, have to be a matter for negotiations;
3) that the overall aim is to enhance, and not to undermine, deterrence; and
4) that East–West negotiations should aim to achieve security with reduced levels of offensive system on both sides.[7]

This joint understanding provided British support for SDI research conditional upon its objective being to enhance deterrence without seeking strategic superiority over the Soviet Union. In terms of arms control, any SDI deployment was to be based on further negotiations with regard to the 1972 ABM Treaty and concurrent with arms reduction talks. These conditions were to become the public basis for allied participation in SDI research.

The eagerness of the US Administration for allied participation became very evident in 1985. Speaking on SDI in February, Reagan declared: 'In many areas of this [SDI] research, technical progress appears very promising. We are eager to be joined in this research by our allies, and look forward to collaboration with you.'[8] Later that same month, during a return visit to Washington to address a Joint Session of Congress, Thatcher announced 'if we are to maintain deterrence' that is 'why I firmly support President Reagan's decision to pursue research into defence against ballistic nuclear missiles'. She also expressed her hope 'that our [British] scientists will share in this research'.[9]

WEINBERGER'S 'INVITATION'

At the NATO Nuclear Planning Group meeting in March 1985 US Secretary of Defense Caspar Weinberger publicly confronted his NATO allies with a request to officially declare their intentions as to entering into government-to-government agreements with the United States on SDI research.[10] Further, he asked that they make their responses known within 60 days. In the meeting's communiqué, the NATO Defence Ministers lent public support to SDI as they 'welcome the United States invitation for Allies to consider participation in the [SDI] research programme'. But they balanced this with an explicit statement of the context in which support for SDI was given: 'the aim of which is to enhance stability and deterrence at reduced levels of offensive nuclear forces' and 'within the terms of the ABM Treaty'.[11] They thus provided an allied consensus behind the earlier Reagan–Thatcher Camp David 'understanding'.

Privately, however, there were alliance-wide denunciations by NATO governments of what amounted to an undisguised American 'ultimatum'. In the face of this the Reagan Administration was forced to retreat from Weinberger's 'acknowledgement' deadline. But it continued to argue that developing strategic defences for a 'point defence' of the US nuclear deterrent would enhance NATO deterrence strategy. This point was repeatedly made by Vice-President George Bush during his seven-nation 'whirlwind' tour of European capitals in June.[12] Further, such a limited 'point defence', if the existing technologies could be developed and integrated together, could, according to the then US Ambassador to NATO, David Abshire, also have applications for an anti-tactical ballistic missile (ATBM) defence in Europe.[13]

By the end of the year, the Reagan Administration had restructured its arguments in support of this 'new' goal of using SDI to 'enhance deterrence' by protecting the American nuclear deterrent in the United States and in Europe. In his February 1986 Defense Department Report to Congress, Weinberger listed the 'cogent themes' on SDI's direction and scope:

> The aim of SDI is to secure and deploy a thoroughly reliable defense against Soviet *strategic* and *intermediate-range* missiles. Our research program to determine if we can do this is well under way.
> U.S. and allied security remains indivisible. The SDI program is designed to enhance allied security as well as U.S. security. We will continue to work closely with our allies.[14]

SDI research was thus meant to be seen as strengthening the alliance's deterrence policy both strategic and within the European theatre.

US MOTIVES FOR SEEKING ALLIED PARTICIPATION

A number of reasons have been put forward for the Reagan Administration's interest in involving its allies. According to former French Foreign Minister Claude Cheysson, the SDI research programme had three identifiable American policy objectives. First was the hope of making American ICBM sites invulnerable. Second there was the desire to promote a good moral image on the United States at least in Reagan's eyes. Thirdly, it was hoped that SDI research would permit the United States 'to recover their leadership in certain areas of the high technology of tomorrow'.[15]

The main motivation has generally been felt to be domestic American politics. By building up a supportive foreign constituency among major allied governments, the Administration could gain further leverage with Congress in appropriating the massive funding requested. Also such allied support could swing individual Congressional members who were not already firmly committed either way to climb on the 'SDI bandwagon'. In the words of the then French Minister of Defense, Quiles, the real purpose of the SDI is 'to create a consensus within American society'.[16]

A secondary reason was to enlarge the 'pool' of technological expertise upon which the Strategic Defense Initiative Organisation (SDIO) could draw in assessing the potential 'emerging technologies'. But this was felt by Europeans to be marginal in view of the Administration's strong encouragement for increased SDI involvement of the American scientific community, especially within the universities. Rather the perception was that the SDI programme, with its proposed US$26 billion for research in the first five years, would probably result in a personnel 'brain drain' to the United States as the SDIO went shopping for technology and the research scientists to go with it.

Even as an alliance-wide research effort, the SDI programme was not intended by the American government as a charitable distribution of financial assistance to allied industries. Even prior to the series of 'memorandums of understanding' in 1986, the West Europeans, as well as Japan and Canada, had expressed fears that the American Pentagon which operates the SDIO would control any technology resulting from the programme, regardless of its origins. Among European officials and businessmen, memories of the Reagan Administration's embargo on US technology vis-à-vis European participation in the Soviet Siberian pipeline project are still fresh.[17]

In addition, they feared that the United States would use the SDI-generated technologies to forge ahead in the high-technology 'market war', at the expense of its allies. In addition to retaining control over the resultant technology, the United States could simply outspend Europe on promising research areas as well as luring the best European scientists and engineers to America with SDI dollars. In the view of E. P. Thompson, one of the END founders, SDI's goal was not to enhance deterrence at all, 'but to enhance the competitiveness and technological supremacy of United States industry'. In effect, the Reagan Administration would be 'permitted' to make a massive government investment for US technologicial superiority in the name of 'safeguarding the Free World'.[18]

ALLIED RESPONSES TO 'STAR WARS II'

In considering their individual national responses, the allies, especially the Europeans, tended to share a number of key concerns.[19] First, high-technology research contracts would provide a welcome boost to domestic companies in need of short-term business, but that consideration needed to be weighed alongside the national interests of the country as a whole. Secondly, in view of the benefits of an external source of research funds, the transfer of US technology and the possible technological–industrial boom from SDI contracts, it was thought to be better to get a share of the 'windfall', regardless how small, though allied governments differed as to whether a governmental agreement would provide a stronger framework from which to negotiate contracts with the SDIO. Thirdly, by participating in SDI research, European as well as Japanese high-technology industries would be better able to remain with American high-technology corporations at the 'cutting edge' in a number of areas of technological research. Fourthly, as the Reagan Administration was committed to research into 'emerging technologies' for strategic defences, such SDI research could be seen as making necessary preparations for defence if (or when) deterrence might actually *fail*. Also it would be better to make the best of the apparent American commitment for the sake of alliance cohesion, while still making allies' consternation as to the future of strategic defences known to the Americans in bilateral talks, NATO meetings, and other confidential forums. And finally, by supporting a move toward relying on strategic defences as opposed to deterrence based on a strategic 'balance of terror' of nuclear offensive forces, allied governments would 'reap some demagogic gain' over domestic peace movements and disarmament campaigns. Individual leaders could gain the appearance of supporting the call for nuclear disarmament by backing a research effort into possible non-nuclear defences, even while not explicitly dropping their official support for nuclear weapons for deterrence.

Basically, Reagan's call for a SDI research programme and Weinberger's subsequent 'invitation' to participate forced all their allies to make a choice: whether to participate in SDI research or not. Such a high-profile decision which allowed for no middle position in fact generated three types of responses. The first and quickest response was from those allies who officially 'declined' to participate. This group included Australia, Denmark, Norway, Greece and, initially, France.

The second type of response was that there would be no official government-to-government agreement on terms for participation. Rather individual companies could participate if they wished. This was the position taken by Canada. In its September 1985 decision after holding coast-to-coast public hearings on SDI, the Canadian Government under Brian Mulroney stated that it was opposed to further escalation of the Soviet–American arms race but that SDI research was 'both consistent with the ABM Treaty and prudent in the light of significant Soviet research and ABM deployment'.[20] While declining the 'official invitation', the Mulroney Government left the door open for participation by Canadian contractors to tender for SDI contracts or subcontract to American SDI contractors.[21]

Initially France reacted with a mixture of 'scepticism, bewilderment, and a mild dose of embarrassment' over Reagan's SDI proposal, though it relatively soon began distancing itself from what was seen as an American political initiative which would only offer up research 'crumbs' in the form of subcontracts to American SDI contractors.[22] Worried over the possibility of an American *démarche* ahead of European-generated technology and faced with Weinberger's 1985 'invitation', the French Government a month afterwards launched 'Eureka', a European-based civilian high-technology research programme into some of the same technologies as the SDI programme. After a cool initial reception, a number of European countries have joined 'Eureka' as the commercial and technological returns from SDI contracts prove to be much less than hoped for. France, for its part, has now adopted a response similar to that of Canada. While refusing the political attachment of an official SDI agreement, the

French Government has shown a new official willingness to help French companies win SDI contracts. According to Premier Jacques Chirac, 'we do not want to ignore the technical aspects of this research, and we are encouraging French firms to work with, let's say, US companies and the SDI organization in this field'.[23]

In the face of the US 'invitation' and subsequent 'sales tours' of senior Administration officials to Europe, the third type of response was bilateral negotiations of a 'memorandum of understanding' whereby companies and laboratories of the participating country would be permitted to bid for SDI contracts along with American ones *or* in consortium with them. Great Britain was the first ally to reach such an agreement when, in December 1985, it signed a secret memorandum which was declared to be based upon the 1984 Camp David agreement. The British Government under Thatcher had originally sought a guaranteed slice of the proposed US$26 billion in SDI research funds for being the first Western ally to sign. Though guaranteed contracts of up to US$2 billion were reportedly asked for, Great Britain in the end signed without any guaranteed amount or specific contracts.[24]

Though this first agreement provided leverage with Congress over the release of further SDI funding and with other allied governments to negotiate such agreements, there were already by February 1986 complaints from British companies about how poor a deal the Government had accepted. In response, government officials suggested that contract terms be re-negotiated on a contractor–SDIO basis. By the end of the year, Great Britain had been awarded less than US$30 million in SDI contracts as opposed to the Government's 'hopes' of a guaranteed larger portion. Three of its contracts involved research work on defensive systems that could be used in Europe against short-range nuclear missiles.[25]

After the signing of the British memorandum, Weinberger visited Bonn for discussions with West German Chancellor Helmut Kohl, who had reportedly been anxious to be the first NATO ally to sign a SDI accord.[26] The Kohl Government justified its support for SDI in terms of the commercial technological benefits that would accrue to German industries; or, alternatively, the loss that would result if German industry did not remain at the edge of high-technology research alongside its American and Japanese competitors. But Kohl restated the allied position that SDI must not destabilise deterrence, decouple American and West European security interests, nor limit NATO's nuclear and conventional defence options.[27] In March, West

German Economic Minister Martin Bangeman signed a SDI participation memorandum and a second on transfer of technology, with Defense Secretary Weinberger.

Despite Bangeman's claims to having obtained a good agreement, the accidental release of the secret technology memorandum established that there would be no free exchange of technical knowledge and that the US Defense Department retained all rights over the resultant technology, including the possibility of declaring German technology classified if it was integrated into SDI technology.[28] In fact the United States obliged West Germany to enforce stricter limits over its high-technology exports to Eastern Europe than had obtained previously under the Western Bloc's CoCom restrictions. Further, it was agreed that the West German Defence Ministry would actively promote German companies' participation and liaison between them and the SDIO in Washington.[29] In his September 1986 political farewell speech, Helmut Schmidt pointed out that, despite the Kohl Government's portrayal of SDI as a civilian programme, even though German industry would only pick up 'the crumbs', the United States regarded its SDI memorandum with Bonn as a military and strategic programme.[30]

At the same time as Schmidt was censuring the West German SDI accord, Italy was signing its negotiated SDI 'memorandum'. Previously the national Union of Scientists for Disarmament had made to the Italian Chamber of Deputies strong representations highly critical of Italy's becoming involved. Despite such warnings, unconfirmed press reports continued to hint at substantial contracts available to Italian companies after an agreement was reached. After the official signing, the then Foreign Minister Giulio Andreotti acknowledged that the terms of the secret Italian SDI accord were along similar lines to those signed by Great Britain and West Germany.[31]

Among the other NATO members, Spain, with the fifth largest economy in Europe, has shown a lack of interest in SDI participation. Part of the reason for this is no doubt the Socialist Government's concern with keeping 'Star Wars' off the country's political agenda after the narrow referendum victory on remaining in NATO. A number of the smaller West European countries continue to talk about SDI-funded research but generally lack the specific technologies required to compete for contracts. But, according to press reports in the autumn of 1986, US Administration officials had already privately conceded that SDI memoranda with allied governments were more important for reasons of diplomacy than of technology. Hence the Reagan Administration's desire for alliance-wide support might still result in some SDI contract spin-offs to the smaller allied industries via consortium with American corporations.

Among the 'invited' non-NATO allies, the Australian Government, despite its original refusal, announced in April 1986 that it was no longer opposed to the participation of its domestic companies in SDI research, though it would still not seek a bilateral accord.[32] The following month Israel signed a 'classified' SDI memorandum, becoming the third 'signed-up' ally. As with the other memoranda, the terms of participation were not disclosed. Then, in November, it contracted to undertake SDI-funded research on tactical ballistic missile defence systems. Israel's interest in this research area appears primarily motivated by defence fears of missile launches from within the Middle East region, particularly the Soviet-supplied short-range SS-21 and possibly intermediate-range SS-23 missiles.[33]

Though the government of Prime Minister Yashuhiro Nakasone approved Japanese participation in SDI research in September 1986, it attached the decision to five principles of understanding, among them that such research conformed with the 1972 ABM Treaty and that the United States would continue to negotiate with the Soviet Union on arms control while maintaining consultations with its allies. But the approval stops short of guaranteed Japanese participation. As with European high-technology industries, Japanese high-technology companies are worried that any SDI participation would effectively leave resultant technology patents as the property of the US Defense Department and thus deprive Japan of the rights to exploit commercially the new technology.[34] Though dismayed by the US Administration's 1987 'public' debate on a partial SDI 'early deployment', the embarrassment resulting from Toshiba Machine Company's sale of sensitive milling technology to the Soviet Union is reported to have pressured Japan into accepting similar terms as the other 'signed-up' allies. While the Japanese signing has been welcomed as showing further allied support for SDI, extensive Japanese participation presently seems unlikely in view ot the American-imposed restrictions upon commercial use of any technological developments.[35]

Of the information that has become public via media reports, those allied governments which have entered into bilateral 'memoranda' have reportedly accepted harsh terms in exchange for SDI financial 'crumbs'. Those terms worsened in August 1986 when Congress passed an amendment, despite the opposition of Administration supporters, requiring all future SDI contracts to be placed inside the

United States unless the Defense Department certified that the work in question could not be done by domestic industries.[36] As a result, future foreign contracts are likely to be primarily awarded to allied companies which excel in a specifically-required technology or agree to operate in consortium with American corporations. But political criteria such as the necessity of ensuring continued West European political support for SDI and alliance solidarity cannot totally be discounted as possible considerations.

'CONTRACT WARS'

Over the initial four years of SDI contracts, there has been a relatively unchanged pattern of contract awards. Of the US$10.9 billion distributed in 3300 SDI contracts, foreign firms were given less than one per cent of the total amount, according to a Federation of American Scientists' report.[37] Approximately US$85 million was awarded to allied industries whose government had signed a bilateral 'memorandum'. Among these countries, West Germany received US$48 million, Great Britain US$29 million, Israel US$10 million, and Italy US$2 million, while France, which chose not to sign an official accord, had US$3 million in SDI contracts.[38] By comparison, American corporations had during the same period received 73 per cent of the SDI contract awards, followed by US national laboratories with 14 per cent and universities with 6 per cent. Among the five largest SDI contractors, Lockheed Corporation received US$1024 million in contracts, followed by General Motors with US$730 million, TRW with US$570 million, Lawrence Livermore National Laboratory with US$552 million and McDonnell Douglas with US$485 million.

Even prior to the release of these disproportionate figures, there were widespread public perceptions in Europe and elsewhere that allied industries had only received the 'small change' from the SDI programme. Without financial benefits to offset the harsh patent and transfer terms imposed upon allied participation, public dislike of the American SDI programme has grown, especially in Western Europe. In a Marplan poll taken in Great Britain, France, West Germany and Italy during early 1987, the majority of those responses favoured not getting involved in SDI at all, as opposed to either SDI participation or development of their own system.[39]

A 'SDI' DEFENCE FOR WESTERN EUROPE: 'STAR WARS III'?

After early concerns about a 'SDI-defended' United States decoupling its security interests from Europe and the subsequent American call for 'strategic defences' to reinforce current deterrent policy, a number of voices in Europe have begun to call for an ATBM system there, a so-called European Defence Initiative or Star Wars III. The development of an ATBM defence as a shield for large population centres is considered unlikely. Even a limited ballistic missile defence of selected components of the US 'assured destruction capability' (ICBM sites, Strategic Air Command airfields, C^3I facilities, and the national command authority) is currently perceived as unfeasible. On the other hand, 'battlefield' applications of antitactical ballistic missiles are thought to be considerable, especially if improvements could be made in 'sensors, kill mechanisms, command and control, battlefield management, etc.'.[40] Also a tactical system, even if created out of SDI-generated technology, would not be covered under the 1972 ABM Treaty.

During his December 1985 visit to Bonn, Weinberger attacked the notion of a separate 'European Defence Initiative' on the grounds that a parallel European programme would be financially wasteful and politically 'problematic' as it could imply a split in the alliance. What he 'personally' preferred was an SDI shared by the Atlantic Community. In fact, American research had already begun to develop new means of defending the already-deployed US Pershing II and cruise missiles in Europe.[41] At the same time, a London *Guardian* editorial suggested that

> because the SDI is both scientifically and strategically flawed it does not follow that an improved and conventional European defence system, with a similar set of initials and using techniques which may be similar in origin, is equally objectionable. Advocates of improved conventional defence – the rapier instead of the bludgeon – have to rely on greater sophistication in the weaponry. British technology could be better employed in tightening NATO's capabilities in Europe than in chasing Mr Weinberger's moonbeams.[42]

Other critics argue that any perceived need for a European version of SDI is based on unreliable evaluations of the Soviet military threat.

And instead of supporting a 'European Defence Initiative', greater effort should be made to reduce East and West conventional and nuclear forces.[43]

During the NATO defence ministers' meeting in March 1986, it was reported that Weinberger informed the assembled ministers that Washington would start accepting European firms' bids for 'architectural studies' for developing missile defences for West Europe.[44] By December, Weinberger was able to announce that more than two dozen West European companies, as part of seven US–European consortia, had been awarded contracts for studies on how SDI technologies could be used to defend against short-range nuclear missiles.[45] As the French had feared, European companies had become subcontractors to American-held SDI contracts.

The likely result of allied participation, especially in view of the national interests of West Europeans and Canadians, is that a NATO-deployed ATBM system composed of some components of SDI-generated technology seems almost inevitable. (But of course questions of the effectiveness of such technology, integrating it with current 'off-the-shelf' technologies, and the time period needed to deploy even a rudimentary ATBM in Europe still remain unresolved at the present.) In fact, the West German Minister of Defence Manfred Wörner has argued for just such an anti-missile defence for NATO Europe.[46] If a successful ATBM system could be deployed, would a Western Europe protected from INF and shorter-range nuclear missiles be tempted to 'decouple' from the United States and its ICBM strategic balance with the Soviet Union? Or would the continuing numerical superiority of Soviet/Warsaw Pact forces over those of Western Europe necessitate a continuing Atlantic security community?

Canada is militarily linked to the United States through the North American Aerospace Defense Command (NORAD), in addition to NATO. Though the NORAD agreement was renewed only recently, there was considerable debate as to whether a SDI-generated BMD system would be integrated into the NORAD system, thus drawing Canada through the back door into American plans for future deployment of 'strategic defences'. In 1985, the US Department of Defense awarded two contracts to Canadian firms to produce studies on the feasibility of space-based radar surveillance systems to detect cruise missiles and bombers: the 'air-breathing threat'. In view of Canadian technical expertise in space surveillance and monitoring systems, further contracts or subcontracts from US SDI contractors seems likely.

But, reiterating the position of other NATO allies, Mulroney recently warned that, while Canada continued to support SDI research, 'extreme care must be taken to ensure that [strategic] defences are not integrated with existing forces in such a way as to create fears of a first strike' and not to 'allow strategic defences to undermine the arms control process and existing agreements'.[47] But Canadian participation under the NORAD umbrella in a SDI-generated tactical air defence system against Soviet bombers and aircraft/submarine-launched cruise missiles remains a serious possibility.

SDI AND ARMS CONTROL

Basically, SDI research has affected the Soviet–American arms control process in three ways. First, the development and ultimate testing of SDI components in space is generally thought to contravene the 1972 ABM Treaty. To counter the image of 'breaking' that treaty, the Reagan Administration has argued for a 'looser', more permissive interpretation which would allow extensive testing of space-based defence systems, as opposed to the traditional or 'narrow' interpretation. In line with the 1984 Camp David 'understanding' and the 1985 NATO Defence Ministers' communiqué, a number of the United States' closest allies have called for the Reagan Administration to stay within the traditional view. Yet, despite the possibility of a collapse of the ABM treaty over planned American tests of SDI components, Secretary of State George Shultz has cautioned NATO allies against opposing such tests.[48]

Then, in early 1987, Reagan and his top aides further undermined the ABM treaty when they 'publicly' discussed Pentagon proposals for an early deployment of a partial space-based system. Despite assurances from Shultz that no decision had been taken and that it would probably not be taken until 1988,[49] the Defense Department has continued to call for an 'early deployment' using existing technology and weapons systems. Weinberger has continued to stress, 'with adequate funding for the S.D.I. program', that 'phased deployment could begin as early as 1994 or 1995'.[50] Once again, the Reagan Administration initiated a divisive 'public' debate without allied consultation, this time over deployment and in contradiction of the 1984 Camp David 'understanding'.

But such a 'public' debate on an 'early-deployment' decision could also be seen as a means of gaining additional leverage with Congress which has become increasingly reluctant to agree to the multi-billion dollar SDI expenditures requested by the Administration. But the 'Executive–Congressional' confrontation over SDI funding has further dampened allied support for SDI and the availability of future contracts, while increasing their unease with the Reagan Administration's management style. As a result, Shultz was quickly despatched to Europe to explain the Administration's position on 'early deployment' in an attempt to defuse a possible Alliance crisis over SDI.[51]

Secondly, prior to October 1986, the SDI programme as an American bargaining chip appeared to be a realistic arms control option. But at the Reykjavik summit with Soviet General-Secretary Mikhail Gorbachev, Reagan dissipated that belief by refusing to trade away his vision of developing 'strategic defences' against Soviet ICBMs in exchange for significant cuts in both American and Soviet strategic nuclear warheads. Further, he alarmed West European leaders with his willingness, without prior consultation with his NATO allies, to contemplate scrapping all strategic ballistic missiles within a scheduled time period.[52] After the summit, Reagan argued that 'SDI is America's insurance policy that the Soviet Union would keep the commitments made at Reykjavik'.[53]

In pursuit of Alliance solidarity and lucrative research contracts, the European allies as well as Canada may have aided the Reagan Administration's sacrifice of a possible American–Soviet strategic and INF warhead reduction at the Reykjavik summit. Their 'failure' to declare that development of an SDI system would ultimately prove 'unworkable' technologically, politically, or militarily enabled Reagan to refuse to include SDI 'research' in a multi-weapon package deal and 'creditably' walk away from the first possible nuclear *disarmament* agreement since the start of the atomic age.

And thirdly, continued SDI research has the capacity to develop technological components which, while perhaps enabling a partial SDI deployment, could be used to create an ATBM system in Western Europe. Such a system would not be in breach of the ABM Treaty. Despite the impact of such an ATBM deployment on East–West relations, research in this direction is proceeding. But such a SDI-generated theatre defence would be unnecessary if the superpowers continue to work for arms reduction in Europe in the wake of the historic December 1987 Intermediate Nuclear Forces (INF) agreement which globally eliminated two classes of American and Soviet nuclear missiles.

PROSPECTS FOR THE WESTERN ALLIANCE

In the area of allied domestic politics, the NATO Governments have repeatedly reaffirmed their commitment to the December 1984 Camp David points. Despite this allied consensus, the Reagan Administration's 'track record' on consultations with its allies is one of absence or *post hoc* effort. Rather, despite Weinberger's SDI 'invitation' being subsequently withdrawn, it forced each of the Western allies to choose publicly whether or not to enter into an official participation 'memorandum' on SDI research. Though such memoranda have not resulted in sizeable financial or commercial gains, the Canadian and subsequent French decision *not* to enter into an official agreement may be seen in the future as depriving their companies of governmental support in dealing with the SDIO while still being perceived internationally as participating in 'Star Wars – possibly the worst of both positions.

As for economic benefits derived from SDI contracts, it is now apparent that both Great Britain and West Germany were forced to accept less than they had hoped for in their official agreements, for example in respect of guaranteed amounts of funding, areas of research, access to US technology, or proprietary rights over resultant technology. Though the agreements signed by Italy, Israel and now Japan are also 'classified', there is no reason to believe that they were granted any more favourable terms.

And finally, Reagan's SDI proposal undermined alliance deterrence policy and, in the case of Britain and France, national nuclear deterrent forces, by calling for a shift from nuclear deterrence to strategic defences. Just as the European allies had to make a considerable effort to swing domestic political consensus behind the 1981 INF deployments, so too will they have to expend considerable political capital to gain support for any SDI deployment, even a partial one. This will be even more costly in view of the lack of any substantial commercial compensation. Further, with US Congressional support for SDI funding waning, alliance cohesion could be seriously split in the future if a subsequent US Administration after Reagan decided to seriously cut or even terminate the SDI programme.

At present, the general European consensus appears to be that it would be happiest with the SDI programme being traded for an East–West strategic nuclear weapons reduction agreement, possibly after yielding whatever commercial dividends can be derived from research contracts within Europe. The situation in Canada is basically the same. As such dividends have increasingly proved to be smaller than anticipated and, as Reagan's refusal to use it as a bargaining chip is repeatedly demonstrated, the West Europeans and most likely America's other industrial allies will prove even more intractable on the question of future SDI research and any early systems deployment.

Currently the outcome most to be feared from current SDI research is the development of technology suitable for deploying an ATBM system in Western Europe, though components could be used elsewhere as well. Such deployments are likely to generate renewed Soviet fears of nuclear strikes across its long borders reminiscent of the 'US containment strategy' period of the 1950s, only this time from behind SDI-generated 'regional' shields.[54] Further such ATBM systems could become field test prototypes for a future SDI system or even the basis for a Western strategic ABM system.[55]

Notes

1. *New York Times*, 24 March 1983.
2. Ibid., 30 March 1983. In a July 1986 letter to Gorbachev, Reagan was reported by the *Washington Post* to have again offered to share SDI technology if an agreement could be worked out; cited in *Globe and Mail* (Toronto) 4 August 1986.
3. Christoph Bertram, 'Strategic Defense and the Western Alliance', *Daedalus*, vol. 114, no. 3 (1985) p. 281.
4. *New York Times*, 13 November 1985.
5. Bertram, 'Strategic Defense and the Western Alliance', p. 294.
6. George W. Ball, 'The War for Star Wars', *New York Review of Books, 11 April 1985*.
7. US Department of State, *The Strategic Defense Initiative* (Washington, DC, 1985), p. 3.
8. *New York Times*, 4 February 1985.
9. Ibid., 22 February 1985.
10. And subsequently Australia, Israel, Japan and South Korea.
11. NATO Nuclear Planning Group Communiqué, reprinted in *NATO Review*, vol. 33, no. 2 (1985) p. 33.
12. *Globe and Mail*, 4 July 1985.
13. David M. Abshire, 'SDI – The Path to a More Mature Deterrent', *NATO Review*, vol. 33, no. 2 (1985) pp. 8–16. For a fuller analysis of this view, see Manfred R. Hamm and W. Bruce Weinrod, 'The Transatlantic Politics of Strategic Defense', *Orbis*, vol. 29, no. 4 (1986) pp. 709–34.
14. Caspar W. Weinberger, *Annual Report to the Congress, Fiscal Year 1987* (Washington, DC, 1986) p. 292. Emphasis added.
15. 'Interview with M. Claude Cheyson', *Libération* (Paris), 3 May 1985.

16. 'Interview with Paul Quiles', *Manchester Guardian Weekly*, 5 January 1986, p. 14.
17. For a useful analysis of that 'alliance crisis', see Anthony Binkel, *Ally versus Ally: America, Europe and the Siberian Pipeline Crisis* (New York, 1986).
18. E. P. Thompson, 'Folly's Comet', in E. P. Thompson (ed.), *Star Wars* (Harmondsworth, 1985) p. 119.
19. For an excellent analysis of SDI issues prior to 1986, see Michael Lucas, 'SDI and Europe', *World Policy Journal* (New York), vol. 3, no. 2 (1986) pp. 219–49.
20. See Gregory Wirick, *Canadian Responses to the Strategic Defense Initiative* (Ottawa, 1986).
21. Lenny Glynn and Emily Laux, 'Star Flaws', *Report on Business Magazine* (Toronto), August 1986, p. 23.
22. For a detailed analysis of the French response see John Fenske, 'France and the Strategic Defence Initiative', *International Affairs* (London), vol. 62, no. 2 (1985–6) pp. 231–46.
23. 'Interview with Jacques Chirac', *Time Magazine*, 6 April 1987, p. 38.
24. *Manchester Guardian Weekly*, 15 December 1985, p. 3. Also see Trevor Taylor, 'Britain's response to the Strategic Defence Initiative', *International Affairs* (London), vol. 62, no. 2 (1985–6) pp. 217–30.
25. *Manchester Guardian Weekly*, 14 December 1986, p. 6.
26. For a good review of the German SDI debate, see Christoph Bluth, 'SDI: the challenge to West Germany', *International Affairs* (London), vol. 62, no. 2, (1985–6) pp. 247–64.
27. *Christian Science Monitor*, 12 March 1986.
28. Committee on Energy, Research and Technology European Parliament (Strasbourg), *Working Document PE 105.753*, WG(VS1)3928E, 25 April 1986.
29. *Der Spiegel* (Hamburg), 14, 21 and 23 April 1986. Translations kindly provided by Peter Gerlach.
30. *New York Times*, 11 September 1986.
31. *Globe and Mail*, 8 August 1986; and *New York Times*, 18 September 1986. Information on the pre-accord Italian SDI debate was kindly provided by Paolo Farinella of the University of Pisa.
32. *New York Times*, 5 April 1986.
33. Ibid., 6 November 1986 and 29 July 1987.
34. Ibid., 10 September 1986; and *Asahi Evening News* (Tokyo), 24 November 1986.
35. *Christian Science Monitor* (Boston), 18 February and 22 July 1987; and *New York Times*, 22 July 1987.
36. *Manchester Guardian Weekly*, 17 August 1986, p. 6.
37. *Christian Science Monitor*, 22 April 1987.
38. Steven A. Hildreth and Alice C. Maroni, *The Strategic Defense Initiative: Program Facts* (Congressional Research Service, Issue Brief IB–85170, Washington DC, 1987) p. 3.
39. *Manchester Guardian Weekly*, 22 February 1987, p. 4.
40. See Deborah Nutter Miner and Alan H. Rutan, 'What role for limited BMD?', *Survival*, vol. 29, no. 2 (1987) pp. 118–37.
41. *Manchester Guardian Weekly*, 15 December 1985, p. 3.

42. Ibid., p. 1.
43. See, for example, Matthew Evengelista, 'Exploiting the Soviet "Threat" to Europe', *Bulletin of the Atomic Scientists*, January/February 1987, pp. 14–18.
44. *New York Times*, 22 March 1986; and *Aviation Week & Space Technology*, 19 May 1986, pp. 24–6.
45. *Globe and Mail,* 5 December 1986.
46. Manfred Wörner, 'A Missile Defense for NATO Europe', *Strategic Review*, vol. 14, no. 2 (Winter 1986) pp. 13–20.
47. *Globe and Mail*, 25 May 1987.
48. Ibid., 12 February 1987.
49. *New York Times*, 4 February 1987.
50. Caspar W. Weinberger, 'It's Time to Get S.D.I. off the Ground', *New York Times*, 21 August 1987.
51. *Manchester Guardian Weekly*, 15 February 1987, p. 4.
52. For a good post-summit assessment, see Christoph Bertram 'Why Reykjavik upset the European allies', *Arms Control Today*, January/February 1987, pp. 15–18.
53. *Manchester Guardian Weekly*, 19 October 1986.
54. For an example of these fears, see V. Beletsky, 'What lies behind the "European Defence Initiative" Project?', *International Affairs* (Moscow), June 1986, pp. 49–55.
55. The author is grateful to Francesco Calogero, to David Carlton and to Jürgen Altmann for drawing his attention to a number of points during the preparation of this paper, though all errors or omissions are his own.

11 The Technical Feasiblity of Strategic Defence

Dietrich Schroeer

INTRODUCTION

A political scientist has said that 'Star Wars is a boon to contentious scientists.'[1] This is an expression of concern that technological possibilities might become the most important factors determining the desirability of strategic defences. Science and technology are indeed not the most important aspects of the debate about strategic defence. None the less, one must have some appreciation for that technology, in order to comprehend how unimportant it really is. If decision-makers do not understand the relevant technologies, they may be overwhelmed by contentious scientists and other people claiming to possess special expertise.

The question controling the political debate is whether 'Star Wars' can work. But that question is unclear. What does the expression 'Star Wars' mean: the Strategic Defense Initiative (SDI) research programme to study the technical possibilities; a defence of retaliatory strategic forces, such as Intercontinental Ballistic Missile (ICBM) silos; a general reorientation toward defences; a population defence that can significantly reduce civilian casualties in a nuclear war; or mutual assured survival? What is the meaning of feasibility: will the weapons work as projected; can a strategic-defence system work; are the economics of strategic defence bearable; which strategic objectives of an anti-nuclear defence are feasible?

This paper will briefly describe some weapons for strategic defence and when they might become available for use in defensive systems. It will consider strategic defence systems, and when these might become useful. Finally, there will be a review of what strategic objectives may be achievable, and at what cost. This survey is to clarify how rational people can disagree so strongly about an issue that is so strongly based on technologies.

192 *The Technical Feasibility of Strategic Defence*

THE TECHNOLOGIES OF STRATEGIC DEFENCE

Discussion of strategic defences is complicated. They can involve many different weapons to attack missiles and warheads. These weapons can be deployed in various systems and locations. The weapons systems can be combined to form strategic defences of various levels of capability. The objectives of strategic defence inevitably affect the defensive configurations. Figure 11.1 illustrates the technical complexity of the systems that are usually under discussion when strategic defences are being considered; the term 'Star Wars' symbolises this complexity. The following outline of strategic defences is intended to show that such simple terms as 'strategic defence' or 'Star Wars' are inadequate when asking about technical feasibility. The feasibility question will either have to be focused on some specific sub-system, or will have to be couched in terms of reaching some specific strategic objective.

Weapons

Missiles or Re-entry Vehicles (RVs) may be intercepted by means of interceptor rockets. New interceptor technologies appear to make non-nuclear interception possible by means of high-accuracy target-seeking guidance mechanisms. These interceptors might be based on the ground, in the style of the Anti-Ballistic Missile (ABM) defence systems deployed in the early 1970s. They conceivably might also be based in space on a satellite, launched to intercept for example RVs during their mid-course flight; but problems of flight time would then make large numbers of satellites necessary.

Kinetic-Energy Weapons (KEWs) could intercept RVs or ICBMs. By customary usage that term KEW refers to weapons such as electromagnetic railguns that fire either inert or small target-seeking objects with no warheads. They would destroy by direct contact only. To avoid being disabled by air resistance, these KEWs will need to be based in and fired at targets in space.

Directed-Energy Weapons (DEWs) generate beams of light or of atomic particles that travel towards a target at or near the speed of light. An electron-beam weapon might be based on the ground for short-range interception; while neutral-hydrogen beams might be used for longer-range interception in space. Laser light beams could be generated either in space or on the ground; in the latter case air

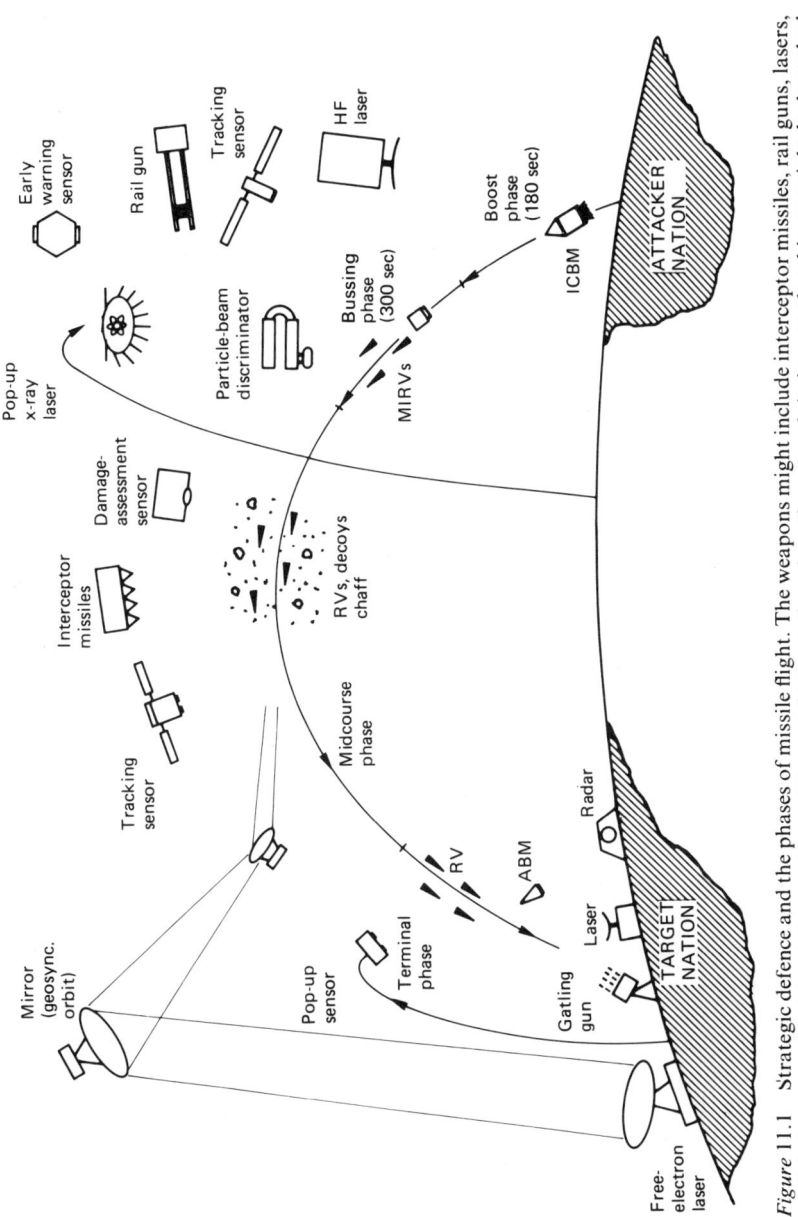

Figure 11.1 Strategic defence and the phases of missile flight. The weapons might include interceptor missiles, rail guns, lasers, particle-beam accelerators and x-ray lasers. They might be stationed on the ground, in low-earth orbit, or might be launched into space as soon as launches of enemy missiles are detected. The defences might operate during the boost, bussing, midcourse, and re-entry phases of the missile flight. Various sensors for the surveillance, acquisition, tracking, and kill assessment functions are indicated.

absorption would have to be taken into account. X-ray lasers are a subset of DEWs. They are unique because they would be powered by a nuclear explosion. They would either have to be based in space, or launched into space in some pop-up mode during the defensive engagement.

Weapons Systems

A strategic defence would involve not only weapons, but also various adjuncts, forming a total system. Figure 11.1. indicates some of these adjuncts. Early warning satellites in geosynchronous orbit at an altitude 36 000 km above the earth are to detect the heat released by rocket-engine plumes during missile launches. Other sensor satellites in lower orbits would use radar, light, and neutral particle beams to distinguish between missiles, re-entry vehicles, decoys, and chaff; and to track the missiles and the RVs precisely enough to aim the weapons. Some sensing satellites would determine whether an interception by the defence has been successful and, if not, determine the miss vector for a possible follow-up interception. Unless the weapons are to operate completely independently, some control stations in space or on the ground would manage the whole system of weapons and sensors. The battle-management stations would communicate with, as well as link, the sensors and the weaponry.

Layered Defences

The flight of ICBMs consists of several phases. An effective strategic defence should contain layers to exploit the differing vulnerabilities of missiles and RVs during these flight phases. Figure 11.1 sketches these flight phases and suggests the differing weapons used during each phase.

Boost Phase
Immediately after an ICBM is launched, it is in its boost phase. During this phase the rocket engine fires, accelerating the missile to its final ballistic velocity. It lasts 300 seconds for the current generation of Soviet ICBMs, and 180 seconds for the new US MX missile; fast-burn boosters with firing times as short as 50 seconds are thought possible.[2] As the boost phase progresses, the missile sheds its stages until the payload reaches its final ballistic velocity. Interception of an

ICBM during its boost phase would mean the destruction of all its warheads, as many as ten for the current generation of missiles. During the boost phase, the missile's rocket plume is very bright and hot, so that both visible and infra-red detectors sense it. Furthermore the missile is relatively vulnerable because it contains flammable fuel inside thin-skinned fuel tanks.

Bussing Phases
At the end of the boost phase, the missile payload goes into its bussing phase, lasting about 500 seconds for the MX missile for example.[3] During this phase, the 'bus' platform carrying the Multiple Independently-Targeted Re-entry Vehicles (MIRVs) uses small thrusters to change its orientation, and then fires the MIRVs sequentially towards different targets. The bus platform will also begin to release decoys and metallic chaff to hide the real RVs. During the bussing phase, the bus and RVs are relatively hard to detect, since no large rockets are fired. The number of targets to be analysed and intercepted increases rapidly as this phase progresses.

Mid-Course Phase
Once the re-entry vehicles have been dispersed by the bus, they will fly towards their targets in ballistic trajectories under the influence of the earth's gravitational force. The RVs will be surrounded by decoy warheads, perhaps formed by metal-coated balloons, and by clouds of radar-reflecting metallic chaff. The only energy emitted by the RVs will be due to the fact that they are still warm; they may be visible against the cold background of space. Even though the ballistic phase may last as long as 1200 seconds,[4] the RVs will be hard to detect and difficult to distinguish from the accompanying material.

Re-entry Phase
During the final phase of their flight, the re-entry vehicles carrying the warheads penetrate into the atmosphere, which reaches to about 100 km above the earth's surface. During the re-entry phase, which may last 100 seconds or so,[5] the lighter decoys and the chaff will be stripped away from the heavier RVs. Thus managers of a strategic defence need not have to worry about decoys, if only they can wait long enough during the re-entry phase. The air resistance will cause the RVs to become very hot. They will then be detectable with optical and infra-red sensors as they glow brightly.

Multiplicative Defence Effects

From this description of a missile's flight, and from Figure 11.1, it is clear that a system for strategic defence can operate during many different parts of missile flight. Whether a missile or RV can be successfully intercepted during its flight will depend on the mixture of weapons and the phase of missile flight during the attack.

This multiplicity of layers represents an opportunity for a strategic defence. A strategic defence might well be most effective if it were to attack missiles and RVs several times, and if it were deployed in layers, each layer intercepting targets during a different phase of missile flight. The opportunity is that no single layer of defence might have to be very effective in order to have a very effective total defensive system. Thus four independent sequential layers of defence, each 50 per cent effective, would lead to a penetration of only 6 per cent of the attacking warheads. The current claims of possible highly effective strategic defences rely heavily on such multiplicative effects. Obviously a multiplicity of weapons would have to be developed for a layered defence, the cost of multiple sets of defensive systems would go up, and the co-ordination among the defensive layers would present problems.

THE TECHNOLOGICAL FEASIBILITY OF SDI WEAPONS

The technical feasibility of strategic defences may best be discussed in two parts, first in terms of the weapons to be employed, and then in terms of incorporating the weapons into a functioning system. The current funding allocations for the research and development (R&D) programme of the SDI give some indications of the current enthusiasms. The appropriations for the SDI Organisation for the fiscal year 1986/7 is \$3·0 billion, with 33 per cent allocated to work on directed-energy weapons, 21 per cent allocated to kinetic-energy weapons, 26 per cent allocated to research and development on surveillance, acquisition, tracking and kill assessment functions, 10 per cent for battle management, and 10 per cent for other functions. A brief survey of the various weapons being considered for strategic defences can give an impression of the current rate of progress in the research.

Anti-ballistic Missiles

The technology for ABM defences has improved considerably since the early 1970s, when the United States deployed its 'Safeguard' system (now discontinued).[6] The improvements have largely come in the employment of homing sensors, which guide the interceptor rockets to the warhead, and in the sensors for detecting and tracking the interceptors and for managing the battle. Both the US Anti-satellite (ASAT) System,[7] and the Homing-Overlay interceptors[8] use infra-red detectors to home in on warm objects. Both have had some success in interceptions. Consequently it appears possible to develop and deploy a terminal defence involving a homing warhead to intercept incoming re-entry vehicles, and destroying the target by contact. The primary questions are now about the relative effectiveness and costs of such systems.

Kinetic-energy Weapons

Kinetic-energy Weapons (KEWs) are designed to destroy a target by causing an inert object to collide with it at high speeds. Progress is being made in developing the new KEW technology of electromagnetic railguns.[9] These weapons accelerate objects to very high speeds by means of electric and magnetic fields generated by very large currents. Such guns might aim inert objects at a target, perhaps in the style of a machine gun; or they might accelerate objects with target-seeking sensors ('smart rocks').[10] In either case, the kinetic energy of the interceptor would be so high that mere contact would suffice to destroy the target. The problem with these Directed-energy Weapons (DEWs) is reaching the target missile or RV before it passes out of range. In boost-phase defence the interceptor would have to travel thousands of kilometres in perhaps 100 seconds. Thus it is thought that ballistic velocities of 40 km/s are needed for the KE interceptors.[11] If the interceptors are to carry sensors, then they might have a mass of tens of kilograms.[12] To be useful, the railgun would have to be able to fire tens or hundreds of interceptors in perhaps a hundred seconds. The current railgun technology is able to accelerate a 0·1 kg mass to 4 km/s, shooting twice a day.[13] While progress is being made in this technology, the goal of using 'smart rocks' as interceptors is at present far out of reach. Current interest in railguns has come to focus on their use to protect battle satellites from ASAT attacks.

Directed-energy Weapons

The term Directed-energy Weapon (DEW) has come to stand for a weapon using light or particle beams to deliver energy to a target. DEWs have the very appealing feature that the destructive energy is delivered to the target at, or nearly at, the speed of light. Hence longer ranges to the targets create only a problem of beam intensity, not of energy-delivery time. This feature makes DEW technology symbolic of the technical advances that would have to be made if a reasonably effective strategic defence is to become feasible. DEWs have generic operational requirements, which might be labelled beam generation, beam focusing, beam transmission, and target damage mechanisms.

Particle Beams Particle beams for strategic defence are likely to be of two kinds. Electrons might be usable for short-range defences within the atmosphere, beams of neutral hydrogen for defences in space. Both beams would be generated by high-energy particle accelerators, and would be focused and aimed by electric and magnetic fields. Both beams would penetrate the target, depositing energy throughout it. Damage could be inflicted on the target by melting its skin, igniting its fuel or explosives, or disabling its electronic circuits.

Electron Beams Beams of charged particles are strongly absorbed by air, so that their range in the atmosphere is relatively short.[14] The particles within the beam repel each other, threatening to broaden it unacceptably. The earth's magnetic fields deflect the beam in partially unpredictable and uncorrectable ways.

A pulse technique can eliminate these problems in air. When an intense beam of electrons travels through air, it heats the air as it is absorbed, essentially generating a channel that is partially evacuated. A series of beam pulses may be able to drill a tunnel in air, through which subsequent beam pulses can travel without major absorption. Positive charges build up on the outside of the evacuated channel. These act to keep the negatively charged beam in a coherently narrow beam, and protect it from beam deflection by magnetic fields.[15] This technology is an off-shoot of an interest of the US Navy in ship-board defence against cruise missiles (the Chair Heritage programme).

An electron-beam defence would work only in the air, and only at relatively short range. It actually would not exploit the fact that such high-energy electrons travel at nearly the speed of light. Since many beam pulses would be needed to evacuate a channel for beam propagation, and since these pulses would be separated in time, the beam would have to be pre-aimed towards a spot through which the

RV would be expected to pass, hence a lead time of at least a fraction of a second would be involved.
Such beam propagation is currently under study. A strategic defence in air against RVs may be projected to require a 10 000-ampere beam of 500-MeV electrons, with the accelerator able to generate 10 000 pulses per second. Currently an electron accelerator is under test which can generate a 10 000 ampere beam of 50-MeV electrons, with a pulse repetition rate of 10 per second.[16] Tests of the propagation of such a beam in air over 50 metres is planned.[17] The electron-beam weapon technology is still in its infancy.

Neutral-Particle Beams A neutral particle beam might be suitable for use at longer ranges in space. It would be unaffected by the earth's magnetic field, and would not be spread through repulsion between the beam particles. The particle of choice for such a beam would probably be neutral hydrogen, H°. It would be produced in a high-energy accelerator as a beam of negatively-charged H^-, which can be accelerated, shaped, and focused by electromagnetic fields. After acceleration, the beam would be neutralised by passing it through a stripper, where the excess electron would be removed from each H^- ion.

It is thought that a 5-ampere beam of 500-MeV hydrogen ions might have to be generated in order to destroy one RV in space at a range of 3000 km within $\frac{1}{2}$ second. The current best accelerator produces 0·15-ampere beams of 5-MeV H^- ions; in 1986 construction began on an accelerator which will produce H^- ions; with a 100-MeV energy and the same current. Plans are to test the functioning of such an accelerator, at low energies in space, in the late 1980s.

In the late 1970s there was a brief wave of enthusiasm for Particle-Beam Weapons in strategic defence.[18] That enthusiasm has waned, as a general judgement has developed that Particle-Beam Weapons are a less mature technology than laser weapons.[19] Some see H° beams as most promising discriminating between RVs and decoys during the ballistic phase of missile flight, rather than as a weapon to destroy RVs.

Lasers
It may be useful to illustrate the problems and possibilities of advanced strategic defence technologies by examining one example in some detail. Chemical lasers are a DEW technology which demonstrates all the considerations involved in analysing the feasibility of a

weapon technology, and represents the changing enthusiasms of technologists for favoured technologies. Many different types of chemical lasers are under consideration for strategic defence. They are all devices which convert some chemical or electrical energy into intense beams of narrowly-focused light. This laser light then transmits some fraction of that input energy to the target at the speed of light. The light is absorbed by a surface layer of the target, producing damage of the surface layer by melting, or generating a shock-wave.

The initial question about strategic-defence lasers is how well they can focus the light they emit onto a small spot at a target some large distance away from the laser. If the size of this spot is very small, then relatively little energy will have to be carried by the whole beam, since a small hole in the target presumably would be as efficacious in destruction as a large hole. This critical parameter of laser performance is the fluence, the energy deposited per unit area on the target. A laser focusing 20 MW (20 million watts) of light with a wavelength of 2·7 μm (10^{-6} m) onto a target 3000 km away by means of a 10-meter diameter mirror can have a maximum energy intensity on the target of 2500 watts/cm^2. This could destroy an ICBM within eight seconds, if it has the resistance of 20 kJ/cm^2 typical of future generations of Soviet missiles. Doubling the wavelength would reduce the light intensity by a factor of four, doubling the mirror size would quadruple the light for intensity, and doubling the distance to the target would reduce the light intensity by a factor of four. Any faults, for example in the focusing, would reduce this maximum possible intensity.

Current emphasis for strategic defence is on two types of lasers, chemical lasers because they are the current leaders in performance, and free-electron lasers because they hold the most promise for the future and are developing rapidly. Chemical lasers using hydrogen and fluorine as fuel and lasing medium currently lead in power output. A 2·2-MW laser using fluorine and deuterium (an isotope of hydrogen) has been operated;[20] a 2-MW HF laser of a design that can be scaled up in power output is being tested. The DF laser could be used within the atmosphere, the HF laser can be used only in space since its light is absorbed by the atmosphere. Since an HF laser for space-based strategic defence would need to be quite large, interest has actually been shifting toward the so-called free-electron lasers.[21] These have the major advantage that they can be made to emit light of very short wavelength, so that much smaller mirrors could focus the beam tightly enough to be useful for long-range interception. However, the accelerators required for free-electron lasers would be massive, hence they would have to be stationed on the ground. The light from a free-electron laser would then have to be directed towards the target by a series of space-based mirrors as shown in Figure 11.1.

Laser Station A laser weapon will include not only a chamber in which the light beam is generated, but also a supply of fuel and a mirror to focus the laser beam.[22] For an HF laser weapon intended for boost-phase defence, the hydrogen and fluorine gases flow from storage tanks into a combustion chamber in which they are burnt to generate hot HF gas. When that gas flows into the semi-vacuum of a laser cavity, the hot HF molecules release their energy as a laser beam. The cool HF gas then flows out into space. The laser light beam is then expanded, and finally focused on a distant target by a large mirror. The laser battle satellite will carry peripherals, such as sensors and communications antennas.

Laser Weapon Requirement Table 11.1 sketches the requirements imposed on laser weapons to be deployed in various alternative strategic defence systems. The requirements for an ASAT laser system are included for comparison purposes. The parameters of the best laser weapons currently available are also listed. The table illustrates that the timetable for possible deployment of strategic defence depends very much on the objective of the defence. Lasers with a power output adequate for a ground-based terminal defence may already be under development. However, the level of performance requisite for a space-based HF laser weapon for boost-phase defence is several orders of magnitude higher than the current performance levels. The energy output required for free-electron lasers that are to be ground-based for mid-course strategic defence is many orders of magnitude higher than the current levels of performance. It is interesting to note that the first capability to be achieved will be anti-satellite interception.

It is difficult to predict when these various weapons systems might become available for deployment. Extrapolations of technological capabilities into the future are notoriously unreliable. Yet it may be instructive to perform such an extrapolation for laser weapons, assuming that current development trends continue. In the past, the maximum power output of lasers has tended to double roughly every two and a half years.[23] New laser technologies have often grown even more rapidly, but only until they have caught up with earlier, more highly-developed technologies. Figure 11.2 shows when the feasibility

Table 11.1 Requirement for several laser weapons of possible interest for defensive systems

	ASAT[1]	Terminal defence[2]	Boost-phase defence[3]	Mid-course defence[4]
Laser type	HF-chem.	DF-chem.	HF-chem.	Free e
Laser wavelength	2·7 μm	3·8 μm	2·7 μm	0·5 μm
Laser location	space	ground	space	ground
Target distance	3000 km	10 km	3000 km	75 000 km
Mirror diameter	4 m	4 m	10 m	50*/26/2 m
Laser output	2·5 MW	2 MW	20 MW	1000 MW
Time/shot, max range	75 sec	0·16 sec	8 sec	0·66 sec
Beam size at target	2·5 m	1·2 m	1 m	0·9 m
Incident energy to kill	56 W/cm^2	150 kJ/cm^2	20 kJ/cm^2	50 kJ/cm^2
Fuel energy content	1·4 MJ/kg	1·4 MJ/kg	1·4 MJ/kg	10 MJ/kg
Fuel per shot	720 kg	1·1 kg	560 kg	330 kg
		Under development		
Project		Alpha		
Laser location		ground		
Mirror diameter		4 m		
Power output		2 MW		

[1] A space-based ASAT system using an HF chemical laser with a 3000-km range.
[2] A ground-based DF chemical laser, to be used in a short-range terminal defence system.
[3] A space-based HF chemical laser, to attack ICBMs during the boost phase.
[4] A ground-based free-electron laser, using space-based reflectors to attack RVs during their mid-course flight phase.
* The three mirror diameters for this system refer to the ground-based laser-beam focusing mirror, the reflecting mirror in geosynchronous orbit, and the orbital battle mirror with a range of 300 km.
Energy absorption by the atmosphere is assumed to be 50 per cent, and the lasers are assumed 20 per cent efficient.

of various laser weapons systems might be established, assuming such a two-and-a-half-year doubling time applies for their future development growth rate. For example, HF lasers with a power output of 20 MW for boost-phase defence might be shown to be feasible by the mid-1990s. Typically a five- to eight-year development period elapses between the establishment of feasibility and the completed construction of a prototype weapon.[24] Thus deployment of laser weapons in a boost-phase defence might become possible around the turn of this century. These extrapolations make no judgements about the performance of such defensive systems, nor about the economics of building such defences. They do give some indication as to when enough may be known to make an informed decision about deployment. Figure 11.2 shows that a ground-based laser weapon could be available for terminal defence, or for ASAT interceptions, well before the turn of this century. A free-electron laser for mid-course defence, on the other hand, would seem unavailable as a prototype until several decades into the next century. Similar projections have been made by Harold Brown, the former US Secretary of Defense.[25]

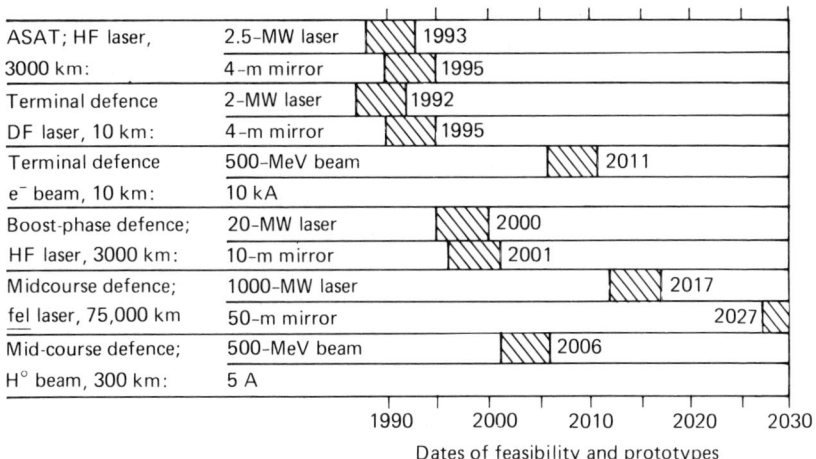

Figure 11.2 Estimates of the times when the feasibility of various strategic-defence weapons might be established, and when they might be available for deployment. The time interval marked by slanted lines indicates the period between demonstrated feasibility and development of a prototype.

X-ray Lasers

One type of laser warrants special discussion. An x-ray laser converts the energy released in a nuclear explosion into high-energy photons (x-rays) and directs this energy as a narrow beam in a specific direction. An operational x-ray laser might consist of a 300-kt nuclear explosive, surrounded by ten to a hundred bundles of thousands of very thin metallic rods, each several metres in length.[26] Perhaps one-tenth of a per cent of the energy of the nuclear explosive might be focused by these rods as a beam spot of 30 metres at a distance of 3000 km.[27] Each of these bundles could be aimed in a separate direction, so that as many as 100 RVs might be attacked simultaneously. The nuclear explosion destroys the x-ray laser microseconds after the laser has fired, so that such a laser could operate only once.

The appeal of such an x-ray laser is its high energy-to-mass ratio. Many, including Edward Teller,[28] believe that any part of a strategic defence that is permanently located in space on a satellite will be vulnerable to attack. In their view, as much as possible of a strategic defence should therefore be based on the ground, and be launched into space only after an attack has begun. Because nuclear weapons are relatively light-weight, they would be suitable for such a 'pop-up defence', as it is often called.

The drawbacks to x-ray lasers come from the same sources as the advantages. X-ray lasers involve the explosions of nuclear devices, yet the new-style strategic defences are supposed to make nuclear weapons obsolete. The fact that x-ray lasers might be stored on the ground until the attack has commenced also implies a delay time in the final deployment of those lasers. X-rays are absorbed by even thin layers of air, so that x-ray lasers can work only above the atmosphere. Hence x-ray lasers cannot function until after they have reached outer space. X-ray lasers therefore are unlikely to be useful for boost-phase defence; during the launch time of the x-ray lasers, the boost phase of the opponent missiles may well be completed – particularly if fast-burn boosters are developed for ICBMs.

The potential of x-ray lasers is the subject of much controversy. A group of x-ray laser researchers at the Los Alamos National Laboratory, supported by Teller, is very enthusiastic about the progress and future of x-ray lasers.[29] Much money is being spent on the development of x-ray lasers, mostly on nuclear tests to activate them.[30] The enthusiasm of outside technical experts for x-ray lasers has been more oscillatory, dampened for example by the controversy of 1985, in which early reports of tremendous improvements in x-ray laser output were soon followed by revelations of equipment malfunction.[31]

Currently the x-ray laser programme is seen by most as a future-oriented research programme, with the existing energy output nowhere near that required for a useful weapon. The technology is so exotic, and so scientifically and technologically interesting, that its development programme seems almost to have a life of its own, independent of any contact with the real requirements of weapons for strategic defence.[32] In fact much of the criticism of x-ray lasers for strategic defence has focused on time constraints and strategic-stability questions, rather than on matters of technical feasibility as such.

STRATEGIC DEFENCE SYSTEMS

The technical requirements for a functioning strategic defensive system are judged by many to be far higher than those for the weapons incorporated into the system.

Operational Requirements

A strategic defence system must perform a variety of weapons-related functions. It must detect the targets to be destroyed, distinguishing between ICBMs or RVs and decoys. It must track the targets, and based on that tracking, must aim its weapons in the right directions and focus their beams on the point where the targets will be when the interceptions take place. Then each weapon must be fired. If more than one shot is to be taken at a target, the result of the first firing has to be analysed to evaluate the damage and to determine the miss vector. The process from tracking through to damage assessment will have to be repeated until the observed damage is judged sufficient or the target is passed on to the next weapon.

Not only must the defensive system perform many functions, but there must be many stations, such as satellites, containing defensive weapons. Most of the strategic defences are likely to be located in space, particularly for boost-phase defences. Satellites close to the earth are constantly moving with respect to the earth's surface. To have at least some battle satellites in orbit above the opponent's missile launch sites it will therefore be necessary to place into orbit a large number of satellites.

For a satellite-based weapon with an intercept range of 3000 km, at least 43 satellites must be in orbit in order that at least one weapon will be within 3000 km of every opponent missile.[33] If the number of launchers to be intercepted exceeds the interception capacity of a single battle station, then more satellites will have to be placed in orbit. The number actually required depends upon the distribution of enemy targets, the burn-time of the boosters, the weapon-beam intensity, and the time required to re-aim the weapon from one target to another.[34]

Because the number of missiles and RVs to be intercepted is likely to be very large, each battle station will have to attack many targets. Consequently each battle station will have to be massive, as well as complex. Table 11.2 indicates that for an HF-laser boost-phase

Table 11.2 The configuration of a space-based boost-phase defensive system, using HF lasers, that is to be adequate to fire a single shot at every Soviet ICBM during its boost phase

Laser type	HF
Laser power	20 MW
Laser focusing mirror	10-m diameter
Altitude of laser station	300 km
Number of laser stations	120
Average range for laser shots	1 300 km
Number of shots per station	400
Average fuel per shot	82 kg
Average time per shot	1·1 sec
Total shots available (120 × 400)	48 000
Total fuel (48 000 × 82 kg)	3 900 tonnes
Total station mass (2 × fuel mass)	7 800 tonnes
Polar-orbit shuttle capacity	15 tonnes
Number of shuttle flights	520
Launching time at 2 flights/month	22 years

Note: The booster hardness is assumed to be 20 kJ/cm^2, the time during which the booster can be attacked is 150 seconds, and the light-energy obtained from the HF fuel is assumed to be 280 kJ/kg. The retargeting time is assumed to be zero.

defence, 120 20-MW HF lasers with 10 m diameter mirrors might be needed to fire one shot at each of 1000 enemy missiles within 150 seconds. With an average fuel consumption of 82 kg per shot, this would represent 3900 tonnes of fuel. If one assumes that the mass of the battle stations is roughly equal to the mass of the stored fuel, then a total payload of 7800 tonnes would have to be lifted into orbit for a single-shot boost-phase defence. That represents 520 15-tonne payloads for the current American space shuttle fleet.

Other strategic defence systems would have different weapon configurations. But the demands placed on an HF-laser system are probably representative of those imposed on other strategic defence weapons systems, in terms of complexity, multiplicity of functions, numbers of weapons stations in orbit, and amounts of material involved. This judgement appears to be shared by strategic defence planners, who are asking for the development of a larger space shuttle for the future.[35] If the time scale of development for such a larger space shuttle is similar to that of the current space shuttle, then a decade might pass between taking a development decision and having a significant number of shuttles deployed.

Battle Management

A strategic defence will require extensive battle management because the defence battle environment will be very confused, and because the multiple layers of defence will have to interact.

A strategic defence battle will be operating in a very confused environment, where information from many sensors will have to be analysed very rapidly, with uncertainty in much of the data. Because of the time constraints, most decisions for a strategic defence will be made by computers. In programming the computers, the confusion will have to be anticipated, and planned for.

If a multi-layered defence is to be effective, the layers ought to be coupled, and that coupling should be managed. Ideally, such a management system would track the ICBMs and RVs from 'birth' to 'death'; it would distinguish the ICBMs and RVs from the decoys, and pass that information on to all the defence layers; it would decide which defence weapon should attack each target; and at the end of an attack it should decide whether to have the weapon repeat the attack, pass the target on to another weapon in the same defence layer, or pass the target on to the next layer. These decisions will have to be made in fractions of seconds and hence computer control of these operations is essential.

There is a technical consensus that this battle management is likely to be the hardest part of an extensive strategic defence.[36] Concerns about the difficulties of managing a strategic defence have so far focused on the problem of developing a computer programme to perform this management. Can a computer programme with 10 to 100 million lines of programme code be written?[37] Opponents of 'Star Wars' point out that no computer programmes can be made error-free, particularly if it is never realistically tested. Proponents of strategic defence point to functioning computer-based systems, such as the telephone network, where errors in one part of the system can be corrected by other parts of the system. The disagreements in this debate are as much about the objectives of the battle management system as about its technical capabilities. The opponents talk about the unfeasibility of a perfect defence; the proponents talk about the feasibility of some (generally unspecified) lesser level of defence.

Countermeasures

The opponent will probably respond to a strategic defence with countermeasures. While the effectiveness of countermeasures is hard to evaluate before a specific defence system is proposed, it may be worth mentioning a few of them. The debate relating to most countermeasures is concerned with relative costs and benefits; often it focuses on the additional weight a countermeasure imposes on the offensive system, and the consequent effect on the payload which can be delivered to the target.

Hardening of Missiles
Because of their fragility, ICBMs are thought to be vulnerable to attack during the boost phase. Hardening of a missile's skin might protect it against holes being burned through it, and against the shock generated at the missile surface. The costs of such a hardening countermeasure would come in the consequent loss of missile payload; some argue that significant protection of the missile skin would considerably reduce the number of warheads that can be carried, while others argue that such effects would be relatively minor.[38] This debate cannot be readily settled without studying the destructive mechanisms in detail, and evaluating actual missile designs that are to provide such protection.

Fast-boost Missiles
The boost phase of an ICBM lasts only a short time. It may be possible to develop rockets whose boost would be completed in 50 seconds or so[39] within the earth's atmosphere. Endowing missiles with shorter boost times would reduce the effectiveness of a strategic defence. Not only would the defence have less time to intercept the ICBMs, but, further, those defences that cannot penetrate the atmosphere, such as x-ray laser beams, will become totally ineffective.

Shortening boost-phase times may generate several costs. One cost may be a reduction in payload. While some argue that payload losses for such missiles would be relatively small,[40] others argue that this loss has not been properly evaluated for a realistic rocket design.[41] Shortened boost times would increase the stresses on such a rocket, as it would be passing through denser parts of the atmosphere at higher velocities. Its construction would therefore have to be stronger, resulting in increased missile weight and reduced payload. If the bussing phase is also to be completed rapidly, RV accuracy may suffer because of unpredictable interactions with the air. Decoys cannot be released inside the atmosphere.

The debate on the feasibility of fast-boost missiles has so far been carried out mainly in the context of x-ray lasers. Such lasers would be useless for attacking ICBMs during launch if their boost-phase was completed within the atmosphere. The concern about this countermeasure is the payload loss for such a flight modification, rather than its technical feasibility. An important question is how readily the Soviet Union itself could develop and deploy such fast-boosting missiles.

Decoys
An obvious countermeasure against a strategic defence will be decoys. As the missile bus releases MIRVs it will also release balloons coated with metal and clouds of metallic chaff, and may break up into RV-sized chunks of material. An effective strategic defence must distinguish between such decoys and clouds of chaff and the real RVs. Discrimination can be passive, by looking at the emissions of light and heat from the mixture of RVs and decoys and chaff (the 'threat cloud'). But it will probably also involve active examinations of the 'threat cloud', irradiating it with some energy, say a radar beam, and then studying the return emissions.

Return radar signals can give information about the location and size of the target. Visible light can discriminate between targets and decoys on the basis of reflectivity and shape. Intense laser beams may 'tap' possible decoys; their recoil under the impact will indicate their mass.[42] Some of the most exotic DEW technologies may find their first uses in discrimination. Neutral-particle beams are being developed in part to irradiate the 'threat cloud'; the hydrogen nuclei in the beam will create many neutrons in massive RVs, but few in lightweight decoys.

The effectiveness of decoys as countermeasures depends not only on their technical feasibility, but also on cost–benefit ratios. Decoys cost both money and missile payloads; in turn, discrimination measures also cost money and involve launches into space. Sources of radiation to illuminate decoys will have to be coupled to related sensors. The resulting information will have to be fed into the strategic defence management systems. The cost effectiveness of various decoys is difficult to estimate now, since the strategic defence configuration is unknown. Some experts do predict that the cost of decoys will be cheaper than the cost of strategic defences,[43] while other experts are optimistic about the progress in discrimination techniques.[44]

ASATs

Anti-satellite systems could be a counter to space-based strategic defences. The improved ASAT systems currently under development by the United States use technologies related to strategic defences. Some proponents of strategic defences, including Teller, accept the argument that ASATs pose a major danger, and want to launch strategic defences into space only after the attack has been launched in the so-called 'pop-up' technique.

One of the concerns of the SDI R&D programme is to develop protection of satellites against such attacks.[45] One source of enthusiasm for the rail-gun concept of KE weaponry is its potential use in defending battle satellites. Even a relatively slow 'rock' fired by a rail gun would be sufficiently fast to intercept a weapon attacking a battle satellite. As indicated in Figure 11.2, ASAT weaponry will become feasible long before a strategic defence system itself becomes feasible. The costs of deploying effective ASAT systems, and of developing defences against them must be more closely studied before any cost-benefit estimates can be made.[46]

More Missiles

The ultimate countermeasure against a strategic defence would be to increase the number of missiles launched, and to increase the number of MIRV warheads carried by each missile. The Soviet Union has indicated that one of its responses to a strategic defence would be the deployment of more missiles.[47] Paul H. Nitze, the arms control adviser to the US President and the Secretary of State, has said that a strategic defence should not be deployed unless it can be cost-effective at the margin, that is unless it would cost less to build additional defences than it would cost to build additional offensive missiles.[48] The debate about the relative costs of more missiles and more defence has been extensive. It has almost been a litmus test of pro- and anti-SDI sentiment to ask whether the number of defensive satellites would have to scale linearly with, or as the square root of, the number of missiles to be intercepted.[49] That numerical question has not been settled, and the answer depends to a considerable extent on the particular system to be deployed, and on its defensive objectives.

There does appear to be a technical consensus that any strategic defence can be overcome if the opponent is willing to spend enough money on additional offensive weapons and on countermeasures such as decoys. The cost effectiveness of offence versus defence is presently indeterminate.[50] It surely will depend on the objectives of the defence;

a boost-phase defence designed to introduce uncertainty into an enemy first-strike attack will have a very different calculus from a four-layer near-perfect defence of urban populations.

CONCLUSION

If we pose the simplistic question: 'Is strategic defence technically feasible?' then the simplistic answer is that 'For some amount of money, over some time period, some strategic defence can be developed and deployed.' The fact that the answer is so unspecific indicates that the original question was indeed simplistic. The question should specify not only the objectives to be met, but also the criteria by which feasibility is to be measures.

In Figure 11.2 dates of estimated technical feasibilities were given for various strategic defence weapons systems. As has already been pointed out, systemic problems are likely to extend the establishment of technical feasibility even further into the future. But the technical feasibility depends on the objective to be met by the strategic defence. Table 11.3 lists some of these possible objectives. A very rough measure of cost is indicated for each system. The estimated time of availability takes into account only the development time of the weapon technologies needed for the specific objectives; it does not take into account delays introduced by system problems.

Silo Defence

Figure 11.2 suggests that technologies are now available for strategic defences that are designed to strengthen deterrence by protecting retaliatory missiles. Laser weapons of sufficient power and mirrors of adequate size for possible use in short-range terminal defences are now under development, as are ABM defences utilising short-range interceptor missiles with homing guidance and non-nuclear warheads. It is not settled whether a strategic defence of missile silos would be economically viable. Cost figures for an extensive defence of this type have ranged from tens of billions to a hundred billion dollars.[51] The debate over the ABM system of 1969 was to a large extent over the question whether overcoming such a limited defensive system may not be less expensive than the defence.[52] None the less there may be considerable leverage in such a silo defence. The opponent would

Table 11.3 Possible objectives of strategic defences

Strategic objective	Defensive strategy	DEW deployment		
		Weapons	Date	Cost
Deterrence by threat of retaliation	preferential terminal defence; to preserve retaliatory capability	ground-based lasers or charged-particle beams, or ground-based ABMs	1995	$100B
Deterrence by denial	terminal defence plus 25% area defence; to disrupt first strike	some space-based DEW boost-phase plus two-layer ABM	2000	$100–300B
Transition to defensive regime	90% effective area defense; damage limitation	DEW boost, DEW and KEW mid-course, two-layer ABM	2000–30	$500–1000B
Mutual assured survival	essentially perfect defence; protect populations	all types of DEW, KEW defences, all flight phases	2030	$1000B+ (impossible)

have to be sure of destroying all missile silos, while the strategic defence would have to preserve only some limited amount of its retaliatory capability. But the problem with silo defence is not so much technical feasibility as the economics, which can only be worked out for some specific defence deployment.

Deterrence by Denial

The second level of strategic defences might be an extension of deterrence by denial. This defensive strategy would protect as many military assets as possible. Its objective would be to deny the opponent any hope of inflicting significant military damage; its purpose would be to introduce sufficiently large uncertainties into the mind of the opponent about the possible military success of a first strike. Such a defence would not have to be perfect; it might be sufficient if capable of intercepting some select fraction, say 25 per cent, of incoming warheads. It might also provide some protection against a nuclear attack originating from an accidental missile launch, or a third nuclear nation.

It would be desirable to have some boost-phase interceptions as part of such a defence, since that defence layer provides such a large leverage in destroying several warheads with one attack. But if specific military targets are to be protected, subsequent layers of defence will be responsible for intercepting selected warheads. Since the availability of mid-course defences appears to be furthest in the future, a strategic defence system for deterrence by denial would therefore probably combine boost-phase and terminal defences. It would not be tied to the availability of an extensive battle management capability; the boost-phase defence would simply be a screen to reduce the requirements imposed on the terminal defence; and the terminal defence would require relatively little in the way of battle management.

Cost of a defence for deterrence by denial cannot now be established; clearly they would depend on the level of the desired defences. The wider the terminal coverage, and the more complete the boost-phase defence, the larger will be the cost. Costs as high as $300 billion have been cited by former US Secretary of Defense Robert S. McNamara.[53] The boost-phase defence would introduce considerable additional costs, since enough battle satellites would have to be deployed in space to cover the Soviet launch sites at all times.

The development of strategic defences for deterrence by denial appears to be the goal of most of those who work on strategic defence weapons. Many believe that such limited defences may be feasible, and want to make them cost effective.

Damage Limitation

The new aspect of strategic defence introduced by Reagan in his 'Star Wars' speech of 1983 is the concept of population defence. The level of protection could range from some damage limitation to perfect defence. As already indicated, some damage limitation could be achieved by a combination of boost-phase defence plus extensive terminal defences. As the desired level of protection goes much higher, the required interception capability against a full-scale nuclear attack goes to 90 per cent and higher. Then the number of defensive layers, their effectiveness, and the extent of coupling through battle management, all becomes very large.

The higher the required level of effectiveness of the defence, the further into the future stretches the time-scale over which such a defence might become available. Demonstrations of feasibility for a damage-limiting defence will, therefore, most likely not come until well into the next century; the systems problems will become paramount. The costs for a good damage-denying defence system, operating at an imperfect level of, say, 90 per cent, have been placed at $500 to $1000 billion.[54] Such cost estimates are, however, exceedingly uncertain, since they are based on very little knowledge of what such a defensive system might look like. They will clearly depend on the level of defensive performance desired.

Perfect Population Defence

Reagan's 1983 'Star Wars' speech proposed the goal of perfect population defence. It is a goal which Secretary of Defense Caspar Weinberger has endorsed,[55] and it is still implied by Reagan as remaining his objective. But the technical consensus say that a perfect defence is impossible against a nuclear attack deliberately aimed at civilian targets.[56] Since even a very few nuclear warheads are sufficient to inflict unacceptable damage on any society, and since so many delivery methods exist for nuclear warheads, it would indeed seem technically unfeasible to develop a strategic defence that is so extensive and so reliable that it can reduce the number of deliverable warheads below the level of unacceptable destruction.

Making Nuclear Weapons Obsolete

The policy of the Reagan Administration in fact appears to aim at a different usage of strategic defences. One might call that policy the obsolescence of nuclear weapons. It replaces questions of technical feasibility with questions of political feasibility.

The original 'Star Wars' proposal by Reagan spoke of making ICBMs obsolete. In this scheme the deployment of strategic defences is to occur in parallel with reductions of offensive strategic weapons. The concept is to use strategic defences to make a first strike by ICBMs useless. Once ICBMs become useless for anything other than retaliatory missions, then it might become easier to give them up through arms control agreements.[57] At the same time, the strategic defences that make ICBMs obsolete (useless), can also defend populations against those limited nuclear weapons that might still be deployed during the transition to a defence-dominated world. Ultimately strategic defences might act as insurance against a few nuclear weapons that might be deployed by third countries or be produced in secret violation of disarmament treaties.

One version of the Administration's approach to strategic defence has been formulated by Nitze.[58] His proposals recognise that strategic weapons can be potentially destabilising. They take into account the possible technological limitations of strategic defences, and the possible cost–benefit ratios. Nitze has proposed that strategic defences must satisfy two criteria before their deployment can be justified.[59]

The first Nitze criterion relates to arms-race stability. Nitze believes that strategic defences must be cost-effective at the margin. That is, if additional offensive weapons were to be deployed in an effort to overcome strategic defences, it must be cheaper to build additional defences to overcome those additional offensive weapons than it is to build those additional offensive weapons. This criterion is intended to establish arms-race stability, to insure that there is no benefit to be gained by building up the offensive weapons arsenal.

The second Nitze criterion relates to crisis stability. Nitze argues that strategic defences must not increase the chance of a nuclear war by making a pre-emptive first strike more attractive during a time of crisis. Such instability might occur for some limited strategic defences, as for a defence designed to limit damage to populations. While such a defence might not be effective for intercepting all warheads of an enemy first strike, it might appear to be quite effective against an enemy retaliatory second strike. Nitze argues that a transition to a defence-oriented world should not present such a temptation.

If the strategic offenses are limited, strategic defences might indeed become technically feasible. However, it is widely accepted that the only way to achieve such 'technically feasible' disarmament is by political negotiations, and by a 'Transition Treaty' to govern the process of disarming offensively as defences are built up. Thus, the success of the Reagan Administration's strategic defence programme will ultimately be judged not by the progress of the technologies of the Strategic Defence Initiative, but by the acceptance by the Soviet Union of a defensively-oriented world, and by the establishment of a Transition Treaty for such a defence-dominated world.

Notes

1. L. Freedman, 'The "Star Wars" Debate': The Western Alliance and Strategic Defence' in International Institute for Strategic Studies, *New Technologies and Western Security Policy*, Adelphi Paper no. 199 (London, 1985) p. 43.
2. A. Carter, *Directed Energy Missile Defense in Space: A Background Paper* (Office of Technology Assessment, Washington, DC, 1984).
3. Ibid.
4. Ibid.
5. Ibid.
6. R. L. Garwin and H. A. Bethe, 'Anti-Ballistic-Missile Systems', *Scientific American*, vol. 218, no. 3 (March 1968) pp. 13–23. See also, for example, A. Chayes and J. B. Wiesner (eds), *ABM: An Evaluation of the Decision to Deploy an Antiballistic Missile System* (New York, 1969); and J. J. Holst and W. Schneider, Jr. (eds), *Why ABM?: Policy Issues in the Missile Defence Controversy* (New York, 1969).
7. US Congress, Office of Technology Assessment (OTA), *Anti-Satellite Weapons: Countermeasures and Arms Control* (Washington, DC, 1985); and R. L. Garwin, K. Gottfried and D. L. Hafner, 'Antisatellite Weapons', *Scientific American*, vol. 250, no. 4 (June 1984) pp. 27–37.
8. 'HEDI Program Plans Missile Interception Test', *Aviation Week and Space Technology*, vol. 124, no. 12 (24 March 1986) pp. 28–9; and W. Pincus, 'Land-Based Missile Defense May be Ready in Late '90s', *Washington Post*, 30 June 1985, p. 1.
9. P. Grier and S. Armstrong, 'Star Wars', Will It Work? Cannons in Space', *Christian Science Monitor*, 5 November 1985, p. 20; 'Railgun Experiments Strive for High Velocity, Repetition', *Aviation Week and Space Technology*, vol. 124, no. 4 (27 January 1986) p. 21; and 'Electromagnetic Launcher Facility Begins Operating in California', ibid., pp. 92–3.
10. Grier and Armstrong, 'Star Wars'.
11. 'Railgun Experiments' *Aviation Week and Space Technology*.
12. Ibid.
13. 'Electromagnetic Launcher Facility', ibid.
14. G. Bekefi, B. T. Feld, J. Parmentola, and K. Tsipis, 'Particle beam weapons: a technical assessment', *Nature*, vol. 284 (1980) pp. 219–25.
15. J. Parmentola and K. Tsipis, 'Particle Beam Weapons', *Scientific American*, vol. 240, no. 4 (April 1979) pp. 54–65.
16. M. A. Dornheim, 'Scientists Produce Weapons-Grade Electron Beam from Accelerator', *Aviation Week and Space Technology*, vol. 123, no. 15 (14 October 1985) pp. 87–8.
17. 'Sandia Laser Experiment May Aid Beam Weapon Development', ibid., vol. 122 no. 16 (22 April 1985) p. 26.
18. General Keegan's position in 1977 had been that well before 1980 the Soviets would 'have technically and scientifically solved the problem of the ballistic missile threat', and by 1980 would have tested such a ballistic missile defence. (See 'Charged Particle Beams: Anatomy of a Defense Scare', *F.A.S. Public Interest Report*, vol. 30, no. 6 (June 1977) pp. 1–2.)

See also N. Wade, 'Particle Beams as ABM Weapons', *Science*, vol. 196 (1977) pp. 407–8; and 'Charged Debate Erupts over Russian Beam Weapon', ibid., pp. 957–9.
19. J. Hecht, *Beam Weapons: The Next Arms Race* (New York, 1984) p. 158.
20. C. A. Robinson, Jr, 'BMD Research Draws Strategic Focus', *Aviation Week and Space Technology*, vol. 120, no. 25 (18 June 1984) pp. 84–93; and M. A. Dornheim, 'Missile Destroyed in First SDI Test at High-Energy Laser Facility', ibid., vol. 123, no. 23 (23 September 1985) pp. 17–19.
21. Hecht, *Beam Weapons*, p. 78; W. Sweet, 'Modified SDI stresses rockets and free-electron lasers', *Physics Today*, vol. 39, no. 1 (January 1986) pp. 53–5; 'Abrahamson Cites Potential of Ground-Based Laser Defense', *Aviation Week and Space Technology*, vol. 123, no. 15 (14 October 1985) pp. 23–3; and B. M. Greeley, Jr, 'SDIO Stresses Gains in ICBM Intercept', ibid., vol. 124, no. 20 (19 May 1986) pp. 24–5.
22. K. Tsipis, 'Laser Weapons', *Scientific American*, vol. 245, no. 6 (December 1981) pp. 35–41.
23. The growth of the power output of lasers is discussed, for example, by J. F. Coneybear, 'The Use of Lasers for the Transmission of Power', *Progress in Astronautics and Aeronautics*, vol. 61 (1978) pp. 279–310. For example, in 1970 a 20 kW Chemical laser was available, while a 2-MW HF laser is supposed to become operational after 1987. That would represent 6·6 doubling periods over 17 years, or a doubling time of about 2·5 years.
24. H. Brown, 'Is SDI Technically Feasible?', *Foreign Affairs*, vol. 64, no. 3 (1986) pp. 435–54.
25. E. Teller, 'Defense: Retaliation or Protection', in R. F. Staar (ed.), *Arms Control: Myth Versus Reality* (Stanford, California, 1984) pp. 102–16.
26. S. D. Drell, P. J. Farley, and D. Holloway, *The Reagan Strategic Defense Initiative: A Technical, Political and Arms Control Assessment* (Stanford, California, 1984).
27. Ibid; and E. Walbridge, 'Angle constraint for nuclear-pumped x-ray laser weapon', *Nature*, vol. 310 (1984) pp. 180–2.
28. Teller, 'Defense: Retaliation or Protection'.
29. Ibid.
30. R. J. Smith, 'X-Ray Laser Budget Grows as Public Information Declines', *Science*, vol. 232 (1986) pp. 152–3.
31. R. J. Smith, 'Experts Cast Doubt on X-ray Laser', *Science*, vol. 230 (1985) pp. 646–8; 'Lab Officials Squabble Over X-Ray Laser', ibid., p. 923; 'Livermore Acknowledges X-Ray Laser Problems', ibid., p. 1023.
32. W. J. Broad, *Star Warriors* (New York, 1985).
33. Carter, *Directed Energy Missile Defense in Space*, p. 14, figure 3.4.
34. R. L. Garwin, 'How Many Orbiting Lasers for Boost Phase Intercept?', *Nature*, vol. 315 (1985) pp. 286–90.
35. T. O'Toole, 'President Orders Study of Bigger Space Shuttle', *Washington Post*, 3 March 1985, p. 12; and B. M. Greeley, Jr, 'NASA/Defense Dept. Study Examines Launcher Concepts', *Aviation Week and Space Technology*, vol. 124, no. 26 (30 June 1986) pp. 22–3.
36. C. W. Cordry, 'Fitting various advances into single systems may be

difficult', *Baltimore Sun*, 19 March 1985, p. 1; and R. R. Ropelewski, 'Battle Management, C³I Network Challenges Resources of SDI Office', *Aviation Week and Space Technology*, vol. 123, no. 3 (15 July 1985) pp. 19–21.
37. W. J. Broad has reported that 'According to one estimate, the software [to keep 'star wars' running smoothly during a fast paced attack] would contain nearly 10 million lines of code, by far the largest program ever written', (*New York Times*, 5 February, 1985, p. C–1.). See also R. J. Smith, 'Star Wars Grants Attract Universities', *Science*, vol. 228 (1985) p. 304.
38. 'Letters to the Editor', *Physics Today*, vol. 39, no. 3 (March 1986) pp. 9–15, 142–8.
39. Carter, *Directed Energy Missile Defense in Space*; and Drell, Farley, and Holloway, *The Reagan Strategic Defense Initiative*.
40. Drell, Farley and Holloway, *The Reagan Strategic Defense Initiative*.
41. R. Jastrow, 'The War Against "Star Wars"', *Commentary*, vol. 78, no. 6, (December 1984) pp. 19–25.
42. Ibid.
43. Carter, *Directed Energy Missile Defense in Space*, p. 69.
44. *The Fletcher Report: The Strategic Defense Initiative: Defense Technologies Studies for the DoD* (Washington, DC, 1984) p. 10.
45. Z. Brzezsinski, R. Jastrow, and M. Kampelman, 'Defense in Space is Not "Star Wars"', *New York Times Magazine*, 27 January 1985, pp. 28–9.
46. OTA, *Anti-Satellite Weapons: Countermeasures and Arms Control*, pp. 75–88.
47. S. Talbott, 'Putting It on the Table: Star Wars the big obstacle as the U.S. and Soviets return to Geneva', *Time*, vol. 125, no. 10 (11 March 1985) pp. 6–11; and S. M. Meyer, 'Soviet Strategic programmes and the US SDI', *Survival*, vol. 27, no. 6 (1985) pp. 274–92.
48. P. Nitze, 'On the Road to a More Stable Peace', address to the Philadelphia World Affairs Council, 20 February 1985.
49. W. D. Hartung, R. W. De Grasse, Jr, R. Nimroody, S. Daggett, and J. Brugman, *The Strategic Defense Initiative: Costs, Contractors and Consequences* (Washington, DC, 1985) Appendix I.
50. G. Field and D. Spergel, 'Cost of Space-Based Laser Ballistic Missile Defense', *Science*, vol. 231 (1986) pp. 1387–93; and R. Jastrow, *Making Nuclear Weapons Obsolete*, (Boston, 1985) pp. 128–31.
51. From a US Department of Defense study on laser weapons (1982) printed in *Strategic Defense and Anti-Satellite Weapons* (Hearing before the Committee on Foreign Relations, United States Senate, 98th congress, Second Session, Washington, DC, 1984) p. 76.
52. Garwin and Bethe, 'Anti-Ballistic-Missile Systems'; Chayes and Wiesner (eds), *ABM*; and Holst and Schneider (eds), *Why ABM?*
53. C. Mohr, 'McNamara and Brown Question Missile Defense', *New York Times*, 1 April 1986.
54. Ibid.; and W. Hartung and R. Nimroody, 'Star Wars: What Price Strategic Defense?', *Council of Economic Priorities Newsletter* (January 1985) pp. 1–6; C. Mohr, 'Space Lasers Might Stop Half of Missile Attack, Expert Says', *New York Times*, 31 March 1983, p. 20; R. de Lauer,

Testimony on HR3073 People Protection Act (Hearings before the Research and Development and Investigations Subcommittee of the House Committee on Armed Services, Washington, DC, 10 November 1983) p. 26; 'Star Wars "may cost $670 bn"', *Financial Times*, 23 July 1986, p. 5; and C. Mohr, 'U.S. Anti-Missile Defense Is Affordable, Study Says', *New York Times*, 24 July 1986.
55. C. W. Weinberger, 'Strategic Defense in Perspective', *Defense 86* (January/February 1986) pp. 3–6.
56. R. J. Smith, 'Weapons Bureaucracy Spurns Star Wars Gold', *Science*, vol. 224 (1984) pp. 32–4; *F.A.S. Public Interest Report*, vol. 38, no. 3 (March 1985) p. 3; and Carter, *Directed Energy Missile Defense in Space*, p. 81.
57. G. A. Keyworth II, 'The Case for Arms Control and the Strategic Defense Initiative', *Arms Control Today*, vol. 15, no. 3 (April 1985) pp. 1, 2, 8; Brent Scowcroft quoted in T. Wicker, '"Stars Wars" vs the MX', *New York Times*, 15 March 1985, p. 27; and C. Mohr, 'What Moscow Might Do in Replying to "Star Wars"', *New York Times*, 6 March 1985, p. 1.
58. P. H. Nitze, 'The Promise of SDI', address before the American Defense Preparedness Association, Washington, DC, 18 March 1986.
59. Nitze, 'On the Road to a More Stable Peace'.

12 Directed-Energy Weapons, Strategic Defence and Arms Control
Dietrich Schroeer

INTRODUCTION

This chapter will examine the relationship between the directed-energy weapon (DEW) technologies of strategic defence and arms control. The relationship between arms control and strategic defence is largely a political matter. But for DEWs, the most exotic of the strategic-defence weapons, that relationship is bounded by technological feasibilities. These technological bounds make it worthwhile to examine the specific relationship between DEWs and arms control. The technological feasibilities of DEWs will be taken as described in the preceding chapter.[1] It is intended then to examine the effect of these strategic-defence technologies on stability and arms control. Finally, there is an examination of methods for directing the new DEW defence technologies into desirable channels, that is applying arms control to strategic defence.

THE TECHNOLOGIES OF DIRECTED-ENERGY WEAPONS

The most relevant conclusions about DEW technologies from the preceding chapter are as follows. For a ground-based terminal defence, a 2MW HF laser with a 4m diameter mirror might be useful. Both of these technologies are currently under development, so that deployment might conceivably come in the early 1990s. Thus the technology for strategic defence to enforce deterrence by retaliation is at hand. The only question is whether such a defence is cost-effective and is desirable from a stability perspective.

For a space-based strategic defence against ICBMs during their boost phase, one set of technological requirements might include about 185 satellites each housing a 10m mirror coupled to a 20MW HF laser. These mirrors might be proved feasible by 1996, the lasers by 1995. Prototypes might be available five years later. Hence deployment of such a defence component might begin around the turn of the century. Such a defence could make possible a more extensive defence of military assets, leading to an enhancement of deterrence by denying the enemy the achievement of military objectives. If this defence is extensive enough it might also offer some protection against accidental launches and against attacks by smaller nuclear powers.

Mid-course defences might require the development of ground-based lasers, with relay mirrors in geosynchronous orbit and battle mirrors in low-earth orbits. The ground-based mirror might have to be as large as 50 metres and contain adaptive optics to correct for atmospheric distortions of the laser beam. The laser might be a free-electron laser with a power output of 1000 MW. Extrapolations suggest that these technologies will not be available as prototypes until perhaps the second decade of the next century. A strategic defence, which is intended to limit damage to populations, will most probably have to include such mid-course defences; this suggests that truly significant damage-limiting strategic defences will not be available for deployment until several decades into the next century.

The most important problem faced in developing extensive strategic defences will be in the systems developments. These problems grow as the strategic defence becomes more extensive and effective. The technical consensus is that it is most unlikely that a near-perfect population defence will ever be available against a strategic attack that is specifically aimed at population centres.

The present state of DEW technologies therefore says that some strategic defence can be carried out with the time-scale and cost depending on the objective to be met. Assured full-scale population defence appears to be impossible in a world of large numbers of Intercontinental Ballistic Missiles (ICBMs), Submarine-launched Ballistic Missiles (SLBMs), bombers and other delivery systems, and in a world armed with ingenious countermeasures. Some form of arms control would appear necessary to achieve a state of mutual assured survival. Another important technical conclusion is that any DEW technology for strategic defence appears to be even more suitable for anti-satellite purposes.

THE EFFECTS OF DIRECTED-ENERGY WEAPONS ON ARMS CONTROL

Introduction

The development of DEW technologies for strategic defence is likely to have several effects on efforts to achieve and maintain arms control; in fact, it challenges traditional arms control. The possibilities of such new defensive technologies as DEWs were indirectly taken into account in the 1972 Anti-Ballistic Missile (ABM) Treaty. In his 1983 'Star Wars' speech, President Ronald Reagan, however, asked for a reorientation in strategic affairs toward defences. In this reorientation, the ABM Treaty is a hindrance rather than a cornerstone, and DEW defences are thought to be very desirable, even essential.

This conflict between the ABM Treaty and possible uses of DEWs is symptomatic of the two-sided relationship between DEWs and arms control. The possibility of using DEWs for global strategic defence requires a re-examination of the objectives of arms control, a reconsideration of what aspects of that technology are desirable, and consideration as to how one might use arms control to allow the desirable while controlling the undesirable. However, the development of high-technology DEWs is also likely to have more immediate effects on the further militarisation of space, the development of Anti-Satellite (ASAT) weapons, the ABM Treaty, and on arms control as a process.

The Militarisation of Space

The development of strategic defences will increase the military uses of space. While considerable activity related to military command, control, communication and intelligence (C^3I) is already located in space,[2] so far no weapons have been positioned there. A boost-phase strategic defence alone would involve the deployment of more than a hundred large armed satellite battle stations.

Large increases in the military utilisation of space would politicise space far beyond the current level. Secrecy would be invoked in virtually all space activities, as civilian space efforts would make up a decreasingly small fraction of all work in space. A new larger space shuttle would be a military device, since no pressing civilian needs for it are foreseeable.

Anti-Satellite Development

The development of anti-satellite weapons is intimately linked to that of strategic defences, particularly for ASAT systems based on DEWs. Since DEW technology would be usable for ASAT purposes at a much lower level of performance than would be required for strategic defence, any development of DEW-based strategic defences would automatically produce ASAT weapons. Furthermore, ASAT systems would become very desirable to threaten deployed strategic defences.

Even if research and development on advanced strategic defences never produces a useful system, the capabilities of ASAT weapons will be enhanced. Many DEW technologies, such as beam generators, and tracking, aiming and management systems, are usable in ASAT systems. Research, development and deployment of advanced strategic defences represent an automatic commitment to research and development of ASAT systems.

Directed-Energy Weapons and the Outer Space and Limited Test-Ban treaties.

The continuing development and the possible future deployment of DEWs as part of strategic defences will, possibly quite soon, have an impact on several existing arms-control agreements, including the Outer-Space and Test-Ban Treaties.

The Outer Space Treaty of 1967 forbids the emplacement of weapons of mass destruction in space. Article IV says that 'States Party to the Treaty undertake not to place in orbit around the earth any objects carrying nuclear weapons or any other kinds of weapons of mass destruction...'[3] Most of the contemplated strategic defences using DEWs would not violate this prohibition, since DEWs cannot readily be used to create mass destruction.[4] The energy released, while quite concentrated, is also quite small. The total energy contained in a 8-sec shot from a 20 MW laser aiming over 3000 km at an ICBM in the boost phase, would be about 160 MJ, which is equivalent to the energy released by the explosion of about 40 kg of TNT. The energy released in a 40 KT nuclear explosion is a million times larger.

However the emplacement in space of nuclear explosives to fuel x-ray lasers would be forbidden under this treaty. Pop-up techniques, in which the x-ray lasers with their nuclear explosives are launched into space without going into a permanent orbit, would not be prohibited by this treaty.

The Limited Test-Ban Treaty of 1963 forbids the explosion of nuclear weapons above ground. Article I states that 'Each of the Parties to this Treaty undertakes ... not to carry out any nuclear ... explosion ... in the atmosphere ... beyond its limits including outer space ...'.[5] This language affects DEW systems directly by preventing any tests of x-ray lasers in space. It affects them indirectly by forbidding tests of countermeasures involving nuclear explosions as, for example, the generation of black-outs of radar systems. This ban on nuclear explosions in space therefore prevents a complete evaluation of the capabilities and problems of DEW systems. That increases the uncertainty about the reliability and effectiveness both of the defence systems and of the countermeasures designed to overcome them.

Directed-Energy Weapons and the ABM Treaty

The greatest impact of developing DEWs will be on the ABM Treaty of 1972. The ABM Treaty limits the deployment of missile-based anti-ballistic defences, and places some restrictions on the testing of ballistic-missile systems. Article II of the Treaty defines anti-ballistic missile systems broadly: '... an ABM system is a system to counter strategic ballistic missiles or their elements in flight trajectory, currently consisting of ...'.[6] DEW strategic defences would seem to fit this definition of ABM systems. The ABM Treaty appears to forbid the development, testing and deployment of space-based DEW defences,[7] when Article V says that 'Each Party undertakes not to develop, test or deploy ABM systems or components which are sea-based, air-based, space-based or mobile land-based'.[8] Deployment of ground-based DEW systems as part of a terminal defence around a missile silo complex or the national capital appear to be allowed, since such defences using ABM missiles are allowed. However, the US Arms Control and Disarmament Agency has interpreted the Treaty as forbidding such deployment unless the Parties consult and amend the Treaty.[9] Certainly the definition of the laser equivalent of a launcher might be difficult to establish.

The effect of the ABM Treaty on the development and testing of components of DEW defences is more problematical. Tests of fixed land-based ABM systems are allowed under the ABM Treaty, although only at clearly specified ABM test ranges; Article IV says that 'The limitations [on deployment of ABM systems or their components] ... shall not apply to ABM systems or their components used for development or testing, and located within current or additionally agreed test ranges'.[10] Thus tests of ground-based DEW defences at these ranges would seem to be allowed.[11] In contrast, since DEW tests in earth orbit would not be of fixed land-based components, such tests would seem to violate the Treaty in its existing form.

However, the issue concerning the development and testing of exotic non-missile ABM systems is confused by the Agreed Statement D, which says that '... in the event ABM systems based on other physical principles and including components capable of substituting for ABM interceptor missiles, ABM launchers, or ABM radars are created in the future, specific limitations on such systems and their components would be subject to discussions in accordance with Article XIII and agreement in accordance with Article XIV of the Treaty'.[12] This might be taken to mean that non-missile defences would be banned only on the basis of new agreements reached after discussions, implying that DEW defensive systems would be allowed unless forbidden after discussions. Most international lawyers and negotiators of the ABM Treaty have argued that the Treaty as a whole prohibits any ABM activities that are not specifically allowed.[13] However the Reagan Administration has interpreted Agreed Statement D as permitting not only research, but testing and development of exotic new technologies such as beam weapons.[14] Most outsiders to the Reagan Administration think this broad interpretation of the ABM Treaty is wrong.[15] And for the time being, Secretary of State George P. Shultz has stated that the 'SDI research program ... will continue to be conducted in accordance with a restrictive interpretation of the treaty's obligations'.[16] But there has been the repeated threat by members of the Reagan Administration that this 'broad' interpretation shall be invoked to allow advanced SDI tests in space to take place.[17]

The ABM Treaty does demand that tests of ABM components be distinguishable from other military and civilian activities. Article XII.3 says that 'Each Party undertakes not to use deliberate concealment measures which impede verification by national technical means of compliance with the provisions of this Treaty'.[18] Considerable co-operative measures might have to be undertaken if such distinctions were to be made clear and unambiguous for DEW developments.

A major concern is how soon part of the SDI research programme might violate some provisions of the ABM Treaty.[19] The answer to that concern hinges on the definition of the words 'develop' and 'component'. The US Department of Defense has interpreted the ABM Treaty as allowing three types of development and testing.[20] First is conceptual design or laboratory testing: this could be laboratory testing of ABM-related equipment before it is turned into a prototype or a breadboard model for field testing. Second is 'field testing' of devices that are not ABM components or prototypes of ABM components: this depends critically on the distinction between components that might be directly usable in strategic defences, and various adjuncts or sub-components that would have to be integrated with other sub-components to perform the function of one of the three components recognised in the 1972 ABM Treaty – that is, interception (as an ABM missile), launching (as an ABM launcher) or guidance to interception (as one of the ABM radars). Third is 'field testing' of fixed land-based components; this is specifically allowed at agreed ABM test ranges.

The Department of Defense justifies various proposed SDI tests by placing them within one or the other of these permitted categories.[21] Several demonstration projects of the SDI DEW programme are of particular concern. The Alpha laser and LODE optics experiments are justified as being ground based, to be done 'under roof', and incapable of achieving ABM performance levels. The revised Talon Gold Acquisition, Tracking and Aiming demonstration programme is initially to involve only ground-based laboratory experiments. Then, in its space-based development phase, it is to involve only parts of the required technologies that would be needed in a complete tracking system. And it supposedly will not be capable of performing at a level adequate for an operational defence. In justifying all these activities, the Department of Defense emphasises the arguments that these SDI developments will involve sub-systems that would be only parts of a complete ABM-equivalent component, or will not be prototypes useful in an ABM mode.

T. K. Longstreth, J. E. Pike and J. B. Rhinelander are not persuaded that all of these DEW tests are consistent with the ABM Treaty.[22] For example, the Talon Gold tracking technology, since it has a resolution that is adequate for some ABM functions, would seem to be equivalent in function to ABM radars. Difficult questions would be raised if a full-scale demonstration of the whole laser triad were to take place in orbit in the early 1990s.

In the short term, the greatest challenge from the SDI research programme to the ABM Treaty will probably come from space-based sensors that could be useful for missile-based and kinetic-energy defences as well as for DEW-based defences. These sensors can be interpreted as being equivalent to one or the other of the perimeter-acquisition or missile-site radars that are limited by the ABM Treaty. Whether or not the SDI programme is inconsistent with the ABM Treaty depends to some extent on interpretations of treaty language. The problems introduced by insufficient clarity in treaty language has already been demonstrated in the debate about several possible Soviet violations of the ABM Treaty.[23] US Senator Albert Gore, among others, has proposed negotiations to define more carefully the terms 'components', 'development' and 'testing' in the ABM Treaty.[24] In practice, such clarification could be sought in the Standing Consultative Commission established under Article III.

One additional limitation is imposed by the ABM Treaty on strategic defences involving third parties. The Agreed Statement G provides that '... the Treaty includes the obligation of the US and the USSR not to provide to other States technical descriptions or blueprints specially worked out for the construction of ABM systems and their components limited by the Treaty'.[25] This may affect the ability of European nations to participate in the R&D portion of the SDI programme. It would also seem that the technology of strategic defences could not be shared by the United States with its NATO allies once it is developed. Under Article IX of the ABM Treaty, ABM systems also cannot be deployed in other countries: '... each Party undertakes not to transfer to other States, and not to deploy outside its national territory, ABM systems or their components ...'.[26] This limitation might raise problems if strategic defences were to be deployed to protect Western Europe; it is already raising concern in Great Britain because of the upgrading of the Fylingdales Ballistic Missile Early Warning System (BMEWS) radar to a phase-array configuration.

The SDI programme on DEWs does not now violate the ABM Treaty. But it may have to do so in the early 1990s if certain space-based tests are to explore boost-phase and mid-course defences. Even some of the earlier testing programmes are, however, only permissible if the concepts of 'development', 'components' and 'ABM-capable', are very narrowly interpreted. Violations may come very soon if a push is made within the SDI programme for earlier demonstrations of feasibility for some less exotic technologies. Any reinterpretations of the ABM Treaty will necessarily allow the Soviet research programme to perform similar tests.

Effects of Directed-Energy Weaponry on the Arms Control Process

The ultimate objective of the SDI-programme in Reagan's view is to allow the replacement of deterrence through retaliation by a policy of mutual assured survival to be achieved by making nuclear weapons obsolete.[27] For the realisable future that ultimate goal is expressed in terms of enhancing deterrence by eliminating the high-accuracy ICBMs which threaten a first-strike capability.[28] In general, the desire is for a defence-dominated world.

This defensive reorientation will have an impact on arms control both in a national and an international sense. The desire for a defence reorientation has revealed a major doctrinal clash within American arms control circles. The clash is between those who see mutual assured destruction as an unavoidable fact of the nuclear age, and those who insist that something must be done now to eliminate it. Many of the objections to the SDI programme are based on judgements that a defence-dominated strategic future is impossible as long as nuclear weapons exist, and that the fruitless search for that future is itself destabilising.

A similar clash has arisen internationally. The concept of a defence-oriented future has become a guiding principle for the United States in the current arms control talks with the Soviet Union.[29] In the past deterence through the threat of retaliation has been seen as the only feasible policy for the use of strategic nuclear weapons. Therefore the objective of arms control so far has been to maintain crisis and arms-race stability, to control these deterrent forces in such a way as to eliminate any incentives for either a pre-emptive first strike during a time of crisis or for engaging in a nuclear arms race. The ABM Treaty is generally seen as an expression of the belief that strategic defences are destabilising in these two senses. Now the United States wants to use strategic defence to deny the Soviet Union its military objectives, rather than threatening retaliatory punishment; and wants to couple a decrease in offensive nuclear weapons with the build-up of strategic area defences, so that in the long run damage to populations in a nuclear war can be minimised.

One of the objectives of the current arms control negotiations is to persuade the Soviet Union that the replacement of strategic offences by strategic defences makes doctrinal sense. Injecting such a radically new doctrine into arms control negotiations makes them more difficult. The problem will be to induce the Soviet Union to co-operate in a transition to deterrence through defence.[30]

The SDI research programme is itself a major point of contention in current arms control talks. SDI research and development may itself be a hindrance to reaching arms control agreements.[31] Many believe that the SDI, with its threat of possible defensive deployments, has brought the Soviet Union back to the negotiating table.[32] Now the Soviet Union demands that research on strategic defences be strictly limited as a precondition for achieving any agreement on strategic weapons.[33] Yet the Reagan Administration continues to hold the view that a transition to strategic defences is the key to any future arms control and to strategic stability. If the two sides are serious in their arguments, then this doctrinal conflict may be insoluble.[34]

ARMS CONTROL OF DIRECTED-ENERGY WEAPONS

Beyond understanding the effects of DEWs on arms control, one needs to consider possible arms control of such weapons. Is the development and deployment of DEW strategic defence technologies desirable? If so, how can this development be guided into configurations that are consistent with the relevant strategic objectives?

Objectives of DEW Arms Control

Arms control can have a variety of objectives, some of them possibly mutually contradictory. Arms controllers are interested in limiting and reducing nuclear weapons, both in numbers and in kind. But they also want to reduce the probability of nuclear war. These two goals emphasise different aspects of strategic stability. Arms-race stability is a condition in which no nation has an incentive to increase the levels of its armaments. Crisis stability is a condition in which no nation has an incentive to attack the opponent in a pre-emptive first strike during a crisis. The ideal goal of the new defence orientation carries arms-race stability to its logical conclusion of eliminating all nuclear arms. It proposes to use effective strategic defences to make nuclear weapons no longer useful implements in international security affairs. That goal imposes an additional requirement of transitional stability, a condition in which the transition towards such a defensive state should at no time increase the likelihood of a nuclear war. These arms-control objectives have various implications for DEWs.

Economics and the Control of DEWs

Strategic defences will be quite expensive, particularly when they focus on area defence of populations, and when they require the development of DEWs. Avoiding such a large new economic defence burden could be an objective of arms control.

Most analysts, even those strongly opposed to strategic defences, support a research programme on such defences.[35] They cite the need to avoid technological surprise, and the desirability of developing appropriate countermeasures to defensive deployments by the opponent. Some, however, are concerned that the research expenditures in the SDI programme are too large, that the research is already going beyond exploring the feasibility of defensive systems.[36]

Some SDI critics worry that, once the defensive technologies become available, it may become difficult to make dispassionate policy decisions concerning deployment. The fear of such technological imperatives is not universally accepted. Jonathan B. Stein has in fact argued that the SDI programme was proposed against the judgement of technical experts.[37] But those worried about such a technological momentum (and about a possible institutional momentum as well),[38] are not reassured by recurrent demands for the rapid deployment of some defences,[39] nor by the vision of the Director of the SDI Organization, James Abrahamson, that 'It is the responsibility of the SDI program to ensure the availability of technological options ... [in case of need ... and to] grasp the opportunity associated with a defensive system'.[40]

In contrast, other arguments in favour of research on high-technology strategic defences are flavoured with technological optimism. Banning military DEW research might eliminate some civilian spin-offs. To achieve a verifiable limitation of military-oriented DEW research, some related civilian research might also have to be controlled.

The argument is made by many that the United States is already engaged in a development competition in the field of strategic defence.[41] Since the United States has a significant lead in many of the technologies of DEW systems, such as sensors, computers, and electronic management, should it not exploit that technological advantage?

Arguments about the economic feasibility of deployment go beyond those about research and development. In the past the deployment of some weapons systems has initiated mutual arms races, with no ultimate net military benefits to either side.[42] Some claim that the development of strategic defences, including DEW systems, would generate a new spiral in the arms race.[43] They believe that this new arms race should be halted before it leads to a deterioration in the strategic balance, at great expense.

It seems reasonable to demand of strategic defences that they be cheaper than any offences deployed to counter them. Paul H. Nitze, the Reagan Administration's senior arms control adviser, has proposed as a criterion for the deployment of a strategic defence that it must be 'cost-effective at the margin, that is, it must be cheap enough to add additional defensive capability, so that the other side has no incentive to add additional offensive capability to overcome the defense'.[44] Cost-effectiveness can of course be calculated several other ways. One might instead compare the costs of deploying full defensive and full offensive systems, or compare the full costs of a defensive system with the marginal costs of adding enough off-setting offences.[45] For either definition, the question arises whether enough knowledge about such cost-effectiveness will exist at the time that deployment decisions are to be taken, and whether the criteria can be applied to SDI technology in a completely analytical fashion, once the technology has become available.

DEWs and Stability

Arms control is supposed to increase strategic stability. Stability in international relations improves as risk-taking is discouraged. Stability increases with improved knowledge of the opponent's capabilities and predictability of his behaviour, reduction of tensions, and decreased incentives for pre-emptive attacks during crises. Strategic defences in space in one sense are intrinsically destabilising. They are a tempting target for a pre-emptive attack in times of crisis, just as they would also be an important target early in any superpower conflict. For this reason, the invulnerability of strategic defences has been given as one criterion for judging their desirability.[46]

Ideally the goal of strategic planning should be to decrease both the chance of a nuclear war breaking out, and its consequences if one were to take place. These two goals may not always be mutually consistent. The emphasis of the doctrine of deterrence by threat of massive retaliation has been on decreasing the probability of nuclear war by making the consequences unacceptably large. In contrast, strategic defence, with its DEWs, would aim to decrease the probability of nuclear war by decreasing the benefits resulting from the use of nuclear weapons. Proponents of the limiting of strategic defences argue that any defensive activities designed to decrease the consequences of a nuclear exchange, also increase the chances of such an exchange taking place. Since they see mutual assured destruction as a fact of life, they believe that strategic defences are destabilising on several levels.

DEW ASAT systems and stability   Anti-satellite capabilities are an inevitable adjunct of strategic defences. ASAT systems, particularly those employing DEWs, can affect strategic stability in several ways. Satellites now perform functions of surveillance, warning and communications. Those functions that support second-strike forces are usually seen as stabilising, while those that support first-strike capabilities are generally judged as destabilising.

An ASAT system is sometimes seen as a deterrent against use by an opponent of his own ASAT system. But a large and capable DEW ASAT system, which could attack many satellites instantly and simultaneously, would probably be seen by an opponent as a destabilising component of a first-strike threat.

Defences of military assets and strategic stability   Strategic defences including DEWs might be useful in the defence of militarily important targets, such as ICBM silos. Such point defences are said to preserve crisis stability, since they remove incentives for a pre-emptive first strike in a crisis.

Defences of military assets may also contribute to arms-race stability. If the Soviet Union were to insist on maintaining whatever first-strike capability it had prior to an American defensive deployment, even an imperfect defence of military targets might force the deployment of a very large compensatory offensive force. The leverage arises because the point defence can select which military assets it wants to protect, while the pre-emptive offence would want to be certain of being able to attack successfully all military targets. When relatively small defensive expenditures can only be offset by large offensive costs, arms-race stability is enhanced. This justification for defences works only if the defences are reasonably inexpensive, and if a realistic first-strike threat exists.

The objective of strategic defences initially was couched in terms of getting rid of nuclear weapons altogether. Gradually the focus has come to be the elimination of the most destabilising nuclear weapons, the highly-accurate MIRVed land-based ICBMs. The hope is that even an incomplete strategic defence will cause the Soviet Union to judge that a first strike with ICBMs cannot accomplish its military objectives. Then it will recognise that offensive missiles are of little use, are obsolescent, and will agree to limit them.[47] The measure of success for this strategy of deterrence by denial (of military objectives) will be the resulting level of arms reductions. However, many believe that the most likely response of the Soviet Union to such strategic defences will instead be to build up its offensive strategic forces.[48]

Damage limitation and strategic instability Proponents of a limited area ballistic missile defence may agree that effective protection of populations against large-scale nuclear attacks is impossible. None the less, they see value in some damage-limiting capability, and would support the deployment of such defences. They argue that even a partial defence could intercept small numbers of ICBMs launched accidentally by a superpower, or deliberately by smaller nuclear powers. Such a defence would decrease the damage caused by a limited launch, and thereby reduce the possibility of an accidental full-scale nuclear conflict. In this sense such a capability would represent increased stability. However, since such a defence would defend populations, it might have to be so extensive that it would threaten to negate the Soviet retaliatory capability that might survive an American first strike. That possibility would increase crisis instability.

If deployed by the Soviet Union, such damage-limiting area defence might threaten the usefulness of the nuclear deterrents of France and Great Britain. This might trigger nuclear arms build-ups by the second-rank nuclear powers.[49] On the other hand, the existence of strategic defences might discourage some presently non-nuclear countries from ever developing their own strategic nuclear forces.

A damage-limiting defence might generate tensions within NATO. On the one hand, some Americans believe that an effective strategic defence would enhance the credibility of the American nuclear commitment to the defence of Western Europe, by increasing the probability that the American President would indeed authorise the use of tactical nuclear weapons in the face of a successful Soviet conventional attack. In short, the United States might go further in the defence of Europe if it knew that it could better survive a small escalatory nuclear strike by Soviet forces.

On the other hand, European concerns about the renewed American interest in strategic defences have been mostly about the contrary possibility. Europeans wonder whether they would still be protected by the American nuclear umbrella if the United States were to develop significant population defences. Would a defended United States still see its vital interests involved in Europe, or would the United States then leave Europe vulnerable to a Soviet nuclear threat? Europeans instinctively fear any defensive measures by the United States as the start of a retreat to 'Fortress America'.[50] From the European perspective, an invasion of Western Europe by the Soviet Union can best be prevented if the Soviet Union accepts that the United States might retaliate with a nuclear strike in a response to an attack on any member of NATO.[51] In an attempt to defuse this concern, the United States has promised that strategic defences could protect Europe as well as American territory.

Europeans also fear the effect of strategic defence on stability in the conventional arms area. Might the expenditures on strategic defence significantly reduce the money available for conventional forces? Would an effective nuclear defence put renewed emphasis on conventional forces in Europe, laying bare NATO's conventional inferiority?

Arms control faces a major challenge in dealing with damage-limiting strategic defences. It will be difficult to permit the deployment of defences that reduce the effects of nuclear attacks, without increasing the instabilities in the superpower balance. The interest of West European nations in strategic defences are significantly different from American interests; arms control must not leave them feeling more vulnerable, and hence less stable.

The elimination of MAD The ultimate objective for strategic defence could be the elimination of mutual assured destruction as a fact. The dream could be an essentially perfect defensive screen over the United States and its allies. Reagan's speech of March 1983, for the first time since the development of nuclear weapons, held out the hope of releasing civilisation from the threat of nuclear annihilation. But a perfect strategic defence is technically impossible. Stability with strategic defences can only be achieved if no offensive threat is there, needing to be deterred. Therefore the long-term goal has become a combination of build-up of strategic defences simultaneously with the reduction of strategic offences. In going through the transition toward a perfect defence, a regime of great potential instabilities must be transversed. As strategic defences are developed, any asymmetries in them present a great danger. Even if strategic defence technologies were shared between the two superpowers, there would come a time during the deployment period when the defence of one side would be effective enough to threaten the assured-destruction capability of the other side. This would generate crisis instability, causing the lagging nation to consider a pre-emptive strike at times of great tension.[52] Even if perfectly symmetric area defences were deployed, uncertainties about the leakage rates of the defences could produce instabilities.[53] Therefore, in order to achieve continuing crisis stability, it would seem that the strategic offences should be reduced simultaneously.

Is DEW Arms Control Desirable?
The debate about the economic acceptability of strategic defences may be resolved in time, although not necessarily before a deployment decision is made. If strategic defence is indeed as expensive as its opponents claim, then the electoral 'market-place' may settle the issue of large-scale defensive deployments even without arms control.

The critical debate about controlling strategic defences most probably lies rather in the destabilisation in strategic affairs that may occur prior to deployment of full-scale strategic defences. Arms control might help limit this destabilisation. The proponents of arms control for strategic defence must be convincing in their arguments that even the search for a strategic defence is likely to be destabilising, increasing the probability of a nuclear war. Freeman Dyson makes the type of argument that must be countered by the proponents of defence arms control. He argues for a defence orientation in a non-quantitative manner. He accepts that so many people would die in any nuclear war, even with defence, that the number of lives possibly saved by defences cannot be used in any cost–benefit analysis of defences. None the less, he feels that, on moral grounds, an effort ought to be made to save some lives in case of nuclear war.[54]

In return, the proponents of the development of strategic defences should not use the promise of making nuclear weapons impotent and obsolete as an argument against arms control of such defences. The elimination of the state of mutual assured destruction by means of strategic defences alone seems so unlikely in any foreseeable future that as a goal it should not affect public policy decisions, not even the decision whether or not to submit strategic defence to arms control.

The debate about the arms control of strategic defence could be much clearer if the distinction between defences of military assets and of populations were always kept in mind and clearly stated. The objective of disturbing enemy first-strike planning by protecting military targets is very different from the objective of mitigating the consequences of a nuclear war by area defences of populations. These objectives, and the weapons systems to achieve them, differ greatly in cost and feasibility; the former could use existing technologies, the latter must be space-based, and would use DEWs. They differ greatly in their effects on strategic stability. They most likely will also differ in the extent to which they could be subjected to arms control measures. Only by keeping these objectives clearly distinct can reasonable judgements be made on the desirability of subjecting defensive technologies to arms control.

Possible Arms Control for Directed-energy Weapons

The future path of DEW arms control obviously differs depending on the strategic objectives of such control. To preserve deterrence through retaliation, a careful clarification of the 1972 ABM Treaty might be sufficient. To achieve mutual assured survival through the obsolescence of ICBMs and nuclear weapons, a totally different type of treaty would be required to manage the transition through possible instabilities on the way to a defence-orientated strategic balance. Some simple treaties falling well short of direct DEW arms control might be useful to achieve limited objectives. It might, for example, be desirable to remove some of the uncertainties in space activities. There is a broad concensus that 'rules of the road' for space activities might act as confidence-building measures.[55]

Arms control measures aimed specifically at DEW development and deployment would not only have the many objectives described above, but would also need to focus on a variety of systems ranging from ASATs to global defences; and they could impose limitations ranging from restrictions on some weapons-related research and development, all the way up to prohibiting the deployment of dedicated strategic defence systems. In many instances, the control of DEWs would have to be coupled to control of those non-DEWs that could perform the same functions.

Total DEW Ban
The arms control objectives of crisis stability and arms-race stability could be achieved by retaining deterrence by the threat of retaliation. That could be served by a total ban on all strategic defences, in particular on the newer high technologies of DEWs for space-based area defences. Such arms control could be achieved by retaining and strengthening the 1972 ABM Treaty. Improvements would have to come in several respects. For DEW systems the distinction between point defences and area defences is hard to establish. Therefore, it might be best to ban all point defences, or at least such defences should be clearly restricted to weapons that cannot be used for area defence, such as short-range ABM missile interceptors or ground-based kinetic-energy weapons. Some research would presumably would have to be allowed – because of the need to avoid possible break-outs by the opponent, because it cannot be monitored, and because of its connection with civilian developments. The distinction between research, development and testing would have to be spelled out much more carefully than in the past, as would the nature of those components whose development or testing is to be allowed.

The emphasis in a treaty to control DEW strategic defences should be on limiting the tests of components dedicated and usable in strategic defences, and on controlling the deployment of strategic defensive systems. An arms control agreement to ban DEW-based strategic defence, which could perhaps be a renegotiated ABM Treaty, might include the following provisions.

Banning dedicated components The development and testing of dedicated components of a potential DEW-defence system would have to be controlled. This might include, for example, banning space tests and deployment of lasers with a brightness above some value, say 1 watt/cm^2 at a range of 1000 km, or the testing of a mirror system in earth orbit that can rotate, say, faster than one degree per second. Such limitations would be analogous to the provisions in Agreed Statement B of the ABM Treaty, limiting the power output of certain types of radar.

Limits on dedicated components would, however, create considerable difficulties. Such a ban might interfere with the development of some civilian technologies. Writing such a treaty would not be easy, since the possible configurations of future defensive systems are at present not known. Distinctions between DEWs and non-weapons on the basis of such parameters as brightness and slew rates can be written, but, unless the thresholds are set very low, they may not be sufficient. Clearly the terms 'ABM capable', 'components', and 'development', need to be defined much more explicitly than was the case for the ABM Treaty.

Banning systems tests   If a complete ban on DEW defensive systems is desired, then it would be necessary to ban tests of any systems that might be dedicated to that purpose.[56] The obvious difficulty is to distinguish a dedicated DEW system from one intended for some alternative use, such as exploring the atmosphere or tracking satellites. A primary distinction might be based on the fact that a DEW defence system must be able to react to multiple targets. Thus, a DEW treaty might contain the rule that any space-based directed-energy source may not be test-fired more than once an hour in different directions. This would allow civilian tests, while preventing militarily significant developments. But a similar attempt in the ABM Treaty to distinguish radar units for defensive purposes from those monitoring ICBM tests and tracking satellites has led to controversy about the purposes of the Soviet radar system at Krasnoyarsk.[57]

Banning systems deployment   A ban on the deployment of complete DEW defence systems would be easiest to define and monitor, since so many highly-capable components would have to be deployed as part of an interactive whole. Defining the difference between a dedicated system and a random collection of non-dedicated components would present political problems; any residual capability from non-dedicated components might well make a DEW strategic defence treaty politically unacceptable.

DEW arms control and ASAT activities   A strong coupling exists between uses of DEWs in strategic defences and in ASAT systems. To establish a truly successful, non-controversial, verifiable, and enforceable ban on DEW defences, ASAT systems using DEWs would also have to be banned. The problem is that the development and deployment of DEW-based ASAT systems allows the exploration of DEW defensive systems at lower power levels. That would create opportunities for possible technological break-outs.

Thus a ban on the development of DEW defences should incorporate into the ABM Treaty an ASAT Treaty banning DEW weapons. Possible ASAT treaties have been discussed in the past.[58] None of these treaties specifically mentions DEWs as possible components of ASAT systems. These proposals have generated controversies as to whether the destruction of existing ASAT systems could be verified, about the residual ASAT capabilities of non-dedicated systems such as a the space shuttle, about the distinctions between ground-based and space-based systems, and about the impact of a ban on civilian space developments. The controversies would be even greater if a DEW treaty were to ban ASAT systems, while allowing the development of strategic defences.

The connection between ASAT and strategic-defence capabilities in the DEW area holds even more strongly in the reverse direction. Any strategic defence capability utilising DEWs automatically generates an ASAT capability, since any DEW capable of destroying missiles or re-entry vehicles (RVs) in flight could also destroy a satellite. Any effective ASAT Treaty would have to forbid the testing and deployment of any DEW components that might be relevant to the operation of an anti-satellite system.

Directed-Energy weapons in Point Defences

In an arms control agreement limiting strategic defences, it might be desirable to allow some defence of military assets related to the retaliatory capability, such as missile silos. Such a point defence treaty would not necessarily have to permit the development of DEWs, since point defences could adequately be based on conventional missiles, or perhaps on kinetic-energy weapons, such as railguns. After all, the 1972 ABM Treaty does permit some point defence.

If certain forms of short-range ground-based DEW point defences were to be permitted, while banning space-based DEW area defences, the 1972 ABM Treaty could be used as the basis for an agreement. The development of fairly powerful ground-based lasers, and the improvement of relevant short-range tracking and control systems, would have to be allowed. If the number of defensive systems were to be limited, some equivalence would have to be defined between lasers and ABM missile launchers.

The greatest difficulties arise in describing the allowed deployments in such a way as to restrict their usefulness only to point defence. The problem is that DEWs are so useful because of their ability to attack targets instantaneously even at long ranges. This capability inevitably blurs the distinction between point defence and area defence. The coverage of a ground-based laser defence would include an area limited only by the earth's curvature; therefore DEWs could be restricted to point defence only by imposing limits on their power output and their sensors. The ABM Treaty is being threatened by the concern that the Soviet SA-12 air defence missile might have a limited capability in a defence against ICBMs. Since the gradations between capabilities of DEWs for point and area defence are likely to be even less distinct than for ABM interceptors, the problem of imposing a point defence limitation on DEWs may be very great.

A treaty allowing DEW point defences would face all the other problems outlined for a total DEW ban, such as distinguishing between civilian and military acitivies. But these problems may be even worse when point defences are permitted, since more varied military research, development, testing and deployment would then be allowed, all of which might increase this confusion. Any allowed work on DEWs, whether directed toward ASAT missions or terminal defences, will greatly increase verification problems.

Directed Energy Weapons in Population Defences
If the decision were made to permit strategic defences of populations, the ABM Treaty would have to be replaced by an arms control agreement to manage the transition from deterrence through the unstable regime of damage limitation, to mutual survival, and to maintain that final stable state. This transition would go through a period when increases in defences would have to be carefully balanced by decreases in offensive weapons, whether these were in high-accuracy ICBMs, or all nuclear forces. The problem is that global strategic defences, say by boost-phase interception, will enhance the first-strike capability of the offensive strategic forces; the defences would be more effective in intercepting an enemy retaliatory second strike than in intercepting a first strike. Consequently, the transition to a defence orientation would require a Transition Treaty that ensures co-operation to maintain crisis and arms-race stability.

Weinberg and Barkenbus have suggested that this transition could be undertaken unilaterally in a process that carefully and exactly balances the increases in defence for one side by the decreases in retaliatory forces for the same side.[59] For a terminal defence of retaliatory missiles this management process might work, if the defences were calculated to keep the surviving retaliatory missiles constant in the face of an opponent's first strike. But it is uncertain whether such a unilateral arrangement could work for a global strategic defence, based, for example, on DEWs in space.

The basic design feature of a Transition Arms Control Treaty (TACT) would best balance mutual defensive deployments with mutual cuts in the offensive first-strike potential. As long as delivery systems with accurate multiple warheads exist, whether these be ICBMs or SLBMs, or even stealth bombers with several Cruise missiles, defences will be destabilising, since they will tend to make a pre-emptive first strike seem attractive. The current American negotiating strategy is to use the deployment of strategic defences to persuade the Soviet Union that high-accuracy ICBMs are useless and should be given up. It might be better to reverse the process. Perhaps limits to reduce first-strike offensive weapons should be negotiated first, in order that strategic defences can be deployed without being seen as destabilising and threatening.

There exists no precedent for a TACT. It would mix drastic philosophical changes with complex trade-offs between non-comparable weapons systems; it would attempt to control unknown technologies; and it would require a great deal of co-operation between the treaty partners. It would seem that the Soviet Union will have a veto on whether such a transition can be undertaken. A transition treaty would be, for both conceptual and practical reasons, orders of magnitude more difficult to achieve than past arms control treaties. There is no evidence that enough thought has been given so far to the possible shape of a reasonable and achievable TACT; there is little appreciation of what would be involved in its development.

Verification of Directed-energy Weapons Arms Control Agreement

One major factor in the arms control of strategic defences involving DEWs will be the ability to verify any relevant arms control agreements.[60] Whether DEW arms control agreements can be verified hinges on what is meant by verification.

One must appreciate that verification problems may arise not only from inadequate technologies, but also from difficulties with the verification process itself. Verification starts with the 'negotiations', in which are developed the rules of the treaty, the constraints on the technology, the co-operative measures to help verification, and the procedures for settling disputes and cancelling the treaty.[61] The next step is the 'monitoring' process, in which data are obtained about the compliance with the treaty, and the data are interpreted. Many think of this as 'verification' proper. Then comes the 'evaluation' process in which the results of the monitoring process are used to evaluate whether a treaty is being obeyed. This might involve inter-agency review committees, or later a meeting of treaty members, as in the Standing Consultative Committee that was set up for the SALT I treaty. Finally, based on the results of the monitoring and evaluation steps, some 'enforcement' procedure may be invoked to enforce obedience to the treaty, leading as a last resort to abrogation. Monitoring is only a part of this whole process. It may not even be as important as the 'semi-political' evaluation process, where judgements are made as to what 'adequate' verification might be.[62]

Verification Technologies and DEW Treaties

Verification technologies cover a wide range from covert means, such as espionage, through listening to telephone conversations and clipping newspapers, to various space-based surveillance devices.[63] The whole electromagnetic spectrum is covered by these technologies, from the radar microwaves that track the flight of missiles and satellites, through infra-red radiation to detect missile launches and power generation, visible light to photograph objects such as laser installations, and ultraviolet radiation to see through clouds, all the way to x-rays and gamma-rays to watch for nuclear explosions. All of these channels might be exploited for monitoring DEW arms control.

Verification technology relevant to DEWs is constantly improving. This is true, for example, for photographic methods, including satellite live-time imaging with charge-coupled sensors. Optical photographic ground resolution of the order of 10 cm is becoming possible.

What Aspects of Directed-energy Weaponry are Verifiable?

Visual detection A ground resolution of 10cm should be adequate for most monitoring purposes of DEWs, as long as enough money and analysts are available. The major components involved in a useful DEW strategic defence system would include mirrors 4m and more in diameter, lasers with dimensions in excess of 1m, particle-beam accelerators 20m or more in length, and various large space-based sensors. These features are all large compared to a resolution of 10cm, and hence would be detectable and identifiable by visual means, unless kept permanently under cover.

Some technological parameters that might distinguish strategic defence systems from others (such as ASAT systems) may not be as easy to measure. Thus determining the slewing rate of a laser mirror and its aiming accuracy would probably require the collation of many different kinds of information, as is now required to determine the weight of the warheads in ICBMs (a parameter important in monitoring the SALT II Treaty).

Infrared detection The generation of useful directed-energy beams will release large amounts of energy. It has been reported that existing infra-red sensors can detect human body heat at a range of hundreds of kilometres. A space-based laser would eject about a million times as much waste thermal energy into space. Even the impact of the heat on a target would release easily observable amounts of thermal energy. Therefore the testing and operation of DEWs in space should be easy to monitor.

Electronic intelligence If ever a DEW were to be tested as a part of a defence system, extensive communications would be needed to coordinate the components of the system. This communicating should be readily detectable, even though it might be encrypted. Thus monitoring the testing and operation of a DEW system should be feasible by observing electronic communications.

The verification of arms control, that might be imposed on DEW defensive technologies, should therefore present no insurmountable technical monitoring problem. Space is wide open, hence all defensive activities related to space could probably be detected and monitored. The difficulties of DEW verification will probably lie elsewhere. For example, the distinction between military and civilian activities would not only be hard to detect, but might in fact be at times non-existent. For instance, docking manoeuvres are useful not only for civilian resupplying of space stations, but also for an ASAT satellite approaching a target or a satellite refuelling a DEW system. Thus docking manoeuvres can be seen, but their purposes cannot be easily determined.

Verification of a Directed-energy Weapons Ban
From a technological perspective a ban on DEW strategic defences can probably be quite adequately monitored. The relevant develop-

ment, testing, and deployment should be observable because of the large physical size of the devices, the amount of power being consumed, and the necessary communication between components. The verification problem will begin at the evaluation stage, where the thresholds between allowed and forbidden components, development and research, and dedicated and non-dedicated capabilities become intermingled with political realities. Thus those drafting DEW treaties must pay great attention to making the evaluation process as easy and comprehensive as possible. Treaties can be made more verifiable if they are written very carefully to prevent intentional or unexpected exceptions which might make the treaty meaningless or create mistrust and suspicion. The less the treaty allows, the more verifiable it will probably be. Many past difficulties with arms control treaties have arisen when one side or the other included exceptions for a pet project.

In fact the technology may not be the major factor which limits the verification of arms control agreements that might include DEWs. Verification technology is good now and is constantly getting better. Rather the verification problems will arise for several other reasons. First, the provisions of a DEW Treaty, like those of most other treaties in the past, are likely to be pushed to the limit. The inherent uncertainties of monitoring processes then mean that it becomes impossible to verify treaty provisions with absolute certainty. Secondly, the verification process for a treaty dealing with such a high technology as DEWs will involve a multiplicity of monitoring technologies, some of which may themselves be secret. Thirdly, civilian and military uses of such advanced technologies will be so intermingled that the intentions of activities will have to be evaluated. Finally, since there is unlikely to be a consensus on the desirability of any DEW agreement, politics will play a large role in the evaluative process. Each of these problems is aggravated when there is no openness and trust between treaty partners, as is the case now between the United States and the Soviet Union.

Politics impinges directly on verification during the evaluation process, as the question of certainty arises. Technical verification will always leave some residual uncertainties; absolute knowledge can never be obtained. If DEW treaties cannot be made foolproof, then some techniques must be developed that can reduce the mutual suspicions to a level that is commensurate with the actual danger to national security posed by possible cheating. For example, discussions of possible violations must be possible. The Standing Consultative Commission seems to have worked well at times for the evaluation part of verifying the SALT treaties. But now politics have become a larger part of this 'judgemental' aspect of the verification process. The arms control process has become more tightly coupled to other political activities. When linkages exist, as in the coupling of the non-passage of the SALT II Treaty to the Soviet invasion of Afghanistan, then arms control will be that much harder. Then verification may become the whipping-boy for political failures.

CONCLUSION

The public policy issue of DEWs, strategic defences, and arms control, is extensively governed by technological aspects. That which is desirable must still be shaped to fit that which is technologically feasible. The stated purpose of the Strategic Defense Initiative (SDI) is to clarify the technological feasibility of various defensive technologies, in order to guide political judgements. However, many political debates and judgements have come before the technological limits are known. This is partially due to the way in which the SDI programme was first proposed, with a stated goal of making nuclear weapons 'impotent and obsolete'. The policy debate has, therefore, been unclear and emotional, as desirability and feasibility have become all too frequently confused with each other. Unfortunately, the strategic debates and those on arms control cannot be delayed until the technological issues have been completely resolved.

The defensive capabilities being developed as part of the SDI require some arms control, no matter what the strategic goals might be for the resulting systems. Such arms control is particularly important for any DEWs that might become available. If the decision were to limit or ban defensive technologies, an extension and expansion of the current ABM Treaty might serve. But if strategic defence is to do more than preserve deterrence, then a transition treaty will have to be negotiated to manage the reduction of offensive armaments as defences are increased. In either case it is hard to conceive how anything can be accomplished without the co-operation of the Soviet Union.

Several conclusions can be drawn specifically about DEW arms control. It seems difficult, and may well be undesirable, to limit research on DEWs. But work on strategic DEW defences ought to be made distinct from civilian and conventional military applications of directed-energy beams. Any treaties dealing with DEWs should try to incorporate co-operative measures to distinguish work on strategic defences. In general, more care is needed in writing future arms control agreements involving DEWs than was the case for the ABM Treaty. The potential and shape of these technologies are as yet unknown, so that it may be better to specify those developments that are allowed, rather than those that are forbidden. Any DEW limitations ought to come at the development stage, but certainly must apply to testing and deployment. The emphasis should be on controlling dedicated systems.

DEW arms control could take place for several different levels of DEW applications. Applications of DEWs to ASAT systems and to strategic defences are so tightly coupled that one cannot limit one while letting the other go uncontrolled. It may be tempting to allow some use of DEWs in point defences while forbidding area defences, but a treaty to impose such controls would be hard to write and monitor. A transition treaty to help manage the necessary offensive reductions is without precedent in complexity and required co-operation. The shape of such a treaty ought to be explored now, in order to judge how feasible it might be to go through the transition to a defensive world without generating dangerous levels of instability.

For the verification of DEW treaties, monitoring technologies seem good enough to keep track of future progress, but only if enough effort is invested in the collection and analysis of data. However the political aspects of verification may present problems. Politics have come to play an increasing role in the evaluation part of the verification process. Consequently in some cases the technology itself has been questioned and is being used as an excuse for rejecting arms control. Technical aspects of treaty verification cannot overcome poor treaties and poorly exercised political control. But verification is not usually the limiting factor on what can be done in arms control.

Notes

1. D. Schroeer, 'The Technical Feasibility of Strategic Defence', ch. 11, above. See also D. Schroeer, *Directed-Energy Weapons and Strategic Defence: A Primer*, Adelphi Paper no. 221 (London, 1987).
2. B. Jasani (ed.), *Outer Space: A New Dimension of the Arms Race* (London, 1982).

3. Jasani (ed.), *Outer Space*, p. 371.
4. C. L. Herzenberg, 'Nuclear Winter and Strategic Defense Initiative', *Physics and Society*, vol. 15, no. 1 (January, 1986) pp. 2–5; this article raises the spectre of starting fires in cities by means of space-based lasers. See also C. Norman, 'The Dark Side of SDI', *Science*, vol. 235 (1987) pp. 962–3.
5. Jasani (ed.), *Outer Space*, p. 368.
6. B. Jasani (ed.), *Space Weapons: The Arms Control Dilemma* (London, 1984) p. 34.
7. A. B. Sherr, *Legal Issues of the 'Star Wars' Defense Program* (Boston, 1984); he says on p.3 that 'a space-based laser, or other directed energy weapon, as envisioned under the Strategic Defense Initiative [clearly would] fall within this provision [that each party undertakes not to develop, test, or deploy ABM systems or components which are sea-based, air-based, space-based or mobile land-based]'.
8. B. Jasani (ed.), *Outer Space*, p. 376.
9. *The Arms Control Impact Statement for 1984*, prepared by the US Arms Control and Disarmament Agency, says that '. . . although the Treaty allows the development and testing of fixed land-based ABM systems and components, based on other physical principles (such as lasers or particle beams) . . . the Treaty prohibits the deployment of such fixed, land-based systems and components unless the Parties consult and amend the Treaty'. Quoted in A. Chayes, A. H. Chayes and E. Spitzer, 'Space Weapons: The Legal Context', *Daedalus*, Summer 1985, pp. 193–218.
10. Jasani (ed.), *Outer Space*, p. 376.
11. US Arms Control and Disarmament Agency, *The Arms Control Impact Statement*.
12. Jasani (ed.), *Outer Space*, p. 380.
13. Sherr, *Legal Issues of the 'Star Wars' Defense Program*, p. 3.
14. See for example C. Mohr, 'Beyond the U.S. "Star Wars" Debate: The question of Moscow's Reaction', *New York Times*, 17 October 1985, p. 6; and P. H. Nitze, 'Permitted and Prohibited Activities under the ABM Treaty', address before the International Law Weekend Group, New York City, 31 October 1986. 'Agreed Statement D. . . permits the creation – i.e. the development and testing – of, for example, space-based ABM systems that are based on "other physical principles" and their components. A careful reading of the treaty text and review of the negotiating record demonstrate that . . . the restrictions of Article v of the Treaty do not apply to ABM systems based on other physical principles and their components.'
15. J. B. Rhinelander, 'Reagan's "Exotic" Interpretation of the ABM Treaty', *Arms Control Today*, vol. 15, no. 8 (October 1985) pp. 3–6; and B. B. Auster, 'Treaty Reinterpretation Under Attack', ibid, vol. 17, no. 1 (January/February 1987) pp. 11–12.
16. See, for example, 'Excerpts from a Speech by Shultz at North Atlantic Assembly Meeting', *New York Times*, 15 October 1985, p. 4; and M. Krepon, 'Dormant Threat to the ABM Treaty', *Bulletin of the Atomic Scientists*, vol. 42, no. 1 (January 1986) pp. 31–4.
17. M. R. Gordon, 'A Tug of War Erupts on Missile Treaty Data', *New York*

Times, 15 July 1986, p. 20; and M. R. Gordon, 'U.S. Said to be Near Ruling on Meaning of '72 ABM Treaty: Looser Interpretation Would Allow Wider Experiments with Systems in Space', *New York Times*, 5 February 1987, pp. 1,6.
18. Jasani (ed.), *Outer Space*, p. 378.
19. T. K. Longstreth, J. E. Pike, and J. B. Rhinelander, *The Impact of U.S. and Soviet Ballistic Missile Defense Programs on the ABM Treaty* (3rd edition, Washington, DC, 1985); and US Department of Defense, *SDI Research in Compliance with ABM Treaty: Report to Congress* (Washington, DC, 1985); particularly Appendix B, 'The Strategic Defense Initiative (SDI) and the ABM Treaty', pp. B1–B9.
20. Ibid., pp.B4–B6.
21. Ibid., pp.B6–B9.
22. Longstreth, Pike and Rhinelander, *The Impact of U.S. and Soviet Missile Defense Programs*.
23. Ibid.
24. Senator Gore proposes negotiating to clarify the differences between research and development, which components can be tested, and which types of tests are not permissible; see F. Lewis, 'A Chance to Bargain', *New York Times*, 4 April 1985, p. 85.
25. Jasani (ed.), *Outer Space*, p. 376.
26. Ibid, p. 377.
27. For the full text of Reagan's 'Star Wars' speech see *New York Times*, 14 March 1983, p. 20.
28. Department of Defense, *SDI Research in Compliance with ABM Treaty*, pp. B6–B9.
29. B. Gwertzman, 'Minimum Goals set on Space Weapons', *New York Times*, 21 February 1985, p. 1. Paul H. Nitze, special advisor on arms control to Reagan and Shultz, said in a speech delivered to the Philadelphia World Affairs Council, 20 February 1985; 'We are even now looking forward to a period of transition to a more stable world, with greatly reduced levels of nuclear arms and an enhanced ability to deter war based on an increasing contribution of non-nuclear defenses against offensive nuclear arms.'
30. Ibid; and US State Department, 'The Strategic Defense Initiative', *State Department Fact Sheet*, 4 June 1985.
31. G. Kennan, M. Bundy, G. Smith, and R. McNamara, 'The President's Choice: Star Wars or Arms Control', *Foreign Affairs*, vol. 62, no. 3 (Winter 1984/5) pp. 264–78.
32. C. Bertram, 'Strategic Defense and the Western Alliance', *Daedalus*, Summer 1985, pp. 279–96. Some disagree on this point. See, for example, J. Mendelsohn and J. P. Rubin, 'SDI as Negotiating Leverage', *Arms Control Today*, vol. 16, no. 9 (December 1986) pp. 6–9.
33. P. Quinn–Judge, 'Soviets say summit proposals on SDI, arms form single package', *Christian Science Monitor*, 17 October 1986, p. 10.
34. P. Taubman, 'Gorbachev Angrily Accuses Reagan of Scuttling an Accord at Reykjavik', *New York Times*, 13 October 1986, p. A8; and B. Gwertzman, 'Reagan–Gorbachev Talks End in Stalemate as U.S. Rejects

Demand to Curb "Star Wars"', *New York Times*, 13 October 1986, pp. A1, A8.
35. L. Gelb, 'Vision of Space Defense Posing New Challenges', *New York Times*, 3 March 1985, pp. A1, A16–A18; he said that 'Officials and critics alike agree that some research is desirable, if only on the grounds of prudence and as a check against Soviet projects'.
36. M. Bundy, 'The Real Relation Between Star Wars and Arms Control', *Arms Control Today*, vol. 15, no. 3 (April 1985) pp. 1–4; on p. 3 he said that 'No one can or should oppose a sensibly designed program of research in this field ... but this requirement can be met with research on a budgetary level so far below the one the Administration now projects'.
37. J. B. Stein, *From H-Bomb to Star Wars: The Politics of Strategic Decision Making* (Lexington, Massachusetts, 1984).
38. Gwertzmann, 'Reagan–Gorbachev Talks', *New York Times*, 13 October 1986.
39. M. R. Gordon, 'Reagan and Aides Meet on Plan for Early "Star Wars" Deployment', *New York Times*, 2 February 1987, p. A2.
40. An interview with Lt. Gen. James Abrahamson, Director of the SDI Organization, by the US Information Agency, 26 March 1985.
41. US Department of Defense, *Soviet Military Power* (Washington, DC, 1985) pp. 42–59.
42. G. T. Allison and F. A. Morris, 'Armaments and Arms Control: Exploring the Determinants of Military Weapons', in F. A. Long and G. W. Rathjens (eds), *Arms, Defense Policy and Arms Control* (New York, 1976) pp. 99–124.
43. J. Tirman (ed.), *The Fallacy of Star Wars*, (New York, 1984).
44. Gwertzman, 'Minimum Goals', *New York Times*, 21 February 1985.
45. W. Hartung and R. Nimroody, 'Star Wars: What Price Strategic Defense?', *Council on Economic Priorities Newsletter*, January 1985, pp. 1–6.
46. Gwertzman, 'Minimum Goals', *New York Times*, 21 February 1985.
47. G. A. Keyworth, 'The Case for Arms Control and the Strategic Defense Initiative', *Arms Control Today*, vol. 15, no. 3 (April 1985) pp. 1, 2, 8: on p. 8 he says that 'When they [the Soviets] look seriously at the loss of utility on their ICBMs as a preemptive force, they will have no choice but to admit the age of the ICBM as the dominant weapon is passing ... If ICBMs serve only to retaliate ... both sides can consider truly massive reductions in ICBM warheads'.
48. Brent Scowcroft, President Gerald Ford's National Security Advisor, and Chairman of the MX Advisory Commission, said that 'As a practical matter, it would be very difficult to induce the Soviets to reduce their offensive forces if they faced the prospects of a strategic defense ... Potentially they ["Star Wars" and arms control objectives] are in contradiction'. (T. Wicker, "Star Wars" vs the MX', *New York Times*, 15 March 1985, p. 27.) Some high officials hope 'Star Wars' will force the Soviets to give up ICBMs, others expect the programme is 'more likely ... to encourage an offensive arms race', (C. Mohr, 'What Moscow Might Do in Replying to "Star Wars"', *New York Times*, 6 March 1985, p.1).

49. R. Hutchinson, 'Chevaline: UK's response to Soviet ABM system', *Jane's Defence Weekly*, 15 December 1984, pp. 1068–9.
50. Bertram, 'Strategic Defense and the Western Alliance'; and D. S. Yost, 'European Anxieties about Ballistic Missile Defense', *Washington Quarterly*, vol. 7, no. 4, (Fall 1984) pp. 112–29.
51. J. Mearsheimer, 'Nuclear Weapons and Deterrence in Europe', *International Security*, vol. 9, no. 3 (Winter 1984–85) pp. 19–46.
52. A Legault and G. Lindsey, *The Dynamics of the Nuclear Balance* (revised edn, Ithaca, New York, 1976).
53. C. L. Glaser, 'Star wars bad even if it works', *Bulletin of the Atomic Scientists*, vol. 41, no. 3 (March 1985) pp. 13–16; he argues that if the defence were to work it would lead to instability: the possibility of a slight leakage, whether real or perceived, would be dangerous – and, otherwise, the conventional balance would become critical. See also P. D. Zimmerman, 'Pork Bellies and SDI', *Foreign Affairs*, no. 63, Summer 1986, pp. 76–87.
54. F. Dyson, *Weapons and Hope* (New York, 1984). He says that 'The theoretical antagonism between defense and deterrence disappears as soon as it is understood that all counting of the lives saved by defense is illusory...' (p. 26).
55. Jasani (ed.). *Space Weapons*. See, for example, 'Appendix 2. Treaties and treaty proposals which contain provisions aimed at some form of arms control in space'. (pp. 211–49.); and US Congress, Office of Technology Assessment, *Anti-Satellite Weapons: Countermeasures and Arms Control* (Washington, DC, 1985).
56. F. Hussain, *Impact of Weapons Test Restrictions*, Adelphi Paper, no. 165 (London, 1983), for example, pp. 39–47.
57. 'The bulk of the U.S. intelligence community [believes] it is designed primarily to provide early warning of a ballistic missile attack by Trident submarines ... and is situated at Abalakova primarily as a cost-cutting measure ... only slight ballistic missile defense capability'. (R. J. Smith, 'U.S. Experts Condemn Soviet Radar: Most experts agree that the Abalakova radar violates SALT I, but they differ on its strategic significance', *Science*, 22 March 1985, pp. 1442–4).
58. W. Slocombe, 'Approaches to an ASAT Treaty', in Jasani (ed.). *Space Weapons*, pp. 145–55; Union of Concerned Scientists, *Anti-Satellite Weapons: Arms Control or Arms Race?* (Washington, DC, 1983) pp. 33–5; and Committee on International Security and Arms Control, National Academy of Sciences, *Nuclear Arms Control: Background and Issues* (Washington, DC, 1985).
59. A. M. Weinberg and J. N. Barkenbus, 'Stabilizing Star Wars', *Foreign Policy*, no. 54, Spring 1984, pp. 164–70.
60. For a good overview of verification as a part of arms control see W. C. Potter (ed.), *Verification and SALT: The Challenge of Strategic Deception* (Boulder, Colorado, 1980).
61. R. A. Scribner, T. Ralston, and W. Metz, *The Verification Challenge: Problems and Promise of Strategic Nuclear Arms Control Verification* (Boston, Massachusetts, 1985).

62. See, for example, articles by J. Welch, A. Carnesale, R. Perle, and A. Katz on 'adequate' versus 'full' verification in R. Pfaltzgraaf, U. Ra'anan, and W. Milberg (eds), *Intelligence Policy and National Security* (London, 1981).
63. W. V. Kennedy, *The Intelligence War* (London, 1983).

Part III
Regional Aspects of the Arms Race

13 Nuclear Weapons and Coercive Diplomacy: Their Impact on the Developing World

K. Subrahmanyam

In spite of the efforts of the overwhelming majority of the nations of the world to outlaw nuclear weapons, their use and threat of use through successive resolutions in the UN General Assembly, nuclear weapons continue to remain legitimate weapons and a currency of power in international relations, owing to the opposition of the NATO countries. The Non-proliferation Treaty (NPT) has had the impact of legitimising the nuclear arsenals in the hands of five nuclear weapon powers and has resulted in galloping proliferation of nuclear arsenals in the five proclaimed nuclear weapon states and their further proliferation into new ocean areas. Today nuclear war-fighting infrastructure (stockpiles, testing facilities, access to nuclear weapon carriers, command, control, communication and intelligence network) encompasses 65 nations and territories all over the globe.[1]

Of the four categories of weapons of mass destruction – biological, chemical, radiological and nuclear – the latter are in a special category. There is a convention outlawing biological weapons. The use of chemicals in war was outlawed under the Geneva Protocol of 1925 and a more comprehensive draft treaty on outlawing chemical weapons is, it is hoped, nearing finalisation between the United States and the Soviet Union. A draft treaty outlawing radiological weapons was prepared by the two major powers and its finalisation has been held up mainly because of certain lacunae in the draft. Only on nuclear weapons are there no negotiations to outlaw and delegitimise them. The Soviet Union has of course proposed elimination of all nuclear weapons by the year 2000. And the NPT mentions in sub-paragraph 12 of its preamble the desire to ease international tensions to facilitate the liquidation of all the existing stockpiles and the elimination from national arsenals of nuclear weapons and the means of their delivery. At present, however, no discussions are taking place to outlaw the fourth category of instruments of mass destruction as has happened in the case of the other three.

On the other hand, nuclear weapons have come to be associated with the exercise of deterrence, not by all nations of the world but by a privileged few. It is argued that nuclear deterrence has preserved peace in the territories of the industrialised nations over the last four decades and nuclear deterrent doctrine and the threat of use of nuclear weapons are integral to the security policy of the NATO states. Though the threat focused on is that in Europe, nuclear weapons are deployed all around the globe and are not restricted to the area which is perceived to be threatened.

While efforts are made to delegitimise the other weapons of mass destruction, in the case of nuclear weapons their possession is held to be invested with a privileged status. If the true purpose of the so-called NPT was to halt proliferation of nuclear weapons, that logic would have demanded that those who abjured development and possession of weapons should be monitoring those who were still responsible for the proliferation of weapons. Those who had scrupulously abided by the objective of non-proliferation should have been entrusted with greater responsibility than those who were continually reneging on their obligations under the Treaty. Instead of controlling the proliferators, however, this Treaty allows them unlimited licence to proliferate and seeks to impose obligations on the majority who have no intention of indulging in proliferation. This is analogous to five gangsters locking up all the peaceful citizenry in a town to ensure that peace will be maintained.

Those who possessed the weapons exempted themselves from all inspection and safeguards. While there has so far been no report of diversion of fissile materials from safeguarded reactors there is considerable evidence of fissile materials having been diverted from an unsafeguarded military facility – NUMEC, Apollo, Pennsylvania – and having resulted in a nuclear arsenal being established in another nation. So long as there are unsafeguarded military facilities producing weapons-grade fissile materials there is no way of preventing thefts and leakages and it is admitted that there is a black and grey market on such materials in the world today.[2] The traces of Pu-239 in the New York water supply reported by Mayor Koch could have originated only in material obtained in a military reprocessing facility or a weapon laboratory. It is quite obvious that the International Atomic Energy Agency (IAEA) safeguards system cannot be effective so long as there are leakages and thefts from the military facilities. There have been continuous reports of vast quantities of weapons-grade material being unaccounted for. Just to quote a recent instance, the US Energy department discovered that in five months in 1983/4 two plants at Oak Ridge and Kentucky alone had 180 kilograms of enriched uranium unaccounted for.[3] The safeguards system of IAEA is not so much intended as a means to safeguard diversion of weapons-grade material but is an instrument of technological hegemony which is used to distinguish the privileged lawless proliferators from the underprivileged nations who have foresworn nuclear weapons. The docile and supine IAEA does not highlight the fact that inspection is a farce, with dozens of unsafeguarded military facilities vulnerable to leakage and theft.

The supporters of the NPT argue that the greater the number of decision-making centres having control over nuclear weapons the higher the probability of a nuclear war breaking out. This argument has today become a part of received wisdom. Yet this argument is fallacious and based on a propagated myth that in a nuclear weapon country there is a single decision-making centre controlling the release of all nuclear weapons. This is not true. In fact the nuclear weapon submarines are not under the strict control of national authorities and are capable of firing their weapons if the Captain, the first officer and the weapons officer jointly decide to act.[4] The task force on nuclear terrorism has admitted that the quick reaction alert nuclear weapons are not under the electronic locking system.[5] It is obvious that they cannot be if they are to perform their role. If the supporters of the argument that the more decision centres there are controlling nuclear weapons the greater the probability of war are logical they should accept that the addition of each nuclear missile submarine and each unit with quick reaction alert weapons is equivalent to a new nuclear weapon state being added. In fact at present there are not just five or six (if Israel is included) nuclear decision-making centres. There are hundreds. If the present system is stable enough an addition of another small nuclear force is not likely to augment the risk of nuclear war breaking out as propagated by the apologists of the NPT.

Underlying this attitude towards the NPT is an unmistakable racist bias which assumes that even the officers manning nuclear missile submarines and in charge of quick reaction alert weapons in the four

White nations and China are likely to be more responsible than the heads of states and governments of threshold nuclear weapon countries.

It is evident that the NPT was not intended to stop the rapid proliferation of nuclear weapons in the five nuclear arsenals and sheltered client states like Israel, nor to stop the proliferation of nuclear weapons to all oceans and to various territories all over the world. The nuclear weapon powers were free to proliferate to autonomous decision-makers the power to release nuclear weapons and these decision-makers may include nationals of countries which have acceded to the NPT with a presumed non-nuclear weapon status. The Treaty was not meant to safeguard the leakage and theft of weapons-grade missile materials and the safeguard system is a farce.

What was the purpose underlying the Treaty? The Treaty was to reconfirm the Yalta system of international management. It is not fortuitous that the five nuclear weapon powers were the five permanent members envisaged at Yalta and that the sponsors of the Treaty were the three present at Yalta. The two powers, France and China, who did not participate at Yalta have also stayed out of the NPT. The purpose of the treaty was to legitimise nuclear weapons in the hands of five nuclear weapon powers as a currency of power and to establish a hegemonic relationship between them and the rest of the world. Subsequently the Strategic Arms Limitation Talks and now the current arms control negotiations including those on the Strategic Defense Initiative were and are intended to further stratify the international power hierarchy into two supreme dominating powers, three lesser dominating powers and the rest of the nations. This structure is not very dissimilar to that which prevailed before the Second World War, when the British and French empires were supreme dominating empires followed by lesser ones: Dutch, Portuguese, Italian and Belgian.

Today both President Ronald Reagan and General Secretary Mikhail Gorbachev jointly subscribe to the view that a nuclear war cannot be won and therefore ought not to be initiated. If this is a genuine perception – and there is no reason to doubt it – how is one to explain the accumulation of nuclear arsenals on both sides, the efforts to introduce weapons into space and the continuing adherence to the doctrine that, if necessary, the NATO nations will use nuclear weapons to ensure the security of Western Europe? In order to explain this apparent paradox one has to analyse and understand the changes that have come about in strategic thought over the last four decades. This paradox goes along with another one – the industrialised nations and nuclear weapon powers are responsible for over 85 per cent of global military expenditure and have been doing so for the last four decades, and yet there has been no major conflict in the territories of industrialised nations and nuclear weapon powers. Nor has the world seen a comparable period of four decades of highly armed peace in the history of the most combustible area of the world – Europe – and the phenomenon of coexistence of two global navies sailing cheek by jowl without escalating into war.

These paradoxes can be satisfactorily explained if one moves away from the Clausewitzian maxim that war is a continuation of politics by other means. Nuclear weapons as well as the new weapon technologies have changed that and the industrialised world has imperceptibly fallen back on the wisdom of the ancient Chinese philosopher, Sun Tzu: 'to subdue the enemy without fighting is the acme of skill'.[6] Today in respect of international relations among the industrialised countries war is no longer a viable instrument because of high risk of escalation to nuclear level. War was a viable instrument of policy so long as the use of force could be controlled politically. An extensive literature is now available highlighting the point that, in all probability, in a nuclear war between two nuclear weapon nations centralised control over firing of weapons will be lost after the first few shots. War was a viable instrument of policy when the use of force was applied to the destruction of the adversary's force and thereafter holding out threat of pain and punishment against the population of the adversary which compelled him to accept the imposition of the will of the victor. Ever since the advent of air arms and particularly of nuclear-tipped long-range missiles, however, the infliction of pain and destruction on the adversary's population is not contingent upon gaining a victory in the battlefield over him. In a sense the term victory itself calls for fresh definition. If victory is to be meaningfully related to the attainment of desirable political objectives in terms of affordable and worthwhile costs it is difficult to talk of victory in a nuclear war or even in the case of high-intensity and high-technology conventional war.

War has lost its relevance as an instrument of policy in the industrialised world but not in the developing world, where inter-state wars of two categories are possible. The first is the category of conventional war that took place during the Second World War, in which it is still necessary to vanquish the adversary's armed force before one can place his population at peril and impose one's will. One saw this category of hostilities in the Arab–Israeli, Indo–

Pakistan and China–Vietnam wars and has seen it taking place between Iraq and Iran over the last several years. The second category is a war of total asymmetry, like the ones in Korea, Indochina and Algeria, in South African strikes against its neighbours; and in Israeli, US, and French strikes against developing countries. Here one side can only defend itself and cannot carry the war into the adversary's territory even through air strikes. In these circumstances, while there has been no war in the territories of industrialised nations, they have used their armed forces extensively in wars in the developing world. In other words peace among the industrialised nations does not necessarily mean they they have been at peace with the rest of the world. War in the sense of use of force by one nation against another continues to be an effective instrument of policy in the developing world.

Declaring war has become *passé*. It is termed police action, intervention, assertion of international legal rights, ensuring security of one's population, pre-emptive action, support for freedom fighters (if they are on one's own side) but never war. In this era there is no clear-cut divide between war and peace. In the continuum of international transactions from peaceful diplomacy at one end to war at the other there is a wide spectrum of coercive diplomacy. Mere deterrence is coercive diplomacy nearer to the diplomacy end. Covert intervention; arms supplies on a selective basis; acquisition of bases and access facilities; demonstration of use of force by deployment of units of armed forces; overt intervention in support of one side in a continuing conflict; nuclear alerts; and overt armed intervention come towards the other end of the spectrum. War and peace were discontinuous states in international relations. Coercive diplomacy, on the other hand, is a continuum in which coercion and diplomacy are used in different mixes as the occasion warrants.

Since this has become the age of coercive diplomacy superseding the age of war as an instrument of international politics most of the meaningful actors on the international scene maintain the necessary wherewithal for coercive diplomacy. The result is a state of armed twilight peace among industrial nations and a number of interventions, demonstrations of use of force and inter-state wars involving both developed and developing nations in the latter area.

In the exercise of this coercive diplomacy nuclear weapons and their carriers have acquired a symbolic value as the ultimate instrument of deterrence in the industrialised world and punishment in the developing world. The policy of not disclosing which ship is a nuclear weapon carrier is not so much intended to ensure security of information on military capability *vis-à-vis* a nuclear adversary as to convey a sense of intimidation to all other nations. The US anger against New Zealand is not that the security of the South Pacific could not be safeguarded without sending nuclear armed ships to New Zealand but that New Zealand's stand challenged one of the basic postures of general international nuclear intimidation *vis-à-vis* non-nuclear weapon nations. The practice of coercive diplomacy involves keeping all nations in a state of general nuclear intimidation. This is evident from the kind of guarantee extended by the United States and Great Britain in respect of their nuclear posture. They will 'not use nuclear weapons against any non-nuclear weapon state party to the Non Proliferation Treaty or any comparable internationally binding commitment not to acquire nuclear explosive devices, except in the case of an attack on the United States, its territories or armed forces or its allies by such a state allied to a nuclear weapon state or associated with a nuclear weapon state in carrying out or sustaining the attack'.[7] This guarantee will permit the Americans and the British to use nuclear weapons when their own forces launch an offensive against another nation and the other nation, in its defence, counters their forces. The phrase 'associated with a nuclear weapon state in carrying out or sustaining the attack' is vague enough to be interpreted to one's own convenience.

The pronouncements of various people in authority tend to reinforce the coercive aspect involved in the world-wide deployment of nuclear weapons. In July 1975 US Secretary of Defense James Schlesinger said 'we will make use of nuclear weapons should we be faced with obvious aggression likely to result in defeat in an area of great importance to the US in terms of foreign policy'.[8] In February 1980, after the Soviet intervention in Afghanistan and amid speculation on the future security of the Persian Gulf, a top Pentagon official said the United States was considering the possibility of using theatre atomic weapons outside Western Europe where they were now confined.[9] Secretary of Defense Caspar Weinberger, testifying before the Senate during his Confirmation Hearing on the issue of whether he would have used nuclear weapons in Vietnam, said '... if it is a serious enough situation to warrant a war and warrant the committal of US forces, we owe it to them to be ready and not necessarily to do it, but be ready to utilise the strength that we have'.[10]

The unresolved controversy about contingent plans of Great Britain to use a nuclear weapon against an Argentinian city[11] in case one of the British capital ships had been successfully attacked by the Argentine Air Force would fit in with the above wording of the so-called British guarantee and therefore has certain plausible credibility. The guarantee in fact warns the non-nuclear weapon nations that in case of conflict with the United States or Great Britain any attempt to defend themselves may result in nuclear weapons being used against them.

Use of nuclear weapons against non-nuclear weapon nations will not involve initiation of a nuclear war in which it is recognised there will be no victory. It may not even be necessary actually to use the weapon: even the implied threat of use will achieve the purpose of securing anticipatory compliance of non-nuclear nations to the demands of the nuclear weapon power. This will be coercive diplomacy at its best and constitute the acme of skill according to Sun Tzu. Hence the refusal of three nuclear weapon powers to agree to a no-first-use pledge or to discuss the outlawing of nuclear weapons. If the assertion that the Americans and the British need a possible first use option doctrine to deter a Soviet conventional threat is to be taken seriously at its face value then they should be in a position to give a categorical and a caveat-free no-first-use pledge in respect of all non-nuclear weapon nations.

The refusal by the Western nations to give a no-first-use pledge has no operational significance in deterring the Soviet Union in Europe. It flies in the face of the Reagan–Gorbachev joint declaration that a nuclear war cannot be won and therefore ought not to be initiated. The refusal to give a no-first-use pledge and the statement that a nuclear war ought not to be initiated since there will be no winners can be reconciled within the framework of only one logic. Nuclear weapons are intended to be used in coercive diplomacy against non-nuclear weapon nations in circumstances which will not result in a nuclear war, in the sense that only one side will be resorting to nuclear threats, overt or implied, or to demonstrative use of a nuclear weapon or two.

This will no doubt be denied vehemently and it will be asserted that there is absolutely no documentary substantiation for this thesis. As the empires were built up and the developing world was colonised there was never a blueprint for such a development. When the British East India Company was adding to the territories under the Company's jurisdiction the Company's directors were protesting against that policy. The imperialists thought they were on a civilising mission which the Lord had cast upon them as the White Man's burden. The conscious drive to acquire colonies in the developing world came almost one century after imperialist conquests got under way. Similarly, those who would exercise coercive diplomacy through use and threat of use of nuclear weapons may not be conscious of that possibility today but may only be buying options at this stage, though there is adequate collateral evidence to suggest that they may not be all that innocent. In this context the old adage that it is not the current intention but the capability that counts is very relevant. The Western nuclear weapon powers are not prepared to forgo nuclear weapons as a currency of power available for their use under various circumstances – with the possibility of their resorting to its use *vis-à-vis* the Soviet Union being rated as very low and irrational even by their own leadership.

The nuclear issue has got inextricably linked up with security situations in the developing world. Except for the Berlin crisis all the nuclear threats held out were in respect of crises in the developing world: Korea (1953), Suez (1956), Quemoy-Matsu (1958), Cuba (1962), the Arab–Israeli war of 1973 and the South Atlantic war (1982). Successive US Secretaries of State have held that the major difference with the Soviet Union was in respect of its non-co-operative response in tense situations in the developing world.[12] At the 1985 Geneva Summit, while the Soviet Union pressed for high priority for arms control, for the US regional issues (Central America, Southern Africa, West Asia, South-West Asia and South-East Asia) claimed higher priority. The linkage thesis popular in the 1970s postulated that, having reached parity in strategic arsenals, the Soviet Union had developed an increasing proclivity for intervention in the developing world. No doubt this is an untenable proposition, but the result has been an increasing nuclearisation of the oceans in the vicinity of developing nations and increasing access of nuclear weapon carriers to facilities in the developing world.[13]

According to the understanding contained in SALT any weapon carrier tested for a particular nuclear weapon capability is to be deemed to be deployed with such capability. Following on from this, P3 C Orion aircraft touching various facilities in the Indian Ocean countries should be deemed to carry nuclear depth-charges. Diego Garcia, with an airfield which can take B-52 bombers which carry nuclear weapons, should be deemed a nuclear base. The carrier task force permanently deployed in the Indian Ocean and all ships which can carry nuclear weapons of various categories are to be deemed deployed with that capability.

Increases in the deployment of SS-20s caused understandable concern in Western Europe. It was also argued that any negotiated reduction of SS-20 missiles in Europe should not result in their transfer to Siberia, thereby increasing the threat to China and Japan. But there is hardly a word in the international press about deployment of seaborne nuclear weapons in the neighbourhood of developing nations by countries which refuse to give even a no-first-use pledge. It would appear that security of nations falls into two categories. While the security of the Western industrialised world, of China and of Japan are sacrosanct, the security of developing nations is of little concern to the NATO nations. There was a time China, too, was included in the latter category and subjected to various threats and intimidations: including nuclear threats. But the concern which was totally absent in respect of a non-nuclear China is all too evident for a nuclear-armed China. The lesson to be drawn from this double standard is too obvious to need elaboration.

A reference was made earlier to the guarantee extended by the Americans and the British to non-nuclear nations which is more of a threat than a guarantee. That guarantee referred to non-nuclear weapon states which are parties to the NPT or any other comparable internationally binding commitment. The Tlatelolco Treaty – the Latin American Nuclear-weapon-free Zone Treaty – used to be held up as an example for non-nuclear weapon states to promote their security. It has been disclosed that the United States has contingency plans to deploy nuclear weapons in case hostilities are anticipated.[14] In other words, the Nuclear-weapon-free Zone – like the NPT – is binding only on the second-class non-nuclear weapon nations and it is not binding on nuclear weapon powers when they anticipate a need to discard their obligations.

Recently the ASEAN nations have mooted a proposal to have a Nuclear-weapon-free Zone in Southeast Asia. But they have been sternly told that such a NWFZ will not contribute to peace and stability because it would include the Subic Bay and Clark air force bases in the Philippines.[15] New Zealand, the country which contributed its manpower to fight two world wars, cannot have alliance protection unless it submits itself to nuclear hegemony. Here too an interesting question arises which has not been debated in the international press. The Nordic members of NATO are not supposed to permit deployment of nuclear weapons in their territories (which presumably includes their territorial waters) except in anticipation of hostilities. If the sensitivity of Nordic countries which are part of the

NATO area are respected, why could not the same apply to New Zealand? Or is it the case that the Nordic states' non-nuclear policy is only on paper, like Japan's three non-nuclear principles which turn a blind eye to US nuclear weapons on board ships? One is at the same time aware of the opposition to the concept of a Nordic NWFZ on the part of the United States. In other words, nations cannot have a NWFZ unless it suits the convenience of nuclear weapon powers.

It is quite obvious that visits of nuclear weapon carriers to New Zealand or the Subic Bay and Clark air force bases have little to do with deterring the Soviets who have joined in the declaration that a nuclear war cannot be won and should not be initiated. But bases overseas, the deployment of nuclear weapons on ships close to the shores of developing nations and the refusal to give a no-first-use pledge taken together form a framework in which nuclear weapons constitute an instrument of coercive diplomacy and currency of power.

The Brookings Institution has carried out a study on use of force without war.[16] The data has been further updated by Philip Zelikow up to 1982.[17] According to these studies, in the period 1946–82, the United States resorted to demonstration of force without war on 259 occasions. The Soviet Union had totalled 167 instances up to March 1979. Only 15 per cent of these demonstrations related to Europe in the case of the United States. In the case of the Soviet Union the analogous percentage was 49.7. In both cases, with the passage of time, the instances of demonstration of force without war tended to decrease in respect of Europe and increase in respect of the developing world.

The nuclear issue tends to be debated as though it mostly concerns the industrialised world, and the developing countries are brought in only with reference to the proliferation question. In the present context the developing countries face the risk of coercive diplomacy directed against them and in the exercise of that coercive diplomacy nuclear weapons play a significant role. The new central command, the only one to be created other than NATO, encompasses the vast area of the Indian Ocean and the nineteen developing countries and forces earmarked for the command will have nuclear capabilities of various types.

So long as such a threat of coercive diplomacy involving nuclear weapons persists some of the leading developing nations will have to keep their nuclear options open or practise a policy of nuclear ambiguity.

Notes

 1. See William Arkin and Richard Fieldhouse, *Nuclear Battlefields: Global Links in the Nuclear Arms Race* (Cambridge, Mass., 1985).
 2. P. K. S. Namboodiri, 'Nuclear Terrorism' in K. Subrahmanyam (ed.), *India and the Nuclear Challenge* (Delhi, 1986).
 3. Ibid., pp. 124–5; 129–30.
 4. Joseph Volz and Alton Slagle, 'Nuclear Subs on their own', *Daily News* (New York), 19 October 1983.
 5. See Paul Leventhal and Yonah Alexander (eds), *Preventing Nuclear Terrorism* (Lexington, Mass., 1987) pp. 15–17. Mention is made of improvements necessary to overcome deficiencies and of balancing security against operational responsiveness. Mention is also made of US naval weapons and also many tactical nuclear weapons not having electronic permissive action links.
 6. Sun Tzu, *The Art of War* (London, 1963), p. 97.
 7. United Nations, *Study on Nuclear Weapons* (E. 68-IX-V, New York, 1980), appendix II.
 8. Quoted in Inder Khosla, 'Use of Nuclear Weapons', *IDSA Journal*, vol. 13 (1980–1) p. 477.
 9. Christopher Paine, 'On the Beach: The Rapid Deployment Force and the Nuclear Arms Race', *MERIP Report*, vol. 13, no. 1 (1983) pp. 3–11.
10. US Senate Armed Services Committee, 'Nomination of Caspar Weinberger to be Secretary of Defense', 6 January 1981.
11. *New Statesman*, 24 and 31 August 1984.
12. Zbigniew Brzezinski, *Power and Discipline* (London, 1983) p. 148; and 'Confirmation Hearings of George Shultz', *Facts on File*, 1982, p. 505.
13. See C. Raja Mohan, 'Global Nuclearisation' in K. Subrahmanyam (ed.), *Nuclear Proliferation and International Security* (Delhi, 1985). See also Jasjit Singh, 'Threat of Nuclear Weapons' in Subrahmanyam (ed.), *India and the Nuclear Challenge*.
14. Judith Berken, C. S. Hey-Maestre and P. J. Saado-Liorens, 'Violating the Treaty of Tlatelolco', *Arms Control Today*, January 1985, pp. 4–5; and Leslie Gelb, 'US upsets Allies with Secret Plan to Place N Arms on their Soil', *International Herald Tribune*, 14 February 1985.
15. *International Herald Tribune*, 12 February 1987; and *Defense and Foreign Affairs Weekly*, 30 March–5 April 1987.
16. Barry M. Blechman and Stephen S. Kaplan, *Force Without War: US Armed Forces as a Political Instrument* (Washington, DC, 1978).
17. Philip Zelikow, 'Force Without War, 1975–82', *The Journal of Strategic Studies*, vol. 7, no. 1 (1984) pp. 29–54.

14 The Concept of Nuclear-Weapon-Free Zones

Olga Šuković

INTRODUCTION

The concept of Nuclear-weapon-free Zones (NWFZs) has been advocated by many countries over the last three decades as a means of halting the spread of nuclear weapons. However during the last few years two major, but opposite, trends have been discernible: an increased interest on the part of states in the creation of NWFZs; and a growing concern over the viability of such zones in some regions of the world, or in general. While the signing of the new Treaty on the South Pacific Nuclear-Free Zone is evidence of the first trend, the failure of the Group of Governmental Experts appointed by the United Nations Secretary-General to complete a study on NWFZs in all its aspects revealed that there were some differences even among experts concerning the concept of such zones. In particular, the viability of such zones was questioned in the light of the new findings on the climatic effects of eventual use of nuclear weapons (so-called 'nuclear winter') and the Chernobyl accident. Having in mind these two trends, it seems appropriate at this stage to re-examine the existing zones and proposals and analyse the basic questions which are essential to the establishment of NWFZs in future.

Partial disarmament measures have long been advocated within or outside the United Nations in parallel with more comprehensive approaches, such as general and complete disarmament. One of these measures is the establishment of NWFZs, considered by many as a very practical means of preventing the horizontal proliferation of nuclear weapons through banning them from certain areas. In addition, the establishment of such zones is considered as an effective means of assuring Non-nuclear-weapon States (NNWSs) in these zones against the use of nuclear weapons, thus increasing their security. Lately the concept has been supported as an arms control and confidence-building measure.

Several proposals for the establishment of NWFZs have been made since the mid-1950s. The concept received particular attention in 1975, when, pursuant to Resolution 326 (XXIX), the *Comprehensive Study of the Question of Nuclear-Weapon-Free Zones in All Its Aspects*, carried out by an *ad hoc* group of governmental experts, was submitted to the UN General Assembly.[1] The experts reached consensus on a number of principles that would have to be taken into account in creating such zones when appropriate conditions existed, but they could not agree on certain other principles. In 1982 the General Assembly created a new group of governmental experts to review and supplement the 1975 study on the subject. However it was not able to reach agreement on the study as a whole and on the conclusions in particular.

The concept was further elaborated in 1978 by the General Assembly at its Tenth Special Session, when in its Final Document it was stated that the establishment of NWFZs on the basis of arrangements freely arrived at among the states of the region concerned constituted an important disarmament measure, and that the process of establishing such zones in different parts of the world would be encouraged with the ultimate objective of achieving a world entirely free of nuclear weapons.[2]

Despite the attention given to the concept of NWFZs, two such zones have been actually established in populated areas, namely in Latin America in 1967 and on 6 August 1985 when a new Treaty on a South Pacific Nuclear-Free Zone was signed. Efforts to exclude nuclear weapons from certain regions or environments can be classified into four categories: treaties prohibiting nuclear weapons in certain geographical areas; treaties prohibiting them in certain environments; declarations proclaiming certain regions or countries denuclearised; and studies on the question of the creation of NWFZs.

The Antarctic Treaty of 1959 belongs to the first category; it ensures that Antarctica shall be used exclusively for peaceful purposes and prohibits, *inter alia*, any measure of a military nature, any nuclear explosions and the disposal of radioactive waste there. The Treaty for the Prohibition of Nuclear Weapons in Latin America (Treaty of Tlatelolco) established the first NWFZ within an inhabited area. The

South Pacific Nuclear-Free Zone Treaty established a second such zone in a populated area.

Treaties belonging to the second category exclude nuclear weapons from such environments as outer space (Treaty on Principles Governing the Activities of States in the Exploration and Use of Outer Space, including the Moon and Other Celestial Bodies), the sea-bed and the ocean floor (Treaty on the Prohibition of the Emplacement of Nuclear Weapons and Other Weapons of Mass Destruction on the Sea-Bed and Ocean Floor and in the Subsoil thereof) and the Moon (Agreement Governing the Activities of States on the Moon and Other Celestial Bodies). An example of the third category is the Declaration of Denuclearisation of Africa of 1964. Falling into the fourth category are the comprehensive studies which have already been mentioned.

In this chapter analysis will be confined to three aspects: treaties concerning the existing NWFZs; proposals for the creation of further NWFZs; and the concept of NWFZs.

EXISTING NWFZs

Several of the above-mentioned treaties could be analysed here if one took account of the wider concept of denuclearisation of certain environments. But in fact only two treaties will be mentioned in this section because they are measures which exclude nuclear weapons or nuclear explosive devices from the territories of the state parties, while the other treaties exclude nuclear weapons and other weapons of mass destruction from certain environments or territories which do not belong to specific states or are outside state jurisdiction.

Until now, as already mentioned, only two treaties have been signed on NWFZs in the narrow sense: The Treaty for the Prohibition of Nuclear Weapons in Latin America (Treaty of Tlatelolco) and The South Pacific Nuclear-Free Zone Treaty (Treaty of Rarotonga). The Treaty of Tlatelolco (signed on 14 February 1967) defines the obligations of the states parties to the Treaty and the zone of its application and establishes the International Agency for the Prohibition of Nuclear Weapons in Latin America (OPANAL) to ensure compliance with the Treaty, together with a control system that includes the application of International Atomic Energy Agency (IAEA) safeguards to peaceful nuclear activities. The Treaty has two Additional

Protocols relating to undertakings to be entered into by states outside the Zone having *de jure* or *de facto* responsibility for territories lying within the Treaty's geographic zone, which would thereby commit themselves to apply the status of denuclearisation in respect of such territories (Additional Protocol I); and the Nuclear-weapon States (NWSs) which would undertake not to use or threaten the use of nuclear weapons against parties to the Treaty (Additional Protocol II). As of December 1985, the Treaty was in force for 23 Latin American states which had ratified it and had waived the requirements set out in paragraph 1 of Article 28. All NWSs had adhered to Additional Protocol II, while Additional Protocol I has been signed and ratified by the Netherlands, the United Kingdom and the United States. France has signed it, but has not yet ratified it.[3]

The Treaty of Rarotonga (signed on 6 August 1985) establishes the second NWFZ and defines the obligations of the contracting States and the zone of its application. Similar to the Treaty of Tlatelolco, it establishes within the South Pacific Forum a Consultative Committee for consultation and co-operation on any matter in relation to the Treaty or for reviewing its operation (Annex 3 to the Treaty). At the same time, the Treaty establishes a control system for the purpose of verifying compliance of states with their obligations under the Treaty, which comprise, *inter alia*, the application of safeguards by the IAEA to their peaceful nuclear activities (as provided for in Annex 2).[4]

PROPOSALS FOR THE CREATION OF NWFZs

Proposals have been made for the establishment of NWFZs in various other regions of the world, namely Africa, Asia, Europe and the Middle East.

Africa

Since 1960, the African states have adopted or sponsored the adoption of a series of decisions aimed at making the continent of Africa a NWFZ. *The Declaration on Denuclearisation of Africa* was a statement adopted by the Organisation of African Unity (OAU) in July 1964, and it was endorsed by the UN General Assembly on 3 December 1965 (Resolution 2033 (xx)). At the same time, the General Assembly called upon all states to refrain from testing, manufacturing, using or deploying nuclear weapons on the continent of Africa as well as from transferring such weapons, scientific data or technical assistance, either directly or indirectly, in any form which might be used to assist in the manufacture or use of nuclear weapons in Africa.

There is a general consensus in the international community in favour of the establishment of a NWFZ in Africa (expressed through numerous resolutions of the UN General Assembly, the OAU and the Non-Aligned Movement). Meanwhile, grave concern has been expressed by the African and other states at South Africa's nuclear capability and this is considered a major obstacle to the denuclearisation of Africa.

Asia

The question of establishing a NWFZ in South Asia has been discussed in the United Nations since 1974 when the General Assembly adopted two resolutions (32065 A and B (XXIX)) initiated by India and Pakistan and reflecting their views concerning such a zone. Since 1976 the UN General Assembly has adopted each year only one resolution which reaffirms its endorsement, in principle, of the concept of a NWFZ in South Asia and urges states of the region to make all efforts to establish such a zone. However, India has repeatedly stated that the existence of nuclear weapons in Asia and in the Pacific and the presence of foreign military bases in the Indian Ocean make the situation inappropriate for the establishment of a NWFZ in the sub-region of South Asia.

Europe

Various proposals have been made for the establishment of NWFZs relating to certain parts of Europe, particularly the Balkans, Central Europe and Northern Europe. It should be noted that Europe differs from other regions in the world, particularly in that the region is still characterised by the greatest concentration of troops and armaments, both conventional and nuclear.

Proposals for the establishment of a NWFZ in the Balkans date back to 1957 when Romania proposed the establishment of an area of peace in the Balkans free of foreign military bases and later, in 1959, reiterated that initiative in more detail. In 1959 also the Soviet Union suggested the creation of such zones in the Balkans and the Adriatic.

Since the beginning of the 1980s, the idea of turning the Balkans into a NWFZ has once again become the focus of attention in most of the countries in the region. While in bilateral and multilateral declarations and statements Bulgaria, Greece, Romania and Yugoslavia have supported the transformation of the Balkans into a NWFZ, or into a zone of peace and co-operation free of nuclear weapons, Turkey has stated that the security of the Balkans is related to that of Europe as a whole and that one could not be isolated from the other, and therefore that security could not be attained by establishing a NWFZ in the Balkans in present conditions. Albania has also stated that 'in the present situation of international relations of the Balkan States, the creation of a zone without nuclear weapons in this region would have no practical effect, either for the security of the Balkan countries, or that of the world'.[5]

Proposals for a NWFZ in Central Europe were put forward on numerous occasions in the 1950s. In 1956 the Soviet Union proposed that a zone be created in Central Europe where armaments should be subject to limitations and inspection and the stationing of any atomic or hydrogen weapons would be prohibited. Poland later developed the idea of establishing a NWFZ into a full-fledged plan for Central Europe, namely the Rapacki Plan of 1957. The Plan was subsequently revised in 1958, 1962 and 1964. Since then, Poland has repeated its proposals. Thus, in 1982, the Polish Seim and other national institutions expressed the belief that the creation of such a zone would still constitute a valid and constructive measure.

On 8 December 1982 the Swedish Government approached 28 governments in Europe and North America, asking them to express their views on the proposal originally suggested by the Independent Commission for Disarmament and Security Issues (The Palme Commission) 'to create a zone free of battlefield nuclear weapons extending from Central Europe to the outermost northern and southern flanks of the two alliances' (originally it was suggested that the zone would be 300 kilometres).[6] However, owing to different views among European States, no practical measures have been taken.

The idea of establishing a NWFZ in Northern Europe was suggested for the first time in 1959 by the Soviet Union. In the late 1950s and early 1960s, several suggestions were made regarding the establishment of such a zone in the Nordic and Baltic area. However the idea has been advocated primarily by Finland. In May 1963 the President of Finland suggested that the Nordic countries should establish a NWFZ which would only confirm, through mutual undertakings, the existing *de facto* situation of the absence of nuclear weapons without impairing the security of the Nordic countries or affecting the balance of power in the world. While the matter has been discussed from time to time during the last two decades, the different attitudes of the Nordic countries have not made it possible to proceed to concrete negotiations and to the implementation of the Finnish proposal. In the 1980s the debate on a NWFZ in Northern Europe has gained a fresh momentum in the Nordic countries. Also the Soviet Union has expressed its readiness to contribute to the establishment of such a zone in Northern Europe, not only by committing itself to respect the status of such a zone, but also by its readiness to consider the question of certain, even substantial measures relating to its own territory adjacent to the zone, which would promote the strengthening of its nuclear weapon-free status.

The Middle East

It is generally accepted that the creation of a NWFZ in the Middle East would greatly enhance international security and peace, particularly having in mind the situation in that region. Such a proposal was initiated by Egypt and Iran in 1974, when the UN General Assembly adopted Resolution 3263 (XXIX) in which it commended the idea of establishing such a zone in the Middle East, and considered that it was indispensable that all concerned parties in the area 'proclaim their intention to refrain, on a reciprocal basis, from producing, testing, obtaining, acquiring or in any other way possessing nuclear weapons'. Since 1980 the General Assembly resolutions on the subject have been adopted by consensus, expressing wide acceptance in the General Assembly of the proposal and its wide support in the region itself. Although Israel joined the consensus on the subject, it has expressed several reservations regarding the approach suggested in those resolutions.

At the same time, there has been increasing concern about Israel's reported nuclear-weapons capability. In the UN *Study on Israeli Nuclear Armament*, the Group of Experts was unable to conclude definitely whether or not Israel was at present in possession of nuclear weapons, but stressed that the possession of such weapons by Israel would be a seriously destabilising factor in the already tense situation prevailing in the Middle East.[7]

THE CONCEPT OF NWFZs

Numerous questions have been raised so far, either during the creation of the existing NWFZs, or during discussions of proposals for creating new ones, or in the course of the UN studies on the subject. Here we will concentrate only on the more important of these.

Definition of the Concept

There have been a few attempts to define the concept of a NWFZ but none of them has received general approval. The most comprehensive definition thus far is that adopted by the United Nations General Assembly on 11 December 1965. In its Resolution 3472 B (xxx), it defined the concept of a NWFZ as follows:

> A nuclear-weapon-free zone shall, as a general rule, be deemed to be any zone, recognized as such by the General Assembly of the United Nations, which any group of States, in the free exercise of their sovereignty, has established by virtue of a treaty or convention whereby:
> (a) The statute of total absence of nuclear weapons to which the zone shall be subject, including the procedure for the delimitation of the zone, is defined;
> (b) An international system of verification and control is established to guarantee compliance with the obligations deriving from that statute.

Further impetus to the concept was given in the Final Document of the Tenth Special Session of the General Assembly, adopted by consensus, referring to the concept of a NWFZ in the following manner:

> The establishment of NWFZs on the basis of arrangements freely arrived at among the States of the region concerned constitutes an important disarmament measure. ... The process of establishing such zones in different parts of the world should be encouraged with the ultimate objective of achieving a world free of nuclear weapons. In the process of establishing such zones, the characteristics of each region should be taken into account. The States participating in such zones should undertake to comply fully with

all the objectives, purposes and principles of the agreements establishing the zones, thus ensuring that they are genuinely free from nuclear weapons.[8]

The concept has been also discussed in the United Nations Disarmament Commission in the framework of agenda item 4 concerning various aspects of the arms race, particularly the nuclear arms race and nuclear disarmament. Although the Contact Group established to deal with this item has been unable to reach consensus on a complete set of recommendations, the Disarmament Commission submitted in 1984 to the 39th Session of the General Assembly 'Compilation of proposals for recommendations on agenda item 4', in which the following recommendation appeared without brackets, indicating general acceptance:

> The establishment of nuclear-weapon-free zones in different parts of the world on the basis of agreements and or arrangements freely arrived at among the States of the region concerned constitute an important disarmament measure and should be encouraged, with the ultimate objective of achieving a world entirely free of nuclear weapons. In the process of establishing such zones, the characteristics of each region should be fully complied with and the effective respect for the status of such zones by nuclear-weapon States should be subject to adequate verification procedures, thus ensuring that the zones are genuinely free from nuclear weapons.[9]

The two existing treaties on NWFZs, those on Latin America and the South Pacific, do not define the concept as such. However, while the Parties to the Rarotonga Treaty in its Preamble express their belief that 'regional arms control measures can contribute to global efforts to reverse the nuclear arms race and promote the national security of each country in the region and the common security of all', the Tlatelolco Treaty is somewhat more explicit. For there it is stated

> that the military denuclearisation of Latin America – being understood to mean the undertaking entered into internationally in this Treaty to keep their territories forever free from nuclear weapons – will constitute a measure which will spare their peoples from the squandering of their limited resources on nuclear armaments and will protect them against possible nuclear attack on their territories, and will also constitute a significant contribution towards

preventing the proliferation of nuclear weapons and a powerful factor for general and complete disarmament.

However, the Group of Experts appointed by the Secretary-General pursuant to General Assembly resolution 37/99 F of 13 December 1982 in order to undertake a study to review and supplement the *Comprehensive Study of the Question of Nuclear-Weapon-Free Zones in All Its Aspects* did not reach consensus on a definition of the concept of a NWFZ. In addition, there are differences in opinion among states as to the need to define the concept as such. Some of them consider that it would not be practical to lay down a uniform set of rules for strictly defining the NWFZ concept. The states participating in a NWFZ should be free to decide what measures they consider appropriate to the requirements of their specific region. Taking into account the particular characteristics of a given region and the fact that security perceptions of states of that region could vary widely, it would be appropriate to leave to the states in question the freedom to decide on the concept and the obligations concerning such zones. On the other hand, some elements of general definition of the zone concept could be useful as guidelines which might be of assistance in the efforts for the establishment of further NWFZs.

Responsibilities of Zonal States

There are some differences between the obligations undertaken by State Parties to the Tlatelolco and the Rarotonga Treaties. Under the Treaty of Tlatelolco (Article 1), the Contracting Parties undertake to use exclusively for peaceful purposes the nuclear material and facilities under their jurisdiction and to prohibit and prevent in their respective territories:

(a) The testing, use, manufacture, production or acquisition by any means whatsoever of any nuclear weapons, by the Parties themselves directly or indirectly, on behalf of anyone else or in any other way, and
(b) The receipt, storage, installation, deployment and any form of possession of any nuclear weapons, directly or indirectly, by the Parties themselves, by anyone on their behalf or in any other way.

Under the Rarotonga Treaty, each signatory undertakes:

(a) not to manufacture or otherwise acquire, possess or have control over any nuclear explosive device by any means anywhere inside or outside the South Pacific Nuclear-Free Zone;
(b) not to seek or receive any assistance in the manufacture or acquisition of any nuclear explosive device;
(c) not to take any action to assist or encourage the manufacture or acquisition of any nuclear explosive device by any State.

Besides this basic difference in prohibiting only nuclear weapons (in the case of Latin America) and prohibiting any nuclear explosive device (in the case of the South Pacific), the Treaty of Rarotonga goes beyond the Tlatelolco Treaty in two important respects: it bans the testing of nuclear explosive devices (in other words it does not make a distinction between testing of nuclear devices for warlike or for peaceful purposes) and it bans the dumping of radioactive waste.

There are different views among states and experts on the issue of nuclear explosions for peaceful purposes. According to some, nuclear explosive devices intended for peaceful purposes could also be used as weapons, owing to the fact that, for the time being, there is no way to distinguish between the explosive devices for military or peaceful purposes. Hence, they argue, the development and production of such devices by zonal states would violate one of the principal purposes of the zones. Moreover, they point out, peaceful-explosions services are available from NWSs under Article V of the Non-Proliferation Treaty, with the assistance of the IAEA.

Opponents of this approach stress the inalienable right of all states to use nuclear energy for peaceful purposes and the right to exploit such benefits. Hence they contend that peaceful nuclear explosions should be available to all parties to a NWFZ treaty. This view has found an expression in the Tlatelolco Treaty, allowing explosions of nuclear devices for peaceful purposes under certain conditions. However the conditions attached to the relevant clause in the Treaty are interpreted by most countries as in practice prohibiting the manufacturing of nuclear explosive devices for peaceful purposes unless or until nuclear devices are developed which cannot be used as weapons – a condition which is never likely to be fulfilled.

It is interesting to note that the NWSs have expressed different opinions on this question in relation to the Tlatelolco Treaty. Thus Great Britain, in ratifying the Additional Protocols to the Treaty, declared that it did not recognise the right of Parties to the Treaty to carry out explosions of nuclear devices for peaceful purposes unless and until advances in technology had made possible the development of devices for such explosions which were not capable of being used for weapon purposes.[10] The Soviet Union made a similar declaration, stating that the carrying out by any Party to the Treaty of explosions of nuclear devices for peaceful purposes would be a violation of the obligations under Article 1 and would be incompatible with non-nuclear status.[11] On the other hand, the United States, while ratifying Protocol II, stated that it would not prevent it collaborating with the Parties to the Treaty for the purpose of carrying out explosions of nuclear devices for peaceful purposes.[12]

Another controversial question is the right of transit and transportation of nuclear weapons within or through the zone. There are different views on the question of whether the transit of nuclear weapons through a NWFZ should be permitted or prohibited, or whether the legal instrument establishing such zones needs to contain specific provisions in this respect. The Treaty of Tlatelolco does not exclude explicitly either the transit or transportation of nuclear weapons through the Zone. The NWSs have taken different attitudes towards this question. Thus the United States, while ratifying Protocol II, made a statement in which, *inter alia*, it held that the Treaty did not affect the right of the Parties to grant or deny transport and transit privileges to non-Parties.[13]

On signing Additional Protocol II China stated that all nuclear countries must undertake and implement the undertaking to prohibit the passage of any means of transportation and delivery of nuclear weapons through Latin American territory, territorial seas or airspace. Similarly the Soviet Union stated that it reaffirmed its position that authorising the transit of nuclear weapons in any form would be contrary to the objective of the Treaty.[14]

Opposing these views, France stated that it took note of the interpretation of the Treaty given by the Preparatory Commission for Denuclearisation of Latin America and reproduced in the Final Act, according to which the Treaty did not apply to transit, the granting or denying of which lay within the exclusive competence of each State Party in accordance with the pertinent principles and rules of international law.[15]

The Treaty of Rarotonga does not prohibit the transit of nuclear armed ships or aircraft and leaves the decision to the state concerned.

Responsibilities of Non-Zonal States

The question of support for the creation of and respect for a NWFZ from beyond the region, and particularly by the five NWSs, is also treated in a different manner in the two existing treaties; and there are different opinions among governments and experts. In the Final Document of the Tenth Special Session of the General Assembly it is stated:

> With respect to such zones, the nuclear-weapon States in turn are called upon to give undertakings, the modalities of which are to be negotiated with the competent authority of each zone, in particular:
> (a) To respect strictly the status of the NWFZ;
> (b) To refrain from the use or threat of use of nuclear weapons against the States of the zone.

Other extra-zonal states should fully respect the status of the NWFZ and refrain from assisting in the introduction and manufacture of nuclear weapons therein and in the acquisition of nuclear weapons by zonal states. Their responsibilities could, depending on the specific characteristics and circumstances, be expressed in a legally binding form or in other forms such as unilateral declarations or other international documents.

In the case of Latin America the question of responsibilities of the NWSs and other non-zonal states have been solved through two Additional Protocols. While, on the basis of Additional Protocol I, its signatory States undertake to apply the status of denuclearisation in respect of territories for which, *de jure* or *de facto*, they are responsible internationally, and which lie within the geographical zone established in the Treaty, in Additional Protocol II it is stipulated that the Parties to that Protocol (the NWSs) would fully respect the status of denuclearisation of Latin America and would undertake not to use or threaten to use nuclear weapons against the Contracting Parties to the Treaty of Tlatelolco.

While it is more or less accepted that NWSs should undertake an obligation to respect the status of the NWFZ and not to use nuclear weapons against such zones, there are differences of opinion among governments and experts as to the extent of these obligations and whether such undertakings should be undertaken in an internationally legally-binding instrument or in such instruments as unilateral or multilateral declarations.

A question also arises as to whether the entry into force of such a treaty should be conditional upon the acceptance of certain obligations by the NWSs. During the elaboration of the Treaty of Tlatelolco two different views were expressed among the Contracting States and as a result a compromise solution was accepted as incorporated in Article 28 of that Treaty. One view was that the Treaty should enter into force, in accordance with the generally accepted applicable rule in such cases, between those States which had ratified it, on the date at which the respective instruments of ratification were deposited. The states supporting the second position, on the contrary, held that the Treaty, even though it had been signed and ratified by all the States Members of the Preparatory Commission, should enter into force only when four prerequisites had been fulfilled. Essentially these are the prerequisites appearing in Paragraph 1 of Article 28 of the Treaty, which may be summed up as follows: signature and ratification of the Treaty and the additional Protocols I and II by all States to which the three instruments in question are open for signature, and the conclusion of agreements with the IAEA on the application of its system of safeguards by all the Signatory States to the Treaty and to additional Protocols I and II. The solution was found by incorporating the four requirements in Article 28, Paragraph 1, but at the same time stipulating that 'All signatory States shall have the imprescriptible right to waive, wholly or in part, the requirements laid down in the preceding paragraph.'

Since one of the requirements for entry into force of the Treaty was the signature and ratification of the Additional Protocols I and II by the NWSs and by other States which have *de facto* or *de jure* jurisidiction over the territories within the Zone, it is obvious that there were two opinions among State Parties to the Treaty of Tlatelolco as to whether undertakings of the NWSs towards the denuclearised zone were preconditions for the establishment of that Zone.[16]

Having in mind the case of Latin America, the State Parties to the Treaty of Rarotonga did not make the entry of the Treaty into force dependent on the signature and ratification of its Protocols 1, 2 and 3 by the NWSs, but simply stated that it would enter into force on the date of deposit of the eighth instrument of ratification (Article 15, Paragraph 1).

According to Protocol 1, the Parties to that Protocol would

undertake to apply, in respect to the territories for which they are internationally responsible and which are situated within the South Pacific Nuclear-Free-Zone, the prohibitions contained in Articles 3, 5 and 6 in so far as they relate to the manufacture, stationing and testing of any nuclear explosive device within these territories and the safeguards in article 8(2)(c) and Annex 2 of the Treaty (Article 1).

By signing and ratifying Protocol 2, the NWSs would undertake not to contribute to any act which constitutes a violation of the Treaty or its Protocols (Article 1), as well as not to use or threaten to use any nuclear explosive device against the Parties to the Treaty or any territory within the South Pacific Nuclear-Free-Zone for which a State that has become a Party to Protocol 1 is internationally responsible.

Under Protocol 3 the NWSs are called upon to undertake not to test any nuclear explosive device anywhere within the South Pacific Nuclear-Free-Zone (Article 1).[17]

Geographical Scope of NWFZs

As far as the size of NWFZs is concerned, there is no rule which could be applied to every case. The extent of a zone would depend upon the specific characteristics of the region and the precise objectives to be realised, as well as the intentions of the parties to a given agreement.

So far as the proposals advanced so far are concerned, it is apparent that they have ranged from a single state proclaiming itself or even part of itself as a NWFZ, to plans for whole continents and for areas adjacent to the zone, including in some cases large portions of the high seas and vast areas of the ocean over which no state has jurisdiction.

The question of geographical scope has been raised in the context of the proposals for the creation of NWFZs in Northern Europe, in the Balkans, and particularly lately in connection with the creation of a zone which would be free of battlefield-nuclear-weapons in Central Europe. According to some states, one of the main obstacles to the creation of a NWFZ in Northern Europe is the presence of nuclear weapons in the area adjacent to the zone, particularly the nuclear weapons stationed in the Soviet Union. It seems that this obstacle could be lessened in the future following the stated readiness of the Soviets to undertake certain obligations in regard to their own territory. According to news reports, during a recent visit to Finland,

Yegor Lygachev expressed a Soviet willingness to withdraw nuclear missiles from the Kola peninsula and from around Leningrad.[18]

In the Tlatelolco Treaty the geographical scope of the NWFZ is defined in a rather broad manner. For it is stipulated that the zone of application of the Treaty is the whole of the territories for which the Treaty is in force and that, upon fulfilment of the requirements of Article 28, Paragraph 1, the zone of application shall also be that which is situated in the Western Hemisphere within given limits (except the continental part of the United States and its territorial waters). In other words, the zone of application of the Treaty of Tlatelolco would, upon the fulfilment of certain requirements, include large areas in the Atlantic and the Pacific Oceans, hundreds of kilometres off the coast of Latin America, in addition to the territories of the countries concerned. It seems that international law regarding the freedom of the seas did not stand in the way of banning nuclear weapons from the high seas under the Treaty of Tlatelolco.

In the case of the Treaty of Rarotonga, we are presented with two possible definitions. First, the scope of the Treaty in geographical terms is defined by membership of the South Pacific Forum. Therefore the nuclear prohibition will almost certainly be applied in Australia (and its territories), the Cook Islands, Fiji, Kiributi, Naura, New Zealand (and its Territories), Niue, Papua New Guinea, the Solomon Islands, Tonga, Tuvala and Samoa. In addition, if Great Britain, France and the United States sign the Protocols to the Treaty, its application would be extended also to their South Pacific Territories. But although the actual area of application of the nuclear prohibition is confined to the territories of the Forum countries, and of the dependencies for which administering powers sign, the Treaty defines the geographical scope of the South Pacific Nuclear-Free-Zone in much broader fashion. The boundaries stretch from the border of the Latin American NWFZ in the east, to the west coast of Australia in the west, and from the border of the Antarctic Zone in the south to the equator – with some extension into the northern hemisphere to include Kiributi. As this Zone includes a vast area of ocean over which the Treaty signatories do not have jurisdiction and in relation to which the Treaty does not seek to apply any nuclear prohibition, this concept of the region is termed as a 'picture frame' approach and represents an intended area of application.[19]

On the basis of the existing treaties on NWFZs, proposals put forward for the establishment of such zones in different parts of the world, and the views expressed by states and experts, it could be concluded that the scope of application of a given treaty on the creation of a NWFZ should be determined by the states participating in such arrangements taking into account the specific characteristics of the zone and the security requirements of the states concerned.

Verification

As already mentioned in connection with the definition of the concept of a NWFZ, the General Assembly considered that the establishment of an international system of verification and control to guarantee compliance with the obligations deriving from the denuclearised status of a NWFZ was an essential part of the concept. In the case of Latin America, the control system for verifying whether the Contracting Parties comply with their obligations under the Treaty has two components: application of IAEA safeguards to their nuclear activities on the basis of multilateral or bilateral agreements concluded with the IAEA and verification through OPANAL, which could carry, through its Council, special inspections in a case of violation of the Treaty.

A similar solution has been accepted in the South Pacific case: verification of treaty obligations is provided by the application of IAEA safeguards to peaceful nuclear activities and by giving a controlling body, the Consultative Committee, the power to direct a special inspection team to investigate any suspected violation on the territory of a Member State. While acquisition of nuclear weapons could be detected by the IAEA inspectors, nuclear testing could be detected by the seismic monitoring network in Australia and New Zealand.

In addressing the question of verification in the context of NWFZs many of the problems present in discussing arms control measures in general arise, such as whether it is possible to verify treaty provisions concerning the high seas or other areas not under national jurisdiction; the practical difficulties of detecting and monitoring ships and especially submerged submarines; the problem of verification in a case when a NWS participates in a zonal arrangement with only a part of its territory, or when a zonal state is a member of an alliance with a NWS. In addition, one should bear in mind the fact that verification of undertakings of the NWSs and Non-Zonal States in the matter of the NWFZ in Latin America is not envisaged.

It seems that, in order to ensure that a NWFZ will function effectively, it is necessary to devise a system of verification to provide adequate assurances that all zonal arrangements are strictly observed by contracting parties, by the NWSs and by all other extra-zonal states. The precise nature, scope and modalities of the verification system could vary from zone to zone; and, although it is desirable to solve the problem during the negotiation of an arrangement for the creation of such a zone, the problem of verification and its effectiveness should not prevent states from accepting such an arrangement if other security requirements are satisfied.

It is generally accepted that international organisations or regional bodies could play a role in verification activities in relation to NWFZs. In accordance with its Statute and on the request of the zonal states concerned, such a role could be assumed by the IAEA (as in the cases of Latin America and the South Pacific) or the states concerned could create a special organisation or use some regional bodies for that purpose. The precise mandate of such bodies would have to be defined in the treaty establishing the zone.

CONCLUSION

As illustrated by the foregoing analysis of the existing treaties, proposals for the creation of NWFZs and the concept of such zones, there are differences of opinion among states in relation to many questions. While in the early 1950s and 1960s it seemed that the concept was accepted as a practical means of preventing the horizontal proliferation of nuclear weapons and as an effective means of insuring Non-nuclear-weapon States in such zones against the use or threat to use nuclear weapons by the NWSs, later these basic assumptions were questioned by some states in the light of some new developments. It has been argued that the Non-proliferation Treaty (NPT) has already fulfilled the primary reason for creation of such zones and that the guarantees given by the NWSs through unilateral declarations have made redundant the assurances by those states through additional regional arrangements not to use nuclear weapons against the zones.

Some doubts have also been expressed as to the viability of NWFZs in the face of the escalating nuclear arms race among the NWSs. In addition, some reservations have been expressed on the efficiency of partial disarmament measures, particularly in the context of the

'Nuclear Winter' findings and the Chernobyl accident which confirmed once again that state boundaries provide no protection from the consequences of an accident or from the effects of a large-scale use of nuclear weapons in case of war.

Having in mind the scepticism expressed by some states and experts concerning the viability of the concept of NWFZs, on the one hand, and the renewed interest of some states in creating such zones in different parts of the world, on the other, it would appear that the concept of NWFZs should be looked upon as an arms control and confidence-building measure as well as as a measure intended to strengthen the global nuclear non-proliferation regime.

Notes

1. United Nations, *Comprehensive Study of the Question of Nuclear-Weapon-Free Zones in All Its Aspects* (New York, 1975).
2. United Nations, *Official Records of the General Assembly, Tenth Special Session*, Supplement No. 4 (A/S-10/4), sect. III, paras 60–1.
3. US Arms Control and Disarmament Agency, *Arms Control and Disarmament Agreements: Texts and Histories of Negotiations* (Washington, DC, 1980) pp. 59–81.
4. Stockholm International Peace Research Institute (SIPRI), *World Armaments and Disarmament: SIPRI Yearbook 1986* (London, 1986) pp. 509–19.
5. *Zeri i Popullit*, 12 June 1983.
6. Independent Commission on Disarmament and Security Issues, *Common Security: A Programme for Disarmament* (London, 1982).
7. United Nations, *Study on Israeli Nuclear Armament* (New York, 1982), paras 82 and 83.
8. United Nations, Doc. A/S-10/4.
9. United Nations, *Official Records of the General Assembly, Thirty-ninth Session, Supplement No. 42 (A/39/42), annex* IX, recommendation no. 14.
10. SIPRI, *SIPRI Yearbook 1986*, p. 579.
11. Ibid., p. 580.
12. Ibid., p. 579.
13. Ibid., pp. 579–80.
14. Ibid., pp. 578–80.
15. Ibid.
16. Alfonso Garcia Robles, 'The Treaty for the Prohibition of Nuclear Weapons in Latin America (Treaty of Tlatelolco)', SIPRI, *SIPRI Yearbook of World Armaments and Disarmament, 1969/70* (Stockholm, 1970) pp. 218–56.
17. Greg E. Fry, 'The South Pacific nuclear-free zone', SIPRI, *SIPRI Yearbook 1986*, pp. 499–508.
18. *Politika* (Belgrade), 14 November 1986.
19. Fry, 'The South Pacific nuclear-free zone', p. 503.

15 Brazil and Disarmament
Ernst W. Hamburger

INTRODUCTION

Disarmament is not an important issue in Brazilian politics or in the media. Why this is so will be briefly analysed later. Two related issues are, however, often discussed in the media: the Brazilian armaments industry, which mainly developed during the last decade; and the Nuclear Programme which is a plan for the construction of nuclear power plants, but which in the public mind is always connected with nuclear war and destruction. These will be considered below. Attention will also be given in this chapter to the general issue of nuclear disarmament in Latin America and the Brazilian position relative to world disarmament.

PUBLIC CONCERN ABOUT DISARMAMENT IN BRAZIL

Interest in the issues relating to disarmament is very small in Brazil. Other problems are of more immediate interest. Up to very recently, it was believed that a global nuclear war in the northern hemisphere would not directly affect the countries in the southern hemisphere. Only the recent studies of the climatic effects of a nuclear war have shown that a Nuclear Winter would also destroy life and civilisation in the south. However the situation concerning nuclear war is clearly outside Brazil's control and depends essentially on the two superpowers. Thus it is felt to be their problem and not Brazil's.

Brazil is moreover a very stratified country in which a relatively small fraction of the population takes part in debating public policy. Of the population of about 130 million, about 50 million watch television and only about 20 million read newspapers. Very little about disarmament is published in the newspapers or in the electronic media. Disarmament negotiations and demonstrations against nuclear weapons in northern countries are, however, reported in despatches of international news agencies. There is a clear feeling of sympathy for disarmament but few proposals for action or discussion in Brazil. Public debates about disarmament usually attract few people.

Brazil is undergoing, at present, the final stages of transition from 21 years of military government to democracy. The military regime started as a relatively mild dictatorship during the period 1964–8, passed through a period of tyranny from 1969 to 1974 and again a gradually liberalising dictatorship prevailed from 1974 to 1984. At present military influence is still considerable but political freedoms and a free press exist. Political parties in Brazil do not have, in general, precise positions on issues of foreign policy. National independence *vis-à-vis* foreign powers is the main concern. There is apparent consensus among parties that Brazil should not construct nuclear bombs because it would be a very expensive programme and of doubtful utility. However, this is not a campaign issue and debates in the Parliament are very rare. There seems to be no objection among politicians to the announced intention of constructing a nuclear-powered submarine and the rapid expansion of the conventional arms industry is not criticised.

Peace movements are not strong in Brazil. Ecological movements are much stronger, since the destruction of the natural habitat and resources is a very fast-moving and dangerous process in Brazil. In São Paulo there are two main peace organisations, both related to, but formally independent of, left-wing political parties: 'Movimento Pacifista Brasileiro' and 'Conselho de Defesa da Paz'. In Rio de Janeiro also these organisations and others exist. There are also a few local committees such as 'Comite Londrinense pela Paz' and also Brazilian chapters of international organisations such as International Physicians for Prevention of Nuclear War. In 1985 an international Pugwash meeting was held in Campinas followed by a public discussion of the disarmament issues at the meeting of the Brazilian Association for the Advancement of Science. The Catholic Church in Brazil has a position in favour of peace and disarmament but is more concerned with more immediate problems of social justice such as agrarian reform and diminution of poverty.

Academic interest in the subject is modest. Several books have been published. There is a journal *Política e Estratégia* dedicated to strategic subjects which contains articles mostly conservative in tone and related to the military establishment; and there have been studies from economic and sociological points of view about the arms industry, particularly at the University of Campinas.

Some scientific societies, particularly the Sociedade Brasileira de Fisica and the Sociedade Brasileira para o Progresso da Ciencia, have been concerned with disarmament and with the nuclear programme. Ever since the public announcement, in 1975, of a nuclear agreement with West Germany for construction of nuclear power plants, the scientific societies have actively criticised the plan, mainly for technical and economic reasons but also because of the suspicion of military motivations.

Even in academic circles the interest in disarmament is limited. For example, a course on Causes and Consequences of a Nuclear War which the present writer organised at the University of São Paulo, in 1984, attracted only about 70 of the 30 000 students and 4 000 faculty.

THE ARMS INDUSTRY IN BRAZIL

The armaments industry in Brazil has had striking success in developing rapidly, obtaining foreign technology, supplying a large part of the needs of Brazilian armed forces, and obtaining a foreign market for the export of arms. Brazil now ranks third among third-world weapons producers, after India and Israel, and first among third-world exporters, slightly in front of Israel.

From the point of view of economic development, and also of technological independence, this branch of industry is paradigmatic, an example which is to be followed in other branches. In a short time, about ten years, production leaped from a small value to such a large one that it now contributes significantly to the national balance of foreign payments, and it is controlled solely by Brazilian interests. Other industries which grew rapidly, such as the automobile industry, are almost totally controlled by multinational corporations.

Up to and after the Second World War, Brazil depended almost totally on the import of weapons, mainly from the United States, transferred under a military agreement between the two governments. At the time of the Vietnam War the United States restricted its weapon exports, and Brazil started to import also from European countries. During the Jimmy Carter Administration US weapons sales were restricted even more, owing to the campaign against violations of human rights; the Brazilian government then severed the military agreement in 1977 and relied almost totally on internal production and imports from Europe.

Long before this, however, the foundations for a future weapons industry had been laid. During the war, the first large steel mill was built. In 1946 the Air Force established the Centro Técnico de Aeronáutica (CTA) in the city of São José dos Campos, near São Paulo, on the road to Rio, a town which is considered today the centre of the weapons industry. The CTA contained a research institute and a modern engineering school (ITA) based on American models, with the collaboration of US professors. Graduates from ITA have been important in the arms industry and other technology-intensive industries. In these years also a plan for providing the state of São Paulo with abundant hydroelectric energy was formulated; during the last decades many hydroelectric plants were built, and electricity was made available for industrialisation. The automobile industry started about 1951, with factories of General Motors, Ford, Volkswagen and other multinational companies. As a consequence, there was a rapid development of the metallurgical industry.

Industry in general grew rapidly during and after the war, and imported goods were replaced with home-made ones. A wide and diversified industrial base was created. The electronic industry started by building radio receivers and later television sets with imported components, but today makes small computers and other advanced goods. However, Brazil is still dependent on imports in this area.

Even with a broad civilian industrial base, the weapons industry only succeeded because of continuous and intelligent government support. For example, the aircraft factory EMBRAER, located near CTA in São José dos Campos, had the prototypes of its first aircraft developed for it by CTA (with the help of foreign technicians), and built the first batch of aircraft to meet government orders for the Air Force and the Ministry of Agriculture. A special government taskforce co-ordinated the efforts of private companies (which were encouraged by tax exemptions and similar advantages to participate in the weapons programme) and of government institutions (military arsenals, research institutes and government departments) in a general plan to prepare and maintain favourable conditions for this particular branch of industry. Also the kind of technology employed in the weapons was carefully chosen to take into account the limited capability of the country and also emphasised relatively simple, uncomplicated but rugged equipment: combat cars (smaller and cheaper than tanks which are also made), short-range rockets, training aircraft (also used as small passenger aircraft), guns and ammunition. In the case of aircraft, both civilian and military applications were foreseen and also both internal use and export. The concern of the military government with counter-insurgency in Brazil, principally during the 1970s, must also have influenced the technology chosen. However, owing to international conditions, the export of arms soon became the dominant activity of the Brazilian weapons industry. It is thus seen as an economically beneficial activity which helps to pay the huge foreign debt of the country and creates jobs. Of course Brazilian weapons are not the most sophisticated or modern, but they have proved useful in the limited wars of recent years. The weapons industry thus has strong support: it employs many people, makes money for the country and makes the country stronger and more independent. Since most of the rich countries manufacture and sell weapons, why should Brazil not do the same?

The success of the weapons industry is seen as proof that it is possible rapidly to develop new and highly technological manufactures in Brazil, if there is a definite desire to do so, in spite of foreign technological advance. It is hoped that the example will be followed in other branches, such as computer manufacture. It is clear, however, that private Brazilian enterprise is not capable of developing such a project alone: government support is essential, for planning, co-ordination, tax exemption, tariff increases on foreign competitors and, as a large customer, to guarantee a minimum market for the produce.

It is not easy to argue, in present-day Brazil, that the weapons industry is bad for society. Even in times of peace and with a democratic regime, there is much worry about personal security against assault and robbery. Hence many people buy small arms or even employ armed guards for protection. Violence is particularly prevalent in the great cities, where social inequalities are blatant.

THE NUCLEAR PROGRAMME

After the Second World War the first nuclear accelerators were installed in Brazil, in São Paulo: a Betatron (1948) and a Van de Graaff (1953). Extraction of ores of rare earth and radioactive elements and their export at extremely low prices led to the establishment of controlling regulations. The National Research Council, established in 1951, assumed responsibility for nuclear matters. In 1957 a swimming pool reactor was bought from the United States and a small Nuclear Energy Institute was established in São Paulo. Another institute, in Minas Gerais, tried to design reactors based on thorium. After the military coup in 1964 no great progress was made; the attempt to build reactors in Brazil was abandoned, and a power reactor was purchased from Westinghouse, to be installed on the beach of Angra dos Reis, between Rio and São Paulo. In 1975 the government announced a large programme in collaboration with West Germany whereby nine power reactors would be installed by 1990. The reactors would be partially built in Brazil. This programme has been much criticised by scientific societies. One reactor is being installed next to the Westinghouse one. But the economic recession has prevented the fulfilment of the programme. Only two of the planned nine reactors will be built and, furthermore, much later than originally planned. The programme has also been much criticised in the media because it is very expensive, increases the foreign debt and does not rely much on Brazilian expertise. Moreover the reactors are located near a large city (Rio de Janeiro), endangering a beautiful beach; and the proposed enrichment method ('jet nozzle') is not technologically proven. Suspicions that this programme has military purposes seem to be unfounded. There has existed for some years, however, a so-called parallel nuclear programme which is largely confidential and unknown. The Navy plans to build a nuclear-powered submarine and to develop a reactor for this purpose. The government denies the intention to build bombs. In August 1986 a newspaper denounced the existence of deep wells dug in an area reserved for military proving-grounds, which might be intended for tests of nuclear weapons, but again this was denied.

NUCLEAR DISARMAMENT IN LATIN AMERICA

Brazil, like India and Argentina, refused to sign the Non-proliferation Treaty of 1968 because it does not limit the nuclear-weapon powers themselves but only seeks to control non-nuclear-weapon countries. Brazil did sign the Treaty of Tlatelolco in 1962, which declares Latin America a non-nuclear region, that is, forbids any nuclear weapons to be located there. It has been signed also by the nuclear-weapon powers even though they are not Latin Americans. However, the Tlatelolco Treaty will only really come into effect when all Latin

American countries have signed, and Cuba refuses to sign because it brands the Treaty as a piece of US imperialism. All other Latin American countries have signed.

There is an old rivalry between the two principal South American countries, Argentina and Brazil. Argentina's efforts to develop nuclear energy independently date from the early 1950s, and the country is considered to be more advanced in nuclear technology than Brazil. The danger of a little local arms race between the two countries is real. The Physical Societies of Brazil and Argentina (the Sociedade Brasileira de Fisica and the Associacion Fisica Argentina) have, during the last few years, made great efforts to prevent such a race and to bring about an agreement and collaboration between the two countries in nuclear matters. Such an agreement was recently reached between the two (now civilian) Presidents Raúl Alfonsin and José Sarney, and there are hopes of establishing a collaboration programme for development of nuclear technology. It is felt that such a programme is perhaps more important than inspection procedures to ensure the maintenance of the agreement.

The Brazilian government has always declared in favour of peace and disarmament in its foreign policy, and the present writer believes this corresponds to popular feelings. However, very little real diplomatic pressure has been put on the superpowers to take effective steps towards disarmament: Brazil does not seem to be different from other non-nuclear-weapon countries in this respect.

16 China's Defence Policy
Shu Yuan H. Chang

INTRODUCTION

China is gradually adjusting its status from isolationist to internationalist. When Chinese policy-makers ponder their defence strategy, they look around first at their suspicious neighbours on the other side of very long borders. In the far west lies Afghanistan, struggling with Soviet occupation. To the south is Vietnam, supported by the Soviet Union and currently competing with China for influence in Southeast Asia. The rest of the border, over 4360 miles, is shared with the Soviet Union which has one million or more troops on the line.[1]

Although China is opening its door and improving political and economic relations with the West, it can feel the nuclear tension involving two superpowers and even Great Britain and France. Both Chinese political and military leaders realise the need to upgrade outdated military hardware and armed forces to encounter possible foreign invasion with modern weapons.[2] Mao Zedong's doctrine of 'people's war' is no longer adequate today to defend one billion people. China exploded its first atomic bomb in 1964 and its first hydrogen bomb in 1967. By 1980 China was holding a nuclear test estimated at between 200 and 1000 kilotons. According to the *SIPRI Yearbook 1986*, Chinese nuclear forces comprise between 300 and 400 warheads, 120 to 150 bombers, 165 to 225 land-based missiles, and 26 to 38 submarine-based missiles. Chinese scientists who are familiar with their nuclear technology have denied these numbers, which, if correct, would put China in a similar position to Great Britain. 'If we had so much', they confide, 'we would not have to worry so much.'

China's second Artillery Corps, however, has developed a good command of strategic guided missiles, including intercontinental ballistic missiles and long-range missiles. The size of the missiles will be reduced in the near future while their mobility will be increased. As part of the country's national defence modernisation effort, China will strive to reduce the technological gap between itself and the rest of the world in this field.[3] Recently the Chinese National Defence

Science, Technology and Industry Commission has also improved its capability for launching communications satellites into space. Some research institutes and companies in Western Europe, the United States and Asia have been negotiating with China to launch satellites. Undoubtedly this will help boost China's nuclear capability.[4]

As for the People's Liberation Army (PLA) there are four million servicemen, supported, when necessary, by a lightly armed Basic People's Militia of another four million men and women, and an unarmed Ordinary People's Militia of about six million.[5]

CHINA'S POSITION ON NUCLEAR WEAPONS

With 41 other nations in 1982, China made its official no-first-use declaration in the General Debate of the Second United Nations Special Session on Disarmament. The text read:

> An agreement should be reached by all the nuclear States not to use nuclear weapons. Pending such an agreement, each nuclear State should, without attaching any condition, undertake not to use nuclear weapons against non-nuclear States and nuclear-weapon-free zones, and not to be the first to use such weapons against each other at any time and under any circumstances...[6]

Since then, high-ranking Chinese officials have repeatedly stressed at various international meetings that China opposes the arms race and will never participate in such a race. It will not use nuclear weapons as its small quantity of nuclear warheads is for self-defence only. China, like those who signed the Limited Test Ban Treaty in 1963, will no longer conduct atmospheric nuclear tests. The Chinese decision-makers have further pledged to cut down military forces and curtail defence expenditure.[7] Meanwhile they have urged the two superpowers to reduce nuclear missiles simultaneously and to talk seriously about nuclear disarmament. The Strategic Defense Initiative programme has been denounced. China would even consider constraining its own nuclear arms development if the two superpowers cut back their nuclear arsenals by half.[8]

A speech by Premier Zhao Ziyang at the Chinese People's Rally for World Peace in 1986 typified China's fundamental views and policy on demilitarisation:

The nuclear arms race constitutes a grave threat to world peace and security. The ultimate goal of nuclear disarmament should be the complete prohibition and thorough destruction of nuclear weapons.

The United States and the Soviet Union, with the largest nuclear arsenals, should take the lead in halting the testing, production and deployment of all such weapons, wherever deployed, and destroying them on the spot. This will help create favourable conditions for a widely-representative international conference on nuclear disarmament. All the nuclear-weapon states should then discuss further nuclear disarmament and the destruction of nuclear weapons.

To prevent the outbreak of nuclear war, all nuclear-weapon states should undertake not to be the first to use nuclear weapons in any circumstances, and not to use or threaten to use nuclear weapons against non-nuclear-weapon states or nuclear-weapon-free zones. An international convention should be concluded by all nuclear-weapon states, ensuring the prohibition of the use of these weapons.

There should be simultaneous and balanced reduction, and on-the-spot destruction, of the medium-range nuclear missiles deployed in Europe and Asia by the Soviet Union and the United States.

Along with nuclear arms reduction, there should be drastic reduction of conventional arms. Conventional arms should be used only for defence, and not to threaten the security of other countries.

Outer space should be used exclusively for peaceful purposes, for the benefit of all mankind. No country should develop, test or deploy space weapons in any form. An international agreement on the complete prohibition of space weapons should be concluded as soon as possible.

An international convention on the total banning and destruction of chemical weapons should be reached at an early date. Until then, all countries capable of manufacturing chemical weapons should pledge never to use them and to stop their testing, production, transfer and deployment.

To bring about arms reduction, disarmament agreements must contain necessary and effective measures of verification.

As the question of disarmament concerns the security of all

countries, it should not be monopolized by a few big powers. Any disarmament agreement between them must not jeopardize the interests of other countries. All countries, big or small, militarily strong or weak, should enjoy equal rights to participate in the discussion and settlement of disarmament problems.[9]

CONVENTIONAL DISARMAMENT

Unlike armies in the West, the PLA is more than a group of professional standing soldiers. It is a multi-functional organisation carrying out such various tasks as social construction, economic production and education, and taking part in political affairs. Although the present policies of modernisation clearly divide their functions into four, namely, agriculture, industry, science and technology, and military, the last has to wait until the first three have been fulfilled. Furthermore, officially, the armed forces have to assist economic development before they can have their turn in obtaining badly needed new equipment. The existing defence industry is closely associated with science and technology and the relevant personnel are thus able to contribute to making civilian production better and more profitable. Certainly a disciplined army can provide a good backbone for economic construction and it may thus take a while for the PLA to change its multi-functional role into a purely military one. Until now the Chinese leaders have directed the cadres in service to engage in political and ideological work,[10] law and order duty,[11] and science and research programmes for commercial purposes.[12]

Although China has been slowly reducing its armed forces since 1977, the announcement made in 1985, involving the reorganisation of its military forces by retiring and discharging one million personnel within two years, was the largest systematic and strategic measure it has ever undertaken in this area. Following this announcement, made by Deng Xiaoping on 4 June 1985 at a meeting of the Central Military Commission, senior officers of the army, navy, and air force attending the meeting expressed their support and willingness to set examples themselves, even though half of the cut would affect officers.[13] Two days later, Yang Dezhi, PLA Chief of General Staff, publicly confirmed that the programme was running smoothly and could be completed on schedule.

The streamlining focuses on reducing the number of overlapping organisations in the army and on overstaffing by administrative personnel, according to the published report by the Civil Affairs Military Official.[14] More than half of the PLA's older veterans have retired,[15] while somewhat younger officers have been relocated to posts suitable to their experience and in conformity with their personal wishes to return to their home area, native province, city, or county (except the overpopulated cities such as Shanghai, Beijing, and Tianjing). Those who were formerly involved in frontier defence and wars or who had performed meritorious service are given preferential treatment in job placement. Many cadres, however, have volunteered to be sent to frontier regions in Xinjiang, Qinhai, Ningxia, Yunnan, and so forth.[16] Interviews conducted with several military officers, on the other hand, have revealed a little more of the picture. Decisions on discharge and relocation are made and carried out strictly by the Central Military Commission. 'Not democratic at all', as an air force medical officer confided to the present writer. Whatever or whoever the central office decides to cut or retire, the decision is final. 'No room for discussion or bargaining', commented another officer interviewed. In some areas entire units, including officers and troops, have been either merged or abolished totally. They can neither appeal nor expect explanation. Everyone is simply discharged. As a rule, the demobilised personnel are assigned by local civilian government to be utilised as they are needed. It is local government's responsibility to see to it that they have suitable jobs. Some of the cadres with previous administrative experience take over administrative positions in local government, schools or production plants.

Whether retired, disabled, discharged, or relocated, the person concerned is no longer in the armed forces and his/her retirement pension, discharge benefit, or future retirement has become the responsibility of local government, and thus falls on the civilian, not the military budget. The benefits of his/her family also come under this arrangement.

By the end of March 1986 not only had more than half of the veteran cadres retired but also more than 65 per cent of cadres in the combat units had been replaced by those with formal training in military institutes.[17] The average age of officers at army level and above had decreased by between three and five years. The Government has allocated one billion yuan (nearly 310 million US dollars), an average of 310 US dollars per person, for resettling and re-employing the discharged forces.[18] Jobs for their spouses and schooling for children are also taken care of as much as possible by local government. Facilities for vocational training or further education have been provided to prepare the demobilised officers and soldiers to become competent for new jobs in civilian fields. So far the majority of the cadres being discharged are in their forties with previous high school education. They have been replaced by a much younger and even better-educated group who have recently been promoted to leading posts. Since most of the soldiers have had very little formal education before entering on their duties in military service, they will be required to undertake compulsory secondary education during the Seventh Five-Year-Plan (1986–90). The goal is to have them complete the junior high school level by the end of 1987. All officers and troops have been encouraged to acquire not only military and civilian production know-how but also a basic knowledge of science, technology and management. In the past few years, more than a hundred thousand training courses have been offered to instruct soldiers in civilian skills in agriculture, food processing, trade, transport and so forth.[19]

Priority has also been given to training officers and improving armament research, technology and production. The Central Military Commission will be issuing a new directive focusing on the necessity to reform military academies and their strategic contribution to the teaching and training of armed forces, especially high-ranking cadres. The PLA has over 100 military institutes and schools nation-wide from which more than 200 000 cadres graduated between 1980 and 1985. The Central Military Commission has drawn up a plan to upgrade all chief officers in the combat troops to college education level by the end of the year 2000. Those who are promoted in the combat field must have formal education in military academies afterwards. In general, military education has been improved in military schools and academies, particularly by using computer and other electronic and laser technology and simulation techniques.[20]

The Chinese authorities have also come to appreciate that, to prepare a military system to defend China in a possible future war, the PLA must study the policies and strategies of China's national defence as well as those of major military blocs in a global sense. Such modern military education presented in the classrooms and fields can be delivered by both Chinese and foreign experts. Through exchange programmes, new military procedures to establish army units, officers' ranking system, management, science, technology and equipment can be introduced to China. Even the selection and promotion of leaders ought to be improved. To prevent nepotism, the appointments of new officers has to be more democratic and competitive and based on merit, ability and 'political awareness'. All 'back-doors' should be closed to ensure fairness and justice.[21]

MODERNISATION OF DEFENCE INDUSTRY THROUGH ITS ASSISTANCE TO CIVILIAN INDUSTRY

Military industry also has to be streamlined and shifted towards civilian production, as domestic conventional arms requirements have fallen drastically. It was during the Sixth Five-Year-Plan (1981–5) that rules were drawn up for the defence industry to shift from exclusive military production to serving the civilian sector as well.[22] China's better-equipped defence industry began to assist civilian industry in building nuclear power plants, civil airplanes, satellites, and such equipment and parts as civilians had not been able to produce. The scientific and technological achievements of the military have also been used to modernise other fields of the economy. Transportation, medical instruments, machinery for energy generation, food processing and light industry will eventually benefit.

The responsibility and contract systems implemented in the general economic programme have been extended to arms enterprises and they now have more autonomy in management. Military industry, therefore, has gradually become more independent in producing goods and services. In 1985 alone the production of civilian goods totalled 2·51 billion yuan, 36 per cent of the Ministry of Ordnance's total output value.[23] With more flexible management, efficiency has improved and production has been geared to the needs of civilian markets for profit. In the present Seventh Five-Year-Plan period, the arms industry is rapidly organising a network of export-oriented production bases with emphasis on the expansion of machinery and electrical products.[24]

From the interviews the present writer conducted among retired veteran cadres, young officers, government officials, factory managers, and staff and students in higher educational institutes, it would seem that part of the profits an arms plant earns from making civilian production and from exporting military hardware to foreign countries can be retained for research and study in developing modern weapons. Such expenditures, furthermore, are not considered as part of the national defence budget, as the plant, producing consumer goods, is under local government's administration. The more earnings these military enterprises make, the more money is available to improve weapons without being categorised as defence expenditure. Thus the production of weapons would be guaranteed despite increased emphasis on making consumer goods. Several new weapon systems of advanced international quality have been planned and are expected by the Ministry of Ordnance and Provincial Governments to be in existence by 1990.[25]

Such changes in military output, in fact, consolidate and develop national defence and economic modernisation simultaneously. With local authorities and economic departments co-operating closely, the programmes are more decentralised and function as they are required. For example, the Chinese Air Force, jointly with United China Airlines (UCA), is to initiate an airline in 1986. It will add a flavour of competition to the only air service in China up to 1984, the Civil Aviation Administration of China, and several small new airlines. The UCA was established with the assistance of the Air Force in 1984 to ease the air transportation problem during China's tourist boom. With the fleet of military aircraft the UCA has lent a hand in the development of China's civil aviation. Eventually, the new PLA-UCA airline will extend its influence and obtain co-operation from local governments and increase its service with more up-to-date models. Even its fuel supply, pilots, flight crew, ground staff, maintenance and in-flights meals will be provided by the Air Force. In return, the Air Force will collect 75 per cent of the annual profit for its own military advancement. A very good arrangement indeed.[26]

CONCLUSION AND FUTURE PROSPECTS

Official announcements indicate that China opposes every kind of arms race and will not take part in any. It supports a total ban upon and the complete destruction of nuclear arsenals, outer space devices, and chemical and biological weapons and calls for a drastic reduction of conventional armaments. To uphold this position, China does not station soldiers abroad, nor does it build military bases abroad. China has, in the past few years, converted a large number of military industries into military–civil enterprises and has been in the process of reducing its troops by one million during the period 1985–7. It has taken a major practical step to reform defence systems as veteran cadres are being replaced with younger, modern-minded, and better-trained professional officers. And the profits from utilising the arms industry in civilian production are improving firearms manufacture. Meanwhile, military discipline and technical training are being strengthened with further formal education and by exchanges with foreign defence establishments.

Like all other nations, developed or developing, China has to face its national security problems. It wants to ensure the independence and sovereignty of its territory and to perpetuate its socio-political, economic system based on that territory. The security of China's territory still depends largely on the safety of its long border with its neighbours. Historically and politically, the Soviet Union poses an immediate threat. Chinese Vice-Premier Li Peng claimed in 1986 that the development of Sino-Soviet relations in economics, trade, science, technology, culture and education has been fine, but to normalise the relations between the two countries requires the Soviets to remove three obstacles, namely, Soviet support for Vietnamese aggression in Kampuchea, the Soviet invasion of Afghanistan, and Soviet troops along the Sino-Soviet border and in Mongolia.[27] Permanent physical border lines cannot be changed easily. Ideological border lines are even harder to manipulate, although Moscow is far away and the West is an ocean or a continent away. Hence official announcements also admit that China has been upgrading its military forces and armaments for self-defence.

At present, more than ever before, China needs a peaceful international environment, as well as internal stability, to undergo vital modernisation. In these circumstances China could be sincere about cutting its conventional forces and genuine in seeking world nuclear disarmament. Such domestic and foreign policies could inspire non-nuclear states in Western and Eastern Europe, Japan, Australia, New Zealand and the third-world countries (among which China counts itself) to exert their influence in pressing the two superpowers to come to an agreement on reducing nuclear arsenals, especially now that the Americans and the Soviets are considering cutting back their nuclear forces by 50 per cent. Since 1985 China has proposed that all nuclear states should participate in an international convention prohibiting the use of nuclear weapons.[28] It is time to hold such a meeting as a preliminary action leading towards world demilitarisation.

On the other hand, China could be merely propagandising its intent to be a supporter of world peace, arms control and international co-operation and continuing its modernisation of weaponry, conventional as well as nuclear, like many others who are cautious of their neighbours. In such a case, this may not only complicate and endanger the present triangular Sino-Soviet-American relations but also escalate and prolong the current arms race among nations. If so, regional destabilisation will be encouraged and disarmament measures in general will certainly be more difficult to achieve.

Notes

1. As recently as Summer 1986, a military incident occurred on the Sino-Soviet border. See *International Herald Tribune*, 24–5 August 1986.
2. For a detailed discussion see Ellis Joffs, 'Party and Military in China: Professionalism in Command?', *Problems of Communism*, vol. 32 (1983) pp. 48–63.
3. *China Daily*, 28 January 1986.
4. Ibid., 3 and 4 February 1986; and *Renmin Ribao* [*People's Daily*], 3 and 4 February 1986.
5. *Liberation Army News*, 13 June 1985; and *Time*, 29 April 1985.
6. Frank Blackaby, Jozef Goldblat, and Sverre Lodgaard (eds), *No-First-Use* (London, 1984) pp. 133–43.
7. *China Daily*, 2 October 1985. China's announced military expenditure and budget share have fallen annually since 1977. See Ellis Joffe, 'Party and Military in China', p. 51; *Renmin Ribao*, 16 April 1986; Stockholm International Peace Research Institute, *World Armaments and Disarmament: SIPRI Yearbook 1986* (Oxford, 1986) pp. 219 and 231; and US Arms Control and Disarmament Agency, *World Military Expenditures and Arms Transfers, 1971–1980* (Washington, DC, 1983) p. 44.
8. *China Daily*, 2 October 1985, 18 February 1986, and 8 April 1986; Ministry of Foreign Affairs, China, *Foreign Affairs, China*, September 1984; *New York Times*, 22 June 1983; and *Renmin Ribao*, 1 and 23 January, 6 April, and 15 June 1986.
9. *China Daily*, 22 March 1986; and *Peace* (Chinese People's Association for Peace and Disarmament), April 1986, pp. 2–5.
10. Editorial Committee for Party Literature, Central Committee of the Communist Party of China (ed.), *Selected Works of Deng Xiaoping: 1975–1982* (Beijing, 1984) pp. 127–40 and 269–75.
11. Yang Shangkun, 'Military Should Lead Ahead to Correct Party Discipline', in *Central Government Must Be the Model for the Nation* (Beijing, 1986) pp. 71–8.
12. *Xin-Hua Yuebao* [*Xin-Hua Monthly*], July 1985, pp. 6–8.
13. From the interviews the writer held with several air force officers, it appears that the figure can be 60 per cent or more of cadres.
14. *Renmin Ribao*, 27 July 1985.
15. *China Daily*, 2 April 1986.
16. *Renmin Ribao*, 5 January, 4 May, and 16 June 1986.
17. *China Daily*, 2 April 1986.
18. Ibid., 6 July 1985 and 25 January 1986.
19. *Renmin Ribao*, 6 January, 26–7 February, and 19 June 1986.
20. *China Daily*, 2 April 1986.
21. *Guanming Ribao* [*Guanming Daily*], 4 March 1986 and *Renmin Ribao*, 6 January, 26–7 February, and 19 June 1986.

22. *Renmin Ribao*, 23 December 1985.
23. *China Daily*, 23 January 1986.
24. Ibid, 5 March 1986.
25. Ibid., 23 January and 5 March 1986.
26. For a detailed report see ibid., 11 June 1986.
27. Ibid., 4 April 1986.
28. Ibid, 2 October 1985; and *Peace*, April 1986.

17 Understanding China's Nuclear Disarmament Policy

Qian Xuefeng

The present-day world is experiencing an intensive arms race which has escalated from land to sea, from sea to space. Today outer space has become the next stage in the arms race and will be tomorrow's battlefield. Missiles have been improved in range, accuracy, power and secrecy. The arms race has posed a grave threat to world peace and security. Disarmament, nuclear disarmament in particular, has become the strong aspiration of all peoples. Yet the record of the search for nuclear disarmament since the Hiroshima explosion leaves much to be desired.

Though one of the five nuclear powers in the world for over two decades, China has been surprisingly closed to the outside world. It is only since about a decade ago, under the 'open policy' and with the development of an independent foreign policy, that it has been playing an increasingly active role in world affairs, including the search for nuclear disarmament. So China's nuclear disarmament policy is worthy of attention and study.

First, a brief review of the development of China's nuclear force is necessary. China began its nuclear research in the late 1950s with the assistance of the Soviet Union. As is well known, as the Sino-Soviet dispute sharpened, the Soviets withdrew all their technicians in the early 1960s. In October 1964, however, China exploded its first atomic bomb. In its sixth nuclear test, in June 1967, its first hydrogen bomb was tested. In April 1970 it successfully launched a space satellite. In 1980 it tested an intercontinental ballistic missile successfully. Two years later a submarine-launched ballistic missile was launched. One year after that it launched a space satellite into geostationary orbit. The Stockholm International Peace Research Institute (SIPRI) Yearbook for 1986, *World Armaments and Disarmament*, provides the facts and figures about China's nuclear force by the end of 1985 (see Table 17.1).

China in the last two decades has built up by its own efforts a nuclear force of considerable size. In the opinion of SIPRI, 'China is the only developing country that has a full triad of nuclear force that can threaten the two superpowers, and aside from them is the only other country with ICBM.'[1] Yet, compared with the huge and growing nuclear arsenals of the two superpowers, China's capability is very much limited in size and function.

Table 17.1

Type	Weapon System No. deployed	Range	Warheads Warhead × Yield	No. stockpiled
Aircraft				
Tu-4 Bull	10–30	6100 (km)	1–4 × bombs	10–30
Il-28 Beagle	10–20	1850	1 × 6	10–20
Tu-16 Badger	100	5900	1–3 × 6s	100
Land-based missiles				
CSS-1 (DF2)	40–60	1100	1 × 20kt	40–60
CSS-2 (DF3)	85–125	2600	1 × 2–3Mt	85–125
CSS-3 (DF4)	10	7000	1 × 1–3Mt	20
CSS-4 (DF5)	10	12000	1 × 4–5Mt	20
Submarine-based missiles				
CSS-N-3	26	3300	1 × 200kt–1Mt	26–38

Since the founding of the People's Republic of China in 1949, China's nuclear disarmament policy can be said to have had three phases. The first phase was when China and the Soviet Union were close allies. The second phase started in the early 1960s and lasted until the late 1970s. Thereafter came the third phase.

In the first phase China's and the Soviet Union's nuclear disarmament policies were similar. The early 1960s witnessed continuing tension and hostility between the United States and China. Meanwhile, however, the Sino-Soviet dispute had become public and bilateral relations worsened. China's legitimate seat at the United Nations was still unrestored. National liberation movements were in high spirits in many parts of the world. And China stood in the front line in support of their struggles against imperialism and colonialism.

What China confronted was a hostile, turbulent and rather isolated world. 'People's War' was the dominant strategy. As early as 1946, during an interview with an American journalist, Mao said:

> The basic question is the consciousness of the people. The bomb will not annihilate the people. The people will annihilate the bomb ... The issue of a future war will not be decided by guided missiles or atom bombs. The revolutionary people are always able to find ways and means for overcoming every kind of modern weapon.[2]

World war was seen as inevitable; it could be fought and won by the people and would end in the triumph of socialism. So China regarded the possession of nuclear weapons as a breakthrough against the imperialist 'nuclear monopoly' and the 'co-domination' by the United States and the Soviet Union. It saw its first successful nuclear test as a great inspiration for the people's struggles. As two American scholars wrote at this period: 'The Chinese see arms control and disarmament as an attempt to cut off the nuclear club at two members, who would then, presumably, divide and rule the world.'[3]

The official Xinhua News Agency announced on the same day as the first nuclear test that 'China will never at any time and under any circumstances be the first to use nuclear weapons.' And China's Premier sent letters to many heads of governments explaining China's position. 'Chinese Statement on Arms Control', published in *People's Daily* on 22 November 1964, clearly summed up China's basic position on disarmament, especially on nuclear disarmament. First, China stood for complete prohibition and thorough destruction of nuclear weapons. Secondly, China rejected the Limited Test Ban Treaty (and later the Non-proliferation Treaty) since 'any international disarmament agreement which is arrived at without the full participation of the People's Republic of China cannot, of course, have any binding effect on China'. Thirdly, the pledge not to initiate nuclear weapons. Secondly, China rejected the Limited Test Ban prohibition. Finally, China held that all countries must have their say; negotiations on nuclear disarmament should not just be the business of the five nuclear weapon states.

In 1966, China became embroiled in a ten-year domestic turmoil, namely, the 'Cultural Revolution'. It was not until the downfall of the 'Gang of Four' and the Third Plenary Session of the Central Committee of the Chinese Communist Party in 1978 that things changed for the better. China then began a new chapter in its foreign policy, playing a more active role in world affairs, including participation in the search for nuclear disarmament.

In his speech at a rally to mark the UN International Year of Peace on 21 March 1986, Premier Zhao Ziyang summarised China's current basic position on nuclear disarmament. First, the nuclear arms race constituted a grave threat to world peace and security. The ultimate goal should be the complete prohibition and thorough destruction of nuclear weapons. Secondly, the United States and the Soviet Union which possessed the largest nuclear arsenals should take the lead in halting the testing, production and development of all types of nuclear weapons and they should destroy on the spot anywhere inside or outside their countries all such weapons they had deployed. This would make it possible to create favourable conditions for the convocation of a broadly representative international conference on nuclear disarmament. Thirdly, in order to prevent the outbreak of nuclear war, all nuclear states should undertake not to be the first to use nuclear weapons in any circumstances and not to use or threaten to use nuclear weapons against non-nuclear weapons states or nuclear-free zones. Finally, it was held that conventional disarmament should go together with nuclear disarmament to make the world safer.[4]

The present writer considers that China's current nuclear disarmament policy, which has more continuity with than difference from the past, bears the following characteristics. First, China places primary responsibility for nuclear disarmament on the two superpowers, which possess 95 per cent of the world's nuclear weapons. Genuine disarmament can only be realised by the superpowers taking the lead. In view of the magnitude of their nuclear arsenals, the superpowers should put an immediate end to the qualitative improvement and quantitative increase of their nuclear weapons and their deployment in various regions. China is against proposals aiming at weakening others and attempting to maintain superiority. Such proposals are of no value for preventing and eliminating the threat of nuclear war.

Secondly, China, as a nuclear weapon state, will not shirk its own responsibility. China has, since its first nuclear test in 1964, insisted that it will not be the first to use nuclear weapons at any time and under any circumstances, nor will it use or threaten to use nuclear weapons against non-nuclear-weapon states or nuclear-free zones. If all the nuclear-weapon states, the superpowers in particular, were to reach such an agreement on no-first-use, then it would be counted as a remarkable step towards prevention of a nuclear war at the present time. It should be noted that, so far, China is the only one among the five nuclear-weapon states that stands for a no-first-use pledge without any preconditions.

Thirdly, China has repeatedly pointed out the importance of the disarmament of conventional weapons. Conventional weapons have been used time and time again for acts of aggression. Further, the outbreak of a conventional war in areas with a high concentration of nuclear and conventional weapons involves the danger of escalation into a nuclear war. Therefore, 'only a combination of measures for both nuclear and conventional disarmament can help reduce the danger of war'.[5] This is the point China has stressed more emphatically than any other nuclear weapon state.

Fourthly, learning from historical lessons, China emphasises the equality of all states, no matter whether nuclear or non-nuclear, big or small. They should have their say in the matter of seeking nuclear disarmament which should not be monopolised or dominated by a few countries. After substantial reduction of nuclear weapons by the superpowers, a broadly representative international conference should be convened with the participation of various states, including all nuclear-weapon states.

Such a policy for nuclear disarmament is closely related to China's changing perception of the world and its relationship with the rest of the world. Its approach to nuclear disarmament is part of its independent foreign policy.

The superpowers' rivalry is the major source of turmoil and insecurity in the world, but today it is not simply a bipolar world. The rapid growth of third-world power is one of the greatest events since the Second World War. Many third-world countries have been making unremitting efforts to take control of their own destiny and have become an important force in the world arena. China is the largest third-world country. The world is facing two problems: peace and development. In peace lies the fundamental interest of the Chinese people, who need a peaceful environment for economic modernisation, not only in this century but also in the next. Thus opposing hegemonism, no matter whether global or regional, and preserving world peace are the fundamental goals of China's independent foreign policy. World war is not inevitable; it can be prevented or much delayed. It should not be fought, or it will be a disaster to mankind.

Recent developments in their relationships with other leading states have convinced the Chinese that an independent foreign policy, that is, one of not aligning itself with any other countries or blocs of countries and one of judging issues on their merits, is desirable and beneficial.

China is now embarking on the path of modernisation, including military modernisation for self-defence. Nuclear weapons are of significance to such defence. Yet at the present time and in the foreseeable future China is unlikely to make enormous investment in weaponry, including nuclear arsenals. In fact, it has decided to limit the size of its army; and the percentage of its Gross National Product devoted to military expenditure has been decreasing in recent years. It is in this broad domestic and international framework that China forges its nuclear disarmament policy. Apart from the domestic aspect, China's approach is closely linked with its foreign policy. The historical development of its nuclear disarmament policy reflects the changes and adjustments in the formation and execution of its foreign policy.

China has arrived, though belatedly, in the international arena so far as nuclear disarmament is concerned. It is predicted that 'as its own nuclear arsenal continues to grow and its social environment continues to change China may well have to assume greater responsibility for promoting and maintaining international order'.[6] This is also true in the nuclear disarmament arena.

Notes

1. Stockholm International Peace Research Institute, *World Armaments and Disarmament: SIPRI Yearbook, 1986* (London, 1986), p. 97.
2. *People's Daily*, 6–7 October 1960.
3. Morton H. Halperin and Dwight H. Perkins, *Communist China and Arms Control* (New York, 1965) p. 132.
4. *People's Daily*, 23 March 1986.
5. Ibid.
6. Curt Gasteyger, *Searching for World Security* (New York, 1985) p. 145.

18 The Debate on Alternative Defence Policies in Italy

Paolo Farinella and Maria Clelia Spreafico

INTRODUCTION

From the points of view of foreign policy attitudes and of their military implications, Italy is a peculiar country. After the Fascist period, when strong nationalistic feelings supported an aggressive, expansionistic policy (the Italian 'empire'), in the postwar decades Italian public opinion has been probably one of the least susceptible in Western Europe to nationalistic or militaristic campaigns. In spite of the presence in Italy of a strong Communist Party, which only in the 1960s became openly critical of the Soviet Union, we have the 'paradox' that in the last forty years all the Italian governments have always professed in the fields of foreign and defence policy an almost complete allegiance to the United States and to NATO (certainly more than other countries such as France or Great Britain have done). Finally, being at the same time a corner-stone of NATO's southern flank and a country deeply involved in many complex problems of the Mediterranean region, Italy is in an undoubtedly intricate geopolitical situation, open to a variety of defence and security options. But the debate on these options has been qualitatively and quantitatively limited and has never attracted long-standing attention from public opinion or the main political forces. This situation has begun to change only in very recent times, and in what follows we intend to discuss some examples of and reasons behind this new trend, as well as outlining the main problems which have been addressed.

The Italian case must be seen in the context of the renewed European interest in problems of security and alternative forms of defence. This interest, which dates back to the 1970s, is the outcome of several factors. Firstly, the activity of a strong albeit somewhat intermittent, European-wide Peace Movement has provoked a much more widespread involvement of public opinion in security issues, in particular when problems have arisen concerning the deployment and possible use of nuclear weapons. Significant differences have gradually emerged in the perceptions on the two sides of the Atlantic regarding the possibility of fighting a limited nuclear war. Europeans have learned to see as a real threat to their security not only Soviet military power, but also a possible nuclear conflict between the two blocs limited to European territory, which might arise either from a deliberate decision or, more probably, from a technical error or from crisis instability. This fear is in part motivated by military doctrines and scenarios currently envisaged in the United States, where war-fighting doctrines are often coupled with neo-isolationist stands. Thus, while the periods of outstanding growth in the European Peace Movement occurred after the NATO decision to deploy Euromissiles in 1979 and the failure of the first Geneva negotiations in 1983, a widespread perception has remained up to now in public opinion that the traditional Western defence posture, based on nuclear deterrence down to the battlefield level, is no longer a firm guarantee for security. The recognition of this fact lies behind many explorations and analyses of alternative defence concepts viable for European countries.[1]

Such concepts can be grouped into three basic types. First, we have the non-military and non-violent option. This is the most radical and unconventional alternative to traditional defence postures both in the conventional and in the nuclear version, and envisages the organised resistance of the civilian population as a mean to deter and defeat any external attack.[2] Secondly, there are concepts of military, but non-nuclear, structurally non-offensive and/or territorial-type defence. These are related to the doctrines adopted by several non-aligned or neutral European countries, and aim at effectively deterring and countering an external invasion by placing reliance on a completely non-provocative military posture.[3] Finally, there are 'conventional' military alternatives, which stress the role of conventional military forces without completely abandoning nuclear deterrence (often in the version of 'minimal' nuclear deterrence). These are frequently presented as improvements or integrations of the present NATO strategy rather than in the form of real, self-consistent alternatives.[4]

Coming to the Italian debate, we have already pointed out that it has started quite recently. As a consequence, exploration of these issues has been incomplete and fragmentary, both within the different governmental agencies and institutions and within the Peace Movement. The reasons for this delay in comparison with other European countries are connected with a traditional lack of interest in Italy in the problems and tasks of state institutions, in particular those related to defence, a phenomenon having deep and complex cultural and historical roots. Since the Second World War and the introduction of nuclear arsenals, Italy has been more engaged in establishing a system of complex and delicate political equilibria, and at the same time in promoting a rapid economic growth, than in developing an original and autonomous international stand and a corresponding defence policy – analogous to some extent with the experience of certain other countries, such as the Federal Republic of Germany and Japan. After the choice to join NATO in 1949 (strongly opposed by left-wing parties), the security of the country has been in a sense 'delegated' to supranational institutions in the framework of the Atlantic Alliance. This has been seen as providing a reliable and durable security guarantee, obtained in exchange for the commitment to Western allegiance. At the same time, the few important choices made by the Government on security issues – in particular those leading to deployments of nuclear weapons in the country – have been made with strong concerns for their short-term domestic policy implications.

Another relevant factor is that in Italy there is a long-standing tradition of separation between army and society, between the civilian and military institutions. In particular, and contrasting with what happens on other issues, the power of Parliament to control and direct defence policy is limited. This power is in fact largely concentrated in the hands of the military chiefs, but is often exercised in a sectorial and short-sighted way. The Minister of Defence cannot resort, as in other countries, to autonomous advisory bodies in order to evaluate critically the choices of the military while paying specific attention to the political aspects of the problems. Likewise, many Members of Parliament and policy-makers tend to consider defence issues as 'technical' and to disregard their political implications – even if, frequently, the critical information is not available to them because of the widespread use of military secret and classification procedures. For this reason little is known publicly about the studies carried out in the institutes or research centres of the Ministry of Defence. The Army, the Navy and the Air Force publish three different magazines in which, usually, only the official positions are expressed, and there is no professional-level official publication dealing with general defence problems.[5]

Outside the military establishment, very few research centres are active. Italy is probably one of the few Western European countries having no publicly-funded peace research institute. And research activity is scarce also in the framework of the universities and of the National Research Council (CNR), apart from some (significant) contributions by individual experts in military history, international law or sociology. Indeed, most Italian intellectuals do not seem to believe that the problems of peace, war and defence are worth serious study at a scientific and professional level.

The exceptions to this rule are still very few. We can quote some institutes with diverse political attitudes, such as the Istituto Affari Internazionali, the Istituto Studi e Ricerche sulla Difesa (ISTRID), the Archivio Disarmo, the Centro Studi di Politica Internazionale and the Istituto di Ricerche per il Disarmo, lo Sviluppo e la Pace (IRDISP). Several people have been active within the Italian Pugwash group, the Union of Scientists for Disarmament and the Forum on the Problems of Peace and War. The latter organisation, based in Florence, has recently put together an *ad hoc* study group on alternative security concepts for Italy.

In what follows it is intended briefly to review the recent Italian debate on the different types of defence alternatives, with the purpose of further stimulating this debate and, at the same time, of indicating the actual and possible links with the research and study activities in progress in other countries.

'CONVENTIONAL' MILITARY ALTERNATIVES

In the last few years a significant shift has been taking place in Italian military policy. From the budgetary point of view, defence expenditure has been increasing at a rate higher than for most other Western European countries (from 2.4 per cent to 2.7 per cent of the GNP between 1981 and 1985).[6] Several new, high-technology and very expensive weapon systems are under development: the 'sea control ship' *Garibaldi,* a helicopter carrier equipped with a 'ski-jump' system for vertical/short take-off and landing aircraft (probably Harrier fighters); the new European Fighter Aircraft; the new electronic surveillance, intelligence and communications system CATRIN, designed for battlefield applications; and the anti-submarine warfare-capable helicopter EH-101. Moreover, as regards the role of Italy in NATO, the traditional land defence role on the North-East border is becoming of minor significance when compared with a new role as a support base for naval warfighting and power projection in the Mediterranean area.[7] Naples, the seat of the headquarters of the US Sixth Fleet (whose ships are anchored at Gaeta), is in fact the most important base for the US naval forces in the Mediterranean, and is the location of both the NATO (CINCSOUTH) and American CINCUSNAVEUR) regional commanders. Apparently important military forces in Italy are being reconfigured for the new role, as shown by the presence in the country of bases serving important anti-submarine warfare functions, of nuclear strike aircraft on quick reaction alert status, of nuclear-armed ground-launched cruise missiles based in Sicily and of important surveillance, command, control and communications systems. All these assets confirm the impression that the new role of Italy is the consequence of changing US and NATO perspectives and war plans, putting a greater emphasis on the Mediterranean area and on the long-range, multi-purpose weapons suitable for a variety of conflict scenarios.

At present the Italian military staff appears to be divided or uncertain in the face of these new developments. In a lecture given at ISTRID in September 1986 the Chief of the Defence General Staff, General Bisogniero, stated:

> The cornerstone of the world power balance is still in the East–West relationship, and the logic of blocs is not obsolete, nor will it become obsolete soon ... The increased danger in the Mediterranean depends on the increased influence of the Soviet Union in several countries, which gives rise to a significant threat ... In the face of conflicts in the Mediterranean area, NATO must prepare itself properly and reshape its operational plans and assets.

But only a few weeks later, again at an ISTRID seminar, General Poli, Chief of Staff of the Army, offered this alternative view:

> The fact that the two superpowers counterbalance each other has opened the way to new forms of conflicts, which are often the product of specific local situations ... The ability of the great powers to manage these crises has strongly decreased, and this presents serious security problems for 'intermediate' powers ...

These situations are beyond the province of the Atlantic Alliance ... they need a better co-operation among the rapid deployment forces of the major European countries including Italy.

According to Poli, these premises imply that, for Italy, although a strong priority still lies in the traditional NATO commitment to defend the North-East frontier, the whole national territory has become vulnerable to threats that are different from the traditional ones. As a consequence, and given an almost constant amount of financial resources, the Army must be reorganised in such a way as to give priority to flexibility, speed and mobility. Hence, according to Poli:

> In the coming years we must shift the balance from heavy armoured vehicles to light infantry, equipped with high-technology weapons ... Tanks are losing importance because they have become more vulnerable to new weapon systems and cannot be moved quickly and in large numbers in a territory which is both geographically difficult and densely urbanized.[8]

It is worth noticing that some of these remarks resemble considerations put forward in the framework of alternative defence models devised for central Europe, even if in the Mediterranean context they may have different implications.

Apart from this debate, which is apparently in progress among the military staff, there have been recently a few proposals which, without changing the overall military force structure and the defence policy of the country, could lead to increased crisis stability and to a more clearly defensive force posture. Here we shall briefly summarise them.

The first obvious possibility concerns the reduction and eventual elimination of battlefield nuclear weapons. Excluding Comiso's Cruise missiles, there are about 540 nuclear warheads stationed in Italy, including about 250 aircraft bombs, 50 Lance missile warheads, 70 Nike Hercules missile warheads, 55 nuclear artillery shells, 65 nuclear depth bombs, and 50 warheads for antisubmarine missiles.[9] These weapons are assigned either to US forces in Italy or to Italian forces, but it is unclear whether the ultimate control over their use is entirely in the hands of the Italian government, or whether there are some possible circumstances in which this control might be taken by American authorities or even by military commanders in the field.[10] The military role of these weapons is questioned by many people.

They are held to be anachronistic and suicidal, if they are intended to defend against an overwhelming Warsaw Pact attack in Northern Italy, an unlikely scenario according to most observers. And if they are intended for use in the Mediterranean area, this can be said to be going beyond the limits of NATO obligations. Their reduction and final elimination has been widely advocated in recent times both by some independent analysts[11] and by the Italian Communist Party.[12] A recent poll has shown that, in Italy, the idea of a purely conventional defence, to be implemented together with the other West European countries, is preferred to nuclear options by more than 70 per cent of the citizens, a much larger percentage than in France, Great Britain and West Germany.[13]

A first and more limited step towards the previous goal could be the establishment of a Nuclear-weapon-free Zone (NWFZ) in North-East Italy, with similar commitments for the neighbouring regions of Austria, Yugoslavia and Hungary. A first version of this proposal was referred to the so-called Adria Alp Community, a community of neighbouring regions of Italy, Austria, Yugoslavia and West Germany, which was started in 1978 to foster cultural and economical co-operation.[14] More recently, a revised proposal (including parts of Hungary and excluding Bavaria) has been debated and agreed upon by several peace movement groups in Austria, Yugoslavia and Italy. A draft treaty has been produced.[15] This includes *inter alia* a commitment to eliminate from the NWFZ any foreign military base, and not to carry out military manoeuvres of major proportions in it. An international seminar on this proposal was held in Trieste in September 1986, with the participation of a United Nations observer. Apart from the usual arguments which support the creation of NWFZs, this proposal has two significant merits: first, it fills the gap between the proposed NWFZs in Northern Europe, in the Balkan area, and along the Central Front (in the Palme Commission explicitly recommended a NWFZ starting with Central Europe and extending ultimately from the northern to the southern flanks of the two alliances). This would imply the creation of a wide 'buffer zone' between the two blocs in the whole of Europe. Secondly, it could be an important confidence-building step, possibly fostering reductions in and restructuring of conventional forces in this area as well as improved co-operation and exchanges among four countries which have very different international standpoints but no real open conflicts among themselves. It is clear that the significance of this NWFZ proposal is more political than military: in this region there is a long-standing common 'Mitteleuropean' historical and cultural background; the possible causes of crisis instability are less serious than along the Central Front; and geography undoubtedly is more favourable to the defenders. In Italy, the obstacles appear to come from the military, who are still unwilling to introduce substantial changes in the traditional defence concept based on frontier-based defence, including as a possible option the first use of nuclear weapons. In the regions of Italy included in the proposed NWFZ (the Triveneto regions), many important US and NATO bases are present, including nuclear depots (for example, at Longare and Aviano) and warhead support groups for nuclear artillery, Nike Hercules and Lance missiles.

As in the case of Central Europe, both the Italian media and most civilian and military authorities are accustomed to the idea that there would be a dramatic Italian force inferiority in the event of a Warsaw Pact conventional attack. This is the main rationale for keeping a vast stockpile of battlefield nuclear weapons and for refusing to adopt a no-first-use doctrine. However, this idea is probably incorrect, as recently concluded by Marco De Andreis of IRDISP on the basis of a detailed analysis of the military balance on the Italian north-eastern front. Here we shall summarise and elaborate somewhat on this analysis.

The assumed attack on Italy would come from Hungary. The six Hungarian tank and motor rifle divisions are classified in terms of their readiness level in Categories 2 and 3 (needing 30–45 and 60–90 days for mobilisation, respectively), and therefore could hardly be used for a blitzkrieg attack. These divisions have some 1200 tanks, almost all of which date back to the 1950s. Four Category 1 Soviet divisions are deployed in Hungary (two tank and two motor rifle divisions); according to the NWFZ proposal discussed earlier, these divisions would be withdrawn or displaced to the North-East part of the country. It is possible that, in case of conflict, additional forces from the Soviet military district of Kiev would be added. This is not a likely possibility, however, because these forces (as well as those deployed in Hungary) would be more probably employed along the strategically far more important Central Front. On the Italian side, besides the five Alpine brigades, nine tank and armoured brigades are deployed, with a total of about 130 000 troops (some two-thirds of the field forces of the Italian Army) and about 1200 tanks. Significant artillery, anti-tank and tactical aircraft forces are also available. A comparison between the ground forces on the two sides can be made by scaling down the available estimates for the balance in the Central Front, using the Armoured Division Equivalent (ADE) as basic unit.[16] The Hungarian and Soviet forces deployed in Hungary are worth about four ADEs, while the Italian are also probably equivalent to about three ADEs. This means that both alliances deploy on this front about one-tenth of their total ground forces, and that (as along the Central Front) the force ratio is far from the 3:1 to 5:1 superiority levels that are thought to be needed for a successful surprise attack.

This conclusion is strengthened when geographical and geopolitical factors are taken into account. To reach the Italian border, the Warsaw Pact forces would cross Austria and/or Yugoslavia, where they would probably meet strong and enduring resistance. After crossing the wide Sava and Drava rivers, in order to avoid very narrow Alpine valleys and passes, the Warsaw Pact forces would concentrate towards the 'Gorizia Gap', the only viable access corridor to the Po Valley. This Gap is about 50 km wide, about the same as the four potential breakthrough corridors identified in West Germany. Many military analysts estimate that 0.5–1 ADE/25 km (or 1 brigade per 7–15 km) is an adequate force-to-space ratio for the defenders to hold the front.[17] And even if two-thirds of the forces were put in the line on the corridor with one-third kept in operational reserve), the Italian forces would appear to be sufficient to hold this front. On the other hand, it is not possible to concentrate at will the offensive forces, and it does not seem likely that the Warsaw Pact could place more than three to four ADEs in engaged combat power on 50 km of front, even were these forces available. The resulting force ratio is again of the order of 1·5:1, insufficient for a successful breakthrough. Finally, the corridor to the Po Valley is about 150 km long, and even with an advance rate of 2–5 km/day for the Warsaw Pact forces (high by historical standards), at least several weeks would be needed to complete the offensive. Of course, in case of a prolonged conflict, the evolution of the force ratio would depend on the availability, the readiness and the performances of the reserves, and it is difficult to make this kind of prediction. However, the available data on the conventional balance fail to confirm the official view that nuclear battlefield weapons are an essential ingredient for defending Italy against an overwhelming conventional Warsaw Pact attack. The withdrawal of these weapons from the north-eastern front, possibly in the framework of a NWFZ agreement, should therefore be seen as a reasonable option, which would not impair the security of the country.

The case for restructuring the ground conventional forces in Italy in a non-provocative and purely defensive mode is less compelling than it is in Central Europe, for several reasons. As already noted, crisis instability and pre-emptive attacks are unlikely in this zone. However, especially in case of a NWFZ agreement, a number of steps could be taken which could improve the situation. For instance, tank and armoured forces could be redeployed further to the rear, as well as long-range aircraft ammunition depots and equipment needed to cross large rivers. Furthermore, some agreement could be easily envisaged with Austria and Yugoslavia to ensure their active co-operation with the defensive side in case of open aggression. In Italy the role of territorial forces like the Alpine brigades could be emphasised at the expense of more mobile and armoured forces in a wide belt including the Alps and the part of the Gorizia Corridor just across the border. Here a network of small light infantry units equipped with high-technology anti-tank and anti-aircraft weapons might play the same attrition role as in many non-provocative defence models proposed for West Germany. The interplay of these steps with a NWFZ agreement has the potential for the full implementation of a common security policy in this part of Europe.

Finally, a potentially important issue relates to the Mediterranean role of Italy and the possible alternatives in this context. We need to assess, in particular, whether the concept of non-offensive defence could be applied to the Mediterranean region and in general to maritime defence. This is a complex issue. On the one hand, technological developments, in particular in the field of precision-guided missiles, are making large surface warships increasingly vulnerable, and this can increase the pressure for pre-emptive attacks. On the other hand, along the coasts it is increasingly possible to create defences based on small and short-range ships and on land-based precision weapons that have no offensive capability outside the coastal area – a solution which has recently been proposed for the Baltic region.[18] For the Mediterranean, the situation is very complex because there is no bloc versus bloc confrontation as in Central Europe, and political factors appear much more important then purely military ones. At the same time, the large, nuclear-capable fleets of the two superpowers are, at least potentially, offensively oriented.[19] Clearly a non-offensive military posture by some or even all the Mediterranean countries cannot solve the main political problems, but it could decrease crisis instability (especially the danger of a local crisis escalating to a global conflict) and weaken the present mutual tensions and fears.[20] Italy could play a significant role in this sense, if an active *détente*-oriented foreign policy were coupled with a more clearly defensive posture (which incidentally would be more consistent with Article 11 of the Italian Constitution). Many recent military choices (for example, the *Garibaldi* warship and the Italian Rapid Deployment Force) appear, however, to conform to an opposite trend. Nevertheless, these issues have, in the last few years, been receiving increasing attention.

TERRITORIAL DEFENCE

As far as the North-Eastern Front is concerned, the debate which is presently in progress can be seen as the follow-up to the lively debate on territorial defence which occurred in Italy during the late 1970s, mainly within the military and among the experts on military history (with most papers published in the journal *Rivista Militare*). Apart from a few exceptions, however, the involvement of policy-makers and governmental agencies remained scarce. Moreover, the debate often addressed only very general issues (characteristics, advantages and drawbacks of in-depth defence, compatibility with staying in NATO, and so on), and seldom dealt with an evaluation of the historical, political and military factors relevant for applicability to Italy. Also the significance in this context of new and sophisticated technologies such as precision-guided munitions was rarely appreciated.

The motivations for this debate, started in about 1976, were diverse, ranging from the contemporary restructuring of the Army and of its employment doctrines,[21] to the influence of an active reformist movement among conscripts and junior officers, to the cultural fashion of emphasising the effectiveness of protracted guerrilla warfare. At the political level, most input was provided by the numerous proposals and bills (never approved by Parliament, but widely discussed in the press) presented by Falco Accame, a former Navy officer who also served as an influential Socialist Deputy. Accame's proposals ranged from a sweeping reform of military service to the implementation of forms of civilian-based defence, with a strong emphasis on the dismissal of the traditional frontier-based defence concept (the so-called defence of the 'Gorizia Threshold') and on the adoption of a type of territorial defence closely related to the strategies of European neutral countries and to the Partisan Resistance Movement (which was of course widely active in Northern Italy during the Nazi occupation from 1943 to 1945).[22]

Proposals of a similar kind came about at the same time from some officers of the mountain infantry corps (the 'Alpini'), who have a long-standing tradition of fighting based on troop dispersal and on detailed knowledge of the local terrain.[23] In this debate there were frequent comparisons with and analyses of the defence policies and strategies adopted by countries such as Yugoslavia, Austria, Switzerland, Sweden, France and West Germany, which rely to various degrees on forms of in-depth territorial defence.[24] But the value of these comparisons was recognised as limited, since the situation of Italy is different both from that of neutral and non-aligned countries (in foreign policy, in the socioeconomic conditions and in the degree of urbanisation) and from that of Central Europe (because of involvement in the Mediterranean area and of the importance of naval forces).

An interesting political case, which caused many comments and arguments, occurred in May 1980, when, at an official meeting of his party, the President of the Christian Democrats, Arnaldo Forlani, criticised the prominent role of nuclear weapons in current defence policy and pointed out that Italian armed forces had to be ready to continue resistance and fighting even after a foreign invasion.[25] Most reactions were negative, and the issue was never raised again at an official level. Around the same time, a meeting of experts on territorial defence was organised by ISTRID. As shown by the published proceedings, most of those who attended were sceptical or openly opposed to the adoption by the Italian Army of territorial defence, at least when it was presented as an alternative to frontier-based defence.[26] A short follow-up to this debate by some influential experts resulted, again, in a majority taking a negative line.[27] Possibly as a consequence of this evolution, the *White Book on Defence* republished by the Defence Ministry in 1985 did not include a discussion about defence alternatives[28] (while the 1977 volume had[29]).

The case made against territorial defence was not based mainly on its military limitations, but on the presumed incompatibility with the overall NATO strategy and even with NATO membership. Some people also believed that the issue about territorial defence was not really about the optimal military strategy, but rather a kind of 'Trojan horse' used in order to create a crisis with NATO, to change inter-services relationships (for example, the relative importance of the Army and the Navy), or to modify radically the conscription policy. An important factor in this shifting attitude was probably the campaign carried out by the military in favour of the Euromissile deployment decision and against the rising Peace Movement, a campaign which was seen as inconsistent with a lively 'internal' debate about alternative defence policies. At the same time, the issue was not considered seriously by most left-wing leaders and experts, although there were a very few exceptions, especially in some radical Marxist groups[30] (which were often worrying about a possible *coup d'état* with severe internal repression). The relationship has also often been stressed between territorial defence and a new system of 'regional conscription' (namely that military service would be carried out in the neighbourhood of one's residence for all personnel except some longer-service, highly-trained staff).[31] At present this kind of proposal is being debated in Parliament and, if passed, it will certainly imply a different location of armed forces in the country.

CIVILIAN-BASED DEFENCE

The debate on the potential involvement of the civilian population during a conflict has been developed in Italy from two very different points of view, which bear contrasting political implications but surprisingly enough have sometimes addressed similar problems.

On the one hand, the issue was raised within the military as a response to NATO directives and at about the same time (during the 1970s) that the conventional military doctrines and posture of the country were being questioned.[32] In this context it is important to notice that in Italian the term *difesa civile* has some ambiguity, meaning at the same time 'civil defence' (that is protecting and defending the population from the devastation of war – in particular, nuclear war – which could be in part dealt with in advance by a series of preventive measures[33]) and 'civilian defence', namely the active role of the population in defending the social, economic and political structure of the country from a foreign attack by non-military means.[34] This linguistic ambiguity is reflected in the fact that in Italy during the last decade official military sources have widely discussed the usefulness of a kind of mixture of the two concepts in the framework of an overall national defence strategy. They have stressed the close connection with the military structure and the operations planned during a conflict.[35] The unifying idea was that of ensuring the continuity of social, economic and political life during wartime, with a strong emphasis on measures of centralisation and increased governmental control. Thus, although the new idea that the concept of defence may be applied not only at a military, but also at a social level, was for the first time widely accepted in the military,[36] one gets the impression that the 'civilian' sphere is identified more with the existing public administration and state institutions than with the democratic life of the country and with the active role of the citizens. This might derive in part from the Napoleonic-type, centralised state bureaucracy and organisation which is still characteristic of Italy. But this debate prompted some experts on military doctrines to analyse the relationships between military and non-military forms of defence, frequently referring, for instance, to the work of Adam Roberts. At the same time, the Ministry of Defence circulated official documents on the issue and supported an *ad hoc* study centre. In Parliament an explicit bill for the actual implementation of the *difesa civile,* including elements of civilian-based defence, was also presented in 1979 by Accame.[37]

A completely different attitude has characterised the supporters of civilian-based defence in the non-violent, anti-militaristic and radical groups which have in Italy a long-standing tradition of cultural and political activity.[38] The most important leader of these groups after the Second World War was Aldo Capitini, an original philosopher and pedagogist inspired by the Gandhian experience and influenced by Eastern philosophies as well as by Christian views. Left-wing Catholic groups have also been active in supporting non-violent ethical views. The concept of civilian defence which has been stressed by these groups has strong connections with third-world liberation struggles, with self-management and social struggle experiences carried out by non-violent means, and with the activities of conscientious objectors to military service bearing allegiance to ethical principles.[39] As a consequence, instead of 'civilian defence' these groups prefer to speak about 'non-violent popular defence',[40] while the adversary is more often identified with an inner authoritarian power than with an external invader. (This may explain why Accame's aforementioned proposal was widely criticised.) This choice may also be due to the fact that patriotic or nationalistic feelings are comparatively weak in today's Italy, and other ideals (of social reform, of renewed and improved democracy, and of individual freedom) are much more effective in promoting collective movements and struggles. The activity on civilian-based defence has thus focused mostly on the organisation of study groups, of documentation centres and of training seminars. Several foreign books on civilian defence have been translated into Italian, and also a few historical instances of civilian resistance in Italy during the Second World War have been 'discovered' and investigated. Also noteworthy, in the last few years, is the interest shown in alternative defence proposals (including both territorial and civilian-based defence by the promoters of the campaign for the 'fiscal objection', that is, the refusal to pay taxes for an amount corresponding to military expenditures in the state budget). (Part of these witheld taxes are in fact allocated to support peace research and studies about defence alternatives.) This campaign caused an acute controversy between the Ministry of Defence and some influential Catholic groups and hence helped to popularise new civilian defence and transarmament proposals.[41]

CONCLUSION

In spite of a siginificant delay in comparison with other West European countries, a debate on alternative defence strategies is now in progress in Italy and its developments might be quite important, both because of peculiar historical political factors and because of the key position of the country on the Southern flank of NATO and at the same time also at the centre of the Mediterranean. There is evidence, moreover, that this debate has been recently involving an ever-wider proportion of the main political parties, of the Peace Movement, of the academic community and even of the military. What is not yet clear is whether it will provoke any significant change in the traditional defence policy of the country.[42]

Notes

1. See, for example, P. Cotta-Ramusino and F. Lenci (eds), *Nuclear Weapons and Europe* (*Scientia*, Milan, 1986); G. Bonvincini, 'Piu' opzioni per una sicurezza globale', *Politica Internazionale,* May 1984, pp. 16–24; L. Anderlini, 'I pro e i contro della difesa comune', *Politica Internazionale,* May 1984, pp. 77–82; and C. M. Santoro, 'Europa e Stati Uniti: cooperazione o conflitto?' in C. M. Santoro, *Lo Stile dell' Aquila* (Milan, 1984).
2. Three important books on this defence policy are A. Roberts (ed.), *Civil Resistance as a National Defence Policy* (Harmondsworth, 1969); A. Boserup and A. Mack, *War Without Weapons* (London, 1974); and G. Sharp, *Making Europe Unconquerable* (New York, 1985).
3. See, for example, A. Roberts, *Nations in Arms* (London, 1976); F. Barnaby and E. Boeker, *Defence Without Offence: Non-Nuclear Defence*

for *Europe* (London, 1982); and Alternative Defence Commission, *Defence Without the Bomb* (London, 1983).
4. Two important examples are McGeorge Bundy, G. Kennan, R. S. McNamara and G. Smith, 'Nuclear Weapons and the Atlantic Alliance' *Foreign Affairs*, Spring 1982, pp. 753–67; and *Strengthening Conventional Deterrence in Europe: Report of the European Security Study* (London, 1983).
5. See F. Accame, 'La difesa nazionale: problemi e prospettive' in *La Difesa del Territorio* (Rome, 1980).
6. M. De Andreis, A. Liberati, M. Mare' and P. Miggiano, 'La spesa militare in Italia' in M. De Andreis and P. Miggiano (eds), *L'Italia e la Corsa al Riarmo* (Milan, 1987) pp. 199–244.
7. W. M. Arkin, 'Evolving military and political role of U.S. military forces and nuclear weapons in Italy' in Cotta-Ramusino and Lenci (eds), *Nuclear Weapons and Europe*.
8. M. Sartori 'Forze armate, c'e' contrasto fra i generali', *L'Unita'*, 16 October 1986, p. 6.
9. W. M. Arkin and R. W. Fieldhouse, 'Forze militari americane in Italia' in *Quello che i Russi gia' sanno e gli Italiani non devono sapere* (Rome, 1984).
10. P. Cotta-Ramusino, 'I guardiani dei missili', *Rinascita,* 9 February 1985, pp. 38–9.
11. M. De Andreis, 'The nuclear debate in Italy', *Survival,* vol. 28, no. 3 (1986); P. Cotta-Ramusino 'Tactical nuclear weapons in Europe and control over them', in Cotta-Ramusino and Lenci (eds), *Nuclear Weapons and Europe;* and F. Battistelli, 'E' possibile una difesa non nucleare dell' Europa?', *Testimonianze*, no. 269/270 (1984).
12. Directive of the Italian Communist Party, 'Un disarmo bilanciato e controllato', *L'Unita'*, 16 November 1986.
13. F. Prattico, 'Ivan non fa piu' paura', *La Repubblica,* 16 February 1987.
14. A. Pascolini and C. Villi, 'A challenging proposal: the mittel-european nuclear weapon-free zone', paper presented at the Pugwash Symposium on 'The role of small countries in the security of Europe', Plovdiv, Bulgaria, 30 May–3 June, 1983.
15. Centro Italiano 'Bertrand Russell', *Per un'Europa Libera dalle Armi Nucleari* (Perugia, 1986) pp. 177–88.
16. See B. R. Posen, 'Measuring the European Conventional Balance', *International Security,* vol. 9, no. 3 (1984/85) and references quoted therein.
17. J. J. Mearsheimer, 'Why the Soviets can't win quickly in Central Europe', *International Security,* vol. 7, no. 1 (1982).
18. A. Boserup, A. Karkoszka, A. A. C. von Müller, R. R. Neild and L. Valki, Report on the fifth workshop of the Pugwash study group on conventional forces in Europe, *Pugwash Newsletter,* January 1987, pp. 56–60.
19. G. Nardulli, 'La difesa non provocatoria e il Mediterraneo: La dimensione navale' in *Preprint Forum on the Problems of Peace and War* (Florence, 1987).
20. R. Ragionieri, 'Security and alternative defence policies in the Mediter-

ranean region', paper presented at the Consultation on Non-Nuclear Alternatives in Europe, Bradford, 15–18 July 1986.
21. S. Porcelli, 'Tra difesa ancorata e difesa mobile: un nuovo ruolo per la fanteria nel prossimo futuro', *Rivista Militare*, no. 2 (1975) pp. 54–7; M. Buscemi, 'Difesa ancorata e difesa mobile: un confronto con le dottrine di altri eserciti', ibid., no. 1 (1976) pp. 67–73; L. Salatiello, 'Spunti per una nuova concezione difensiva', ibid., no. 3 (1976) pp. 2–24; and 'Memoria sull'impiego delle Grandi Unita' – Le operazioni difensive', ibid., no. 5 (1977) pp. 2–12.
22. See, for example, F. Accame, 'Il deserto dei tartari alla soglia di Gorizia', *L'Avanti*, 16 May 1979; and F. Accame, 'Difesa nazionale e difesa territoriale', in ISTRID, *La Difesa del Territorio* (Rome, 1980) pp. 83–101.
23. C. Jean, 'Forme particolari di lotta in montagna', *Rivista Militare*, no. 4 (1972) pp. 502–8; L. Manfredi, 'Attualita' e fisionomia futura della brigata alpina', ibid., no. 5 (1977) pp. 24–31; E. Sessich, 'La guerra in montagna, un'ipotesi ancora realistica', ibid., pp. 32–5; and C. Bess, 'Le unita' alpine nella guerra territoriale', ibid., pp. 47–54.
24. L. Lombardi, 'La riorganizzazione dell'esercito francese', ibid., no. 4 (1977) pp. 19–26; F. Stefani, 'Conosciamo la Svizzera', ibid., no. 4 (1978) pp. 46–58; G. Caccamo, 'Guerra territoriale, la dottrina Spannocchi', ibid., no. 1 (1978) pp. 26–31; F. Stefani, 'La Svezia, una neutralita' basata sulla difesa', ibid., no. 1 (1979) pp. 45–56; and G. Buccioli, 'Esercito e paese: interazione per un modello di difesa integrata in Svizzera', ibid., no. 1 (1983) pp. 62–73.
25. A detailed account is given in V. Ilari, 'Difesa civile e guerra territoriale', *'Nord e Sud'*, no. 11 (1980) pp. 172 and 178.
26. ISTRID, *La Difesa del Territorio*.
27. E. Rambaldi, 'Strategia NATO ed esigenze difensive nazionali', *Politica Militare*, no. 6 (1980) pp. 33–8; F. Accame, 'Alcune considerazioni sulla difesa territoriale', ibid., no. 7 (1981) pp. 12–16; V. Ilari, 'Il dibattito sulla difesa territoriale e il suo reale significato', ibid., pp. 17–18; E. Rambaldi, 'Difesa classica o territoriale?', *Rivista Militare*, no. 5 (1980) pp. 2–10; L. Salatiello, 'La difesa avanzata', ibid., pp. 11–25; and C. Bess, 'Considerazioni sulla difesa territoriale', ibid., no. 6 (1980) pp. 2–8.
28. Ministero della Difesa, *La Difesa: Libro Bianco 1985* (Rome, 1985).
29. Ministero della Difesa, *La Difesa: Libro Bianco 1977* (Rome, 1977).
30. See C. De Biasi, 'La difesa popolare rispetto al problema della pace', *Acciaio*, no. 4 (1981) pp. 165–8; and Stella Rossa, *In Caso di Golpe: Manuale Teorico-Pratico per il Cittadino di Resistenza Totale e di Guerra di Popolo, di Guerriglia e di Controguerriglia* (Rome, 1975).
31. E. Milani and P. Barrera, *Modello di Difesa e Strategia di Pace* (Rome, 1983).
32. Ministero della Difesa, *La Difesa: Libro Bianco 1977;* P. Di Marco, 'Il problema della difesa civile', *Rivista Militare*, no. 4 (1978) pp. 59–65; and B. Piazza, 'La difesa civile', lecture given at Centro Militare Studi per la Difesa Civile, Rome, 6 October 1982.

33. M. Pulcinelli, 'Il soccorso sanitario nel disastro atomico', *Rivista Militare* no. 5 (1975) pp. 97–103.
34. ISTRID, 'Difesa militare e difesa civile', *Annuario 1981–82* (Rome, 1981) pp. 153–5; and Centro Alti Studi Militari, Round Table on National Defence, 30th Session, reported in *Rivista Militare*, no. 4 (1979) pp. 2–10.
35. M. Vinciguerra, 'La difesa civile nel contesto della difesa globale', ibid., no. 2 (1979) pp. 35–40; B. Piazza, 'La cooperazione civile–militare, ibid., no. 1, (1980) pp. 58–62; and P. Feniello, 'Difesa nazionale: organizzazione della difesa civile e suoi collegamenti con la difesa militare', ibid., no. 6 (1983) pp. 93–104.
36. F. Salvati, 'Obiezione di coscienza e difesa civile', ibid., no. 3 (1980) pp. 88–91.
37. Camera dei Deputati, VIII Legislatura, *Atti Parlamentari*, no. 53 (1979).
38. P. Barrera and M. Pianta, 'Movimenti per la pace e alternative di difesa in Europa', *Problemi del Socialismo*, no. 1 (1984) pp. 209–29.
39. A. Drago, 'Verso un programma politico di difesa popolare nonviolenta' in *Atti del Convegno Nazionale sulla Difesa Popolare Nonviolenta* (Verona, 1979); and 'Difesa popolare e nonviolenza', *Testimonianze*, 1981, pp. 51–72.
40. M. Soccio, 'Dalla peace research alla difesa popolare nonviolenta' in *Atti del Convegno Nazionale sulla Difesa Popolare Nonviolenta*; and 'Difesa civile e nonviolenza', *Azione Nonviolenta*, no. 4 (1986) pp. 3–4.
41. G. Salio, 'Una strategia mista come alternativa alla difesa militare', ibid., no. 4 (1986) pp. 5–6; A. Zangheri, 'Compromessi senza compromissioni', ibid., p. 6; A. Zangheri, 'Il transarmo', *Rocca*, 15 April 1983; A. Drago and G. Mattai, *L'Obiezione Fiscale alle Spese Militari'* (Turin, 1986); 'La proposta di legge presentata da Democrazia Proletaria', *Azione Nonviolenta*, no. 4 (1984) pp. 23–5; 'Proposta di legge di iniziativa popolare', ibid., no. 4 (1984) p. 26; 'La lettera degli obiettori fiscali al Presidente della Repubblica Cossiga', ibid., no. 5 (1984) pp. 16–17; MIR – Padova, 'Presentazione della legge sulla difesa popolare nonviolenta', ibid., no. 7/8 (1985) p. 23; 'Coordinamento regionale degli obiettori fiscali, "Proposta di legge sulla DPN"', ibid., p. 24.
42. We are grateful for helpful suggestions and discussions to F. Accame, D. Batani, F. Battistelli, M. De Andreis, A. Drago, M. Elena, A. Graziani, C. Jean, P. Miggiano, S. Minni, G. Nardulli, R. Ragionieri and A. Salvato. We also thank the entire staff of *Archivio Disarmo*, Rome, for help with the references.

Index

Abrahamson, J.   160
Abshire, D.   175
Accame   323
Adria Alp Community   316
Afghanistan   3, 107, 293, 301
Albania   272
Alexander the Great   31
Algeria   260
Allen, R.   157
Andreotti, G.   180
Anglo-American (Rush-Bagot)
    Treaty (1817)   131
Antarctic Treaty (1959)   268
Anti-Ballistic Missile (ABM) Treaty
    (1972)   162
  American hositility to   155, 157,
    158
  and DEWs   222, 224–8, 236–40
  possible Soviet violation   121–2,
    123, 238
  SDI a threat to   172, 174, 175,
    178, 183, 185, 186
Anti-Ballistic Missiles   6–7, 196–7
Anti-Satellite weapons
    (ASATs)   210, 223, 232, 238–9
Arab–Israeli wars   259, 263
Argentina   106, 125, 128, 261, 291
arms control
  and DEWs   228–9
  negotiations   1, 36–58, 114–32
  verification of agreements   135–
    47, 241–5
arms race
  conventional   292
  and negotiations   54–5, 58
  stability   215, 229–30
  technological   17
Aron, R.   103, 106
Association of South-East Asian
    Nations (ASEAN)   264
Australia   178, 181, 282, 301
Austria   45, 316, 318, 319, 321

Bangeman, M.   180

Bangladesh   105
Barkenbus, J. N.   240
Beilenson, L., *The Treaty
    Trap*   155–6
Belgium   83, 258
belief systems   *see* mind-sets
Bendetsen, K. R.   159
Bertram, C.   173
Bethe, H.   17
Bisogniero, General   314
Boyer, P.   13
Brazil   2, 286–92
  arms industry in   288–90
  nuclear programme   288, 290–1
  public concern about
    disarmament   286–8
Brezhnev, L.   16
Brown, H.   120, 203
Buchanan, P.   118
Bulgaria   90, 272
Bundy, McG.   158
Bush, G.   175

Caesar   24, 27
Cambodia   106
cameras
  infra-red   145–6
  optical   138–41
Canada   7, 176, 178, 184–5, 186,
    187, 188
Capitini, A.   323
Carter, J.   122, 136, 151, 156, 162,
    288
Casey, W.   157
Catch 22   30
chemical weapons   4, 53, 57, 119,
    255, 295
Cheysson, C.   176
China   2–3, 106, 143, 258, 264,
    293–302
  Civil War   104, 105
  defence industry   299–300
  nuclear forces   293, 304–5
  nuclear policy   294–6, 305–9

China – *cont.*
  People's Liberation Army
    (PLA) 294, 296–9
  on Tlatelolco Treaty 278
Chirac, J. 179
command and control 28–32, 63,
    257 (*see also* information)
  changes in 31–2
  use of computers 207
communications 26 (*see also*
    information)
  breakdown in war 28–30
compliance 135
confidence building measures
    (CBMs) 109, 111
Contadora Group 111
conventional arms 234, 295
  in China 296–9
  in Italy 313–20
conventional disarmament 307, 308
conventional war 2, 100–12
  costs of 109
  frequency, duration and
    destruction (post-1945) 102–4,
    108
  geographical distribution (post-
    1945) 104–6
  limitation of 101, 108
Cook Islands 282
crisis stability 215, 229, 233, 311,
    315
Cuba 263
Cyprus 107, 143
Czechoslovakia 90

damage limitation 213–14, 233–4
De Andreis, M. 317
decoys 209
defence
  of population 214, 221, 240–1
  of silos 211–12
defence policy, Western, post-
    war 11–20
defences
  layered 194–6
  point 121, 239–40
'defensive defence' 111
'defensive superiority' 36, 44, 45–7,
    48, 49, 51, 52

DeLauer, R. 152, 163
Deng Xiaoping 296
denial 43, 44, 212–13
Denmark 82, 83, 178
deterrence
  by denial 212–13
  non-nuclear 45
  nuclear 14–15, 23–34, 40, 42,
    101, 120, 121, 122, 256
deterrence policy 24, 26–7, 33–4
deterrence theory 24–6
  decision-making in 32–3
  presupposes accurate
    information 27–8
Deutsch, K. 24
developing world *see* third world
diplomacy, coercive 5, 260–5
diplomatic solutions 19
  discussion 50, 51, 57
Directed-Energy Weapons
    (DEWs) 192, 197–8, 198–204,
    220–46
  arms control of 229–45
  costs of 230–1
Dolan, P. J. 68
Dulles, J. F. 13
Dunnigan, J. F. 104
Dyson, F. 235

East Germany 90–1
Egypt 128, 273
Eisenhower, D. 14
El Salvador 106
Ethiopia 106
'Eureka' 178
European Defense Initiative (Star
    Wars) 183–5
European Nuclear Disarmament
    Movement (END) 171 (*see
    also* peace movement)

Falkland Islands 125, 128
Falwell, J. 118
Fiji 282
Finland 143, 272, 281
Finletter, T. 12
first-strike
  strategy 14, 15, 170, 240
  weapons 42, 55
  see also pre-emptive strike

fissile material, control of   256–7, 258
Fletcher, J. C.   164
forces, limitations on   111
Ford, G.   122, 151
Forlani, A.   321
France   23, 106, 258, 316, 321
   nuclear forces   7, 82, 87, 166, 172, 233
   and NWFZ treaties   270, 278, 282
Frank, J.   129
Freedman, L.   166

Geneva Protocol (1925)   119, 255
Glasstone, S.   68
Gochman, C. S.   102, 104, 106
Gorbachev, M.   6, 130, 136, 258
Gore, A.   227
Graham, D. O.   158–60
Gray, C. S.   15, 119, 157
Great Britain   23, 128, 143, 174, 258, 316
   attitude to non-nuclear powers   261–2, 264
   Northern Ireland   107
   nuclear weapons   2, 7, 12, 82, 87, 166, 172, 233
   and NWFZ treaties   270, 277–8, 282
   response to SDI   179, 182, 187
Greece   88, 107, 178, 272
Greve, F.   161–3
Guardian   183

Haig, A.   156
Haig, D.   30
Halle, L. J.   129
Harriman, A.   20, 122
Helms, J.   118
Hiroshima   68, 69–70, 75
Hitler, A.   30, 56, 118, 125, 128
Hoffman, F. S.   164
Howard, M.   47
Hungary   91, 316, 317–18
Huntington, S.   47

Iceland   88

Ikle, F. C.   157, 163
India   105, 106, 271, 288, 291
Indo–Pakistan war   259–60
Indochina   106, 260
Indonesia   107
information   26–8, 38–9, 79 (*see also* command and control; communications)
   problem of analysing   27–8
Inter-Continental Ballistic Missiles (ICBM) flight phases   194–5
Intermediate Nuclear Force (INF)
   deployment in Europe (1981)   171, 187
   talks (1983)   128
International Atomic Energy Agency (IAEA)   257, 269, 280, 284
Iran   101, 106, 107, 108, 273
Iraq   101, 106, 107, 108
Israel   106, 128, 260, 288
   a nuclear power   257, 258
   reaction to SDI   181, 182, 187
Italy   23, 66, 258, 310–24
   civilian-based defence   322–4
   conventional military alternatives   313–20
   nuclear weapons in   88, 315–16
   reaction to SDI   180, 182, 187
   role: in Mediterranean   319–20; in NATO   310, 314–15, 317, 324
   territorial defence   320–2
   White Book on Defence   321

Japan   23, 106, 176, 177, 181, 264, 265, 301
Jervis, R.   122
Johnson, L.   11
Jongman, B.   104, 107

Kampuchea   105, 106, 301
Kende, I.   102
Kennan, G. F.   15–16, 122, 158
Keyworth II, G. A.   161, 163, 164
Khrushchev, N.   16
kinetic-energy weapons (KEWs)   192, 197
Kiributi   282
Kirkpatrick, J.   157

Index

Kissinger, H. 17
Koch, Mayor of New York 256
Kohl, H. 179
Korea, North 105
Korea, South 105
Korean war 260, 263
Kull, S. 42

Laos 106
laser weapons 197–8, 200–4, 211
   X-ray lasers 203–4
Lebanon 101
Levine, R. A. 124
Li Peng 301
limitation *see* conventional war; damage; forces
'limited' nuclear war 171
   collateral effects 63
   defined 59, 63
   simulation model:
      assumptions 80–2;
      described 65–6; fall-out 68, 75–8, 77–8; results 91–7;
      thermal radiation 68, 69–73, 77–8; WSEG-10 68
Limited Test Ban Treaty (1963) 129, 143, 224, 294, 306
listening devices, electronic 146–7
Longstreth, T. K. 226
Los Angeles Times 154
Lushbaugh, C. C. 75
Luxembourg 82
Lygachev, Y. 282

McFarlane, R. 161, 163, 164
McNamara, R. S. 17, 103, 107, 158, 213
Mao Zedong 293, 306
Mearsheimer, J. 44
military balance 1, 24, 52, 55
   defined 38
   examined 37–49
   in non-nuclear forces 43–7
   in nuclear forces 40–3, 121, 123
   unmeasurable 38–9, 56
mind-sets 1
   co-operative 115, 122–3, 124, 128, 130, 132
   competitive 115, 120–2, 124, 128, 129, 130, 132
   confrontational 115, 119–20, 124, 125, 129, 131–2
   Manichean 115, 118–19, 125, 128, 130, 131, 132
   pacifist 115, 123–4, 128
Moaz, Z. 102, 104, 106
Mondale, W. 165
Mongolia 301
Mulroney, B. 178, 185
mutual assured destruction (MAD) 154, 159, 166, 228, 234–5
mutual vulnerability 17, 19

Nagasaki 69–70
Nakasone, Y. 181
Napoleon 31
NATO (North Atlantic Treaty Organisation) 23, 39, 48, 82–90, 124, 158
   attitude to developing nations 264
   dependence on nuclear weapons 12, 16, 47, 64
   European Defense Initiative (Star Wars) 183–5
   Italy's role in 310, 314, 317, 324
   Nuclear Operations Plan (NOP) 80
   and SDI 165, 170–1, 173–5
   targets in 82–90
Naura 282
Naval War College Review (1981) 19
negotiaton *see* arms control
Netherlands 88, 258, 270
New York Times Magazine 155
New Zealand 261, 264–5, 282, 301
Nicaragua 106, 111
Nigeria 105
Nitze, P. H. 119, 157, 210, 215
Niue 282
Nixon, R. 140
no-first-use pledge
   China's 294, 295, 306, 307, 308
   NATO's refusal to give 158, 262, 265, 317

Non-Proliferation Treaty (NPT)
  (1968)   129, 255–8, 284, 306
  alleged racist bias in   257–8
  interpretation of   261, 264, 277
  purpose of   258, 291
Norment, H. G.   68
North American Aerospace Defense
  Command (NORAD)   154,
  184–5
Norway   82, 89, 178
nuclear deterrence   *see* deterrence
nuclear energy   292
nuclear weapons   *see* weapons
Nuclear-Weapon-Free Zone
  (NWFZ)   5, 109, 264, 267–85
  in Africa   270–1
  in Asia   271
  in the Balkans   271–2, 316
  defined   274–6
  in Europe   271–3, 316–17, 318,
  319
  geographical scope of   281–3
  in the Middle East   273
  non-zonal states'
  responsibility   279–81
  verification of   283–4
  zonal states' responsibility   276–8
  see also Treaty for the Prohibition
  of Nuclear Weapons in Latin
  America; Treaty on the South
  Pacific Nuclear-Free Zone

Ockham, W.   24
'offensive superiority'   1, 44, 49, 51–
  2, 56
offensive weapons, definition of   56,
  58
Oppenheimer, J. R.   11
Organisation of African Unity
  (OAU), *Declaration of
  Denuclearisation of Africa*
  (1964)   269, 270
outer space   295
  military uses of   222–3 (*see also*
  satellites)
Outer Space Treaty (1967)   223–4,
  269

Pakistan   105, 106, 143, 271

Papua New Guinea   282
Particle Beam Weapons   199–200
Payne, K.   157
peace
  stable   23, 49
  unstable   23–34
peace movements   178, 287
  European   171, 311, 312, 324
Pearson, L. B., 'Canadian
  Memorandum on Atomic
  Warfare'   20
People's Daily   306
Perle, R.   118, 119, 157, 160
Perry, W.   137
Philadelphia Inquirer   161
Philippines   101, 264
Pike, J. E.   226
Pipes, R.   157
Poitiers, battle of (1356)   27
Poland   91, 272
Poli, General   314–15
policy
  Chinese nuclear   294–6, 305–9
  deterrence   24, 26–7, 33–4
  security   30
  Soviet disarmament   305
  war as instrument of   259–60
  Western postwar defence   11–20
political aims
  offensive   42, 47, 48, 49, 56–7
  peaceful   36, 40, 47, 48, 50–4, 57
political power, and military
  power   16, 18
Portugal   82, 89, 258
Powers, T.   15
pre-emptive strike   42, 46, 49, 51,
  52 (*see also* first-strike)
  collateral damages of   63
  consequences of   65

Quemoy-Matsu   263
Quiles, P.   172, 176

radar, used for verification   141–3
Rapacki Plan (1957)   272
Reagan, R.   130, 136, 258 (*see also*
  Strategic Defense Initiative)

Reagan – *cont.*
  as Governor and Presidential Candidate 153–6
  as President 156–64
  retaliation 43, 44, 45
Reykjavik summit 186
Rhinelander, J. B. 226
Roberts, A. 323
Romania 272
Rostow, E. 157
Rotblat, J. 75
Rowny, E. 157

SALT 119, 123, 130, 258, 263
SALT I 55, 56, 140
SALT II 56, 146
sanctions 135–6
satellites 28, 194, 294 (*see also* outer space)
  used for verification 138–42, 145–7
Schlesinger, J. R., 19, 261
Schmidt, H. 180
security policy, paradoxes in 30
seismic stations, used for verification 143–5
Sheer, R. 154–5
sheltering programme 79
Shulman, M. 122
Shultz, G. 119, 156, 163, 185, 186
Singer, J. D. 102
Sivard, R. 104
Small, M. 102
Smith, G. 158
Solomon Islands 282
Somalia 106
South Africa 140, 260, 271
South Atlantic war 263
Soviet Union 2, 11, 14, 16, 122, 295
  attitude to limited nuclear war 64–5
  disarmament policies 305
  in INF talks (1983) 128
  involvement in out-of-area conflicts 107
  Krasnoyarsk radar 121, 123, 238
  non-nuclear forces 45
  reaction to strategic defence 229
  on Tlatelolco Treaty 278, 281–2
  use of force without war 265
Spain 82, 89, 107, 180
Sri Lanka 101, 107
stability/instability *see* arms race; crisis; peace
Stalin, J. 118, 125
Stockholm International Peace Research Institute (SIPRI) 109, 293, 304, 305
Stoll, R. 102
Strategic Arms Reduction Talks (START) 130
strategic defence
  damage limitation 213–14
  deterrence by denial 212–13
  and nuclear weapons 214–15
  population defence 214
  silo defence 211–12
strategic defence systems 194, 205–11, 221
  battle management 207
  costs 210
  countermeasures 207–11
  operational requirements 205–6
strategic defence weapons 192–4
  feasibility of 196–204
Strategic Defense Initiative (SDI) 6–7, 18–19, 122, 222, 294
  alleged pipedream 151–3, 171
  allied reaction to proposal 165–7, 169–73
  effect on arms control 172, 185–6
  effect on deterrence 170, 175, 187
  origin of idea 153–64
  research funds 170, 174, 177–82
  Star Wars I 170
  Star Wars II 173–4, 177–82
Sudan 105
Sudetenland 128
Suez 263
'sufficiency' 1, 3, 36, 40–3, 48, 49, 51, 52, 53, 54, 122
Sun Tzu 259, 262
'supremacy' 1, 42–3, 44, 49, 51–2, 56

Suslov, M.   118
Sweden   45, 272, 321
Switzerland   45, 321
synergistic effects   66, 69, 71

telescopes, optical, used for verification   147
Teller, E.   154, 159, 163, 164, 204
Thatcher, M.   170, 174, 179
third world
  conventional war in   104–8
  and disarmament   308
  war as policy instrument in   259–60, 263–5
Thompson, E. P.   177
Tonga   282
treaties on outer space, the sea bed and the moon   269
Treaty of Ghent (1814)   131
Treaty for the Prohibition of Nuclear Weapons in Latin America (Treaty of Tlatelolco)   264, 268, 269–70, 276–8, 282, 291
Treaty on the South Pacific Nuclear-Free Zone (Treaty of Rarotonga)   267, 268–9, 269–70, 275, 276–8, 280, 282
Truman, H. S.   120, 157
Turkey   89, 107, 143
Tuvala   282
Twining, N.   14–15

unilateral action   19, 36, 50, 52, 57, 124
United Nations   108, 270, 271, 274–6, 279, 305
  Comprehensive Study of the Question of Nuclear-Weapon-Free Zones (1975)   268, 276
  Study on Israeli Nuclear Armament   273
United States   2, 4, 23, 24, 64, 82, 295, 311 (*see also* Strategic Defense Initiative)
  attitude to non-nuclear powers   260, 261–2, 264
  confronters in   120, 121
  development of nuclear policy   1–2, 11, 12, 14, 16, 17
  importance of verification   135, 137
  in INF talks (1983)   128
  involvement in out-of-area conflicts   107
  Manichean thinkers in   118–19
  and NWFZs   270, 271–2, 278, 282
  pressure groups   156–61
  role of Joint Chiefs of Staff   162–3
  suspicion   129–30
  use of force without war   265
  weapons exports restricted   288

verification   56, 295
  adequate   136–7
  of DEWs   241–5
  of NWFZs   283–4
  technical means of   4–5, 135–47; cameras   138–41, 145–6; electronic listening devices   146–7; radar   141–3; satellites   138–42, 145–7; telescopes   147
  views on   119, 120, 121–2, 123, 124
Vessey Jr, J. W.   162
Vietnam   3, 106, 260, 261

war, conventional   *see* conventional war
war as policy instrument   259–60
Warsaw Pact   5, 39, 46, 47, 48, 171
  conventional attack on Italy   316, 317–18
  Single Operational Plan (SIOP)   80
  targets in   90–1
Washington Naval Treaty (1922)   131
Watkins, J.   163
weapons, nuclear
  postwar history of   11–20
  and strategic defence   214–15
Weinberg, A. M.   240
Weinberger, C.   118, 153, 261

Weinberger – *cont*
   SDI 'invitation' to allies 174–5,
     178, 179–80, 183, 184, 185, 187
West Germany 23, 312, 316, 318,
   321
   military sites 89–90
   nuclear power plants for
     Brazil 288, 291
   reaction to SDI 179–80, 182, 187
Wood, L. J. 159
Worner, M. 184

Yalta Axiom 122
Yang Dezhi 296
Yergin, D. 118, 122
Yugoslavia 45, 272, 316, 318, 319,
   321

Zelikow, P. 265
zero-zero option 101, 186
Zhao Ziyang 294, 307